America's
TEST KITCHEN

Also by the Editors at *America's Test Kitchen*

America's Best Lost Recipes

The America's Test Kitchen Family Cookbook

The Best of America's Test Kitchen 2007, 2008

The Best Recipe Series:
The Best International Recipe
The Best Make-Ahead Recipe
The Best 30-Minute Recipe
The Best Light Recipe
The Cook's Illustrated Guide to Grilling & Barbecue
Best American Side Dishes
The New Best Recipe
Cover & Bake
Steaks, Chops, Roasts, and Ribs
Baking Illustrated
Restaurant Favorites at Home
The Best Vegetable Recipes
The Best Italian Classics
The Best American Classics
The Best Soups & Stews

The TV Companion Series:
Test Kitchen Favorites
Cooking at Home with America's Test Kitchen
America's Test Kitchen Live!
Inside America's Test Kitchen
Here in America's Test Kitchen
The America's Test Kitchen Cookbook

834 Kitchen Quick Tips

To order any of our books, visit us at
http://www.cooksillustrated.com
http://www.americastestkitchen.com
or call 800-611-0759

Praise for the Best Recipe Series and Other *America's Test Kitchen* Titles

"This tome definitely raises the bar for all-in-one, basic, must-have cookbooks. . . . Kimball and his company have scored another hit." Portland Oregonian on *The America's Test Kitchen Family Cookbook*

"A foolproof, go-to resource for everyday cooking."
Publishers Weekly on *The America's Test Kitchen Family Cookbook*

"A timesaving tome." The Chicago Tribune on *834 Kitchen Quick Tips*

"For anyone looking for a lighter way of cooking, this book and its 300 recipes would be a most valuable resource."
Providence Journal on *The Best Light Recipe*

"Further proof that practice makes perfect, if not transcendent. . . . If an intermediate cook follows the directions exactly, the results will be better than takeout or mom's." The New York Times on *The New Best Recipe*

"Exceptional renditions with thorough instruction…"
Publishers Weekly on *Cooking at Home with America's Test Kitchen*

"Like a mini-cooking school, the detailed instructions and illustrations ensure that even the most inexperienced cook can follow these recipes with success."
Publishers Weekly on *Best American Side Dishes*

"Makes one-dish dinners a reality for average cooks, with honest ingredients and detailed make-ahead instructions." The New York Times on *Cover & Bake*

"*Steaks, Chops, Roasts & Ribs* conquers every question one could have about all things meat."
The San Francisco Chronicle on *Steaks, Chops, Roasts, and Ribs*

"The best instructional book on baking this reviewer has seen."
Library Journal (starred review) on *Baking Illustrated*

"A must-have for anyone into our nation's cooking traditions—and a good reference, too."
Los Angeles Daily News on *The Best American Classics*

"If you've always wanted to make real Italian dishes as close to the Italian way as we can make them in America, here's a cookbook that shows you how." Pittsburgh Post-Gazette on *The Best Italian Classics*

"*Cook's Illustrated* to the rescue. . . . *Perfect Vegetables* belongs on every cooking reference shelf. Here's to our health." Pittsburgh Tribune-Review on *The Best Vegetable Recipes*

BEHIND THE
SCENES

with AMERICA'S TEST KITCHEN

BEHIND THE SCENES
with AMERICA'S TEST KITCHEN

BY THE EDITORS AT
AMERICA'S TEST KITCHEN

ILLUSTRATIONS
John Burgoyne

PHOTOGRAPHY
Daniel J. van Ackere
Carl Tremblay

AMERICA'S TEST KITCHEN
BROOKLINE, MASSACHUSETTS

America's Test Kitchen
17 Station Street
Brookline, MA 02445

Library of Congress Cataloging-in-Publication Data
The Editors at America's Test Kitchen

Behind the Scenes with America's Test Kitchen
1st Edition

ISBN-13: 978-1-933615-20-2
ISBN-10: 1-933615-20-6
(hardback): $34.95 U.S./$41.50 CAN
I. Cooking. I. Title
2007

Manufactured in the United States of America

10 9 8 7 6 5 4 3 2 1

Distributed by America's Test Kitchen
17 Station Street, Brookline, MA 02445

Senior Editor: Lori Galvin
Associate Editor: Elizabeth Wray Emery
Series Designer: Amy Klee
Designers: Matthew Warnick and Tiffani Beckwith
Photographers: Daniel J. van Ackere, Carl Tremblay, and Keller + Keller
Jacket Photographs: Christopher Churchill and Daniel J. van Ackere
Food Stylists: Marie Piraino and Mary Jane Sawyer
Illustrator: John Burgoyne
Production Director: Guy Rochford
Senior Production Manager: Jessica Lindheimer Quirk
Traffic and Projects Manager: Alice Cummiskey
Color Imaging Specialist: Andrew Mannone
Production and Imaging Specialist: Lauren Pettapiece
Copyeditor: Cheryl Redmond
Proofreader: Jeffrey Schier
Indexer: Elizabeth Parson

CONTENTS

PREFACE

THE SEVEN-YEAR ITCH. THIS BOOK REPRESENTS OUR eighth season on public television, and there must be something to the notion of a seven-year cycle, because we decided to make some changes, starting with bringing back Odd Todd, our science segment animator. You never know what he will do with a topic as simple as cooking and alcohol content. (His first thought was to explore the notion of roasting koala bears. Don't ask.) We introduced a new Letters to the Editor segment; filmed in my office. We also incorporated a great deal of behind-the-scenes kitchen footage. Finally, we freshened up the look of the show, from the opening scene to the transition graphics used to introduce each segments.

My wife and I recently purchased a team of draft horses from a farm up in the Adirondacks. Although they are well-trained, we aren't. Much like cooking, the thrill is in the learning: how to hook-up the hames (the collars), how to put on the harnesses and connect one horse to the other, and how to walk them into the forecart, getting them hooked up, front to back, and snapping the pieces into place. After a lot of training, you finally get to drive them, holding the reins just right to keep the horses under control, and then executing a close turn without too much stopping and starting. And then there is the pure pleasure of sitting on a cart, reins in hand, being pulled along by two large draft horses, an experience that grows in satisfaction.

The same is true in the kitchen. There is the thrill of learning and then the deep pleasure of cooking well, of standing at the stove, master of the pots and pans, of the minute adjustments of the flavors and heat to make a great meal. And this year, our eighth season, we finally got the hang of television. Everything in life that is worthwhile takes time, but that only adds to the pleasure of mastering an art.

I have a lot of fond memories of this year's show. Bridget in a giant witch's hat in the outdoor grilling area, holding on with both hands during a strong gust of wind; Julia getting the giggles and having to go through a half dozen takes to settle down; my selection of the worst-tasting but most expensive dried pasta (Jack's favorite moment); and Adam revealing that an $11 manual knife sharpener actually works. And it was once again a pleasure working with Becky and an all-new talent on America's Test Kitchen, Sandra.

And the food! Penne alla Vodka. Skillet-Barbecued Pork Chops. Slow Cooker Beef Burgundy. Chocolate Pots de Crème. Lemon Layer Cake. And the show is full of great discoveries, too. How to make the Pots de Crème on a stovetop, avoiding a messy oven water bath. How to get great barbecue flavor in a skillet. And how to get a chicken and potato dinner on the table in about half an hour. (The crew weighed themselves in before and after filming: One camera operator gained a full eight pounds in three weeks!)

Over the years, many people have told me that they enjoy the show. And, believe me, I am grateful for any recognition. But when someone says, "After watching your show and using your recipes, I can finally cook," that brings a real smile to my face. So many folks blame themselves for kitchen disasters. And they shouldn't. It was most likely unsound recipes. Anyone can be a good cook if you start with a good recipe. That is what this book and our show are all about. Recipes that have been tested enough times that, if you follow them exactly, they will produce good food. And if you understand why a recipe works, then you are more likely to enjoy success in the kitchen. To that end, our mission is not just to tell you what to do; we also try to explain why.

Finally, a personal thanks from me to you. You have made the show a success and made America's Test Kitchen a fun, exciting place to work. We love our work because you appreciate what we do. It's that simple.

So here's to our eighth season: to the recipes, techniques, and test cooks that make it all worthwhile. Enjoy the book, the season, and the food.

Christopher Kimball
Founder and editor, *Cook's Illustrated* and *Cook's Country*
Host, *America's Test Kitchen*
Brookline, Massachusetts, 2007

WELCOME TO AMERICA'S TEST KITCHEN

AMERICA'S TEST KITCHEN IS A VERY REAL 2,500-SQUARE-foot kitchen located just outside of Boston. It is the home of *Cook's Illustrated* and *Cook's Country* magazines and is the Monday through Friday destination of more than two dozen test cooks, editors, food scientists, tasters, photographers, and cookware specialists. Our mission is to test recipes over and over again until we understand how and why they work and until we arrive at the best version.

Our television show highlights the best recipes developed in the test kitchen during the past year—those recipes that our test kitchen staff makes at home time and time again. These recipes are accompanied by our most exhaustive equipment tests and our most interesting food tastings.

Christopher Kimball, the founder and editor of *Cook's Illustrated* magazine, is host of the show and asks the questions you might ask. It's the job of our chefs, Julia Collin Davison, Bridget Lancaster, Rebecca Hays, Jeremy Sauer, and Sandra Wu, to demonstrate our recipes. The chefs show Chris what works and what doesn't, and they explain why. In the process, they discuss (and show us) the best as well as the worst examples from our development process: dry hamburgers, leaden scones, and low-fat brownies no one wanted to eat.

Adam Ried, our equipment guru, shares the highlights from our detailed testing process in Equipment Corner segments. He brings with him our favorite (and least favorite) gadgets and tools. He tells you which knife sharpeners performed best in a dozen kitchen tests and shows how a good garlic press can produce better tasting dishes.

Jack Bishop is our ingredient expert. He has Chris taste our favorite (and least favorite) brands of common food products—everything from canned tuna and tortilla chips to strawberry preserves and hot cocoa mixes. Chris may not always enjoy these exercises (frozen pizza and soy sauce aren't always a whole lot of fun to taste), but he usually learns something as Jack explains what makes one brand superior to another.

Although there are just eight cooks and editors who appear on the television show, another 50 people worked to make the show a reality. Coordinating producer Melissa Baldino organized many aspects of filming to ensure that taping would run smoothly. Meg Ragland conducted all the historical recipe research. Along with the on-air crew, executive chefs Erin McMurrer and Keith Dresser planned and organized the 26 television episodes shot in May 2007 and ran the "back kitchen," where all the food that appeared on camera originated. Elizabeth Bomze organized the tasting and equipment segments.

During filming, chefs Kenji Alt, Kelley Baker, Meredith Butcher, Matthew Herron, Cali Rich, Bryan Roof, and Diane Unger were in the kitchen from early in the morning to late at night cooking all the food needed on set. Nadia Domeq was charged with making sure all the ingredients we needed were on hand. Kitchen assistants Ena Gudiel, Maria Elena Delgado, Mabelle DelaPuente, and David Lentini also worked long hours. Charles Kelsey, David Pazmiño, Sarah Wilson, and Lynn Clark along with interns Adelaide Parker, Christine Yue, and Kylie Charter helped coordinate the efforts of the kitchen with the television set by readying props, equipment, and food. Meredith Smith led all tours of the test kitchen during filming.

The staff of A La Carte Communications turned our recipes, tastings, testings, and science experiments into a lively television show. Special thanks to executive producers Geoffrey Drummond and Nat Katzman; director and editor Herb Sevush; supervising producer Paul Swenson; director of photography Jan Maliszewski.

We also appreciate the hard work of the video production team, including Stephen Hussar, Michael McEachern, Peter Dingle, Ken Fraser, Patrick Kelly, Gilles Morin, Brenda Coffey, Ken Perham, Jack McPhee, Aaron Frutman, Adam Ducharme, and Stephanie Stender.

We also would like to thank Hope Reed, who handles station relations, and the team at American Public Television that presents the show: Cynthia Fenniman, Chris Funkhauser, Judy Barlow, and Tom Davison. Thanks also for production support from DGA Productions, Boston; Paul Swensen Productions, Santa Rosa, California; and Zebra Productions, New York.

Woodbridge by Robert Mondavi, Kohler, VIVA Towels, Cooking.com, and Valley Fig Growers helped underwrite the show and we thank them for their support. Fresh produce was supplied for the show by Olgo Russo at A. Russo & Sons of Watertown, Massachusetts. Meat was provided by Scott Brueggeman and Wayne J. Tumber of Brueggeman Prime Ltd., Boston, Massachusetts. Live plants and garden items for the show were supplied by Mark Cutler at Mahoney's Garden Center of Brighton, Massachusetts. Aprons for Christopher Kimball were made by Nicole Romano and staff aprons by Crooked Brook. All the props were designed and developed by Foam Props, Woburn, Massachusetts.

We hope this book gives you an inside look at America's Test Kitchen. We are passionate about our work, and we hope you enjoy our recipes as well as reading about the process by which they were created. Our mission is pretty simple. We want to help make you a better cook. We believe that our television show and this book will do just that. If you have comments or questions about the show or the book, contact us at www.americastestkitchen.com.

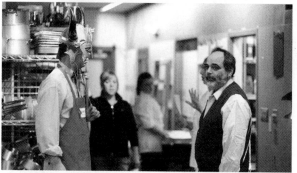

BEHIND THE SCENES WITH AMERICA'S TEST KITCHEN

Adam explains what makes a good safety can opener: a sure grip, smooth operation, and, for easy cleanup, the blade should have minimal contact with food.

EASY SKILLET
suppers

CHAPTER 1

One-dish meals sound like easy weeknight fare, but consider baked ziti. It's the archetypal one-dish meal that's really not—one pot is required for the pasta or noodles, a second is needed for the sauce, and yet a third is used for baking the assembled dish. No wonder it rarely makes an appearance on the weeknight table. Our goal was to streamline all the cooking for this dish into one skillet. And yes, we'd be cooking the ziti in the skillet, too—the test kitchen has had success in the past cooking pasta and noodles in diluted broth or sauce (instead of boiling water). Flavor is paramount, so we would not be taking shortcuts with jarred tomato sauce—we were determined to build our own well-seasoned sauce. Cheese is important to this dish, too, and we would not be skimping—after all, that's what gets all the kids to the table.

Like baked ziti, beef stroganoff is rarely enjoyed on a weeknight. In addition to its fussy preparation, this dish is traditionally made with filet mignon, which most of us frankly consider a bit cost prohibitive for Tuesday night. We'd explore other, less expensive, cuts of beef, but we wouldn't cut corners with tough, gristly meat. And as with our skillet-baked ziti, we'd aim to condense all our steps into one skillet—the beef, the sauce, and the noodles.

BAKED ZITI

WHAT WE WANTED: A streamlined method for this Italian-American favorite that would turn out the perfect ratio of pasta to tomato sauce, blanketed with lots of gooey cheese.

Baked ziti, like lasagna, requires lots of pots and pans and lots of time. The pasta and tomato sauce need to be cooked separately, combined with cheese, and baked for up to an hour in the oven. On top of the time issue, baked ziti can sometimes come out dry, bland, and downright unappealing. Our goal was twofold: We wanted a baked ziti that could be prepared more quickly so that we could enjoy it on a weeknight, and, most important, we wanted this fast baked ziti to be worth eating.

Traditional baked ziti is prepared as follows: The pasta is boiled in one pot and the sauce is prepared in another. The pasta and sauce are combined and transferred to a baking dish where cheese is also added to the mix. The dish goes into the oven and baked until the flavors meld, the dish is heated through, and the top is browned. Our first step toward streamlining the preparation of this dish started

with condensing three pots into one. We chose a skillet, as we've had success in the past with boiling small amounts of pasta (12 ounces or less) in a skillet with a brothy, creamy, or diluted tomato sauce. These thin sauces ensure that there is plenty of moisture to cook the pasta and prevent it from drying out. For our sauce, we chose a combination of crushed tomatoes, water, and heavy cream. The cream adds richness and body to the sauce, so that it coats the pasta evenly and thoroughly. And for seasoning, we turned to crushed red pepper flakes and plenty of garlic—six cloves. We started the sauce by sautéing the garlic and pepper flakes in a skillet. We then added the crushed tomatoes, water, and pasta. Ziti is traditional, but penne works well, too. We covered the skillet and cooked the mixture until the ziti was almost tender. (We didn't want to cook the ziti through because it would cook more in the oven.)

At this point we added the cream to the mixture, along with mozzarella. To keep the dish saucy and prevent it from drying out, we baked it for just 10 minutes in a 475-degree oven. Tasters liked this dish okay, but found the cheesy flavor to be weak. This was easily corrected by adding Parmesan to the mixture, which perked things up nicely. One final addition, minced fresh basil, gave the dish an herbal lift.

We found that this Italian-American dish is best made with some restraint. Just a few really fresh ingredients are all it needs. In addition to the classic version made with tomatoes, mozzarella, and basil, we developed two simple variations—one with vodka and cream and another that combines red wine, olives, and anchovies.

WHAT WE LEARNED: Trade in a multitude of pots usually required for this dish for just one—a skillet. For more flavor in less time, cook the pasta in the skillet with diluted tomato sauce rather than boiling water. Heavy cream adds richness and body to the dish, while a blend of two cheeses—mozzarella for meltability and Parmesan for full flavor—provides just the right balance.

SKILLET BAKED ZITI

serves 4

To complete this recipe in 30 minutes, preheat your oven before assembling your ingredients. If your skillet is not ovensafe, transfer the pasta mixture into a shallow 2-quart casserole dish before sprinkling with the cheese and baking. Packaged preshredded mozzarella is a real time-saver here. Penne can be used in place of the ziti.

    1   tablespoon olive oil
    6   medium garlic cloves, minced or pressed
        through a garlic press (about 2 tablespoons)
    ¼   teaspoon red pepper flakes
        Salt
    1   (28-ounce) can crushed tomatoes
    3   cups water
   12   ounces (3¾ cups) ziti
    ½   cup heavy cream
    1   ounce Parmesan cheese, grated (about ½ cup)
    ¼   cup minced fresh basil leaves
        Ground black pepper
    4   ounces whole milk mozzarella cheese, shredded
        (about 1 cup)

1. Adjust an oven rack to the middle position and heat the oven to 475 degrees.

2. Combine the oil, garlic, pepper flakes, and ½ teaspoon salt in a large ovensafe nonstick skillet and sauté over medium-high heat until fragrant, about 1 minute. Add the crushed tomatoes, water, ziti, and ½ teaspoon salt. Cover and cook, stirring often and adjusting the heat as needed to maintain a vigorous simmer, until the ziti is almost tender, 15 to 18 minutes.

3. Stir in the cream, Parmesan, and basil. Season with salt and pepper to taste. Sprinkle the mozzarella evenly over the ziti. Transfer the skillet to the oven and bake until the cheese has melted and browned, about 10 minutes. Serve.

VARIATION

SKILLET BAKED ZITI WITH PUTTANESCA SAUCE

Anchovies and olives lend zest to this variation.

Add 2 anchovy fillets, rinsed and minced, with the garlic in step 2. Replace the cream with red wine. Add ½ cup pitted Kalamata olives, chopped coarse, with the basil and Parmesan in step 3.

TASTING LAB: Extra-Virgin Olive Oil

IN THE TEST KITCHEN, WE DRIZZLE EXTRA-VIRGIN olive oil over fish, vegetables, soups, pasta dishes, salads, and more. In 2001, we tasted inexpensive supermarket oils and proclaimed DaVinci ($12.99 per liter) our favorite. In subsequent tastings, DaVinci has continued its dominance over other mass-market brands.

But what if price isn't your first consideration? And how do you choose among the hundreds of boutique oils available? Gathering a lineup of 10 best-selling boutique extra-virgin olive oils from a variety of countries, priced at $20 to $56 per liter, we stripped them of their stylish labels and put them through the rigors of a blind tasting, sampling them plain, with French bread, and drizzled over fresh mozzarella. We also added DaVinci oil to the mix to see how it would fare.

Sipped straight up from little cups, the extra-virgin olive oils in our lineup offered a pleasingly wide range of flavors, from fruity and "olive-y" to mild, buttery, and mellow to powerfully green, grassy, and pungent. Why does olive oil have such a wide-ranging flavor profile?

Experts agree that the type of olive, the time of harvest (earlier means greener, more bitter, and pungent; later, more mild and buttery), and processing are the biggest factors. As one expert pointed out, olive oil is really just olive juice, and the quickest, gentlest extraction yields the truest flavors. The best-quality oil comes from olives picked at their peak—deciding exactly when to pick is the chief art of olive oil makers—and processed as quickly as possible without heat (which can coax more oil from the olives but at the expense of flavor).

So how did our oils fare? And why did tasters' scores reveal some clear winners—and clear losers? The big loser in our tasting was DaVinci ($12.99 per liter), our favorite inexpensive oil, which finished dead last. Tasters deemed it "pleasant" but "not complex." Although disappointed, we weren't really surprised. This oil may be better than the other cheap options, but it couldn't compete with high-end products. It makes sense that companies that take the time to make oil in small batches have figured out some secrets to distinguish their oils from mass-market products.

We were surprised, however, that tasters were not impressed with the high-end Italian oils, which finished in fifth through eighth place. Our two top finishers came from Spain, the third from Greece. We needed to explain these unexpected findings.

As we tallied our tasting results, we realized that our two favorite oils—both praised by tasters for their assertive yet well-balanced flavor—were made with a blend of olives. The Columela and Núñez de Prado oils are a mix of intense Picual and mild Hojiblanca olives (the Núñez also adds delicate-flavored Picudo olives), creating a "fruity" olive oil with no elements that were perceived as too strong or mild tasting. By contrast, the other two Spanish oils we tasted, L'Estornell and Pons, were made with only the mild Arbequina olive, and they rated much less favorably.

Darrell Corti, owner of Corti Brothers store in Sacramento, Calif., and chairman of olive oil judging at the Los Angeles County Fair, the top domestic and international olive oil competition in the United States, told us that producers often blend extra-virgin oils from olives with distinct flavors to create the overall flavor profile they want. According to Corti, the best oil is often made from a blend of varietals; the blend may consist of several oils, each one made from a single varietal or from a "field blend," in which different types of olives are picked and then processed together to create a single oil.

Was blending the answer we sought? Maybe not. Ranking nearly as high as the top Spanish oils was a Greek oil, Terra Medi, made only with Koroneiki olives. It's not a blend, yet its balanced character and fruity, rounded flavor, with no harsh notes, made it similar in profile to the two top oils. Additionally, while some of the so-so Italian oils were made from single varietals, others were blends. So blending alone doesn't guarantee great oil.

The choice of olives is one factor that makes a particular oil more or less appealing. With their characteristic green, intense olive flavor and peppery aftertaste, the Italian and Italian-style oils had a few vocal supporters, but the majority of tasters felt that the oils' harsh pungency overwhelmed the olive flavor. What makes these extra-virgin olive oils so pungent and green? According to Paul Vossen of the University of California Cooperative Extension in Sonoma, an International Olive Oil Council–certified olive oil taster, Italian oils came by their signature flavor profile out of necessity—and producers then made it a virtue.

"Tuscany has frost problems, or potential frost problems, so their law requires that they harvest their olives early—by a certain date—and that means they have a green olive oil that is bitter and pungent," said Vossen. "So the Italians just convinced the world that that's how extra-virgin olive oil is supposed to taste. It's marketing. Once you realize that and put it in context, and take it with a grain of salt . . . yes, they make absolutely fabulous extra-virgin olive oils in Italy, but it's really just one style." Darrell Corti agreed. "Americans have been told that they should like very bitter oils, but they don't really like them. The Tuscan oils are bitter."

In the end, balance turned out to be the key factor that determined the winners of our tasting, and we found it in Spanish oils, not Italian oils. Our tasters preferred oils of medium fruity intensity. Italian oils generally fall into the intense category.

In the test kitchen, we'll keep our DaVinci on hand for everyday use, but we'll stock up on our preferred medium fruity Spanish oil, too.

Rating Extra-Virgin Olive Oils

TWENTY AMERICA'S TEST KITCHEN STAFF MEMBERS TASTED 10 NATIONALLY AVAILABLE EXTRA-VIRGIN OLIVE OILS PRICED at more than $20 per liter, along with DaVinci, the test kitchen's favorite inexpensive supermarket extra-virgin oil. We tasted them plain, on French bread, and drizzled over fresh mozzarella. Tasters rated each sample for olive flavor, complexity, and overall appeal. Brands are listed below in order of preference. See www.americastestkitchen.com for up-to-date prices and mail-order sources for top-rated products.

RECOMMENDED
Columela Extra-Virgin Olive Oil (Spain)
$22 for 25.4 oz. ($29/liter)

A blend of intense Picual and mild Hojiblanca olives, this oil took top honors for its fruity flavor and excellent balance. One taster summed it up: "Bold olive flavor and slightly fruity: this is what I think of when I think evoo."

RECOMMENDED
Núñez De Prado Organic Extra-Virgin Olive Oil (Spain)
$27.99 for 16.9 oz. ($56/liter)

"Nutty, fruity, good, with a lot of flavor" was the consensus on this "well-rounded" oil made with Picual, Hojiblanca, and Picudo olives.

RECOMMENDED
Terra Medi Extra-Virgin Olive Oil (Greece)
$9.95 for 17 oz. ($20/liter)

"Rich, olive-y, delicious," wrote one taster, and many agreed. Like the other top oils, this one (made with fruity Koroneiki olives) was praised for having a "great balance of flavor."

RECOMMENDED WITH RESERVATIONS
L'Estornell Extra-Virgin Olive Oil (Spain)
$21.99 for 25.3 oz. ($29/liter)

Made with mild, sweet Arbequina olives, this organic oil won tasters over with "lots of olive flavor," but it lost favor with a few for having "slightly off" notes.

RECOMMENDED WITH RESERVATIONS
Olio Verde Olio Extra Vergine di Oliva (Italy)
$30 for 500 ml. ($60/liter)

"A complex and spicy finish," said one taster about this Sicilian oil pressed from the early-harvest Nocellara del Belice olive. While many loved its "earthy, pungent" flavor, others found it "slightly bitter."

RECOMMENDED WITH RESERVATIONS
Lucini Premium Select Extra-Virgin Olive Oil (Italy)
$14.79 for 500 ml. ($29.58/liter)

"Nutty" and "huge," said tasters, who liked this oil made from a blend of Frantoio, Pendolino, Moraiolo, and Leccino olives. Some found it to have a "really bitter aftertaste."

RECOMMENDED WITH RESERVATIONS
Monini Granfruttato Extra-Virgin Olive Oil (Italy)
$11.49 for 500 ml. ($22.98/liter)

Tasters generally liked this "peppery, bold" oil, which is made with a blend of olives, including Moraiolos that are picked when they are fully ripe. But some complained of its "lingering bitterness."

RECOMMENDED WITH RESERVATIONS
Badia a Coltibuono Extra-Virgin Olive Oil (Italy)
$20 for 16.9 oz. ($40/liter)

This classic Tuscan oil was noted for its "great olive flavor," but others found the aftertaste bitter.

RECOMMENDED WITH RESERVATIONS
Pons Extra-Virgin Olive Oil (Spain)
$21 for 500 ml. ($42/liter)

Arbequina olives are used to create this oil, which tasters described as "rich, buttery, and full bodied," but also "mellow and not assertive."

RECOMMENDED WITH RESERVATIONS
McEvoy Ranch Extra-Virgin Olive Oil (U.S.)
$18.99 for 375 ml. ($50.64/liter)

This organic oil from northern California is a blend of six Tuscan olives. Some tasters liked its "nutty" and "green" flavors, while others found its strong taste overpowering.

BEEF STROGANOFF

WHAT WE WANTED: A method for transforming this classic dish into an easy and inexpensive one-pot meal.

Beef stroganoff is a deceptive dish. While most people think of it as a long-simmering braise, like a beef stew or beef burgundy, it is in fact a simple sauté made with the most tender and expensive cut on the steer, filet mignon. The beef is cooked with wine and stock, finished with cream, and served over egg noodles. But when we spend $25 on filet, we're not going to smother it in gravy. We wanted a cheaper alternative that would make better sense for a weeknight dinner.

Since cheaper cuts of meat are generally tough, we knew we'd have to shift from a quick sauté to a longer braise. The moist heat breaks down the fibers and collagen in meat,

making tough cuts tender. We first tried sliced blade steaks, but they shrank too much. Sirloin tips were up next, and they cooked up tender, but looked odd—with an accordion shape—at the end of cooking. To remedy this, we found that pounding the tips before cutting them into strips compressed the fibers in the meat and helped keep the strips neat and uniform as they cooked.

To braise the beef, we began by searing it in two batches until browned. Then we set the beef aside while we built our braising liquid, or gravy. We sautéed thinly sliced mushrooms together with onion until softened. We then added some flour (to help the gravy thicken) along with equal amounts of chicken and beef broths. Tasters felt that all beef broth tasted a little flat and cutting it with chicken broth helped bring the flavor into balance. As for flavoring the dish, a little restraint helped. We abandoned seasonings like prepared mustard, paprika, and Worcestershire, feeling that they did nothing but cover up the flavor of the beef and mushrooms. Brandy, however, was essential, as it added a welcome depth to the sauce. We then returned the browned beef to the skillet to finish cooking through. And instead of cooking the noodles separately in boiling water, we added them directly to the skillet to cook through alongside the beef in the saucy gravy.

Once the beef was cooked through and the noodles were tender, we finished the dish with sour cream. It's important to fold the sour cream into the dish off the heat to prevent curdling. At last, we had an easy-to-prepare, hearty meal that wouldn't break the bank.

WHAT WE LEARNED: Choose sirloin tips for great beefy flavor without a hefty price tag, but be sure to pound the tips before cutting them into strips—this prevents the meat from curling as it cooks. Build a saucy gravy so that the noodles can cook right in the gravy (instead of boiling them separately). Keep seasonings to a minimum to complement, rather than obscure, the beef and mushrooms.

SKILLET BEEF STROGANOFF

serves 4

Brandy can ignite if added to a hot, empty skillet. Be sure to add the brandy to the skillet after stirring in the broth.

1½	pounds sirloin tips, pounded and cut according to the photos at right
	Salt and ground black pepper
4	tablespoons vegetable oil
10	ounces white mushrooms, sliced thin
1	onion, chopped fine
2	tablespoons unbleached all-purpose flour
1½	cups low-sodium chicken broth
1½	cups low-sodium beef broth
⅓	cup brandy
6	ounces (3 cups) wide egg noodles
⅔	cup sour cream
2	teaspoons juice from 1 lemon

1. Pat the beef dry with paper towels and season with salt and pepper. Heat 1 tablespoon of the oil in a large skillet over medium-high heat until just smoking. Cook half of the beef until well browned, 3 to 4 minutes per side. Transfer to a medium bowl and repeat with 1 more tablespoon of the oil and the remaining beef.

2. Heat the remaining 2 tablespoons oil in the now-empty skillet until shimmering. Cook the mushrooms, onion, and ½ teaspoon salt until the liquid from the mushrooms has evaporated, about 8 minutes. (If the pan becomes too brown, pour the accumulated beef juices into the skillet.) Stir in the flour and cook for 30 seconds. Gradually stir in the broths, then the brandy, and return the beef and accumulated juices to the skillet. Bring to a simmer, cover, and cook over low heat until the beef is tender, 30 to 35 minutes.

TECHNIQUE: Turning Sirloin Tips into Stroganoff

When we were developing our recipe for Skillet Beef Stroganoff, we wanted to use a cut other than the traditional—and expensive—filet mignon. With a little work, we found that sirloin tips (also called flap meat) were a great alternative. Here's how we transformed them into tender, flavorful strips for this recipe.

1. Use a meat pounder to pound the meat to an even ½-inch thickness.

2. Cutting with the grain, slice the pounded meat into strips about 2 inches wide.

3. Slice each piece of meat against the grain into ½-inch strips.

---

3. Stir the noodles into the beef mixture, cover, and cook, stirring occasionally, until the noodles are tender, 10 to 12 minutes. Off the heat, stir in the sour cream and lemon juice. Season with salt and pepper. Serve.

EQUIPMENT CORNER:
Safety Can Openers

WHEN WE LAST LOOKED AT MANUAL CAN OPENERS in January 2002, we chose the Oxo Good Grips standard can opener for its comfort and easy operation. At the time, "safety" can openers were new, and our first opinion was negative—they were difficult to turn and caused liquid to spill out of the side of the can. Since then, the range of safety styles has expanded and their use has become more common (only one of our testers had never used a safety model), meriting a second look.

We purchased five safety styles to compare against our favorite manual can opener, the Oxo Good Grips. A regular can opener attaches to the side of the can and its blade punctures the lid just inside the rim. The operation often produces a sharp-edged lid that falls into the food; it's easy to cut a finger when removing it. A safety can opener attaches to the top of the can and the cutting wheel works from the side, just below the rim, to disconnect the lid from the can. At this point, the edges of both the lid and can are still smooth, and the lid remains perched on the can until it's removed.

We tested the six openers on cans of beans, tomato paste (to judge performance on small cans), and tuna fish (to judge liquid overflow once opened), and rated them on several criteria.

An opener should be comfortable to hold and require minimal pressure to operate—we also gave bonus points to models that could accommodate both left- and right-handed users. The opener should be easy to attach, retain a secure grip on the can, and then detach smoothly.

It's also important for the opener to operate smoothly, requiring only one revolution to open the can. Any liquid or food (such as tuna fish water) should remain in the can during the entire operation, including lid removal.

The opener should complete the job smoothly, as well. Thus, we downgraded models that left sharp tops or edges, especially if there was no way to remove the top without using our fingers. And to speed cleanup, we wanted an opener that had minimal or no contact with food.

What did we find? Three of the five safety models beat our old Oxo standby. The Rösle Can Opener, the Kuhn Rikon Safety Lid Lifter Deluxe Can Opener, and the Oxo Good Grips Smooth Edge Can Opener were all judged to be more comfortable, neater, and safer than the regular Oxo Good Grips. We especially liked the Rösle for the ease with which we could lift the lid after the can was open and the Kuhn Rikon for its adaptability for both left- and right-handed users. The Oxo safety model also performed well, but some of our testers thought it bulky, and left-handed users found it awkward. Superior function is pricey: The winners cost between $20 and $30, while the Oxo regular manual costs $10. Our testers, however, felt the safety and efficiency were worth the price.

Rating Safety Can Openers

WE TESTED FIVE MODELS OF SAFETY CAN OPENERS AND COMPARED THEM TO OUR TOP-RATED MANUAL CAN OPENER. We rated them for performance on small cans, comfort, ability to operate smoothly, and ease of cleanup. The can openers are listed in order of preference. See www.americastestkitchen.com for up-to-date prices and mail-order sources for top-rated products.

RECOMMENDED

Rösle Can Opener, Model #12751

$29.95

The Rösle won points for its compact and sleek design, its ease and efficiency going around the lid, and the simple way the lid is separated and removed (it requires only a slight turn of the wrist to lift it off). Neither the opener nor our fingers ever touched any food. We had one criticism—the instructions could be better written. Given the different design, it's not obvious for a first-time user to know how to attach the opener to the can.

RECOMMENDED

Kuhn Rikon Safety Lid Lifter Deluxe Can Opener, Model #2271

$24.95

The Kuhn Rikon was the best can opener for left-handed users; its large knob was especially comfortable to turn. Some of our heavier-handed users also felt the weightier Kuhn Rikon gave a more secure grip than the Rösle, especially as its handles mimic the style of a conventional can opener. However, removing the can lid was not as smooth as with the Rösle—you need to detach the wheel and use special little lid grippers.

RECOMMENDED

Oxo Good Grips Smooth Edge Can Opener, Model #1049953

$19.95

The Oxo worked efficiently and neatly, but some of our testers found it was too bulky for optimum comfort. It also didn't work well for left-handed users. And, as with the Kuhn Rikon, you use a side set of pincers to remove the can top. However, it is the only one of our recommended models priced under $20.

RECOMMENDED WITH RESERVATIONS

Oxo Good Grips Can Opener, Model #28081

$9.95

Still a good can opener for the price. The cushioned handles established a secure grip on the lid, and the large wheel knob and sharp cutters made for easy turning and opening. However, as with most manual can openers, the lid fell into the can, making for a messy retrieval, and the cutting wheel came into contact with the food, so it required more intensive cleaning.

NOT RECOMMENDED

Kuhn Rikon Safety Lid Lifter Can Opener, Model #2270

$15.95

This is the inexpensive cousin to the Kuhn Rikon model listed as recommended; however, we didn't feel the price savings compensated sufficiently for a poorer performance. It's made of plastic (the Deluxe version is made of stainless steel), and the opener felt flimsy. The handles side-slipped a bit during turning, and some of the testers felt they needed an uncomfortable level of pressure to keep a secure grip on the can.

NOT RECOMMENDED

Good Cook Orbi Safe Cut Can Opener, Model #11836

$12.99

This is a compact model—the entire opener sits on the top of the can—so it's easy for both left- and right-handed users to operate. But the Orbi flunked several of the basic tests: It required a lot of pressure to operate, and it was the only model that stuck going around the lid—in several places, the wheels just spun and we had to reattach the opener. Further, the lid can only be manually removed, making it the only one of our safety openers that risked contact with the food.

In developing our stovetop chicken recipes,
the test kitchen prepared each recipe using a
variety of skillets. Nonstick skillets were favored
over stainless steel and cast-iron for their slick
surface, which prevents food from sticking and
thus makes cleanup easy and quick.

CHICKEN
CHAPTER 2
in a skillet

It's not a surprise that most folks turn to chicken breasts for dinner. They're convenient, low in fat, and, when made right, juicy and satisfying. But chicken boredom is inevitable. We set out to uncover two inspiring chicken dishes that will have everyone looking forward to dinner again.

Parmesan-crusted chicken cutlets are cousin to bread crumb–Parmesan crusted Chicken Milanese and chicken Parmesan. Ideally, the cheese should melt into a chewy, crisp coating that completely envelops the cutlet. The chicken should be moist and juicy—an excellent counterpoint to the rich crust. But perfect renditions of this can be elusive: the cheese can fail to adhere to the chicken, it can turn wet and gummy, or it can overbrown and taste burnt and acrid. We set out to conquer these issues.

Roasting turns chicken moist and flavorful and gives potatoes a deep, earthy flavor with crispy edges. Roasting, however, is also a slow process, which is why most of us consider this dish a Sunday treat. The test kitchen wondered if swapping chicken breasts for a whole chicken, and a skillet for a roasting pan (along with some stovetop cooking), could bring this dish into Tuesday night territory.

Join us as we present two anything-but-dull approaches to chicken breasts that will get everyone to the dinner table on time.

PARMESAN-CRUSTED CHICKEN BREASTS

WHAT WE WANTED: Tender cutlets of chicken coated with a crispy crust of nutty Parmesan cheese.

When it comes to Italian-style chicken cutlets, most people are familiar with two classic recipes: chicken Parmesan (breaded chicken breasts topped with melted Parmesan and mozzarella cheeses and tomato sauce) and chicken Milanese (pan-fried cutlets with a Parmesan-accented breading). Although both offer some degree of Parmesan flavor, they're undeniably more focused on the bread crumbs. So it comes as no surprise that cookbook authors and food magazines have recently begun devising Italian-inspired chicken recipes that put the spotlight on the cheese. In place of the traditional thick layer of breading, Parmesan-crusted chicken offers a thinner, crispy-yet-chewy, wafer-like sheath of Parmesan cheese.

With short ingredient lists including only chicken breasts and Parmesan cheese plus one or two adhesives such as eggs or flour, the recipes we found for this dish seemed straightforward and promising. But variations in cooking technique yielded samples that were far cries from their beautiful descriptions. A baked version was pale, wet, and gummy. And while several pan-fried recipes were nicely browned, their soft coatings were marred by bald spots and tasted surprisingly bitter and burnt. To come up with a superior dish, we'd have to conquer the problems of weak Parmesan flavor and mushy, patchy crusts. We also had to figure out what was causing the acrid flavor in so many recipes. After all, what good is a picture-perfect cutlet if it tastes like a charcoal briquette?

After some initial tests, we knew a few things for sure. First, the chicken would have to be pan-fried, not baked. While baking simply melted the cheese, pan-frying showed potential to deliver the crisp crust we were after. Second, the chicken would have to be cooked in a nonstick skillet to keep the crust from fusing to the bottom of the pan, and it would have to be cooked quickly to prevent the cheese from burning. Boneless, skinless chicken breasts, therefore, were a given, and they had to be fairly thin. For chicken that cooked through in just three minutes, we used ¼-inch-thick cutlets.

For the coating, we began with the breading procedure for classic chicken Milanese (coating the cutlets in flour, followed by beaten egg, followed by bread crumbs), swapping grated Parmesan for both the flour and bread crumb layers. Unfortunately, the grated cheese didn't provide the smooth, dry base necessary for the beaten egg to cling to, producing an uneven crust with soft, eggy patches.

After reintroducing flour as the base layer, the egg and cheese adhered more neatly to the cutlet. But the crust still had a slightly souffléed texture. Omitting the yolks greatly improved matters. The whites clung to the flour and acted like flavorless glue that helped the cheese stick to the chicken.

Now coated with flour, egg whites, and a thin layer of Parmesan, the chicken tasted only faintly of cheese. Looking for big cheese flavor, we tried adding a handful of grated Parmesan to the egg whites. Although cheesier, the mixture was thick, sludgy, and difficult to handle. Adding cheese to the dry base layer of flour was much more successful. Ultimately, we found that equal parts flour and grated cheese kept the binding qualities of the flour intact while contributing a powerful Parmesan boost. Now the coating had two distinct layers of cheese: a fresh, tangy base and a toastier exterior. But the crust was still a little thin and spotty for our liking.

To this point, we'd been using the smallest holes on the box grater to transform the Parmesan into a fine, powdery consistency, which was perfect for whisking into the flour but less impressive when it came to providing a significant outer crust—it was too delicate and lacy. It struck us that the thicker, coarser texture of shredded—rather than finely grated—cheese would provide the bulkier layer we were looking for. With ½ cup of shredded cheese per cutlet, the chicken finally had a substantial crust.

The key to crispness was revealed during a side tasting of preshredded supermarket Parmesan cheese. We noticed that while the flavor of the preshredded cheese was inferior to authentic Parmigiano-Reggiano, it produced chicken that was much crispier and less chewy. Knowing that many of these packaged tub cheeses include starches to prevent caking, we wondered if adding flour to the Parmesan

would do the same thing. The answer was yes: Tossing a mere tablespoon of flour with the outermost layer of shredded cheese filled in any gaps between the cheese and egg white layers, creating a crispier exterior.

Our recipe was coming along, but we still had a major problem. Whenever we cooked the chicken until it looked gorgeous—a deep, dark brown—it tasted burnt. When we underbrowned the chicken (a counterintuitive move), it tasted fine. After some head scratching, we traced the problem back to the Maillard reaction. This chemical effect occurs when amino acids (building blocks for proteins) and sugars in foods are heated, causing them to combine and form new flavor compounds. Most cheeses undergo very little of this reaction when heated, because they don't contain much sugar. Parmesan cheese, however, contains fairly high levels of the sugar galactose, which undergoes the reaction quite readily. As the galactose reacts with sizable amounts of glutamic acid (an amino acid), the formation of bitter tasting substances happens as soon as the cheese starts to brown. Turning the heat down to medium once the cutlets were in the pan—thus keeping browning at bay—allowed the chicken and cheese to cook through without tasting burnt.

We were confident that this Parmesan-crusted chicken, with a perfectly moist, tender interior and a crisp, flavorful cheese crust, could finally live up to its name. By emptying the serving platter in a flash, tasters agreed without saying a word.

WHAT WE LEARNED: To prep the chicken for a cheese coating that will stick, flour the cutlets (add a little Parmesan for a boost of flavor), then dip them in egg white. For a sturdy crust of cheese, grate the Parmesan on the large holes of a box grater. And for a crisp crust, add a little flour to the outer layer of cheese. To prevent the cheese from turning bitter and acrid, cook the cutlets over medium heat just until pale golden on each side.

TECHNIQUE:
Slicing Chicken Breasts into Cutlets

Lay the chicken breast flat on a cutting board, smooth side facing up. Rest one hand on top of the chicken and, using a sharp chef's knife, carefully slice the chicken in half horizontally to yield two thin cutlets.

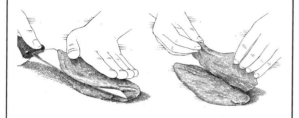

TECHNIQUE:
Two Ways to Cut the Parmesan

An ideal crust requires cheeses of two different textures. A base layer of finely grated Parmesan cut on the smallest holes of a box or Microplane grater (top) is paired with an exterior layer of coarsely shredded Parmesan cut on the largest holes of a box grater (bottom).

Grated

Shredded

PARMESAN-CRUSTED CHICKEN CUTLETS

serves 4

The chicken breasts will be easier to slice into cutlets if you freeze them for 15 minutes until firm but not fully frozen. Note that ½ ounce of the Parmesan is grated on the smallest holes of a box grater (or Microplane rasp grater); the remaining 6 ounces are shredded on the largest holes of the box grater (see photos at left). We like the flavor that authentic Parmigiano-Reggiano lends to this recipe, but a less expensive brand like Boar's Head Parmesan cheese can also be used; however, the resulting cheese crust will be slightly saltier and chewier. Although the portion size (1 cutlet per person) might seem small, these cutlets are rather rich due to the cheese content. To make 8 cutlets, double the ingredients and cook the chicken in 4 batches, transferring the cooked cutlets to a warm oven and wiping out the skillet after each batch.

2	boneless, skinless chicken breasts (8 ounces each), tenderloins removed, breasts trimmed of excess fat and halved horizontally (see the illustrations at left)
	Salt and ground black pepper
¼	cup plus 1 tablespoon unbleached all-purpose flour
½	ounce Parmesan cheese, grated (about ¼ cup) (see note)
3	large egg whites
2	tablespoons minced fresh chives (optional)
6	ounces Parmesan cheese, shredded (about 2 cups) (see note)
4	teaspoons olive oil
1	lemon, cut into wedges

1. Adjust an oven rack to the middle position and heat the oven to 200 degrees. Place the chicken between 2 sheets of plastic wrap and pound to an even ¼-inch thickness. Pat dry with paper towels and season both sides with salt and pepper.

Gummy
Baked chicken has a pale, damp, gummy cheese coating.

Patchy
A spotty, uneven crust is the result of using the wrong "glue."

Dark and Bitter
A dark brown crust looks appealing but tastes bitter and burnt.

2. Set a wire rack on a rimmed baking sheet. Whisk together ¼ cup of the flour and the grated Parmesan in a pie plate. In a medium bowl, whisk the egg whites and chives (if using) together until slightly foamy. In a second pie plate, combine the shredded Parmesan and the remaining tablespoon flour.

3. Using tongs and working with 1 cutlet at a time, coat the chicken in the flour mixture, shaking off the excess. Transfer the chicken to the egg-white mixture; coat evenly and let the excess run off. Coat the chicken with the shredded Parmesan mixture, pressing gently so that the cheese adheres. Place on the wire rack.

4. Heat 2 teaspoons of the oil in a 12-inch nonstick skillet over medium-high heat until shimmering. Place 2 cutlets in the skillet and reduce the heat to medium. Cook until the cheese is pale golden brown, about 3 minutes. While the chicken is cooking, use a thin nonstick spatula to gently separate any cheesy edges that have melted together. Carefully flip the cutlets and continue to cook until the cheese is pale golden brown on the second side and the meat is no longer pink in the center, about 3 minutes. Transfer the chicken to a separate wire rack set on a rimmed baking sheet and keep warm in the oven. Wipe out the skillet with a paper towel and return to medium heat. Add the remaining 2 teaspoons oil and cook the remaining 2 cutlets. Serve immediately with the lemon wedges.

EQUIPMENT CORNER:
Inexpensive Instant-Read Thermometers

WE USE AN INSTANT-READ THERMOMETER FOR QUICKLY checking the status of all our cooking tasks. It should have a broad range to cover high and low temperatures, a stem long enough to reach the interior of large cuts of meat, a way to recalibrate slips in accuracy, and, above all, speed so you don't have to keep the oven door open too long. The most coveted instant-read thermometer in the test kitchen remains the ThermoWorks Super-Fast Thermapen, which meets all of these criteria and produces readings in just five seconds. However, the $85 price tag begs for an affordable alternative.

We ran seven new instant-read thermometers under $25 through a gauntlet of tests, using boiling water, ice water, hot oil, and thick-cut pork chops to compare accuracy, speed, and functionality against our current favorite. The Thermapen is outfitted with a thermocouple sensor, whereas the less expensive models register temperatures with a thermistor, which is a cheaper circuit that comes with a sacrifice in speed and temperature range. However, our testing revealed a worthy stand-in that registered temperatures in only five additional seconds. The CDN ProAccurate Quick Tip Digital Cooking Thermometer DTQ450 ($17.95) further won us over with a temperature range (-4 to 450 degrees F) capable of handling all the tasks we could set before it.

Rating Inexpensive Instant-Read Thermometers

WE RAN SEVEN INSTANT-READ THERMOMETERS THROUGH BOILING WATER, ICE WATER, HOT OIL, AND THICK-CUT pork chops to compare accuracy, speed, and functionality against our current favorite, the $85 Thermapen. The thermometers are listed in order of preference. See www.americastestkitchen.com for up-to-date prices and mail-order sources for top-rated products.

HIGHLY RECOMMENDED
CDN ProAccurate Quick Tip Digital Cooking Thermometer DTQ450

$17.95; Average Response Time: 10 seconds; Probe Length: 4.7 inches

CDN won us over by meeting the testing criteria on all fronts. Quick 10-second readings put it only a step behind the test kitchen's high-end favorite, ThermoWorks Super-Fast Thermapen.

RECOMMENDED
Fieldpiece SPK1

$15.99; Average Response Time: 18 seconds; Probe Length: 3.2 inches

The swing-out, pocketknife probe makes for comfortable high-heat temperature measurements, which the broad range permits (-58 to 392 degrees). No calibration function.

RECOMMENDED
Comark PDT300

$15.27; Average Response Time: 10 seconds; Probe Length: 2.8 inches

While this thermometer does offer a self-calibration button and produces speedy readings, its short probe and limited range (-58 to 300 degrees) make taking temperatures for deep-frying and candy-making out of the question.

RECOMMENDED
ThermoWorks RT301

$14; Average Response Time: 18 seconds; Probe Length: 4.9 inches

Speed makes this thermometer a suitable alternative to the pricier Thermapen from the same company. However, a relatively low maximum temperature limit of 248 degrees and the lack of a calibration button are drawbacks.

RECOMMENDED WITH RESERVATIONS
DeltaTrak 11000

$25; Average Response Time: 28 seconds; Probe Length: 3.9 inches

The slow response time is this thermometer's biggest flaw. It does, however, come with a calibration button and a probe of adequate length.

NOT RECOMMENDED
UEI PDT550

$22.97; Average Response Time: 39 seconds; Probe Length: 3.3 inches

The UEI's only redeeming feature is its broad temperature range (-50 to 571 degrees). Its very slow response time is a big drawback.

NOT RECOMMENDED
Mannix HDT303K

$19.95; Average Response Time: 33 seconds; Probe Length: 2.5 inches

Bringing up the rear, the Mannix lost points across the board for a short stem, limited range, slow response time, and it lacked a self-calibration feature.

SKILLET-ROASTED CHICKEN DINNER

WHAT WE WANTED: A weeknight method for our favorite Sunday dinner that would yield the same moist, juicy chicken and crispy potatoes—in just 30 minutes.

Roasted chicken and potatoes are a classic combination, but you can forget about getting them on the table in 30 minutes, right? For starters, a whole chicken needs to see at least one hour of oven time, and potatoes take somewhere in that time range to get golden brown and crispy. Nevertheless, we were determined to turn this tasty dinner into a simple weeknight standby.

We decided early on that bone-in chicken breasts would take the place of a whole chicken. But even roasted breasts take 40 minutes to cook. That's when we thought of a restaurant method where the chicken is started in a skillet on the stovetop and then finished in a hot oven. Restaurants do this because it frees up burners to cook other dishes. Searing the chicken in the skillet turned the skin nicely brown and crispy and took just five minutes. We then transferred the chicken to a baking dish to finish cooking in a hot oven. But what about our roasted potatoes? We turned to those next.

We chose red potatoes because their tender skin doesn't require peeling—a time-saving measure. We used the same skillet we used for our chicken to cook the potatoes. But in our initial tests we had trouble getting the potatoes simultaneously golden and crisp on the outside and tender on the inside in a reasonable amount of time. After all, we didn't want the potatoes to take longer to cook than the chicken. We then thought of the microwave. While we couldn't produce potatoes with roasted flavor in the microwave, we could use it to jumpstart their cooking. So while the chicken browned in the skillet, we tossed the potatoes with a little olive oil and salt and pepper and popped them into the microwave until they began to soften, about 5 to 7 minutes. Then we added them to the skillet in a single layer and cooked them over medium heat to finish cooking through. In the skillet, the potatoes achieved a deeply caramelized exterior and creamy, moist interior.

As a final flourish, we mimicked the tasty pan juices of a traditional roast chicken by infusing olive oil with lemon juice, garlic, red pepper flakes, and thyme. Drizzled over the chicken and potatoes just before serving, the infused olive oil lent the same moistness and bright flavors of traditional pan juices. In addition, we applied our technique for pan-roasted chicken and potatoes to other tasty combinations, like pan-roasted chicken with baby carrots and pan-roasted chicken with cherry tomatoes and artichokes.

WHAT WE LEARNED: Swap skin-on, bone-in chicken breasts for a whole chicken. Sear the breasts in a skillet for golden brown skin, then transfer the chicken to a baking dish to finish cooking through in the oven. While the chicken browns, jumpstart the potatoes in the microwave until softened, then add the potatoes to the skillet to cook through and crisp. And to finish this dish off, make a quick drizzling oil to mimic the bright herbal pan juices from a traditional roast chicken.

PAN-ROASTED CHICKEN BREASTS WITH POTATOES

serves 4

To complete this recipe in 30 minutes, preheat your oven before assembling your ingredients. If the split breasts are different sizes, check the smaller ones a few minutes early and remove them from the oven if they are done.

    4   bone-in, split chicken breasts
        Salt and ground black pepper
    6   tablespoons olive oil
 1½   pounds red potatoes (4 to 5 medium), cut into
        1-inch wedges
    2   tablespoons juice from 1 lemon
    1   medium garlic clove, minced or pressed through
        a garlic press (about 1 teaspoon)
    1   teaspoon minced fresh thyme leaves
        Pinch red pepper flakes

1. Adjust an oven rack to the lowest position and heat the oven to 450 degrees.

2. Pat the chicken dry with paper towels and season with salt and pepper. Heat 1 tablespoon of the oil in a 12-inch nonstick skillet over medium-high heat until just smoking. Add the chicken and brown well on the skin side, about 5 minutes.

3. Meanwhile, toss the potatoes with 1 more tablespoon of the oil, ½ teaspoon salt, and ¼ teaspoon pepper in a microwave-safe bowl. Cover tightly with plastic wrap. Microwave on high until the potatoes begin to soften, 5 to 10 minutes, shaking the bowl (without removing the plastic) to toss the potatoes halfway through.

4. Transfer the chicken, skin side up, to a baking dish and bake until the thickest part registers 160 degrees on an instant-read thermometer, 15 to 20 minutes.

5. While the chicken bakes, pour off any grease in the skillet, add 1 more tablespoon of the oil, and return to medium heat until shimmering. Drain the microwaved potatoes, then add to the skillet and cook, stirring occasionally, until golden brown and tender, about 10 minutes.

6. Whisk the remaining 3 tablespoons oil, lemon juice, garlic, thyme, and red pepper flakes together. Drizzle the oil mixture over the chicken and potatoes before serving.

VARIATIONS
PAN-ROASTED CHICKEN BREASTS WITH BABY CARROTS

No-prep baby carrots make quick work of this variation.

    4   bone-in, split chicken breasts
        Salt and ground black pepper
    1   tablespoon vegetable oil
 1½   pounds baby carrots
    6   tablespoons unsalted butter
    1   teaspoon sugar
    1   medium shallot, minced (about 3 tablespoons)
    2   teaspoons minced fresh tarragon leaves

1. Adjust an oven rack to the lowest position and heat the oven to 450 degrees.

2. Pat the chicken dry with paper towels and season with salt and pepper. Heat the oil in a 12-inch nonstick skillet over medium-high heat until just smoking. Add the chicken and brown well on the skin side, about 5 minutes.

3. While the chicken browns, toss the carrots with ½ teaspoon salt and ¼ teaspoon pepper in a microwave-safe bowl. Cover tightly with plastic wrap. Microwave on high until the carrots begin to soften, 5 to 7 minutes, shaking the bowl (without removing the plastic) to toss the carrots halfway through.

4. Transfer the chicken, skin side up, to a baking dish and bake until the thickest part registers 160 degrees on an instant-read thermometer, 15 to 20 minutes.

5. While the chicken bakes, pour off any grease in the skillet, add 2 tablespoons of the butter, and return to medium heat until melted. Drain the microwaved carrots, then add to the skillet with the sugar and cook, stirring occasionally, until golden brown and tender, about 10 minutes.

6. Microwave the remaining 4 tablespoons butter with the shallot on 50 percent power until the butter has melted and the shallot is softened, 30 to 60 seconds. Stir in the tarragon. Drizzle the butter mixture over the chicken and carrots before serving.

PAN-ROASTED CHICKEN BREASTS WITH ARTICHOKES AND CHERRY TOMATOES

The artichokes will release a significant amount of water in the microwave as they defrost. To ensure that they brown properly, drain them well before adding them to the skillet.

> 4   bone-in, split chicken breasts
>   Salt and ground black pepper
> 5   tablespoons olive oil
> 2   (9-ounce) packages frozen artichoke hearts
> 1   pint cherry tomatoes, halved
> 2   tablespoons capers, rinsed
> 2   tablespoons juice from 1 lemon
> 1   medium garlic clove, minced or pressed through a garlic press (about 1 teaspoon)
> 1   teaspoon minced fresh oregano leaves
>   Pinch red pepper flakes

1. Adjust an oven rack to the lowest position and heat the oven to 450 degrees.

2. Pat the chicken dry with paper towels and season with salt and pepper. Heat 1 tablespoon of the oil in a 12-inch nonstick skillet over medium-high heat until just smoking. Add the chicken and brown well on the skin side, about 5 minutes.

3. While the chicken browns, toss the artichokes with ½ teaspoon salt and ¼ teaspoon pepper in a microwave-safe bowl. Cover tightly with plastic wrap. Microwave on high until the artichokes begin to soften, 5 to 7 minutes, shaking the bowl (without removing the plastic) to toss the artichokes halfway through. Drain the artichokes well.

4. Transfer the chicken, skin side up, to a baking dish and bake until the thickest part registers 160 degrees on an instant-read thermometer, 15 to 20 minutes.

5. While the chicken bakes, pour off any grease in the skillet, add 1 more tablespoon of the oil, and return to medium heat until shimmering. Add the artichokes to the skillet and cook, stirring occasionally, until golden brown, about 8 minutes. Stir in the tomatoes and capers and cook until the tomatoes are lightly wilted, about 2 minutes.

6. Whisk the remaining 3 tablespoons oil, lemon juice, garlic, oregano, and red pepper flakes together. Drizzle the oil mixture over the chicken and vegetables before serving.

Our recipe for Garlicky Shrimp with Buttered Bread Crumbs starts with extra-large shrimp that are seasoned with salt and pepper and sugar. This step promotes caramelization, which results in cooked shrimp that are juicy and sweet.

TWO WAYS
CHAPTER 3
with shrimp

Shrimp, like other splurges (filet mignon comes to mind), turns a meal into an occasion. We wanted to explore two elegant approaches to shrimp—one hot dish and one cold—and find the very best way to prepare each of them.

What could be simpler than garlicky shrimp baked with buttery bread crumbs? But as the test kitchen made their way through several recipes culled from a variety of cookbooks, things turned out to be far more puzzling. Dry, overcooked shrimp was the primary complaint and second was bread crumbs that turned soggy over the shrimp. We weren't surprised that the dry oven heat was wreaking havoc on the delicate shrimp, but was there a better cooking method? We would need to focus on finding one that would guarantee juicy, flavorful shrimp. At the same time we'd need to figure out how to ensure crisp bread crumbs on the finished dish.

Shrimp salad—plump, sweet shrimp lightly bound together with a creamy dressing. Sounds good, right? But in reality, this dish turns into an amalgam of rubbery, tasteless shrimp awash in an insipid dressing that's heavy on the mayo. Surely there must be a proper way to make a really good shrimp salad. We were determined to develop a recipe that would deliver on all fronts.

IN THIS CHAPTER

THE RECIPES
Garlicky Shrimp with Buttered
  Bread Crumbs

Shrimp Salad
Shrimp Salad with Roasted Red
  Pepper and Basil
Shrimp Salad with Avocado and
  Orange
Spicy Shrimp Salad with Corn and
  Chipotle
Shrimp Salad with Wasabi and
  Pickled Ginger

EQUIPMENT CORNER
Kitchen Timers

TASTING LAB
Tuna

GARLICKY SHRIMP WITH BREAD CRUMBS

WHAT WE WANTED: Plump, juicy shrimp infused with garlic and complemented by a crisp, buttery bread-crumb topping.

Garlicky shrimp with buttery bread crumbs is classic American cooking. Look in any all-purpose cookbook and you'll find a recipe. We found dozens in our library, most of which followed the same basic formula: Poach the shrimp; place them in a baking dish; top with bread crumbs, sherry, melted butter, herbs, and garlic; and bake in a hot oven for 10 to 15 minutes. Unfortunately, the results did not make us nostalgic for the past. The shrimp were often rubbery and bland (no surprise, since they were poached, then baked), while the topping—aside from its slightly crusty surface—was gluey and heavy on raw alcohol flavor. The combination of flavors and textures was appealing (in theory), but this dish needed some serious modernizing.

To avoid poaching and then baking the shrimp, we tossed them with a mixture of melted butter, salt, pepper, garlic, shallots, sherry, and parsley; transferred everything to a baking dish; sprinkled buttered fresh bread crumbs on top; and popped the dish into the oven. After a dozen failures (the shrimp were always too bland and watery), we decided on a more radical solution: trading the baking dish in the oven for a skillet on the stovetop. This would allow us to sear the shrimp (and thus add a flavorful browned exterior) and concentrate the sauce by reducing liquids in the same pan. We planned to use the crumbs as a last-minute topping.

To start, we pan-seared the shrimp in two batches to promote browning rather than steaming. Sprinkling the shrimp with a little sugar also encouraged browning during their short stay in the skillet. Cooking the shrimp completely through caused them to overcook when added to the sauce. Eventually, we hit upon the following strategy: Sear the shrimp on one side and remove them from the pan, build the sauce in the empty pan, and then return the shrimp to let them finish cooking in the sauce.

As for the sauce, we couldn't rely on sherry alone for our liquid component (it was too boozy). Cutting the sherry with bottled clam juice and letting the mixture simmer for several minutes concentrated the flavors and cooked off excess alcohol. (Vermouth can be substituted for the sherry, although amounts of it and the clam juice will differ slightly.) To finish the sauce, we whisked in several tablespoons of cold butter, but the sauce was a bit thin. More butter just made the sauce greasy. We had better luck adding a pinch of flour. This sauce was very good but some felt we were missing something. Then it hit us—lemon juice. Lemon's bright citrusy notes were just the flavor boost our sauce needed.

The crumb topping (toasted in the empty skillet before the shrimp were cooked) was easy. Japanese-style panko was too finely textured, while crumbs made from white sandwich bread became sandy on top and soggy underneath. Chewy supermarket baguette crumbs were sturdy enough to retain a crisp texture even after sitting on top of the saucy shrimp.

After sprinkling the flavorful topping onto the buttery, garlic-infused shrimp, we offered up the results to tasters. Our skillet "casserole" had all the potent flavors and contrasting textures tasters wanted—with none of the usual problems.

WHAT WE LEARNED: For juicy, flavorful shrimp, cook them on the stovetop instead of baking them in the oven. Sear them on one side only (sprinkled with a little sugar to promote browning), remove them from the skillet to build the sauce, then return them to the sauce to gently finish cooking through. For the sauce, augment the sherry with clam juice for best flavor and add butter along with a bit of flour to enrich and thicken it. And for bread crumbs that will stay crisp over the moist shrimp, make them from a chewy supermarket baguette.

GARLICKY SHRIMP WITH BUTTERED BREAD CRUMBS

serves 4

Vermouth can be substituted for the sherry. If using vermouth, increase the amount to ½ cup and reduce the amount of clam juice to ½ cup. To prepare this recipe in a 10-inch skillet, brown the shrimp in 3 batches for about 2 minutes each, using 2 teaspoons oil per batch. Serve the shrimp with rice and either broccoli or asparagus.

1	(3-inch) piece baguette, cut into small pieces
5	tablespoons unsalted butter, cut into 5 pieces
1	small shallot, minced (about 2 tablespoons)
	Salt and ground black pepper
2	tablespoons minced fresh parsley leaves
2	pounds extra-large shrimp (21 to 25 per pound), peeled and deveined
¼	teaspoon sugar
4	teaspoons vegetable oil
4	medium garlic cloves, minced or pressed through a garlic press (about 4 teaspoons)
⅛	teaspoon red pepper flakes
2	teaspoons unbleached all-purpose flour
⅓	cup dry sherry (see note)
⅔	cup bottled clam juice
2	teaspoons juice from 1 lemon, plus 1 lemon, cut into wedges

1. Pulse the bread in a food processor until coarsely ground; you should have about 1 cup crumbs. Melt 1 tablespoon of the butter in a 12-inch nonstick skillet over medium heat. When the foaming subsides, add the crumbs, shallot, ⅛ teaspoon salt, and ⅛ teaspoon pepper. Cook, stirring occasionally, until golden brown, 7 to 10 minutes. Stir in 1 tablespoon of the parsley and transfer to a plate to cool. Wipe out the skillet with paper towels.

2. Thoroughly dry the shrimp with paper towels; toss with the sugar, ¼ teaspoon salt, and ¼ teaspoon pepper in a bowl.

Return the skillet to high heat, add 2 teaspoons of the oil, and heat until shimmering. Add half of the shrimp in a single layer and cook until spotty brown and the edges turn pink, about 3 minutes (do not flip the shrimp). Remove the pan from heat and transfer the shrimp to a large plate. Wipe out the skillet with paper towels. Repeat with the remaining 2 teaspoons oil and shrimp; transfer the shrimp to the plate.

3. Return the skillet to medium heat and add 1 more tablespoon of the butter. When melted, add the garlic and pepper flakes; cook, stirring frequently, until the garlic just begins to color, about 1 minute. Add the flour and cook, stirring frequently, for 1 minute. Increase the heat to medium-high and slowly whisk in the sherry and clam juice. Bring to a simmer and cook until mixture reduces to ¾ cup, 3 to 4 minutes. Whisk in the remaining 3 table-spoons butter, 1 tablespoon at a time. Stir in the lemon juice and remaining tablespoon parsley.

4. Reduce the heat to medium-low, return the shrimp to the pan, and toss to combine. Cook, covered, until the shrimp are pink and cooked through, 2 to 3 minutes. Uncover and sprinkle with the toasted bread crumbs. Serve with the lemon wedges.

BETTER SHRIMP SALAD

WHAT WE WANTED: A recipe for really good shrimp salad, with well-seasoned, tender—not rubbery—shrimp as the star ingredient.

Maybe it's a good thing that most shrimp salads are drowning in a sea of gloppy mayonnaise. The dressing might be bland, but at least it helps camouflage the sorry state of the rubbery, flavorless boiled shrimp. We wanted to find a cooking technique that would deliver perfectly cooked shrimp without the extra work of grilling, roasting, or sautéing. And was it too much to ask that the shrimp have some flavor of its own?

To begin, we rounded up some creamy-style shrimp salad recipes. Most call for boiling a flavorful liquid of white wine, lemon juice, herbs, spices, and water (called a court-bouillon by the French). After the shrimp are submerged into this hot liquid, the pot is removed from the heat and covered for about 10 minutes. Many of the recipes call for quickly shocking the shrimp in an ice bath to prevent over-cooking. Although they looked perfect, shrimp prepared this way were in fact flavorless and tough. Reducing the time the shrimp spent in the liquid did make them more tender, but it did nothing to improve their flavor.

But we had a trick up our sleeves: a technique practiced in the 1970s by the French chef Michel Guérard. He poached proteins by starting them in cold liquid. The cold proteins and broth would heat simultaneously, unlike the traditional poaching technique in which the shrimp proteins immediately turn opaque (and rubbery) upon submersion in hot water. In this way the shrimp would better absorb flavors from the poaching liquid—a kind of turbo-charged flavor injection.

In the test kitchen we took the court-bouillon ingredients—leaving out the white wine, which tasters found overwhelming—and added the shrimp. We then heated the liquid to various temperatures. Too low and the shrimp were mushy; too high and they turned tough. Eventually, we discovered that heating the liquid to a near simmer (165 degrees) was ideal. The shrimp were actually flavorful, and their texture was so firm and crisp that several tasters compared them to lobster.

All we needed now was the perfect deli-style dressing. While mayonnaise provides creamy cohesiveness, we didn't want it to mask the shrimp's flavor or drown out the other ingredients. After testing several amounts, tasters felt a perfect coating was ¼ cup per 1 pound of shrimp. Diced celery, minced shallots, chopped herbs, and fresh lemon juice added unifying aromatic and herbal notes and a pleasant vegetal crunch and acidity. With less mayonnaise, we found we could also add variety to the salads with bolder flavors like chipotle chile, orange, and roasted red pepper.

WHAT WE LEARNED: For best flavor, begin poaching the shrimp in cold liquid—this cooks the shrimp in a gentle, slow manner and allows for more of the poaching liquid's flavors to penetrate the shrimp. For the dressing, don't go overboard with the mayonnaise; just ¼ cup per pound of shrimp is enough to add cohesiveness to the salad without obscuring the flavor of the shrimp—or the dressing's other flavors.

SHRIMP SALAD

serves 4

This recipe can also be prepared with large shrimp (31 to 40 per pound); the cooking time will be 1 to 2 minutes less. The shrimp can be cooked up to 24 hours in advance, but hold off on dressing the salad until ready to serve. The recipe can be easily doubled; cook the shrimp in a 7-quart Dutch oven and increase the cooking time to 12 to 14 minutes. Serve the salad on a bed of greens or on a buttered and grilled bun.

- 1 pound extra-large shrimp (21 to 25 per pound), peeled and deveined
- ¼ cup plus 1 tablespoon juice from 2 to 3 lemons, spent halves reserved
- 5 sprigs plus 1 teaspoon minced fresh parsley leaves
- 3 sprigs plus 1 teaspoon minced fresh tarragon leaves
- 1 teaspoon whole black peppercorns plus ground black pepper
- 1 tablespoon sugar
  Salt
- ¼ cup mayonnaise
- 1 small shallot, minced (about 2 tablespoons)
- 1 small celery rib, minced (about ⅓ cup)

1. Combine the shrimp, ¼ cup lemon juice, reserved lemon halves, parsley sprigs, tarragon sprigs, whole peppercorns, sugar, and 1 teaspoon salt with 2 cups cold water in a medium saucepan. Place the saucepan over medium heat and cook the shrimp, stirring several times, until pink, firm to touch, and the centers are no longer translucent, 8 to 10 minutes (the water should be just bubbling around the edge of the pan and register 165 degrees on an instant-read thermometer). Remove the pan from the heat, cover, and let the shrimp sit in the broth for 2 minutes.

2. Meanwhile, fill a medium bowl with ice water. Drain the shrimp into a colander, and discard the lemon halves,

herbs, and spices. Immediately transfer the shrimp to the ice water to stop cooking and chill thoroughly, about 3 minutes. Remove the shrimp from the ice water and pat dry with paper towels.

3. Whisk together the mayonnaise, shallot, celery, remaining tablespoon lemon juice, minced parsley, and minced tarragon in a medium bowl. Cut the shrimp in half lengthwise and then each half into thirds; add the shrimp to the mayonnaise mixture and toss to combine. Adjust the seasoning with salt and pepper and serve.

VARIATIONS

SHRIMP SALAD WITH ROASTED RED PEPPER AND BASIL

This Italian-style variation is especially good served over bitter greens.

Follow the recipe for Shrimp Salad, omitting the tarragon sprigs from the cooking liquid. Replace the celery, minced parsley, and minced tarragon with ⅓ cup thinly sliced jarred roasted red peppers, 2 teaspoons rinsed capers, and 3 tablespoons chopped fresh basil leaves.

SHRIMP SALAD WITH AVOCADO AND ORANGE

Avocado and orange are a refreshing addition to this salad.

Follow the recipe for Shrimp Salad, omitting the tarragon sprigs from the cooking liquid. Replace the celery, minced parsley, and minced tarragon with 4 halved and thinly sliced radishes; 1 large orange, peeled and cut into ½-inch pieces; ½ ripe avocado, cut into ½-inch pieces; and 2 teaspoons minced fresh mint leaves.

SPICY SHRIMP SALAD WITH CORN AND CHIPOTLE

Chipotle gives this salad a spicy kick; use less if you prefer milder heat.

Follow the recipe for Shrimp Salad, substituting the juice from 3 to 4 limes for the lemon juice (use the spent halves in the cooking liquid) and omitting the tarragon sprigs from the cooking liquid. Replace the celery, minced parsley, and minced tarragon with ½ cup cooked corn kernels, 2 minced chipotle chiles in adobo sauce (about 2 tablespoons), and 1 tablespoon minced fresh cilantro leaves.

SHRIMP SALAD WITH WASABI AND PICKLED GINGER

Follow the recipe for Shrimp Salad, omitting the tarragon sprigs from the cooking liquid. Replace the shallot, minced parsley, and minced tarragon with 2 teaspoons wasabi powder; 2 scallions, white and green parts sliced thin; 2 tablespoons chopped pickled ginger; and 1 tablespoon toasted sesame seeds.

EQUIPMENT CORNER:
Kitchen Timers

IN THE TEST KITCHEN, TIMING IS EVERYTHING. TO THAT end, we tested 10 new models designed to handle multitask timing. We were looking for timers with a range of at least 10 hours (for longer braises, brines, and barbecues) that could count up after the alarm and display two times simultaneously. The compact, easy-to-use single-display Polder Dual Timer/Stopwatch ($19.99) impressed us the most (the previous test kitchen favorite was the single-display Polder Electronic Clock, Timer and Stopwatch, at $5 less). The Taylor Two Event Big Digit Timer/Clock ($10.99) offers the same functions but isn't so easy to use. At half the price, it's our choice for best buy.

Rating Kitchen Timers

WE TESTED 10 MODELS OF KITCHEN TIMERS AND RATED THEM FOR EASE OF USE AND ABILITY TO MULTITASK. THE timers are listed in order of preference. See www.americastestkitchen.com for up-to-date prices and mail-order sources for top-rated products.

RECOMMENDED

Polder Dual Timer/Stopwatch, Model #893

$19.99

Its compact size and easy-to-read display made it the most sensibly designed of the timers tested. When set on the counter, though, it wobbled.

RECOMMENDED

Taylor Two Event Big Digit Timer/Clock, Model #5809

$10

The least expensive of the timers, it still offered all the features we were looking for, making it a best buy. However, the magnetic backing is barely up to the task of keeping this timer mounted.

RECOMMENDED WITH RESERVATIONS

Polder Triple Kitchen Timer/Clock, Model #891-90

$11.99

This model offered all the desired features with one major flaw: Its lack of mounting options requires putting the timer on the counter if a metal surface for magnetic attachment is not available.

RECOMMENDED WITH RESERVATIONS

Bonjour Multi Kitchen Timer with Clock, Model #53459

$16.99

Although the three timers and clean design are strengths, the count-up feature stops once the alarm is silenced.

RECOMMENDED WITH RESERVATIONS

Maverick Triple Timer (manufactured for Williams-Sonoma), Model #TM-03

$18.38

This timer was nearly identical to the Bonjour Multi Kitchen Timer, but minor style differences placed it slightly lower in the rankings. Buttons were close-set and hard to push.

RECOMMENDED WITH RESERVATIONS

Amco Houseworks Magnetic Double Digital Timer, Model #8543

$25

The missing clock and count-up feature put this timer at a disadvantage.

RECOMMENDED WITH RESERVATIONS

West Bend Dual Channel Electronic Timer, Model #40056

$19.99

Functionally, this West Bend timer is a twin to the Amco Houseworks timer. Poor audibility is a drawback, and with no count-up feature, it's impossible to know how long a dish has overcooked.

NOT RECOMMENDED

Bonjour Double Timer with Clock, Model #53460

$24.95

Like it or not, this timer has no place to go but the countertop. The short time range makes it impossible to time long braising or brining.

NOT RECOMMENDED

Bonjour Double Folding Timer with Clock, Model #53461

$24.95

To set the timer upright, the detachable magnet must be removed (and ultimately lost). The controls on the back make it unnecessarily complicated to set. A locking switch must be slid to set and then slid back to lock before the start button will trigger the countdown.

NOT RECOMMENDED

American Innovative Chef's Quad Timer, Model #Quad 4W-US

$19.99

Of all the timers tested, this was the most baffling. A rotary collar to set the time was tough to turn. Once set past an hour, the time goes up in five-minute increments. After two hours, the time can only be set in increments of 15 minutes.

Rating Tuna

TWENTY MEMBERS OF THE AMERICA'S TEST KITCHEN STAFF TASTED EIGHT TUNAS (FIVE CANNED IN WATER, three in water-packed pouches) and rated them for flavor and texture. The tunas are listed below in order of preference and are available in supermarkets.

RECOMMENDED

Chicken of the Sea Solid White Albacore Tuna in Water

$1.39 for 6-ounce can

Tasters liked its "good, mild flavor," "moist texture," "chunky appearance," "large, beautiful flakes," and "taste of the ocean."

RECOMMENDED

StarKist Solid White Albacore Tuna in Water

$1.39 for 6-ounce can

Texture ruled with this "firm," "flaky," and "moist" tuna that was praised for its "fresh taste," "perfect salt level," and "mellow flavor."

RECOMMENDED WITH RESERVATIONS

StarKist Premium Chunk White Albacore Tuna in Water

$3.69 for 7.06-ounce pouch

Seasoning seemed to be the key in this "tangy," "tart," "salty and briny" tuna. Tasters especially appreciated its "clean" and "bright" flavor.

RECOMMENDED WITH RESERVATIONS

Geisha Albacore Solid White Tuna in Water

$1.29 for 6-ounce can

Fans appreciated this tuna's "dense," "meaty," and "chunky" texture, saying that it "looks like real fish." The flavor was deemed "very mild."

RECOMMENDED WITH RESERVATIONS

3 Diamonds Fancy Albacore Solid White Tuna in Water

$1.29 for 6-ounce can

While tasters liked its "juicy and moist" texture, some were put off by this tuna's "strong fish taste." As one taster wrote, "This is why people don't like seafood."

RECOMMENDED WITH RESERVATIONS

Chicken of the Sea Premium Albacore Tuna in Water

$3.67 for 7.1-ounce pouch

This tuna elicited mixed comments, ranging from "clean flavor" to "stinky." A few tasters thought this tuna was "meaty," but there were many complaints about "pre-chewed" texture.

NOT RECOMMENDED

Bumble Bee Solid White Albacore Tuna in Water

$1.29 for 6-ounce can

Tasters compared this "harsh," "sour" tuna to anchovies, sardines, and even "old salmon." The "bloody" appearance and "dry" texture didn't help.

NOT RECOMMENDED

Bumble Bee Premium Albacore Tuna in Water

$3.39 for 7.06-ounce pouch

Several tasters likened this sample to cat food, describing the texture as "previously chewed," "ultra-chopped," and "mealy." Its "strong fishiness" sunk this tuna to the bottom of our list.

TASTING LAB: Tuna

IN RECENT YEARS, POUCHED TUNA HAS APPEARED IN supermarkets, promising a fresher, less processed, better-tasting alternative to canned tuna. But is pouched tuna really better than its canned cousin?

A preliminary tasting showed that tasters had a strong preference for solid white albacore tuna packed in water, which is the mildest variety of processed tuna; chunk light tuna had unappealing strong flavors, and albacore packed in oil was too mushy. We rounded up the top five national brands of canned albacore tuna in water and tasted them blind against three pouched water-packed albacore products.

The results were, in a word, startling. Out of the eight tunas sampled, tasters chose two canned products—Chicken of the Sea and StarKist—as their overall favorites; in fact, canned tunas took four of the top five spots.

Why didn't the pouched products, which require less processing and therefore should have a fresher flavor, swim away with the lead? When it comes to tuna, more flavor is not necessarily a good thing. Our tasters preferred the milder brands (whether pouched or canned) and down-graded Bumble Bee (the big loser in this test) for tasting too fishy. Given the minimal flavor differences in the mild tunas, our tasters focused on texture—and here's where the canned tunas won the race.

Because the cans are about three times as wide as the pouches (1½ inches versus about half an inch), the tuna must be broken down to get it into the pouch; the cans hold larger pieces of fish. Larger pieces mean that canned tuna has larger flakes than pouched tuna. In the end, we found meaty canned tuna was preferred to mushier pouched tuna.

Using a model of a whole pork loin, Chris explains the differences among chops cut from each section. For our Skillet-Barbecued Pork Chops, we prefer bone-in rib chops, which cook up juicy and tender—a perfect match to the dish's tangy barbecue sauce.

RAINY DAY BBQ
CHAPTER 4

pork chops

There's no getting around it—unless your climate is warm year-round, grilling season is limited and often downright short. And even in warm climes, inclement weather can make standing over a grill unpleasant. For these occasions, we wanted an indoor method for one of our favorite barbecued dishes—pork chops. We wanted pork chops with juicy meat and slathered with a smoky, tangy barbecue sauce. But how would we replicate the savory crust of a grilled pork chop? When cooking pork chops indoors, liquid exuded by the chops pools under the meat, inhibiting that flavorful crust from forming. We set out to solve this puzzle.

A cool, creamy macaroni salad is the perfect accompaniment to pork chops, but really good versions of this salad are hard to come by. Too often, the dish is bland and downright dry. Other times, a heavy hand with the mayonnaise-based dressing turns the macaroni greasy. We wanted to find the perfect ratio of macaroni to dressing. And while we didn't want a bland salad, we didn't want to go overboard either—we'd choose our seasonings sensibly to keep in line with the homespun spirit of this popular picnic salad.

SKILLET BBQ PORK CHOPS

WHAT WE WANTED: An indoor method for replicating the tangy, sweet burnished crust and juicy meat of a grilled pork chop.

If we had our way, the calendar would be made of nothing but late-summer afternoons, but alas, the New England grilling season ends abruptly. To enjoy the smoky, salty-sweet flavor of a grilled pork chop coated with a spicy barbecue sauce in the off-season, our only options are going to a restaurant with an indoor grill or attempting it in our own kitchen. Getting smoky, charred flavor into the chops is almost assured when cooking over a live fire outdoors. Back inside, it can be more elusive.

The first order of business was to find a way of giving the pork a nice, evenly charred surface without overcooking the interior. We tried searing the chops in a blazing hot skillet and then turning the heat way down once they developed a good crust, a method we've used to good effect with steak or lamb chops. Aside from the fact that this technique filled our kitchen with billowing smoke and splattered oil, the pork ended up dry and stringy by the time a well-charred crust had developed.

The problem? Pork chops are leaner than steaks or lamb chops and therefore more prone to drying out. Brining improved matters a bit, but it was clear that our technique was going to need an overhaul. Since we've successfully cooked charred, juicy pork chops on an outdoor grill, we wondered what was so different about cooking in a skillet.

For one thing, a piece of meat elevated above the heat source on a grill doesn't remain in contact with the juices released during cooking. In a pan, pork chops end up simmering in their own juices, which lowers the temperature of the cooking surface, leading to meat that overcooks before

it can brown properly. If we couldn't get the pork itself to char properly, why not add another element that would char instead of the pork? We realized that there was already an outdoor technique that would accomplish this exact goal—the dry spice rub.

Though standard fare for a grill, a spice rub is rarely applied to meat meant to be cooked in a skillet; in a hot skillet, the rub (which darkens more readily than the pork

proteins) doesn't just char, it blackens. But by starting with medium heat rather than high, we found we could let the spice rub char while the pork cooked at a gentler pace, which resulted in chops that were perfectly cooked both inside and out. Lowering the heat solved our smoky kitchen problem, as well. For the rub, we settled on a simple mix of five ingredients: cumin and paprika for their pungent, smoky overtones, black pepper for heat, and coriander and brown sugar for their pork-complementing sweetness.

We turned our attention to the barbecue sauce. Starting with the requisite ketchup and molasses, we ran through a battery of taste tests. Hits of Worcestershire sauce and Dijon mustard gave the sauce complexity and heat, and onions and cider vinegar added a pungent kick that tasters liked. We found that grating the onion distributed the onion flavor evenly and made for a smoother sauce. A spoonful of brown sugar helped mellow out and blend the sharper flavors. We figured a couple of teaspoons of our dry spice rub added to our sauce could only improve its flavor. Tasters confirmed our hunch.

Although our sauce was now balanced, we still felt it needed more outdoor flavor. Without the benefit of a live fire with smoldering hickory chips, we had only one place to turn: liquid smoke. In the test kitchen, we generally shun artificial or synthetic ingredients, so we were pleased when hands-on research revealed that liquid smoke is a completely natural product (see "Making Liquid Smoke" on page 38). All suspicions were laid to rest when a batch of sauce to which we had surreptitiously added a teaspoon of liquid smoke swept the next blind tasting. The key to keeping liquid smoke palatable is moderation. When we tried adding more liquid smoke, the flavor was harsh and overwhelming.

Now we had our charred pork and our smoky sauce, but we also had a problem. We had been ignoring something every good outdoor cook knows: The sauce is not merely an accompaniment to the meat—it's an essential part of the cooking process. We had been treating the chops and the sauce as two discrete elements rather than parts of the same entity, applying the sauce only after the meat had been fully cooked. On an outdoor grill, the sauce caramelizes and intensifies, lacquering the chops in a sticky glaze. Could we re-create this process on our stovetop without ruining our pans and splattering hot barbecue sauce all over the kitchen?

Brushing the sauce directly onto the chops while they were still in the pan produced a sticky, burnt mess and a stovetop spotted with sauce. What if instead of bringing the sauce to the pork, we brought the pork to the sauce? We cooked up a new batch of chops, this time removing them from the pan a few minutes early. We were then able to brush the chops with a thin coat of barbecue sauce and wipe out the skillet so we could finish cooking with a clean, hot surface. When the pork chops made a vigorous sizzle as they went back into the hot pan for their second sear, our hopes were high.

We flipped the chops and saw that the sauce had reduced to a sticky, caramelized, smoky glaze that firmly adhered to the meat. Served with the remaining pan-reduced sauce on the side, these skillet-barbecued pork chops with a rib-sticking sauce tasted like the real deal.

WHAT WE LEARNED: Brine the chops for juicy, well-seasoned meat. Coat the chops with a spice rub, which chars much more readily than pork chops and gives the meat the flavor and appearance of real barbecued. Cook the chops over medium heat so that the rub doesn't blacken. Reserve some of the rub to add a spicy kick to the barbecue sauce and add just 1 teaspoon liquid smoke to give the sauce authentic outdoor grill flavor.

TECHNIQUE: Building Outdoor Flavor on the Stovetop

1. Apply Rub: After brining the chops, coat both sides with dry spice rub, pressing gently to adhere.

2. Add Smoke: Combine the sauce ingredients, adding 1 teaspoon of liquid smoke. Too much liquid smoke will overpower the sauce.

3. Sear Chops: Place the chops in the skillet and don't move them until charred black spots (like you'd get on a hot grill grate) develop.

4. Sauce and Sear Again: When the chops are nearly done, remove them from the pan, brush with sauce, and sear again to lacquer the sauce onto the chops.

SKILLET-BARBECUED PORK CHOPS

serves 4

We prefer natural to enhanced pork (pork that has been injected with a salt solution to increase moistness and flavor) for this recipe, though enhanced pork can be used. If using enhanced pork, skip the brining in step 1 and add ½ teaspoon salt to the spice rub. Grate the onion on the large holes of a box grater. In step 5, check your chops after three minutes. If you don't hear a definite sizzle and the chops have not started to brown on the underside, increase the heat to medium-high and continue cooking as directed (follow the indicated temperatures for the remainder of the recipe).

pork chops

- ½ cup table salt or 1 cup Diamond Crystal kosher salt or ¾ cup Morton's kosher salt
- 4 bone-in pork rib chops, ¾ to 1 inch thick (8 to 10 ounces each), trimmed of excess fat, 2 slits cut 2 inches apart through fat and silver skin of each chop according to the illustration on page 37 (see note)
- 4 teaspoons vegetable oil

spice rub

- 1 tablespoon paprika
- 1 tablespoon brown sugar
- 2 teaspoons ground coriander
- 1 teaspoon ground cumin
- 1 teaspoon ground black pepper

sauce

- ½ cup ketchup
- 3 tablespoons light or mild molasses
- 2 tablespoons grated onion (see note)
- 2 tablespoons Worcestershire sauce
- 2 tablespoons Dijon mustard
- 1 tablespoon cider vinegar
- 1 tablespoon brown sugar
- 1 teaspoon liquid smoke

1. FOR THE PORK CHOPS: Dissolve the salt in 2 quarts water in a large bowl or container. Submerge the chops in the brine, cover with plastic wrap, and refrigerate for 30 minutes.

2. FOR THE SPICE RUB: Combine the ingredients in a small bowl. Measure 2 teaspoons of the mixture into a medium bowl and set aside for the sauce. Transfer the remaining spice rub to a pie plate or large plate.

3. FOR THE SAUCE: Whisk the ingredients in the bowl with the reserved spice mixture until thoroughly combined; set aside.

4. Remove the chops from the brine and pat dry with paper towels. Coat both sides of the chops with the spice rub, pressing gently so the rub adheres. Pat the chops to remove excess rub; discard excess rub.

5. Heat 1 tablespoon of the oil in a 12-inch heavy-bottomed nonstick skillet over medium heat until just smoking. Following the illustration at right, place the chops in the skillet in pinwheel formation; cook until browned and charred in spots, 5 to 8 minutes. Flip the chops and continue to cook until the second side is browned and charred and the centers of the chops registers 130 degrees on an instant-read thermometer, 4 to 8 minutes. Remove the skillet from the heat and transfer the chops to a large plate or baking sheet. Lightly brush the top of each chop with about 2 teaspoons of the sauce.

6. Wipe out the pan with paper towels and return to medium heat. Add the remaining teaspoon oil and heat until just smoking. Add the chops to the pan, sauce side down, and cook without moving them until the sauce has caramelized and charred in spots, about 1 minute. While cooking, lightly brush the top of each chop with about 2 teaspoons of the sauce. Turn the chops and cook until the second side is charred and caramelized and the centers of the chops register 140 degrees on instant-read thermometer, 1 to 1½ minutes.

7. Transfer the chops back to the large plate or baking sheet, tent with foil, and let rest 5 minutes. The internal temperature should rise to about 145 degrees. Meanwhile, add the remaining sauce to the pan and cook, over medium heat, scraping the bottom with a wooden spoon to loosen any browned bits, until thickened to ketchup-like consistency and reduced to ⅔ cup, about 3 minutes. Brush each chop with 1 tablespoon of the reduced sauce and serve immediately, passing the remaining sauce at the table.

TECHNIQUE: Searing Chops

Problem: Pork chops buckle during cooking.
Solution: Cut two slits about 2 inches apart through fat and connective tissue.

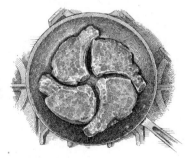

Problem: Pork chops don't fit in pan.
Solution: Arrange pork chops with ribs pointing toward the center of the pan in a pinwheel pattern.

SCIENCE DESK: Making Liquid Smoke

WE WERE AMONG THE MANY PEOPLE WHO ASSUME that there must be some kind of synthetic chemical chicanery going on in the making of "liquid smoke" flavoring. But according to the Colgin Company (which patented modern liquid-smoke production in the early 20th century), that's not the case. Liquid smoke is made by channeling smoke from smoldering wood chips through a condenser, which quickly cools the vapors, causing them to liquefy (just like the drops that form when you breathe on a piece of cold glass). The water-soluble flavor compounds in the smoke are trapped within this liquid, while the nonsoluble, carcinogenic tars and resins are removed by a series of filters, resulting in a clean, smoke-flavored liquid.

Ever the skeptics, we decided the only way the commercial product was going to get our approval was if we could bottle up some smoke ourselves. To do this, we created a small-scale mock-up of the commercial method, involving a duct fan, an ice-chilled siphon, and a glass coil condenser.

In a blind taste test between homemade and store-bought liquid smoke, homemade was the winner, with tasters praising its clean, intense, smoky flavor. But we spent an entire day and $50 on materials to produce just three tablespoons of homemade liquid smoke. Commercial liquid smoke is just fine, especially if you avoid brands with additives like salt, vinegar, or molasses and buy liquid smoke that contains nothing but smoke and water. Wright's Liquid Smoke ($2.99 for 3.5 ounces) is our top-rated brand.

EQUIPMENT CORNER: Chef's Knives

WE ASK A LOT OF OUR CHEF'S KNIVES IN THE TEST kitchen. We want one that's versatile enough to handle almost any cutting task, whether it's mincing delicate herbs or cutting through meat and bones. We want a sharp blade that slices easily, without requiring a lot of force. We want a comfortable handle that doesn't hurt our hands or get slippery when wet or greasy.

We've tested 30 knives in recent years and we know

SHOPPING NOTES: Choosing Chops

Given the number of pork chops we went through to develop this recipe, we thought purchasing "family size" packs of chops would be the logical choice, but we ran into some unpleasant surprises at the bottom of the package.

Looks Like A Good Value
The chops on top look good, but beware of what lies beneath.

Hidden Surprises
The chops they don't want you to see are gristly and unevenly butchered.

Best Bet
Choose a smaller pack where the meat is laid in a single layer so you can see what you are paying for.

what we like. But manufacturers have recently begun offering new designs that challenge many of our assumptions about the classic chef's knife. We've seen unusual handle angles and blades, ergonomic designs for reducing hand fatigue and improving grip, and a variety of other features that promise better handling and easier cutting. Would any of these prove to be a real improvement? We pitted seven innovative knives against the winners of our last comprehensive testing, the Victorinox Fibrox and the Wüsthof Grand Prix. (The Grand Prix has been replaced by the Grand Prix II; we used the new model for this test.)

A good handle should virtually disappear in your grip, making the knife the proverbial "extension of your hand." The knives in our lineup featured handles shaped like metal triangles or wedges, handles tilted upward, handles covered with spongy plastic or pebbled polypropylene, and handles with ergonomic bumps and bulges.

Metal handles on the Chroma Type 301 and Furi FX with Coppertail became slippery when wet or greasy. We continued slipping and sliding with the Wüsthof Grand Prix II's pebble-textured polypropylene handle. The slick plastic grip was heavy and uncomfortable, making the knife feel "angular and awkward."

Testers were more impressed by Alton's Angle, a striking knife designed by Food Network star Alton Brown. Instead of continuing straight from the blade, its handle rises in a 10-degree angle to keep knuckles clear of the cutting board. This provided leverage for hard cuts, but there were some complaints about the exaggerated rocking motion during mincing. The rounded, D-shaped grip was comfortable, but the handle's length made it bump above the wrists of some testers. Testers also had mixed feelings about the bright green ergonomic handle on the Sanelli Premana. Although they liked the "squishy" feel of the handle, they had trouble gripping this knife with chickeny hands.

The one innovative handle that really won testers over was on the Ken Onion knife by Kershaw Shun. (Ken Onion is a well-regarded knife maker.) The short wooden handle arcs downward, with a pronounced bump on the

belly. The metal bolster is cut away to help fingers grip the blade and mercifully extends over the sharp spine to protect the fingers. The wood did not become slippery, and testers reported that the knife felt natural and maneuverable as they worked. A nice touch: The bottom of the bolster stops ½ inch short of the knife's heel, allowing it to pass completely through a sharpening device.

To keep food from sticking as you slice, designers cut dimples all over the blade surface on the Glestain Indented-Blade Gyutou; used rippled steel on the Ken Onion and Alton's Angle knives; and made the MAC Superior blade super-thin and light, with a roughened strip running just

above the cutting edge. In contrast to most of the changes to traditional handle design, we found all of these blade innovations to be successful. These four knives received top scores, winning praise for their agility, ease of use, and precision cutting.

But what made them work, aside from the no-stick blades? One clue came when we realized they were all made by Japanese companies, which are known for their thin-profile knives. We measured the difference in width from spine to blade and found that, indeed, the Japanese knives started out thinner at the spine—as much as 40 percent thinner—than the losing knives and also narrowed less as they neared the cutting edge, with our top Japanese knife, the Glestain, varying by less than 1 millimeter from spine to edge. Why would this matter? As it enters food, your knife can either cut or act as a wedge that pushes the food apart. While a wedge-like blade can be useful for jobs like splitting open a heavy squash, it can rip food and make slicing slower and less precise.

Testers praised the Glestain for its "super-smooth" slicing. Mincing was so efficient it made "parsley almost like dust." It made quick work of raw chicken, onions, and squash, and it stayed sharp throughout testing. The MAC knife, lighter and more utilitarian than the Glestain, was equally sharp and efficient, and testers had high praise for the blades on both Kershaw knives.

So is there a new world order, with Japanese knives taking the lead from traditional Western styles? Not so fast. Our previous test kitchen winner, the very affordable Swiss-made Victorinox Fibrox ($22.95), defeated the best of the innovative newcomers, though just barely. A closer look revealed that, like the Japanese models, its spine starts out thinner and tapers less steeply than other Western knives. This lightweight knife is particularly agile, and the nonslip handle is very comfortable. We found plenty to admire among the top-rated Japanese knives in this test, but we are hard-pressed to pay a premium—sometimes as much as $210—for their innovations.

What do you get when you spend $475 on a chef's knife? You get handmade custom work by Master Bladesmith Bob Kramer of Olympia, Wash. Is this knife markedly better than the competition? Yes. The Kramer knife outperformed every knife we've ever rated. Testers found it exceptionally comfortable, sharp, and agile.

Kramer, a former professional chef, is one of only 100 Master Bladesmiths in America, having passed the American Bladesmith Society's rigorous series of tests. Unlike most bladesmiths, Kramer makes only kitchen cutlery. He uses carbon steel without chromium; this composition makes for a harder, thinner, and sharper blade than most kitchen knives. It will rust and discolor if you don't keep it clean and dry, but the blade is especially sharp and proved durable in our tests.

So why do his knives cost so much? Kramer heat-treats the blades, one at a time, in a seven-step process that takes six hours. He also makes the handles, polishing equatorial burl wood. As for the mass-produced knives made by the competition, Kramer says, "It's like comparing Twinkies to a Grand Marnier soufflé." We agree, but that's one expensive soufflé.

Rating Innovative Chef's Knives

WE TESTED NINE CHEF'S KNIVES AND EVALUATED THEM FOR COMFORT, USER-FRIENDLINESS, SHARPNESS, AND EDGE RETENTION. The knives are listed in order of preference. See www.americastestkitchen.com for up-to-date prices and mail-order sources for top-rated products.

RECOMMENDED
Victorinox Fibrox 8-Inch Chef's Knife
$22.95

"There's a reason we have 20 or 30 of these in this kitchen," said a tester; others agreed, calling it "Old Faithful." They found it notably sharp, with "great maneuverability." In sum: "This is exactly what a knife is supposed to be." At just $22.95, this knife is also a great value.

RECOMMENDED
Glestain Indented-Blade 8.2-Inch Gyutou (Chef's Knife)
$210

Testers appreciated the thin blade's razor sharpness and an enhanced feeling of control. "Effortless cutting—the food jumps away," remarked one tester.

RECOMMENDED
Kershaw Shun 8.25-Inch Ken Onion Chef's Knife
$193.95

This "flashy-looking" knife won points for its "extreme sharpness." A pronounced curve aided the rocking motion. Most testers found it "really comfy," but the tester with the largest hands complained about the "ergonomic bump" on the handle.

RECOMMENDED
MAC Knives 8-Inch Chef's Knife, Superior
$54.95

This "lightweight," "sharp, thin" knife won raves for its "surgical" ability to slice easily through chicken bones and squash. But there were a few complaints that the rounded tip made it harder to pierce food.

RECOMMENDED
Kershaw Shun 8-Inch Alton's Angle Chef's Knife
$130.95

Some testers disliked the angled handle, complaining that it forced a more "exaggerated rocking," while others liked the way it added leverage when cutting squash and bones. Everyone agreed that the blade "cuts beautifully."

RECOMMENDED WITH RESERVATIONS
Sanelli 9.5-Inch Premana Professional Cook's Knife
$33.92

Testers liked the slightly squishy handle. The lightweight blade did well with onions and parsley but on harder tasks felt "cheap" and "had trouble getting through bones."

RECOMMENDED WITH RESERVATIONS
Wüsthof Grand Prix II 8-Inch Cook's Knife
$94.95

This update performed worse than its well-regarded predecessor. The redesigned handle became very slippery when hands were wet. "Looks more comfortable than it actually is," said one tester. Testers complained that the "knife is heavy" and "handle is too long."

RECOMMENDED WITH RESERVATIONS
Furi 8-Inch Cook's Knife with Coppertail, FX Forged
$94.95

This knife made "precision cuts" while dicing onion, but parsley seemed crushed. Testers with larger hands liked the handle more than did those with smaller hands, but all complained about slipperiness when their hands were wet or greasy.

RECOMMENDED WITH RESERVATIONS
Chroma 8-Inch Chef's Knife, Type 301
$81.95

Testers were surprised that the "weird-looking" triangular metal handle felt "bizarrely comfortable" in the palm, but all disliked the metal "nub," which "goes exactly where my thumb wants to go and puts pressure on it." One said simply, "It hurts." The knife was "very sharp."

MACARONI SALAD

WHAT WE WANTED: A picnic-worthy macaroni salad that is flavorful, not bland, and neither too dry nor too greasy.

It's often the simplest dishes that cause us the most trouble in the test kitchen. Macaroni salad is usually thrown together for a barbecue or block party without much thought. Everyone knows the recipe—cooked macaroni and mayonnaise tossed with chopped vegetables and seasonings. Although serviceable, this formula often makes a dry, bland salad. And that's a shame, because a great macaroni salad shouldn't be any more difficult to prepare than a mediocre one.

The main problem is the macaroni, which soaks up the mayonnaise and leaves the salad very dry. Stirring in more mayonnaise makes the salad greasy. So how do you satisfy macaroni's thirst without using an excess of mayonnaise? Our first attempt to solve this problem was to make sure that the macaroni was fully cooked, so that it would not be able to absorb any more moisture. But rather than fixing the problem, this made it worse. The pasta still soaked up the mayonnaise, but now it was also mushy.

Next we cooked the macaroni only till it still had some bite left and rinsed it under cold water before tossing with the mayonnaise. The rinsing cooled the macaroni immediately, and the cooled macaroni soaked up less mayonnaise. But after 10 to 15 minutes, the salad still tended to dry out. We finally hit upon a novel idea: What if we didn't drain the pasta so thoroughly? If the pasta was wet, perhaps it would absorb water rather than mayonnaise. At first even this idea seemed bound to fail. A salad made with damp macaroni looked pretty watery. But after a few minutes the macaroni absorbed the extra water, and the consistency of the salad became perfect. If left for a long time, this salad, too, will dry out a bit, but simply stirring in a few tablespoons of water restores its original creamy consistency.

As for flavorings, we tried combinations of various herbs, vegetables, and spices but found that the obvious choices—onion, celery, parsley, Dijon mustard, cayenne, and lemon juice—worked best. The one somewhat unusual ingredient that our tasters liked was garlic powder. Although raw garlic was too harsh, the powder rounded out the flavor of the salad in a really nice way. Our last thought was that if the macaroni soaked up water, maybe it would also soak up the flavor of the seasonings. After making two salads side by side—one in which the seasonings were tossed with the pasta and allowed to sit briefly before the mayonnaise was added, the other in which everything was tossed together at once—we were surprised by the difference. The pasta tossed with the seasonings first, then the mayonnaise, tasted fresher and brighter. Finally, a word on mayonnaise. Regular mayonnaise tastes best (no surprise here), but low-fat mayonnaise isn't bad in this salad. Nonfat mayonnaise and Miracle Whip should be avoided, though, because of their candy-sweet flavor.

WHAT WE LEARNED: Don't drain the macaroni too thoroughly; the pasta will absorb the excess water as it sits and prevent the finished salad from drying out. Add seasonings to the pasta first and then the mayonnaise, so that the seasonings can penetrate and flavor the macaroni. Garlic powder works best in this salad, as fresh garlic is too harsh.

COOL AND CREAMY MACARONI SALAD

serves 8 to 10

Don't drain the macaroni too well before adding the other ingredients—a little extra moisture will keep the salad from drying out. If you've made the salad ahead of time, simply stir in a little warm water to loosen the texture.

        Salt
 1   pound elbow macaroni
 ½   small red onion, minced
 1   celery rib, minced
 ¼   cup minced fresh parsley leaves
 2   tablespoons juice from 1 lemon
 1   tablespoon Dijon mustard
 ⅛   teaspoon garlic powder
        Pinch cayenne pepper
 1½   cups mayonnaise
        Ground black pepper

1. Bring 4 quarts water to a boil in a large pot. Add 1 table-spoon salt and the macaroni and cook until nearly tender, about 5 minutes. Drain in a colander and rinse with cold water until cool, then drain briefly so that the macaroni remains moist. Transfer to a large bowl.

2. Stir in the onion, celery, parsley, lemon juice, mustard, garlic powder, and cayenne, and let sit until the flavors are absorbed, about 2 minutes. Add the mayonnaise and let sit until the salad texture is no longer watery, 5 to 10 minutes. Season with salt and pepper to taste. Serve. (The salad can be covered and refrigerated for up to 2 days. Check the consistency and seasonings before serving.)

TECHNIQUE:
Mincing Onions with Ease

1. Start with a peeled, quartered onion. Working with one quarter at a time, place the quarter with one flat side down on the cutting board. Make two or three slices across the quarter and down to, but not through, the root end.

2. Turn the quarter onto its other flat side and repeat the slicing.

3. Using the claw grip, with your fingertips folded inward toward your palm to hold the onion in place, cut across the existing slices to make an even dice.

Erin, the test kitchen director, oversees our busy test kitchen, where dishes are being carefully readied for the set. Here, she wastes no time as she portions out tomato sauce while waiting for water to come to a boil for the pasta.

PASTA AND TOMATOES,
CHAPTER 5
reimagined

We don't have anything against spaghetti and meat balls or pasta with marinara, but the world of pasta and tomatoes extends far beyond these popular standbys. One such dish, penne alla vodka, is a delicious take on the pairing—and with vodka and cream added to the mix, a touch elegant too. But a heavy hand with the vodka, or adding it too late in the process (so the alcohol doesn't cook off) often ruins this dish. The cream must also be carefully considered—too much cream dulls rather than enriches the sauce. In order to turn out an estimable version of penne alla vodka, we would need to test each ingredient as well as the process by which they're combined.

Nearly everyone is familiar with the summer favorite Caprese salad—slices of peak summer tomatoes and fresh, milky mozzarella drizzled with olive oil and sprinkled with basil. Less well known is pasta Caprese, where the salad is essentially tossed with hot pasta—the tomatoes warm and sweeten, the basil releases its fragrant oils, and the mozzarella melts into creamy pockets that blend with the pasta, adding richness and heft to an otherwise light dish. But too often this simple-sounding dish fails. When you're working with substandard tomatoes (yes, it happens, even in summer), the dish falls flat. The mozzarella, too, can be particularly vexing, seizing into chewy wads seconds after it hits the hot pasta. Our goal was twofold: We'd need to find a way to boost the flavor of less-than-stellar tomatoes, and we'd need to solve the mystery of why the cheese seizes in this dish—and how to prevent it.

PENNE WITH VODKA

WHAT WE WANTED: Penne tossed with a sophisticated tomato sauce enriched with cream and accented with vodka.

Asked to develop a recipe for penne alla vodka, we phoned our Italian friends. Perhaps their grandmothers might share old family secrets? No such luck. Further research revealed that this unusual recipe for tomato sauce finished with vodka and cream isn't steeped in Italian tradition at all; rather, it's a mostly American creation, the winner of a 1970s recipe contest promoting vodka. An instant classic, penne alla vodka became a featured item on the menus of trendy restaurants, thanks to its simple yet well-thought-out blend of power ingredients. Cream provides luxurious richness. Red pepper flakes ratchet up the heat. Splashes of vodka heighten the flavor of the tomatoes without adding competing flavors.

As with most dishes that look simple on paper, this one finds success in its proportions and timing, as proved by a survey of recipes with identical ingredient lists. Some were absurdly rich, containing more cream than tomatoes; others added too much vodka too late, yielding soupy, boozy sauces. Our goal was to fine-tune this modern classic to strike the right balance of sweet, tangy, spicy, and creamy.

Most recipes for penne alla vodka begin with a basic tomato sauce (canned tomatoes, garlic, and red pepper flakes sautéed in olive oil), but the textures run the gamut from thick-and-chunky to ultra-smooth. Tasters preferred a middle road, so we pureed half the tomatoes (which helped the sauce to cling nicely to the pasta) and cut the rest into chunks. With just 10 minutes of simmering, the sauce had a perfect consistency, but we noticed two recurring problems.

First, the mix of potent ingredients (garlic, red pepper flakes, and vodka) was overwhelming the flavor of the tomatoes, especially their sweetness, a crucial component of the balanced flavor profile we sought. Sautéed minced onion added the right touch of sweetness, and a tablespoon of tomato paste remedied the missing depth of the flavor.

Second, the vodka was out of whack. Besides cutting through the richness, vodka contributes another nuance to the sauce—what tasters identified as "zinginess." As silly as it sounds, the science backs it up. Raw alcohol is an irritant, creating a stinging sensation on the tongue and in the throat. When cooked, alcohol doesn't entirely evaporate, and a mild burning sensation (aka zinginess) is left behind. Many recipes add the vodka along with the heavy cream near the end, but no matter how much restraint we mustered, the sauce tasted boozy. Trial and error taught us to add a liberal amount of vodka along with the tomatoes so that the alcohol mostly—but not completely—cooked off.

To finish the sauce, we swirled in ½ cup of heavy cream for a luxurious but not over-the-top consistency. Letting the penne finish cooking in the sauce (a standard Italian method) encouraged cohesiveness. We garnished the pasta with chopped basil and grated Parmesan. Finally, we had a quick and delicious version of penne alla vodka that struck the flavor balance we'd been looking for.

WHAT WE LEARNED: Puree half the tomatoes and cut the other half into chunks for a sauce that's not too chunky, nor too smooth. To prevent the sauce from tasting boozy, add the vodka early on, with the tomatoes, so that most of the alcohol has time to cook off. Use restraint with the cream—just half a cup gives this sauce enough richness without tasting heavy.

PENNE ALLA VODKA

serves 4

So that the sauce and pasta finish cooking at the same time, drop the pasta into boiling water just after adding the vodka to the sauce.

   1   (28-ounce) can whole tomatoes, drained, liquid
         reserved
   2   tablespoons olive oil
   ½   small onion, minced (about ¼ cup)
   1   tablespoon tomato paste
   2   medium garlic cloves, minced or pressed
         through a garlic press (about 2 teaspoons)
¼–½   teaspoon red pepper flakes
         Salt
   ⅓   cup vodka (see at right)
   ½   cup heavy cream
   1   pound penne
   2   tablespoons finely chopped fresh basil leaves
         Freshly grated Parmesan cheese, for serving

1. Puree half of the tomatoes in a food processor until smooth. Dice the remaining tomatoes into ½-inch pieces, discarding the cores. Combine the pureed and diced tomatoes in a liquid measuring cup (you should have about 1⅔ cups). Add the reserved liquid to equal 2 cups.

2. Heat the oil in a large saucepan over medium heat until shimmering. Add the onion and tomato paste and cook, stirring occasionally, until the onion is light golden around the edges, about 3 minutes. Add the garlic and pepper flakes; cook, stirring constantly, until fragrant, about 30 seconds.

3. Stir in the tomatoes and ½ teaspoon salt. Remove the pan from the heat and add the vodka. Return the pan to medium-high heat and simmer briskly until the alcohol flavor is cooked off, 8 to 10 minutes; stir frequently and lower the heat to medium if the simmering becomes too vigorous. Stir in the cream and cook until hot, about 1 minute.

4. Meanwhile, bring 4 quarts water to a boil in a large Dutch oven over high heat. Add 1 tablespoon salt and the pasta. Cook until just shy of al dente, then drain the pasta, reserving ¼ cup of the cooking water, and transfer the pasta back to the Dutch oven. Add the sauce to the pasta and toss over medium heat until the pasta absorbs some of the sauce, 1 to 2 minutes, adding the reserved cooking water if the sauce is too thick. Stir in the basil and add salt to taste. Divide among pasta bowls and serve immediately, passing the Parmesan separately.

VARIATION

PENNE ALLA VODKA WITH PANCETTA

Heat 1 tablespoon olive oil in a large saucepan over medium-high heat, add 3 ounces thinly sliced pancetta, cut into ½-inch pieces (about ½ cup), and cook until crisp, 6 to 8 minutes. Using a slotted spoon, transfer the pancetta to a small bowl and set aside. Pour off all but 2 tablespoons of the fat from the pan and continue with the recipe for Penne alla Vodka, using the fat in the pan instead of the oil in step 2, reducing the salt to a pinch in step 3, and adding the reserved pancetta to the sauce along with the basil in step 4.

TASTING LAB: Vodka for Cooking

DOES VODKA QUALITY MATTER IN OUR PENNE RECIPE? To find out, we made our recipe with six brands of vodka. The sauce made with Grey Goose (the most expensive vodka; $34) won with its "fresher," "cleaner" flavor. It turns out that cheap vodkas are distilled only once to remove harsh tastes, while "premium" and "super-premium" brands are filtered three or more times.

THE BEST VODKA

You don't necessarily need to cook with Grey Goose, but don't ruin your sauce with vodka you'd never drink on its own.

PASTA CAPRESE

WHAT WE WANTED: A simple-yet-elegant pasta dish showcasing the flavors of summer: sweet tomatoes, fresh basil, and creamy mozzarella.

Legend has it that the popular Caprese trio of garden tomatoes, fresh mozzarella, and basil leaves was introduced in the 1950s at Trattoria Da Vincenzo, a beachside restaurant on the Italian island of Capri. According to creator Margherita Cosentino, the red, white, and green salad of local produce and cheese allowed ladies to "have a nice lunch while still fitting into their bikinis." Swimsuit season or not, the combination became so popular that cooks everywhere took to mixing it with hot pasta, minced garlic, and extra-virgin olive oil for a 15-minute entrée that captures the flavors of summer.

Truth be told, we were skeptical that a recipe would really be required for such a clear-cut dish. Still, we gathered a representative sampling and went into the kitchen. The outcome? Instead of collecting the praise we had expected from our colleagues, we joined them for a few chuckles. The tomatoes, pasta, and basil weren't problems, but the cheese was. In each recipe, it had clumped into an intractable softball-sized wad in the bottom of the pasta bowl. After wrestling a serving out of the dish, things only got worse. The tangles of mozzarella bubble gum were difficult to chew, never mind swallow. The mozzarella was a classic case of Dr. Jekyll and Mr. Hyde: likable and tender at one moment, monstrously tough the next.

When the wisecracks and laughter subsided, several of our colleagues quietly confessed to having experienced the same problem at home.

For these first tests, we had purchased fresh supermarket mozzarella—the kind that comes immersed in plastic tubs of water and is shaped into irregular-sized balls. What if we used regular block-style mozzarella (the low-moisture version often shredded for pizza) instead? It melted nicely and didn't turn chewy, but this inauthentic substitution cheated the dish of its star ingredient, and tasters complained about blandness.

For our next test, we took a big step in the opposite direction and tried water buffalo–milk mozzarella (*mozzarella di bufala*) from a specialty cheese shop. Much softer than the commercial fresh cheese, this handmade mozzarella melted into tender pillows when combined with the pasta—there were no rubbery bits to be found. In addition to the lovely consistency, tasters praised its flavor, which was dripping with milkiness and tang. The next day, we prepared pasta Caprese using handmade cow's-milk mozzarella and achieved the same impressive results. (Intrigued by the differences among the cheeses, we investigated the topic further; see "The Process of Making Mozzarella," on page 49.)

So our problem was solved, as long as we had time to go to the cheese store and were willing to pay the big bucks for handmade cheese, which can easily top $9 per pound. Everyone in the test kitchen agreed this wasn't an acceptable solution. We needed to find a way to use fresh mozzarella from the supermarket.

Our first thought was to thoroughly coat diced mozzarella cubes with olive oil before adding the steaming pasta. This was a step in the right direction, with the oil preventing sticking . . . initially. After a few minutes, however, the nasty clumping problem reemerged.

We wondered what would happen if we put the diced supermarket cheese in the freezer for a few minutes before combining it with the pasta. Could chilling the cheese keep it from melting fully and clumping into wads of bubble gum? We gave this approach a trial run, dicing the mozzarella and chilling it in the freezer for 10 minutes. We then proceeded as usual, combining the firmed-up cheese with the pasta and tomatoes. Success: When added to the hot pasta, the cheese softened but did not fully melt, making the unattractive elastic ropes a thing of the past. It turns out that the proteins in fresh mozzarella begin to melt at about 130 degrees. As the temperature climbs past 130 degrees, the proteins clump together. Freezing the cheese kept it from overheating when tossed with the hot pasta.

With the cheese conundrum solved, we fine-tuned the rest of the recipe, starting with the tomatoes. Juicy, garden-ripe beauties need no adornment, but a sprinkle of sugar can replace the gentle sweetness that is often missing in less-than-perfect specimens. And while Italians would never add an acidic component to a true Caprese recipe, a squeeze of fresh lemon juice (favored over all types of vinegar) did a great job of boosting the flavor of lackluster tomatoes. We also knew from experience that ridding the tomatoes of their seeds before dicing them would preclude a diluted, watery sauce.

In recipes that use raw olive oil, the fruity and spicy nuances of extra-virgin oil make a difference, and this dish is no exception. We added a healthy drizzle of extra-virgin olive oil, then stirred in a minced shallot, a sprinkle of salt, and a few twists of black pepper. Allowing the tomatoes and mozzarella to marinate while the pasta cooked infused them with fruity and subtle garlic flavors. Lengthy marinating times aren't recommended, however, as more than 45 minutes yielded mealy, broken-down tomatoes.

As for the pasta, tasters preferred penne, fusilli, and campanelle over spaghetti, which is commonly used. The short tubular or curly shapes trap the chunky sauce in their nooks and crannies. Freshly chopped basil was the finishing touch to pasta that tasted just like summer.

WHAT WE LEARNED: You can make this dish with supermarket mozzarella if you freeze the diced cheese for just 10 minutes before tossing it with the hot pasta—this helps keep the cheese soft and creamy (instead of dry and clumpy). Otherwise, handmade buffalo- or cow's-milk mozzarella (minus the freezing step) works well. To boost the flavor of less-than-stellar tomatoes, add a little sugar for sweetness and fresh lemon juice for brightness. And don't cut corners with a substandard olive oil—choose a fruity extra-virgin olive oil for best flavor.

SCIENCE DESK:
The Process of Making Mozzarella

WE FOUND THAT ARTISANAL-QUALITY MOZZARELLA melted beautifully in our recipe, but most of the fresh mozzarella we bought at supermarkets melted into bubble gum–like balls. Why the big difference?

To find out, we interviewed Al Scheps of Al Ducci's, a Vermont cheese maker with decades of experience. Scheps explained the art of making mozzarella: Blocks of curd (purchased wholesale or made from scratch) are cut into strips, then immersed in hot (roughly 180-degree) water, where they melt and amalgamate. The cheese maker then reaches into the hot water to gently knead and stretch the mozzarella like taffy, a process known as pasta filata. When the cheese is smooth and shiny, he cuts or tears the cheese into individual portions (the Italian verb *mozzare* means "to cut off"), carefully shapes them into balls, and places them in a salty brine. Freshly made mozzarella cheese, plump and bulging with whey, is extremely perishable and should be eaten within a few days.

Commercial fresh mozzarella is manufactured in much the same way, with one important difference: To facilitate production, the cooking, stretching, kneading, and forming are done by machine, not by hand. Because of this rough handling, the cheese releases an abundance of butterfat and whey. With less fat and less moisture, the product is sturdier and has a shelf life of 90 to 120 days. But vigorous handling also strengthens the protein network in cheese, which causes it to turn tough and ropy when melted.

So what should you buy? In a taste test, the porcelain-white artisanal varieties were favored. Tasters praised their understated, milky flavor and soft texture. Fresh cheeses made by machine were tougher and not as flavorful, but still quite good. Our advice: Buy a handmade cheese if you can. If you end up buying fresh mozzarella at the supermarket, our recipe will turn out great—as long as you remember to freeze the cheese.

PASTA CAPRESE

serves 4 to 6

This dish will be very warm, not hot. The success of this recipe depends on high-quality ingredients, including ripe, in-season tomatoes and a fruity olive oil (the test kitchen prefers Columela Extra-Virgin). Don't skip the step of freezing the mozzarella, as freezing prevents it from turning chewy when it comes in contact with the hot pasta. If handmade buffalo- or cow's-milk mozzarella is available (it's commonly found, packed in water, in gourmet and cheese shops), we highly recommend using it, but skip the step of freezing. Additional lemon juice or up to 1 teaspoon sugar can be added at the end to taste, depending on the ripeness of the tomatoes.

¼	cup extra-virgin olive oil
2–4	teaspoons juice from 1 lemon (see note)
1	small garlic clove, minced or pressed through a garlic press (about ½ teaspoon)
1	small shallot, minced fine (about 2 tablespoons) Salt and ground black pepper
1½	pounds ripe tomatoes, cored, seeded, and cut into ½-inch dice
12	ounces fresh mozzarella cheese, cut into ½-inch cubes (see note)
1	pound short tubular or curly pasta, such as penne, fusilli, or campanelle
¼	cup chopped fresh basil leaves
1	teaspoon sugar (optional; see note)

1. Whisk the oil, 2 teaspoons of the lemon juice, the garlic, shallot, ½ teaspoon salt, and ¼ teaspoon pepper together in a large bowl. Add the tomatoes and gently toss to combine; set aside. Do not marinate the tomatoes for longer than 45 minutes.

2. While the tomatoes are marinating, place the mozzarella on a plate and freeze until slightly firm, about 10 minutes. Bring 4 quarts water to a rolling boil in a stockpot. Add 1 tablespoon salt and the pasta, stir to separate, and cook until al dente. Drain well.

3. Add the pasta and mozzarella to the tomato mixture and gently toss to combine. Let stand 5 minutes. Stir in the basil; season to taste with salt, pepper, and additional lemon juice or sugar, if desired, and serve immediately.

TASTING LAB: Penne

DOMESTIC BRANDS OF DRIED PASTA SUCH AS RONZONI and Mueller's have repeatedly won top honors with our tasters, but now that more specialty brands and Italian imports have hit store shelves, we decided to give fancy pasta—this time in the form of penne—another taste. We tried eight brands, some costing as much as $5 per pound. While none were deemed unacceptable, there were significant differences among the brands we tasted.

Many Italian imports claim to maintain traditional techniques and ingredients such as slow kneading, mixing cold mountain spring water with hard durum semolina, extruding the dough through traditional bronze cast dyes for a coarse texture, and prolonged air-drying. Supposedly, these practices make for stronger flavor and more rustic, sauce-gripping pasta. Yet three expensive imports (Bionaturae, Montebello, and Rustichella d'Abruzzo) landed at the bottom of our rankings. Ronzoni scored in the middle of the pack. Tasters liked three other Italian imports (Benedetto Cavalieri, De Cecco, and Martelli), but top honors went to Mueller's.

Rating Penne

ELEVEN MEMBERS OF THE AMERICA'S TEST KITCHEN STAFF TASTED EIGHT BRANDS OF PENNE COOKED ACCORDING TO package instructions and tossed with olive oil (to prevent sticking) and rated the pasta on flavor and texture. Brands are listed below in order of preference. See www.americastestkitchen.com for up-to-date prices and mail-order sources for top-rated products.

HIGHLY RECOMMENDED
Mueller's Penne Rigate
$1.89 for 16 ounces
Once again beating out Italian imports, this "hearty," "wheaty" pasta earned top honors.

RECOMMENDED
Benedetto Cavalieri Penne Rigate
$4.49 for 17.6 ounces
Made in the "delicate method" —a traditional method using long kneading, slow processing, and drying at low temperature—these imported, oversized "rigatoni-like" quills earned much praise for tasting especially "homemade" and "wheaty."

RECOMMENDED
De Cecco Penne
$1.99 for 16 ounces
Always a top finisher in our tastings, this widely available Italian import garnered praise for its "good texture."

RECOMMENDED
Martelli le Penne Classiche
$5.50 for 17.6 ounces
The priciest pasta of the bunch, this Italian import didn't earn enough points for its "good chew" to merit top rankings.

RECOMMENDED WITH RESERVATIONS
Ronzoni Penne Rigate
$1.19 for 16 ounces
Most tasters found these "pennette-like" tubes too thin for their preference and complained that the pieces became "gummy" as they sat.

RECOMMENDED WITH RESERVATIONS
Bionaturae Organic Penne Rigate
$2.69 for 16 ounces
Organic ingredients and antique bronze dies contributed little to the flavor of this natural foods store staple brand.

RECOMMENDED WITH RESERVATIONS
Montebello Organic Penne Rigate
$2.99 for 16 ounces
While many tasters praised this Italian import's "good, earthy, hearty" flavor, others criticized it for being "unremarkable" and "insubstantial."

RECOMMENDED WITH RESERVATIONS
Rustichella d'Abruzzo Penne
$3.69 for 17.5 ounces
One of the most widely available Italian imports, this pasta was criticized by some for being "nothing special," while others praised its "nice flavor" and "tender, good texture."

EQUIPMENT CORNER: Stockpots

HERE IN THE TEST KITCHEN, WE HAVE 15 STOCKPOTS of varying sizes, and we use them often. Most home kitchens, however, have room for a single stockpot, so it must handle a variety of big jobs—from steaming lobsters and cooking bushels of corn to canning and making huge batches of chili or homemade stock.

So what size is best? After substantial pretesting, we determined that a 12-quart stockpot is the most useful size—it's the "smallest big pot," meaning it can handle most big jobs yet is small enough to store with your other pots and pans. How much do you have to spend to get a good 12-quart stockpot? We bought nine basic stockpots (no fancy steaming or boiling inserts), ranging in price from $25 to $325, and headed into the test kitchen to find out.

We boiled water, cooked mounds of pasta (two pounds of pasta and eight quarts of water at a time), prepared two dozen ears of corn, and made double batches of beef chili in each pot. To evaluate the pots, our testers used digital scales, thermometers, stopwatches, gas and electric burners, and plenty of elbow grease. They handled each stockpot extensively to get a sense of its overall feel (both empty and full) and handle design. We washed the pots repeatedly and practiced stowing them away. What did we find out?

The best stockpot we tested, the $325 All-Clad, impressed us more for what it didn't do—scorch on the bottom or feel awkward or flimsy—than for what it did do; after all, how sexy can a stockpot be, even when it's performing flawlessly? In general, our testers preferred wide stockpots (such as the All-Clad) to tall and narrow ones (such as the Vollrath), as greater width allows you to see and manipulate food better and makes for easier cleaning and storage.

The heavier pots (all weighed without lids) outperformed the lighter models. The four heaviest pots in our testing were made of stainless steel with an aluminum core. Aluminum conducts heat very well and ensures more even cooking and fewer hot spots. The aluminum core also makes the bottom of the pot thicker, which reduces scorching. The lighter pots (including those without aluminum cores) did a fine job cooking corn and pasta—in fact, they heat up faster than the more even-heating pots with aluminum cores. But for cooking applications where sticking and scorching are risks (such as chili), a heavier pot is a must.

Handles matter—a lot. We found that the best handles extend from the pot at least 1¾ inches and are either flat or thick and round, for easy gripping. The All-Clad, Cuisinart, Lincoln, and Arcosteel pots had the best handles—they were easy to grip, even with potholders and a pot full of steaming chili. Pots made by Vollrath and Farberware performed well in cooking tests but were severely downgraded because testers found their thin handles to be awkward and poorly designed.

You can buy a solid, aluminum-core 12-quart stockpot (like the Cuisinart) for $65—or you can drop $325 on the beautiful All-Clad pot, which didn't have a single flaw. If you use a stockpot primarily to boil corn or pasta, it makes sense to buy the Cuisinart model and use the savings to upgrade something else in your kitchen. Whatever your price range, opt for a pot that feels heavy for its size. And when shopping, give the handles a test-run by picking up pots with potholders.

Rating Stockpots

WE TESTED NINE 12-QUART STOCKPOTS AND EVALUATED THEM ACCORDING TO SHAPE, WEIGHT, DESIGN, AND performance (ability to heat evenly and not scorch). The pots are listed in order of preference. See www.americastestkitchen.com for up-to-date prices and mail-order sources for top-rated products.

HIGHLY RECOMMENDED
All-Clad Stainless 12-Quart Stockpot
$324.95; stainless steel with aluminum core; 5.5 lb.

This pot was lauded for being "nice and heavy," with "easy-to-grip" handles. The aluminum core runs up the side of the pot (other pots have aluminum cores only in the bottom, if anywhere) which ensures more even heating than most of us will ever need.

RECOMMENDED
Cuisinart Chef's Classic Stainless 12-Quart Stockpot
$64.95; stainless steel with aluminum core; 4.35 lb.

Very similar to the All-Clad pot, the Cuisinart comes with handles that are "easily grippable." The tilt of the handles made it especially easy to pour out the contents.

RECOMMENDED
Lincoln Foodservice Wear-Ever Professional Series 12-Quart Stockpot
$59.90 (with lid, which must be purchased separately); aluminum; 3.85 lb.

This all-aluminum pot fared well in the test kitchen. Testers loved its "lightweight," "solid feel," and "sturdy raised handles." Aluminum is not as durable as stainless steel, which may lead to problems down the road.

RECOMMENDED WITH RESERVATIONS
Arcosteel 12-Quart Stockpot
$49.95; stainless steel with aluminum core, tempered glass lid, silicone handle covers; 3.7 lb.

This pot heated relatively evenly—there was only a tiny patch of chili stuck after 2½ hours of cooking. The handles are "sturdy" and offer "good control," but this pot was downgraded for dangerous bare spots (no silicone) on the handles.

RECOMMENDED WITH RESERVATIONS
Farberware Classic Series Stainless Steel 12-Quart Stockpot
$70.95; stainless steel with aluminum core; 4.5 lb.

With better handles (these were deemed "uncomfortable" and "slippery"), this heavy aluminum-core pot would have been in the "recommended" category.

RECOMMENDED WITH RESERVATIONS
Vollrath Stainless Intrigue Professional Cookware 12-Quart Stockpot
$88.48 (with lid, which must be purchased separately); stainless steel with aluminum core; 6.35 lb.

This tall and narrow pot "felt tippy" and "cumbersome" and was "harder to pour" and clean than squatter pots. It did, however, cook with very even heat.

RECOMMENDED WITH RESERVATIONS
Endurance R.S.V.P. Stainless Steel 12-Quart Stockpot
$37.95; stainless steel with aluminum core, tempered glass lid; 3.25 lb.

"Shallow," "thin," and "narrow" handles made it hard for testers to grip this pot. This pot heated fairly evenly (thanks to its aluminum core), and there was very little sticking during the chili test.

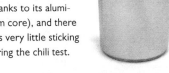

NOT RECOMMENDED
Metro 12-Quart Stockpot
$24.95; stainless steel with tempered glass lid; 2.3 lb.

There was serious burning/sticking at the bottom of this very light pot during the chili test. The handles taper into a point, making it "hard to get your hand in to grip it."

NOT RECOMMENDED
Metro Set of 3 Nested Stockpots with Lids: 8-, 12-, and 16-Quart
$49.99; stainless steel; 1.8 lb.

Testers said this pot, the lightest of the lot, "felt like a toy and would dent too easily." With handles that rise above the top of the pot, it was very awkward to pour because "the leverage is all wrong." There was major sticking and burnt matter on the bottom of the pot after the chili test.

Becky explains that no-boil lasagna noodles are preferred in our Four-Cheese Lasagna for their thin, delicate texture. The test kitchen found that it is necessary to presoak them for 10 minutes so they bake up moist and tender in the finished dish.

FOUR-CHEESE

lasagna

Like another cheesy baked pasta dish—mac and cheese—four-cheese lasagna is unabashedly decadent. But its classic blend of four Italian cheeses (fontina, Parmesan, Gorgonzola, and Gruyère), transforms a childhood favorite into a dish more suited to an adult palate. Each bite of the delicate pasta blanketed with cheese sauce should be savored slowly, in small bites, to really appreciate the sophisticated layers of flavor this dish offers. But we've also suffered through many poor versions of this dish and we bet you have, too. Choosing the wrong cheeses, or the wrong proportions of cheeses, can upset the balance of flavor and yield a heavy, greasy lasagna. And unlike a meat and cheese lasagna, which gets much of its structure from a thick meat sauce and layers of ricotta, four-cheese lasagna has less bulk, relying simply on the pasta and the cheese sauce. The result? Often, a soupy pan of lasagna that's nearly impossible to cut into squares. How could we bulk up our lasagna without upsetting the elegant balance of the dish? The test kitchen set out to solve these problems and more so that you can turn out a foolproof version of this suave Italian classic.

FOUR-CHEESE LASAGNA

WHAT WE WANTED: A refined lasagna; layers of tender noodles bound together by a cheese sauce that is smooth and creamy, not heavy and greasy.

For most people, lasagna brings to mind a thick square with alternating layers of pasta, tomato sauce, gooey cheese, and chunks of ground meat—an unquestionably tasty combination. Four-cheese lasagna offers layers of pasta and cheese bound together with a creamy béchamel sauce. Discerning the uniqueness of each cheese flavor is part of the eating experience. Undeniably rich, but not prohibitively so, this lasagna is not meant to be eaten on its own. It is best served with a green salad, which both complements its richness and frames the dish as an elegant meal. Many of the recipes we tried were heavy and bland, due in large part to the use of plain-tasting cheeses like mozzarella and ricotta. Though some recipes achieved good cheese flavor, they were either soupy, dry, or greasy. Because these recipes lacked a meat sauce, the fillings were thin and the finished products looked flat and insubstantial. We were determined to create a robust cheese lasagna with great structure, creamy texture, and great flavor.

Several quattro formaggi (four-cheese) recipes from northern Italy used a combination of local cheeses, namely fontina, Parmesan, Gorgonzola, and Gruyère. When we tested a lasagna with a mixture of reasonably priced supermarket versions of these varieties, we were greeted by happy tasters. We saw no reason to vary.

The glue that holds the dish together is the béchamel sauce, which is made by thickening milk with a small amount of cooked butter and flour (called a roux). Though this classic white sauce is easy to prepare, finding the right amount and proper texture was a challenge. We made many loose, slippery pans of lasagna, and a number of bone-dry ones, before settling on a sauce made with 3 tablespoons of

butter, ⅓ cup of flour, and 4 cups of milk. Making the sauce with a high ratio of flour to butter (traditional béchamel uses equal amounts) created a thick binder that provided enough heft to keep the layers together. The one remaining problem was the bland, milky flavor, which dulled the overall cheesiness of the dish.

The solution lay in a classic French sauce called velouté, basically roux-thickened broth. Replacing 1½ cups of the milk with chicken broth was the key to balancing the richness of the sauce and bringing forward the cheese flavor. To give the sauce more complexity, we added a shallot and a garlic clove. A bay leaf and a pinch of cayenne stirred into the sauce as it simmered added backbone without overshadowing the other components. To counter the recurring problem of all that cheese causing the lasagna to bake up with pools of unseemly grease on the surface and a slightly curdled texture, we took a cue from the Swiss. Classic fondue recipes include a starch when melting the cheese in order to keep it from becoming oily and gritty. In our next test, we incorporated the cheeses into the sauce, which contained a significant amount of flour, and hoped the starch would trap the oil and keep it from pooling on top of the lasagna. As we pulled the lasagna from the oven, we were thrilled to see no more puddles.

After consulting with our science editor about the chemical structure of various cheeses (see "How Cheese Melts," page 59), we decided that the Gruyère and Parmesan were best mixed into the sauce, as they produced the most oil when cooked, while the fontina and Gorgonzola belonged between the pasta layers, where they helped maintain the dish's creamy texture.

But even after we'd addressed the flavor and texture problems, our assembled lasagna was still squat and dense. Adding more noodles and cheese only made the entire dish heavier and starchier. The value of an open mind

was demonstrated when we returned to an ingredient we had rejected early on, ricotta. It had the characteristics we were looking for: a flavor that didn't stand in the way of the others and a texture that gave the lasagna body without compromising the creamy nature of the sauce. Who knew? The secret to great four-cheese lasagna was a fifth cheese.

Baking the lasagna was our last hurdle, as it was quite delicate and would need only limited time in the oven. Using a technique that has served the test kitchen well, we presoaked the no-boil noodles for 10 minutes before layering them with the other ingredients, which shortened the lasagna's baking time. But the real key was to employ a low-heat/high-heat method. We baked the lasagna, covered, at 350 degrees until it just started to bubble around the edges. We then removed the cover and quickly broiled the lasagna to brown the top. Tasters agreed that this combination cooking method was the final touch that allowed us to deliver on our initial promise to create a sophisticated lasagna.

WHAT WE LEARNED: Replace some of the milk in the béchamel sauce with chicken broth to help highlight, rather than mute, the flavors of the cheese. Use the classic quattro formaggi combination of fontina, Parmesan, Gorgonzola, and Gruyère for the best balance of flavors and richness. Ricotta adds structure and body to the layers. To prevent aged, dry cheeses like Gruyère and Parmesan from separating into pools of grease, fold them into the sauce—the flour in the sauce helps trap the oils in the cheese. And baking the lasagna, covered, at 350 degrees for just 30 minutes and then finishing it under the broiler until just brown, produces delicate layers of tender noodles in a smooth, cheesy sauce.

FOUR-CHEESE LASAGNA

serves 8 to 10

It's important to not overbake the lasagna. Once the sauce starts bubbling around the edges, uncover the lasagna and turn the oven to broil. If your lasagna pan is not broiler-safe, brown the lasagna at 500 degrees for about 10 minutes. Whole milk is best in the sauce, but skim and low-fat milk also work. Supermarket-brand cheeses work fine in this recipe. The Gorgonzola may be omitted, but the flavor of the lasagna won't be as complex. The test kitchen prefers the flavor and texture of Barilla no-boil noodles, but this recipe will work with most brands. One box of Barilla will yield enough noodles for this recipe; you may need 2 boxes of other brands. This lasagna is rich; serve small portions with a green salad.

- 6 ounces Gruyère cheese, shredded (about 1½ cups)
- 2 ounces Parmesan, grated fine (about 1 cup)
- 1½ cups part-skim ricotta cheese
- 1 large egg, lightly beaten
- ¼ teaspoon ground black pepper
- 2 tablespoons plus 2 teaspoons minced fresh parsley leaves
- 3 tablespoons unsalted butter
- 1 medium shallot, minced (about 3 tablespoons)
- 1 medium garlic clove, minced or pressed through a garlic press (about 1 teaspoon)
- ⅓ cup unbleached all-purpose flour
- 2½ cups whole milk
- 1½ cups low-sodium chicken broth
- ½ teaspoon salt
- 1 bay leaf
  Pinch cayenne pepper
- 15 no-boil lasagna noodles
- 8 ounces fontina cheese, rind removed, shredded (about 2 cups)
- 3 ounces Gorgonzola cheese, finely crumbled (about ¾ cup)

1. Place the Gruyère and ½ cup of the Parmesan in a large heatproof bowl. Combine the ricotta, egg, black pepper, and 2 tablespoons of the parsley in a medium bowl. Set both bowls aside.

2. Melt the butter in a medium saucepan over medium heat until foaming; add the shallot and garlic and cook, stirring frequently, until beginning to soften, about 2 minutes. Add the flour and cook, stirring constantly, until thoroughly combined, about 1½ minutes; the mixture should not brown. Gradually whisk in the milk and broth; increase the heat to medium-high and bring to a full boil, whisking frequently. Add the salt, bay leaf, and cayenne; reduce the heat to medium-low and simmer until the sauce thickens and coats the back of a spoon, about 10 minutes, stirring occasionally with a heatproof rubber spatula or wooden spoon and making sure to scrape the bottom and corners of the saucepan (you should have about 4 cups sauce).

3. Remove the saucepan from the heat and discard the bay leaf. Gradually whisk ¼ cup of the sauce into the ricotta mixture. Pour the remaining sauce over the Gruyère mixture and stir until smooth; set aside.

4. Adjust an oven rack to the upper-middle position and heat the oven to 350 degrees. Place the noodles in a 13 by 9-inch baking dish and cover with very hot tap water; soak 10 minutes, agitating the noodles occasionally to prevent sticking. Remove the noodles from the water, place in a single layer on a kitchen towel, and pat dry. Wipe out the baking dish and spray lightly with nonstick cooking spray.

5. Distribute ½ cup of the sauce in the bottom of the baking dish. Place 3 noodles in a single layer on top of the sauce. Spread ½ cup of the ricotta mixture evenly over the noodles and sprinkle evenly with ½ cup of the fontina and 3 tablespoons of the Gorgonzola. Drizzle ½ cup of the sauce evenly over the cheese. Repeat the layering of noodles, ricotta,

fontina, Gorgonzola, and sauce 3 more times. Place the final 3 noodles on top and cover completely with the remaining sauce, spreading with a rubber spatula and allowing it to spill over the noodles. Sprinkle evenly with the remaining ½ cup Parmesan.

6. Spray a large sheet of foil with nonstick cooking spray and cover the lasagna; bake until the edges are just bubbling, 25 to 30 minutes, rotating the pan halfway through the baking time. Remove the foil and turn the oven to broil. Broil until the surface is spotty brown, 3 to 5 minutes. Cool 15 minutes. Sprinkle with the remaining 2 teaspoons parsley; cut into pieces and serve.

VARIATION
FOUR-CHEESE LASAGNA WITH ARTICHOKES AND PROSCIUTTO
Chopped roasted artichoke hearts and prosciutto are flavorful, easy additions to this variation.

1. Adjust an oven rack to the upper-middle position and heat the oven to 450 degrees. Slice 4 ounces of thinly sliced prosciutto into thin strips and set aside. Line a rimmed baking sheet with foil. Toss 2 (9-ounce) packages of frozen artichoke hearts with 1 teaspoon olive oil, ½ teaspoon salt, and ¼ teaspoon black pepper until evenly coated; spread over the prepared baking sheet. Roast, rotating the baking sheet from front to back, until the artichokes are browned at the edges, 20 to 25 minutes. Let the artichokes cool and then chop coarse. Reduce the oven temperature to 350 degrees.

2. Meanwhile, follow the recipe for Four-Cheese Lasagna through step 4. Then distribute ½ cup of the sauce in the bottom of the baking dish. Place 3 noodles in a single layer on top of the sauce. Spread ½ cup of the ricotta mixture evenly over the noodles and sprinkle evenly with ½ cup of the fontina, 3 tablespoons of the gorgonzola, ⅓ cup of the roasted artichokes, and about 2 tablespoons of the prosciutto. Drizzle ½ cup of the sauce evenly over the cheese. Repeat the layering of noodles, ricotta, fontina, Gorgonzola, artichokes, prosciutto, and sauce 3 more times. Place the final 3 noodles on top and cover completely with the remaining sauce, spreading with a rubber spatula and allowing it to spill over the noodles. Sprinkle evenly with the remaining ½ cup Parmesan and bake as directed.

GETTING IT RIGHT: Four Common Problems with Four-Cheese Lasagna

Problem: TOO RUNNY
Solution: Make the béchamel sauce thicker by adding more flour than usual.

Problem: TOO DRY
Solution: Soak the no-boil noodles in hot water and don't skimp on the béchamel sauce.

Problem: TOO GRAINY
Solution: Bake the lasagna as gently as possible to keep the sauce from curdling.

Problem: TOO GREASY
Solution: Stabilize the Gruyère with some flour to keep it from leaving behind pools of grease.

SCIENCE DESK: How Cheese Melts

WHILE DEVELOPING THIS RECIPE, WE WERE SURPRISED by how the cheeses reacted in very different ways when melted. The fontina melted into a creamy, cohesive mass, whereas the Gruyère became greasy and slightly grainy when heated. Why the difference?

It helps to understand that cheese doesn't melt in the true sense, like an ice cube. The protein casein, the solid component that gives cheese its structure, breaks down in the presence of heat. The protein molecules then separate and flow, which gives the appearance of melting.

Relatively young cheeses, such as fontina and mozzarella, have a high moisture content and a weaker protein structure, allowing for the protein to flow at lower temperatures. This higher moisture content means these cheeses have less of a tendency to "break" and become greasy when they melt. On the other hand, aged cheeses, such as Gruyère and cheddar, have less moisture and a stronger protein network, which means they melt at higher temperatures. Once melted, the more-developed protein structures in these cheeses break down, leaving behind a gritty texture. Because there is less moisture in these aged cheeses, they can become unstable and break when melted, releasing the fat and creating the greasiness we had noted in so many of our tests.

Melted Fontina
Young, high-moisture fontina cheese melts smoothly.

Melted Gruyère
Aged, low-moisture Gruyère cheese separates when melted.

SPICY SALAD WITH MUSTARD AND BALSAMIC VINAIGRETTE
serves 8 to 10

This salad makes a perfect partner to our Four-Cheese Lasagna, as the bitter greens and zesty vinaigrette help cut the lasagna's richness.

vinaigrette
- 6 tablespoons extra-virgin olive oil
- 4 teaspoons balsamic vinegar
- 1 tablespoon Dijon mustard
- 1 teaspoon finely minced shallot

- ¼ teaspoon salt
- ⅛ teaspoon ground black pepper
- 4 quarts washed and dried spicy greens, such as arugula, watercress, mizuna, and baby mustard greens

Combine all the dressing ingredients in a jar, seal the lid, and shake vigorously until emulsified, about 20 seconds. Place the greens in a large mixing bowl and drizzle the dressing over the greens a little at a time as you toss the salad. Coat the greens by gently fluffing them with your hands, adding more vinaigrette if the greens seem dry.

TASTING LAB: Balsamic Vinegars

TRADITIONAL AGED BALSAMIC VINEGAR, PRODUCED in the Emilia-Romagna region of Italy, can cost $200 per bottle, making even fine French perfume look like a bargain. You can also walk into any supermarket in America and fork over $2 or $3 for a big bottle of balsamic vinegar. What are you really buying? And which product should you buy?

To find out, we purchased 13 balsamic vinegars ranging in price from just 18 cents per ounce to $60 per ounce. Before going into the tasting room, we wanted to figure out why the same product can cost so little or so much. A crash

TECHNIQUE: Cleaning Greens

Nothing ruins a salad faster than gritty leaves, so the first step in making any salad is cleaning the greens. (Unwashed greens should be carefully stowed away in the crisper drawer with the rubber band or twist tie removed, as the constriction encourages rotting.) Our favorite way to wash small amounts of greens is in the bowl of a salad spinner; larger amounts require a sink. Make sure there is ample room to swish the leaves about and rid them of sand and dirt. The dirt will sink to the bottom. Exceptionally dirty greens (spinach and arugula often fall into this category) may take at least two changes of water.

Do not run water directly from the faucet onto the greens, as the force of the water can bruise them. When you are satisfied that the leaves are grit-free, lift them out of the water, leaving the dirt behind, and spin them dry in a salad spinner. Greens must be quite dry; otherwise, the vinaigrette will slide off and taste diluted. Here are some guidelines for washing, drying, and storing greens:

 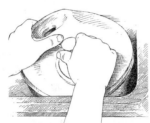  

1. Using your hands, gently move the greens about under water to loosen grit, which should fall to the bottom of the salad spinner bowl. Lift the greens out of the water.

2. If you own a crank-style salad spinner, place it in the corner of your sink. This increases your leverage by pushing the spinner into the floor and walls of the sink.

3. Line the salad spinner with paper towels, then layer in the greens, covering each layer with additional towels. In this manner, the greens will keep for at least 2 days.

4. To store greens for up to a week, loosely roll the greens in paper towels and then place the rolled greens inside a large zipper-lock bag and place in the refrigerator.

course in recent history helped.

Years ago, balsamic vinegar was an obscure product made in northern Italy and so highly valued that many families passed along barrels of aged vinegar as part of a wedding dowry. Fast-forward a generation, and balsamic is now the best-selling vinegar in America, accounting for 45 percent of all supermarket vinegar sales. Of course, none of this popularity would have been possible if balsamic vinegar had remained a $100-an-ounce extravagance.

It turns out there are two kinds of balsamic vinegar, and they're made by entirely different processes. The traditional technique takes a minimum of 12 years, the modern industrial method as little as a few hours. The centuries-old traditional way begins with late-harvest grapes (usually white Trebbiano) grown in Emilia-Romagna. The sweet, raisiny juice, skin, and seeds, called grape must, is boiled in open vats until reduced to about half its original volume. This concentrated must is added to the largest of a battery of wooden barrels, which are kept in uninsulated attics in this region where the summers are hot and the winters frosty. The battery comprises barrels of different woods—including oak, cherry, juniper, and mulberry—and different sizes. The barrels aren't sealed; they have cloth-covered openings on top to allow evaporation. Each year, before the vinegar

one worth using until we hit the lottery?

We began by choosing 10 top-selling, nationally available supermarket balsamic vinegars. All were made in Italy, and their prices ranged from $2.39 to $14 a bottle. We tasted them plain, reduced to a glaze for roasted asparagus, and whisked into a vinaigrette. We also tasted a traditional balsamic vinegar for comparison (see "Gourmet Balsamic Vinegars," page 64).

First the bad news: Tasted straight from the bottle, there was no contest between supermarket and traditional balsamics. Even the best of the commercial bunch—while similarly sweet, brown, and viscous—couldn't compete with the complex, rich flavor of true balsamic vinegar. With notes of honey, fig, raisin, caramel, and wood; a smooth, lingering taste; and an aroma like fine port, traditional balsamic is good enough to sip like liqueur.

But there's some good news as well. You don't need to take out a loan to keep balsamic vinegar in your pantry. The test kitchen made vinaigrette with both a 25-year-old traditional balsamic from Reggio Emilia and the top supermarket brand from our taste tests—and frankly, in dressing, the traditional stuff did not justify its price tag. When we used it in a pan sauce, most of that fine aroma and depth of flavor was cooked away. The lesson was clear: Don't waste your money on pricey traditional balsamic vinegar if you're going to toss it on salad or cook with it. The good stuff works best uncooked, as a drizzle to finish a dish. In vinaigrette or cooked sauce, the sharpness of a supermarket balsamic adds a pleasingly bright contrast to the vinegar's natural sweetness.

Among the 10 supermarket vinegars we tasted, some were quite good, others quite awful. Why? An independent lab test supplied part of the answer. Our top choice contained the most sugar; vinegars with the lowest sugar content occupied four of the bottom five spots on the list. This makes sense—the sweeter supermarket vinegars tasted more like the traditional balsamic. It turns out that our tasters also

maker adds the new must to the largest barrel, he transfers some of its ever-more concentrated contents to the next largest, and so on down the line, before finally removing a liter or two of the oldest vinegar from the smallest barrel. This is traditional balsamic vinegar.

What's more, all this can happen only in two provinces of Emilia-Romagna: Modena and Reggio Emilia, an area designated as a government-protected denomination of origin, or DOP. Each province has its own consortium of experts who approve the balsamic before sealing it in its official 3-ounce bottle (an inverted tulip shape for Reggio Emilia; a ball with a neck for Modena). If you want a guarantee that you're getting true balsamic vinegar, look for the word *tradizionale* and these distinctive bottles—and be prepared to pay dearly.

All those rules are thrown out the window when it comes to commercial balsamic vinegar. With no law defining balsamic vinegar in the United States, manufacturers supply the huge demand any way they can, coloring and sweetening wine vinegar and calling it "balsamic vinegar of Modena." It may not be the real thing, but could we find

Rating Balsamic Vinegars

TWENTY MEMBERS OF AMERICA'S TEST KITCHEN STAFF TASTED 10 SUPERMARKET BALSAMIC VINEGARS THREE WAYS: plain, in a vinaigrette with olive oil and mustard, and cooked into a glaze on asparagus topped with Parmesan cheese and olive oil. The vinegars are listed in order of preference and are available in supermarkets.

RECOMMENDED

Lucini Gran Riserva Balsamico

$14.00 for 8.5 ounces

This was the sweetest and thickest of the vinegars we tasted. Plain, it had a "sweet, nuanced flavor" with a "nice balance" of tart and sweet. In glaze, it was smooth, with no burn. In vinaigrette, it was "very good—to the last drop."

RECOMMENDED

Monari Federzoni Balsamic Vinegar of Modena

$3.39 for 16.9 ounces

A true standout in the vinaigrette, where its acidity lent brightness, winning raves as "extremely smooth and tangy." In glaze, it had "full-bodied" taste.

RECOMMENDED

Ortalli Balsamic Vinegar of Modena

$4.69 for 16.9 ounces

Tasters liked this vinegar's fruity flavor with "musky," "woody," "fermented" tones. In vinaigrette, it was a little too mellow. As a glaze, however, it was "very palatable."

RECOMMENDED WITH RESERVATIONS

Star Balsamic Vinegar of Modena

$2.59 for 8.5 ounces

Plain, it was "lightly fruity," but "too sharp." In glaze, it came across as "candy-like." The tables were turned in the vinaigrette, where its sharpness and sweetness combined to make a "balanced" dressing that was "good, full, and complex."

RECOMMENDED WITH RESERVATIONS

Colavita Balsamic Vinegar of Modena

$4.49 for 17 ounces

Plain, this vinegar was deemed "not impressive one way or another." In vinaigrette, again, it was "tasty enough, but bland"; in the glaze—you guessed it: "Nothing special."

RECOMMENDED WITH RESERVATIONS

Rienzi Balsamic Vinegar of Modena

$3.39 for 17 ounces

Most tasters found this vinegar too tart, even "metallic." In vinaigrette, it was "crisp and light, but harsh." Cooked in glaze, it was more successful, with tasters calling it "complex and delicious, like a good red wine."

RECOMMENDED WITH RESERVATIONS

Progresso Balsamic Vinegar

$2.39 for 12 ounces

Tasters deemed this vinegar "more tangy than sweet," with a "rough finish." Several complained that it was "thin and astringent." In glaze, it was praised for its "oaky flavor."

RECOMMENDED WITH RESERVATIONS

Alessi Balsamic Vinegar

$3.85 for 8.5 ounces

"Too sweet" was the consensus on this vinegar, described as "like vanilla on a bad day." In glaze, it was "like candy with red wine vinegar notes." In the vinaigrette it was "one-dimensional."

RECOMMENDED WITH RESERVATIONS

Modenaceti Balsamic Vinegar of Modena

$4.49 for 16.9 ounces

Tasters noted "hints of richness with some nice fruit," but pointed out that it was "too harsh." "Tastes like wine vinegar with food coloring," noted one.

NOT RECOMMENDED

Pompeian Balsamic Vinegar

$3.69 for 16 ounces

"All harsh hit; no subtlety or character" was the majority opinion. "Bad flavor. I would only color Easter eggs with this," wrote one taster. Said another, "You know the drill: Sip, squint, wince, shudder."

wanted their supermarket balsamic vinegar to be viscous, like traditional balsamics. Lab tests confirmed that higher viscosity tracked with higher rankings.

But sweetness and thickness alone were not enough to guarantee a spot high on our list. The second-sweetest vinegar was also the second most viscous, and it broke the pattern by appearing near the bottom. We were puzzled, until we tested pH levels. This vinegar was the least acidic one tested, and tasters thought it was excessively sweet. So a good supermarket balsamic vinegar must be sweet and thick (like the real deal), but it should also offer a little jolt of acidity.

In the end, we found one supermarket vinegar—Lucini Gran Riserva—that appealed across the board, working well both plain and in the dishes we prepared. The manufacturer told us they use must that is aged in the artisanal way for 10 years, mixed with the company's own wine vinegar. It may have come across as "honey-sweet," but this vinegar offered "a nice compromise between sweet and tangy," with a "nuanced flavor" that came closest to traditional balsamic. We'll admit that it's no 25-year-old consortium-approved marvel. But Lucini Gran Riserva also didn't cost $60 per ounce. In fact, at about $2 per ounce, we'll use this supermarket vinegar at home—when our boss isn't paying the bill.

TASTING LAB:
Gourmet Balsamic Vinegars

WHEN IT COMES TO DRIZZLING VINEGAR OVER BERRIES or a piece of grilled fish, do you have to shell out hundreds of dollars for a traditional vinegar aged for at least 12 years? To find out, we conducted another tasting that included a traditional balsamic approved and bottled by the Reggio Emilia vinegar consortium, Lucini Gran Riserva (winner of our supermarket tasting), and two commercial balsamics sold in gourmet stores. The not-so-surprising news? The 25-year-old Cavalli Gold Seal Extra Vecchio

Aceto Balsamico Tradizionale di Reggio Emilia, at $180 for 3 ounces, topped nearly everyone's list, with tasters waxing poetic about its "pomegranate," "caramel," "smoky" flavor that "coats the tongue" and tastes "amazing." In such rich company, our supermarket winner couldn't compete. Lucini finished last.

But the big surprise was the strong performance of the commercial vinegars we purchased at gourmet stores. They were nearly as good as the 25-year-old vinegar and cost just $3 to $4 per ounce. Tasters praised the Oliviers & Co. Premium Balsamic Vinegar of Modena ($27 for 8.5 ounces) as "fruity, raisiny, and complex," with notes of "wood, smoke, flowers," and described the Rubio Aceto Balsamico di Modena ($35 for 8.5 ounces) as "floral" and "aromatic." Made with aged grape must and, in the case of the Oliviers & Co., good wine vinegar, these gourmet commercial balsamics are reasonably priced options if you want to drizzle balsamic vinegar over food and don't want to pay a fortune.

THE BEST GOURMET BALSAMIC VINEGARS

The $60-per-ounce traditional balsamic vinegar—Cavalli Gold Seal Extra Vecchio Aceto Balsamico Tradizionale di Reggio Emilia (left)—was tasters' favorite, but two gourmet brands, Oliviers & Co. Premium Balsamic Vinegar of Modena (center) and Rubio Aceto Balsamico di Modena (right), were nearly as good—and they cost just $3 to $4 per ounce.

EQUIPMENT CORNER: Box Graters

FOOD PROCESSORS CAN SWIFTLY SHRED POUNDS OF cheese or vegetables, but lugging out the appliance for a chunk of Parmesan or a pair of russet potatoes is impractical. But do you need to risk slicing your knuckles in order to use a box grater? We tested seven models to find out.

We grated block mozzarella, Parmesan cheese, and raw potatoes on each of the graters in our lineup. Mozzarella turned out to be the most forgiving of the three tests we conducted; even the teeth on the wobbly Best Box Grater ($16.95) and the equally unsteady Progressive ProGrip Large Tower Grater ($12.99) required little pressure for a firm bite into the semi-soft cheese. Nonskid bases on the Anolon Box Grater ($24.95), KitchenAid KG300 Box Grater ($19.99), and Oxo Good Grips Box Grater ($14.99) marginally improved stability, but once the plastic-bottomed measuring cup attachments were in place on the Anolon and KitchenAid models, these rubber bases were irrelevant.

Six of the seven graters, including the excessively comprehensive Cuisipro 6-Sided Box Grater ($25.89), featured classically deep punctures—fine for semi-soft cheeses and softer vegetables, but no match for the shallower, razor-sharp edges on the Microplane 34005 Better Box Grater ($24.95). Parmesan shreds, which occasionally chipped and flaked on the other models, fell lithely from these exceptionally sharp blades. However, the Microplane grater's unusually short (under five inches) shredding plane and poorly designed knuckle guard disqualified it from the top ranks. Meanwhile, with its sharp blades and clear, marked container, the Oxo delivered on all fronts, making it our top choice.

Rating Box Graters

WE TESTED SEVEN MODELS OF BOX GRATERS. WE RATED THEM FOR PERFORMANCE IN GRATING CHEESE (BOTH semisoft and hard) and potatoes. Ease of use was also a consideration in our testing. The graters are listed in order of preference. See www.americastestkitchen.com for up-to-date prices and mail-order sources for top-rated products.

RECOMMENDED
Oxo Good Grips Box Grater
$14.99

An all-around good tool. Sharp blades, slim body, and a clear, marked container for easy storage and cleanup. This grater's modest price also makes it a good value.

RECOMMENDED
Cuisipro 6-Sided Box Grater
$25.89

Six blade choices are unnecessary, but at least all of them are sharp. Testers found a few quibbles with the holes' deep punctures, which are fine for semi-soft cheeses and soft vegetables, but not so effective with harder cheeses (like parmesan) and vegetables. Sturdy, comfortable, and equipped with a food-catching base, this is a solid choice all around.

RECOMMENDED WITH RESERVATIONS
Microplane 34005 Better Box Grater
$24.95

To our surprise, this was not the top contender, though, in typical Microplane fashion, the blades were razor-sharp—hard, dry parmesan fell from its blades with ease. An optional knuckle-saving door made shredding food an obstacle, as did the short shredding plane.

RECOMMENDED WITH RESERVATIONS
KitchenAid KG300 Box Grater
$19.99

Testers wanted to like this sturdy, comfortable tool more, but couldn't muster comments beyond "fine" and "ample" for its performance. Plus, its dark base-gripping storage container made viewing the shredding progress difficult.

RECOMMENDED WITH RESERVATIONS
Anolon Box Grater
$24.95

This was a near clone to the KitchenAid model, with a few more drawbacks: a roofed top with a knob grip made viewing progress impossible, as did the even darker unmarked storage container.

NOT RECOMMENDED
Progressive ProGrip Large Tower Grater
$12.99

Not only did this unsteady tripod sport the same unfavorable knob grip as the Anolon, but its supposedly nonskid feet tore off with a little shredding pressure.

NOT RECOMMENDED
Best Box Grater
$16.95

Unsteady to a dangerous degree, this grater is almost flimsy enough to bend in your hand—a problem that is exacerbated by its lack of a flared base.

Four-Cheese Lasagna **page 57**

67

Skillet Baked Ziti **page 5**

Spicy Salad with Mustard and Balsamic Vinaigrette **page 60**

Parmesan-Crusted Chicken Cutlets **page 16**

70

White Chicken Chili **page 110**

Thai-Style Chicken Soup **page 238**

72

Grilled Blackened Red Snapper **page 159**

Roast Salted Turkey **page 124**

Creamy Mashed Potatoes **page 145**

Beer-Braised Short Ribs **page 104**

Skillet Beef Stroganoff **page 9**

Garlicky Shrimp with Buttered Bread Crumbs **page 25**

Grilled Glazed Salmon **page 164**

Kansas City Sticky Ribs **page 149**

Oven-Fried Onion Rings **page 185**

Baked Manicotti **page 86**

82

ITALIAN-AMERICAN
classics

CHAPTER 7

Stuffed manicotti makes a hearty and delicious main course, but in most cases its preparation is best left in the hands of a practiced and patient Italian grandmother. Manicotti may indeed look homey, but blanching and stuffing pasta tubes is a tedious chore and the ricotta filling can be uninspired and watery, making all that effort for naught. We wanted a simpler, easier method for making manicotti that wouldn't test our patience, and we wanted our manicotti to taste as good as it looked—tender noodles, a rich and creamy cheese filling, and a well-seasoned tomato sauce to pull this dish together.

Thick slices of toasted garlic bread make the perfect accompaniment to manicotti and a variety of other dishes—lasagna, spaghetti and meatballs, and minestrone, to name a few. But getting this seemingly simple bread right isn't always so easy. The bread can turn soggy under too much butter, the garlic flavor can be at turns harsh or too faint, and when cheese is added to the mix, a host of other issues become evident (greasy, rubbery cheese for one). We wanted a garlic bread that was full of buttery garlic flavor, and we wanted a crisp crust and chewy, soft interior.

MANICOTTI

WHAT WE WANTED: A simple method for stuffed mani-cotti—one that would produce tender tubes of pasta filled with a rich ricotta blend and topped with a well-seasoned tomato sauce.

We have a love/hate relationship with manicotti. Well-made versions of this Italian-American classic—pasta tubes stuffed with rich ricotta filling and blanketed with tomato sauce—can be eminently satisfying. So what's not to love? Putting it all together. For such a straightforward collection of ingredients (after all, manicotti is just a compilation of pasta, cheese, and tomato sauce), the preparation is surprisingly fussy. Blanching, shocking, draining, and stuffing slippery pasta tubes require more patience (and time) than we usually have. In addition, a survey of manicotti recipes proved that most recipe writers don't get the filling right; too often, the ricotta-based mixture turns out bland and runny.

Testing started with the pasta component. Cheese-stuffed pastas have been consumed in Italy since medieval times, and traditional recipes use either homemade crespelle (thin, eggy, crêpe-like pancakes) or rectangular sheets of homemade pasta as wrappers for the filling. (Both are ter-rific, though neither fit into our streamlined schematic.) Over time, most Italian-American recipes evolved to use ready-made dried pasta shells instead of homemade wrap-pers. For manicotti, pasta tubes are parboiled, shocked in ice water to stop the cooking, drained, and stuffed with ricotta filling. It was on this approach that we focused our attention.

Some recipes require a pastry bag for filling the long, hollow cylinders with ricotta; others explain how to snip the corner from a zipper-lock bag to create a mock pastry bag. Many recipes take a different approach altogether, sug-gesting a small soupspoon for stuffing the tubes. With a bowl of basic ricotta filling at our side, we took a deep breath and gave each method a try. The pastry bag was messy but workable. However, many cooks don't own a pastry bag, and we didn't want to write a recipe requiring a specialty tool. Using a zipper-lock bag to force the ricotta into a slick parboiled pasta tube was maddening; most of the cheese oozed out of the bag, with an embarrassingly small amount actually making it into the tube. The soupspoon was equally frustrating; we eventually gave up on it and used our fingers instead. Noticing our impatience, a colleague suggested slit-ting a blanched noodle lengthwise, packing it with filling, and putting the stuffed tube into a casserole seam side down. Not bad, but this method still called for blanching, shocking, and draining the noodles.

We found a "quick" recipe that seemed worth trying on the back of one of the manicotti boxes. It called for stuff-ing uncooked pasta tubes with ricotta, covering them with a watery sauce, then baking. Filling raw pasta tubes with cheese was marginally easier than stuffing limp parboiled noodles, but it wasn't without missteps: A few shattered along the way. Still, we followed the recipe through, water-ing down a jar of tomato sauce with a cup of boiling water and pouring it over the manicotti. After 45 minutes in the oven, this manicotti was inedible, with some of the pasta shells remaining uncooked and the pink, watered-down sauce tasting, well, like water.

Nearly at wit's end, we remembered the crespelle and fresh pasta sheets, which didn't have any of the assembly problems associated with manicotti tubes. Spreading the filling onto a flat wrapper had to be easier than cramming it into a floppy tube. We scanned the ingredient list on a package of store-bought crêpes, hoping to use them instead of crespelle, but alas, they were far too sugary. Fresh pasta sheets aren't sold at many supermarkets. It was then that we thought of no-boil lasagna noodles. What if we softened the noodles in water, turning them into pliable sheets of pasta? This method worked like a charm. After a quick soak in boiling water, no-boil lasagna noodles could be spread with filling and rolled up in a few easy minutes.

It was a given that ricotta would serve as the base for the filling, but was whole milk, part-skim, or even fat-free ricotta preferable? All were fine, but part-skim ricotta provided the ideal level of richness, allowing the other flavors to shine. In addition to ricotta, shredded low-moisture mozzarella and Parmesan are generally added to the filling. We wondered if other cheeses might fare better. After testing cream cheese, fresh mozzarella, fontina, Asiago, pecorino, and aged provolone, we decided to stick with tradition, opting for mozzarella and Parmesan.

Without eggs, the filling separates, becoming loose and watery. After experimenting with various amounts of whole eggs and yolks, we settled on two whole eggs. But eggs alone didn't completely ward off a runny filling. The proper amounts of mozzarella and Parmesan also proved key; specifically, a generous amount of mozzarella was necessary.

As for seasonings, a few specks of parsley plus salt and pepper are the norm. Looking for improvement, we explored other options, eventually settling on a combination of fresh parsley and basil (dried herbs were too harsh).

A slow-cooked tomato sauce didn't fit into our streamlining goal, so we were relieved when tasters preferred the bright, fresh flavor of a 15-minute sauce made with olive oil, garlic, and diced canned tomatoes pureed in a food processor to give the sauce body quickly. We punched up our quick recipe with fresh basil leaves and a dash of red pepper flakes.

Finally, most baked pasta dishes benefit from a browned, cheesy topping. The best approach was to add a light sprinkling of Parmesan, passing the casserole under the broiler before serving. This, at last, was manicotti that won our complete affection: great tasting and easy to prepare.

WHAT WE LEARNED: No-boil lasagna noodles, which can be spread with the ricotta filling and simply rolled up, are an easier, tasty alternative to hard-to-fill manicotti tubes. Eggs, Parmesan, and an ample amount of mozzarella add richness, flavor, and structure to the ricotta filling. For a quick but brightly flavored tomato sauce, puree canned diced tomatoes and simmer until slightly thickened with sautéed garlic and hot red pepper flakes, and finish with fresh basil.

BAKED MANICOTTI

serves 6 to 8

We prefer Barilla no-boil lasagna noodles for their delicate texture resembling fresh pasta. Note that Pasta Defino and Ronzoni brands contain only 12 no-boil noodles per package; the recipe requires 16 noodles. The manicotti can be prepared through step 5, covered with a sheet of parchment paper, wrapped in aluminum foil, and refrigerated for up to 3 days or frozen for up to 1 month. (If frozen, thaw the manicotti in the refrigerator for 1 to 2 days.) To bake, remove the parchment, replace the aluminum foil, and increase the baking time to 1 to 1¼ hours.

tomato sauce

- 2 (28-ounce) cans diced tomatoes in juice
- 2 tablespoons extra-virgin olive oil
- 3 medium garlic cloves, minced or pressed through a garlic press (about 1 tablespoon)
- ½ teaspoon red pepper flakes, optional
  Salt
- 2 tablespoons chopped fresh basil leaves

cheese filling and pasta

- 3 cups part-skim ricotta cheese
- 4 ounces grated Parmesan cheese (about 2 cups)
- 8 ounces mozzarella, shredded (about 2 cups)
- 2 large eggs, lightly beaten
- ¾ teaspoon salt
- ½ teaspoon ground black pepper
- 2 tablespoons chopped fresh parsley leaves
- 2 tablespoons chopped fresh basil leaves
- 16 no-boil lasagna noodles (see note)

1. FOR THE SAUCE: Adjust an oven rack to the middle position and heat the oven to 375 degrees. Pulse 1 can of the tomatoes with their juice in a food processor until coarsely chopped, 3 or 4 pulses. Transfer to a bowl. Repeat with the remaining can of tomatoes.

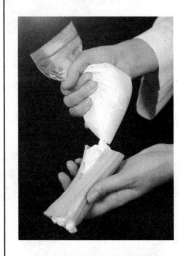

TESTING NOTES: No Shortcut at All

Many recipes replace the traditional pastry bag with a zipper-lock plastic bag. But using a plastic bag to stuff parboiled manicotti shells is a messy, frustrating job that is eliminated by our recipe, which relies on a simple spread and roll-up technique.

2. Heat the oil, garlic, and pepper flakes (if using) in a large saucepan over medium heat until fragrant but not brown, 1 to 2 minutes. Stir in the tomatoes and ½ teaspoon salt and simmer until thickened slightly, about 15 minutes. Stir in the basil; season with salt to taste.

3. FOR THE CHEESE FILLING: Combine the ricotta, 1 cup of the Parmesan, mozzarella, eggs, salt, pepper, and herbs in a medium bowl; set aside.

4. TO ASSEMBLE: Pour 1 inch boiling water into a 13 by 9-inch broiler-safe baking dish, then add the noodles one at a time. Let the noodles soak until pliable, about 5 minutes, separating the noodles with the tip of a sharp knife to prevent sticking. Remove the noodles from the water and place in a single layer on clean kitchen towels; discard the water in the baking dish and dry the baking dish.

5. Spread the bottom of the baking dish evenly with 1½ cups of the sauce. Using a soupspoon, spread ¼ cup of the cheese mixture evenly onto the bottom three-quarters of each noodle (with the short side facing you), leaving the top quarter of the noodle exposed. Roll into a tube shape and arrange in the baking dish seam side down. Top evenly with the remaining sauce, making certain that the pasta is completely covered.

6. Cover the manicotti with aluminum foil. Bake until bubbling, about 40 minutes. Remove the baking dish then remove the foil. Adjust the oven rack to the uppermost position (about 6 inches from the heating element) and heat the broiler. Sprinkle the manicotti evenly with the remaining 1 cup Parmesan. Broil until the cheese is spotty brown, 4 to 6 minutes. Cool 15 minutes, then serve.

VARIATIONS

BAKED MANICOTTI WITH SAUSAGE

Sausage makes for a heartier version of manicotti.

Follow the recipe for Baked Manicotti through step 1. Cook 1 pound hot or sweet Italian sausage, casings removed, in 2 tablespoons olive oil in a large saucepan over medium-high heat, stirring to break the sausage into ½-inch pieces, until no longer pink, about 6 minutes. Continue as directed, adding the garlic and pepper flakes (if using) to the sausage.

BAKED MANICOTTI WITH PROSCIUTTO

Thinly sliced prosciutto is an easy, elegant addition to this variation.

Follow the recipe for Baked Manicotti through step 4. After spreading the bottom of the baking dish evenly with 1½ cups of the sauce, arrange 1 thin slice of prosciutto on each noodle (you will need 16 slices total), before spreading with the cheese as directed.

BAKED MANICOTTI PUTTANESCA

Anchovies, olives, and capers lend a zesty kick to this variation.

Follow the recipe for Baked Manicotti, adding 3 finely minced anchovy fillets to the oil, garlic, and red pepper flakes (if using) in step 2. Add ¼ cup pitted and quartered kalamata olives and 2 tablespoons drained and rinsed capers to the cheese filling in step 3 and proceed as directed.

TECHNIQUE: Assembling Manicotti

1. Soak no-boil lasagna noodles in boiling water for 5 minutes until pliable, using the tip of a paring knife to separate the noodles and prevent sticking.

2. Using a soupspoon, spread about ¼ cup of the filling onto three-quarters of each noodle, leaving the top quarter of the noodle exposed.

3. Roll each noodle by hand and place in the baking dish, seam side down.

CHEESY GARLIC BREAD

WHAT WE WANTED: Toasted slices of chewy bread infused with buttery garlic and topped with gooey cheese.

Based on our experience, garlic bread—with cheese or not—often consists of greasy, soggy bread with a layer of bitter garlic flavor on top and no flavor at all in the middle. Great garlic bread should be light and fluffy on the inside and crunchy on the outside, with the deep perfume of nutty garlic and rich butter throughout. Our first step was to develop a foolproof garlic bread recipe. We could tackle the cheese component later.

We tried raw, roasted, and toasted garlic in combination with butter and olive oil to see which, if any, would yield the right balance of garlic flavor. We mashed the garlic, sliced it, and chopped it. In most cases, the flavors were so bitter and pungent our eyes watered. Starting with minced garlic and cold butter in a pan over low heat brought out the nuttiest flavors, but tasters complained about biting into chunks of sharp garlic. Grating the garlic, we found, ensures smooth, evenly distributed bits of garlic and full flavor, and adding a little water to the pan prevents the garlic from drying out and burning. After a few minutes over low heat, the garlic turned into a sticky, golden paste that was perfect for slathering on bread.

Selecting the bread was easy. Italian supermarket bread was immediately eliminated because of its thin crust and soft, spongy interior. With its crisp crust and chewy interior, a supermarket baguette was a far better choice.

Up to this point, we had been slicing the loaf horizontally and baking the halves open-faced until warm and toasty. The garlic-butter mixture was flavoring the top of the bread, but the rest of the loaf was bland. We solved the problem by wrapping the slathered bread in foil and letting the garlic butter steam for 15 minutes. Unwrapping the bread and opening up the layers for another short stint in the oven made our garlic bread crisp.

As for the cheesy crust, some tasters preferred Parmesan for its potent flavor, while others favored gooey cheeses like mozzarella. Rather than taking the time to grate and shred several cheeses, we picked up a packaged blend of shredded Italian cheeses that satisfied everyone. A quick blast of heat from the broiler melted the cheese and helped crisp the bread even further.

WHAT WE LEARNED: Supermarket baguettes are preferred for their chewy interior and crisp crust. For the garlic butter, slowly sauté grated cloves of garlic with butter and a little water—grating produces finer pieces of garlic for a smoother butter, and the water prevents the garlic from burning. A combination of cheeses, found in packaged Italian cheese blend, gives the bread multiple layers of cheese flavor with little effort. To infuse the bread with buttery garlic flavor, wrap the bread in foil and bake so that the bread "steams." Then, to crisp the crust, remove the foil and bake. To further crisp the crust and brown the cheese, run the bread under the broiler.

CHEESY GARLIC BREAD

serves 6 to 8

The serrated edges on a bread knife can pull off the cheesy crust. To prevent this, place the finished garlic bread cheese side down on a cutting board. Slicing through the crust first (rather than the cheese) will keep the cheese in place. Shredded Italian cheese blend is sold in bags in the supermarket case near other packaged cheeses.

5	medium garlic cloves, peeled and grated
8	tablespoons (1 stick) unsalted butter, softened
½	teaspoon water
¼	teaspoon salt
¼	teaspoon ground black pepper
1	(18- to 20-inch) baguette, sliced in half horizontally
1½	cups shredded Italian cheese blend

1. Adjust an oven rack to the lower-middle position and heat the oven to 400 degrees. Cook the garlic, 1 tablespoon of the butter, and the water in a small nonstick skillet over low heat, stirring occasionally, until straw colored, 7 to 10 minutes.

2. Mix the hot garlic, remaining butter, salt, and pepper in a bowl and spread on the cut sides of the bread. Sandwich the bread back together and wrap the loaf in foil. Place on a baking sheet and bake for 15 minutes.

3. Carefully unwrap the bread and place the halves, buttered sides up, on a baking sheet. Bake until just beginning to color, about 10 minutes. Remove from the oven and set the oven to broil.

4. Sprinkle the bread with the cheese. Broil until the cheese has melted and the bread is crisp, 1 to 2 minutes. Transfer the bread to a cutting board with the cheese side facing down. Cut into pieces. Serve.

TASTING LAB: Parmesan Cheese

THE BUTTERY, NUTTY, SLIGHTLY FRUITY TASTE AND crystalline crunch of genuine Parmigiano-Reggiano cheese is a one-of-a-kind experience. Produced using traditional methods for the past 800 years in one government-designated area of northern Italy, this premium Parmesan has a distinctive flavor that is said to come as much from the region's own geography as from the production process. But is all of this regional emphasis for real, or can really good Parmesan be made anywhere?

Recently, many more brands of shrink-wrapped, wedge-style, American-made Parmesan have been appearing in supermarkets. They're sold at a fraction of the price of the authentic stuff, which can cost up to $33 a pound. But what are you giving up when you buy American? And do you have to go to an upscale cheese shop to get great Parmigiano-Reggiano?

To see how they stacked up, we bought eight nationally distributed brands at the supermarket: six domestic Parmesans and two imported Parmigiano-Reggianos. For the sake of comparison, we also purchased Parmigiano-Reggiano from four gourmet mail-order companies. We paid from $13.99 to $33.60 per pound—plus shipping—for the high-end mail-order cheeses, and the supermarket wedges ranged from $8.49 to $17.17 per pound, with domestic cheeses at the low end of the spectrum.

In Italy, the making of Parmesan is highly codified. Here's how the process works, in brief: Raw, partly skimmed milk from cows that graze in a small area of Emilia-Romagna in northern Italy is warmed and combined with a starter culture (think sourdough) to begin the curdling process. Rennet from calves' stomachs, which contains the coagulating enzyme rennin, is added to facilitate the formation of curds. The curds are stirred, which allows moisture and whey to escape. Eventually, the curds are formed into wheels that weigh about 80 pounds, and the words "Parmigiano-Reggiano" are stenciled onto the exterior. The cheese is submerged in brine (salty water) for several days. This makes the rind a little salty, but most of the cheese is not exposed to the brine.

Finally, the cheese is aged. With aging, moisture levels decline and the cheese's characteristic amino acid crystals form. Aging also allows enzymes to break down the protein structure of the cheese, creating its signature crumbly, craggy texture. By Italian law, Parmigiano-Reggiano must be aged for at least 12 months before it can be sold, and it is usually aged for 24 months.

The process is laborious and time-consuming, which explains the high price tag for this cheese. There are also plenty of places to cut corners, which is one reason why domestic Parmesans are less expensive. But that's not the whole story.

What the cows eat will affect the flavor of their milk and the resulting cheese. In Italy, the cows designated for Parmigiano-Reggiano graze outdoors; in the United States, "most cows are not pastured," said Dean Sommer, cheese and food technologist at the Wisconsin Center for Dairy Research, at the University of Wisconsin-Madison. According to Sommer, American cows generally eat TMR, "total mixed ration," a concentrated feed. (There is a domestic movement toward grazing cows in specially seeded pastures, he added, but it is in the early stages.) The natural grazing changes with the seasons, and so does the cheese flavor—which is why you'll see "spring" and "fall" Parmigiano-Reggiano marketed in gourmet shops.

In addition to the cows' diet, Sommer told us, "there are different and unique microflora and yeasts in the milk from cows in Italy that will be distinct from [those in milk from] the United States or anywhere else." The American practice of heating the milk for pasteurization kills these microorganisms. However, since Italians use raw milk to make Parmesan, these microorganisms add unique flavor components to the cheese. "With raw-milk cheeses, you get extreme highs and lows of flavor," Sommer said. "With pasteurized milk, you won't get those extreme highs, but you also won't get the lows. It's a more consistent product, so it

saves money for the manufacturer."

It's not just the milk that's different in the United States. American cheese makers often use nonanimal rennin to curdle the milk. According to Sommer, it's a "one-hundred percent pure copy" of calves' rennet, and while it works, the flavor is just not the same. "It's almost too perfect a copy from a cheese standpoint," he mused. "Something is missing."

Similarly, the starter cultures differ, with Italians using the whey left from the cheese-making of the day before, while Americans generally purchase starters from enzyme manufacturers. No matter where it comes from, each starter is zealously guarded and cultivated by cheese makers for its unique flavor components. Those variations of flavor don't differ from just nation to nation. Each cheese-making company, and each plant of each company, will have slightly different microorganisms in its environment, which alter the flavor of the cheese being produced. "People will literally take bricks from the walls of the old plant with them to a new plant, in hopes of reestablishing the microflora," said Sommer.

Given all the differences in the manufacturing process on each side of the Atlantic, it shouldn't come as much of a surprise that our tasters easily picked out the imports in our lineup of eight supermarket cheeses (see page 92). The two genuine Parmigiano-Reggianos, sold in supermarkets under brand names Boar's Head and Il Villaggio, were the panel's clear favorites. The domestic cheeses, all made in Wisconsin, presented a wide range of flavors and textures from quite good to rubbery, salty, and bland.

So what made the imported cheeses stand out? Interestingly, though our test kitchen tasters usually like salty foods, the imports had the lowest salt content. Lab tests showed some cheeses to have nearly twice as much salt as others. That's because many American companies produce wheels of cheese that weigh just 20 to 24 pounds, not the 80-pound standard used in Italy. As a result, more of the cheese is exposed to salt during the brining process.

Texture was a big factor for our tasters. The Italian imports had a drier, crumblier texture and crystalline

grains," allowing moisture and whey to escape. American curds are broken up by machine and usually left larger, which causes them to retain more moisture, Sommer said.

Second, as Parmesan ages, it loses moisture and begins to form its characteristic amino acid crystals. At the same time, enzymes break down the protein structure, creating an increasingly crumbly, craggy texture, explained Pat Mugan, vice president of product innovation for Sartori Foods in Wisconsin, which produces SarVecchio Parmesan, the domestic cheese with the longest aging (20 months) and the lowest moisture level in our lineup. "At six months, the cheese would be able to bend; at twenty months, it crumbles," Mugan said. "You see a dramatic difference."

While Italian Parmesans are all aged at least 12 and usually 24 months, for domestic Parmesan the federal standard is 10 months, though a few manufacturers, including Kraft, petitioned (and got temporary permission) to shorten the aging standard to six months, claiming that it does not affect the quality of the cheese. Sommer disagrees: "For a Parmesan, especially, time is critical," he said. "For the first five months of aging, the cheese has hardly any flavor whatsoever. [Flavor development] gradually comes along, picking up speed from around eight months on, when you start getting some really nice flavors." The Kraft products in our lineup performed poorly. The recently introduced Grate-It-Fresh, a chunk of Parmesan sold in a disposable grater, was decried for its "salty," "bland, flat" flavor. Kraft also now produces our previous favorite domestic Parmesan, DiGiorno, using this new shorter aging period, which may help explain why it rated so poorly with our tasters this time.

While our tasters clearly preferred Italian Parmigiano-Reggiano, they also praised the top two domestic cheeses for their pleasingly "nutty" flavor. BelGioioso and SarVecchio were two of the longer-aged of the domestic cheeses, at 10 months and 20 months, respectively. While these cheeses can't really compete with our top-ranked imports, BelGioioso offered "lovely, delicate flavor" for just more than half the price.

crunch. Nearly all of the American cheeses were perceptibly moister, some even to the point of bounciness, with few or no crystals. The laboratory tests bore out our tasters' reactions, with imported cheeses showing lower moisture levels in general. Why is this so? First, even before the cheese is formed into wheels, the size of the curds influences its texture. In Italy, cheese makers use a giant whisk to break curds into pieces described as "the size of wheat

Rating Supermarket Parmesan Cheese

TWENTY AMERICA'S TEST KITCHEN STAFF MEMBERS TASTED EIGHT NATIONALLY AVAILABLE SUPERMARKET BRANDS OF Parmesan cheese three ways: broken into chunks, grated, and cooked in polenta. The results were averaged, and the cheeses are listed in order of preference. An independent laboratory measured the moisture level and salt content (both shown as grams per hundred). Information about aging was provided by manufacturers. The cheeses are listed in order of preference and are available in supermarkets.

RECOMMENDED
Boar's Head Parmigiano-Reggiano

$17.17 per pound; Imported from Italy, aged 24 months; Salt: 1.65 g.; Moisture: 32.46 g

Tasters deemed this sample "best in show" and "authentic," praising its "good crunch" and "nice tangy, nutty" flavor. "Rich" and "complex," this sample had a "very good balance of acid/fruit/nutty/creamy."

RECOMMENDED
Il Villaggio Parmigiano-Reggiano

$16.99 per pound; Imported from Italy, aged 24 months; Salt: 2.21 g; Moisture: 31.11 g

"Nutty, granular, tangy, and tasty" was the verdict, with tasters noting its "good, sharp flavor" and "melt-on-your-tongue feel." In polenta, this cheese was "rich and bold."

RECOMMENDED
BelGioioso Parmesan

$8.99 per pound; Domestic, aged at least 10 months; Salt: 3.19 g; Moisture: 34.78 g

"Mild but complex," this cheese was a little "soft and creamy for a Parmesan," with a "too moist" texture. Grated, it had a "nice and tangy" aroma and "lovely, delicate flavor." In polenta, it was "nutty, well balanced, very good."

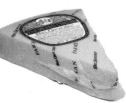

RECOMMENDED
SarVecchio Parmesan (formerly Stravecchio)

$11.99 per pound; Domestic, aged 20 months; Salt: 2.59 g; Moisture: 29.85 g

"Good, interesting flavor; almost has a sharp, lemony note," according to one taster. Another praised the "rich nuttiness" in this "crumbly" cheese "with a slight crunch." One taster summed up: "A Parm with guts!"

RECOMMENDED WITH RESERVATIONS
Rosalia's Trattoria Parmesan

$8.49 per pound; Domestic, aged at least 10 months; Salt: 2.40 g; Moisture: 39.01 g

Tasters disliked its "plastic," "dense and rubbery" texture: "It's like I bit into food from a dollhouse." Grated, it had "nutty flavor and fresh aroma" but was "a bit one-dimensional."

NOT RECOMMENDED
Kraft Grate-It-Fresh Parmesan

$11.40 per pound (sold in plastic grater, 7 ounces for $4.99); Domestic, aged at least 6 months; Salt: 3.57 g; Moisture: 32.82 g

The high salt content showed: "I felt like a deer at a salt lick." Shredded, this cheese's texture was "like dental floss," with flavor that was "artificial." One unhappy taster asked, "Was this grated from a Parm-scented candle?"

NOT RECOMMENDED
Stella Parmesan

$8.98 per pound; Domestic, aged 10 months; Salt: 2.90 g; Moisture: 33.48 g

In chunks, this cheese failed to impress: "Soapy, fake, rubbery. Yuck." Grated, it fared better, with a "nutty, buttery aroma and flavor," though several tasters deemed it "nothing special." In polenta, it was "very bland."

NOT RECOMMENDED
DiGiorno Parmesan

$8.49 per pound; Domestic, aged at least 6 months; Salt: 2.50 g; Moisture: 34.67 g

"Rubbery" came up over and over in tasters' comments. "Like eating candle wax, and the flavor's not much better." Grated, it was "blandsville." In polenta, it was "too mild." "Did you forget to put the cheese in here?"

TASTING LAB: Mail-Order Parmesan

THE INTERNET IS A BIT LIKE EVERYBODY'S CORNER gourmet cheese shop, so we decided to taste a few wedges of imported Parmigiano-Reggiano from four gourmet Web sites to see what kind of quality was available. We ordered from Zingermans.com ($22.50 per pound); Dean & Deluca, which imports a "younger" cheese to lower the cost ($21 per pound, 2-pound minimum, includes Parmigiano knife); Gustiamo.com, which boasts of a 36-month "extra-aged" cheese from a particular dairy ($42 for 1.25 pounds, $33.60 per pound); and iGourmet.com, where we chose both the regular Parmigiano-Reggiano ($13.99 per pound) and an intriguing Vacche Rosse ("Red Cow") Parmigiano-Reggiano ($12.99 for 8 ounces, $25.98 per pound).

We learned that this "Red Cow" Parmesan comes from the red-colored Reggiana cows that were the earliest breed native to the northern Italian region where Parmigiano-Reggiano has been made for centuries. Due to their lower milk yield, these cows were edged out by modern high-yield cows just after World War II. A few traditionalists are bringing them back to make cheese the old-fashioned way. Their milk has a naturally higher fat content, and the cheese is usually aged at least 30 months.

We tasted the cheeses broken into small chunks, and we preferred the iGourmet regular and Vacche Rosse Parmigiano-Reggiano by a landslide, ranking them significantly higher than the other cheeses for complexity of flavor and appealing texture. And when we tasted the regular Parmigiano from iGourmet against our supermarket cheeses (see chart), it was an easy winner.

EQUIPMENT CORNER: Garlic Presses

WE HAVE A CRUSH ON GARLIC IN THE TEST KITCHEN. It appears in more than one-quarter of our recipes, and in most of those we suggest using a garlic press. This is heresy to some professional chefs. Why not just mince? Over the years, we've learned that for the average home cook, a garlic press is faster, easier, and more effective than trying to get a fine, even mince with a chef's knife. More important, garlic's flavor and aroma emerge only as its cell walls are ruptured and release an enzyme called alliinase, so a finely processed clove gives you a better distribution of garlic and fuller garlic flavor throughout the dish. Even our test cooks, trained to mince with a knife, generally grab a garlic press when cooking. And here's the best part: With a good garlic press, you don't even have to stop and peel the cloves.

Americans are using more garlic than ever, and it seems that every kitchen-tool manufacturer is trying to build a better garlic press. Many offer two or three models, traditional and innovative, hoping to catch the eye or the budget of every cook. Prices can range from less than $5 to more than $60. We rounded up nearly two dozen models and bushels of fresh garlic to find the best press for your kitchen.

But then it occurred to us: Beyond how easy it is to squeeze, does your garlic press really matter in your cooking? Will the right garlic press make your food taste better? We were skeptical, but a quick test revealed a surprising answer. We chose seven representative presses and used them to make seven batches of our pasta with garlic and olive oil. It was remarkable to note the wide range of garlic flavor, from mild to robust, when the only difference was the press used to prepare the garlic. Larger chunks of garlic tended to drop to the bottom of the bowl, making most of the dish too bland. And when the pieces were uneven, tiny fragments overcooked to bitterness. Tasters overwhelmingly preferred the samples with the finest and most uniform garlic pieces, which produced a well-developed garlic flavor and consistent texture throughout the dish.

We decided that a garlic press's most important attribute was the ability to produce a fine garlic consistency. We also wanted a press that was simple and comfortable to operate. It should be solidly built, with no contest between the press and the garlic about which is going to break first. It should be able to hold more than one clove and should crush the garlic completely through the sieve, leaving little behind in the hopper. It should handle unpeeled cloves with ease. Finally, it should be simple to clean, by hand or dishwasher, and not require a toothpick to get the last pieces of garlic out.

The more creative garlic gadgets were not successes. The Garlic Twist by NexTrend, a plastic pillbox-shaped device that you twist to chop the garlic inside, could only cut through a peeled, roughly chopped clove. The Genius Garlic Cutter (and a similar model by Moulinex) and the Chef'N Garlic Machine work like a peppermill. We found them slow to use and hard to clean. Such gimmicks sent us back to traditional lever-handled garlic presses. As we squeezed piles of pungent cloves, we began a process of elimination to decide on the 12 presses in our final lineup (see the chart at right).

We had been satisfied with our previous favorite presses, the Zyliss Susi 2 and Zyliss Jumbo, until we noticed that the nonstick coating had peeled off each one in the test kitchen, particularly around the hopper, and a tiny amount of black liquid was sometimes extruded along with the garlic. We sent a damaged press to an independent laboratory to determine what was happening and whether it could be unsafe. As we waited for the lab report, we tested the 12 finalists, including brand-new Zyliss presses. Since all were labeled dishwasher-safe, we ran them through a home dishwasher for 10 cycles. One model, by Amco, fell apart after just six cycles, leaving two halves and a missing hinge pin. And the nonstick coating on the brand-new Zyliss presses peeled—yet again. The lab results also revealed that when the nonstick coating peels off, copper and iron in the aluminum base metal react with the air and sulfur compounds in the garlic, which we sometimes see as a black substance on our extruded garlic. It's not dangerous, but it's not very appealing either.

We downgraded models with removable parts. The Cuisinart's hopper was too easy to put back in the wrong way or lose. We rejected designs such as the potato ricer–style Giant Garlic Press, which offered good leverage with its long handles but was cheaply executed, and the ridiculously expensive Eva Solo Garlic Press with Glass Container ($64.95), which was difficult to squeeze and quickly jammed up.

So which press is the best? Kuhn Rikon's Epicurean Garlic Press ($34.95) was the top performer, producing fine, uniform garlic with minimal effort. Made of solidly constructed stainless steel, it has a luxurious feel, with curved handles that are comfortable to squeeze and a hopper that smoothly and automatically lifts out for cleaning as you open the handles. However, at nearly $35, it's costly. At one-third the price, the chrome-plated Trudeau Garlic Press produced fairly uniform pieces of garlic, had a generous hopper, and was easy to clean.

Rating Garlic Presses

WE TESTED 12 GARLIC PRESSES, PRESSING PEELED AND UNPEELED CLOVES AS WELL AS MULTIPLE CLOVES. WE RAN THE presses through a home dishwasher 10 times to evaluate durability. Presses are listed in order of preference. See www.americastestkitchen.com for up-to-date prices and mail-order sources for top-rated products.

RECOMMENDED

Kuhn Rikon 2315 Epicurean Garlic Press

$34.95

Heavy, solid gliding mechanism, with comfortably curved handles and a hopper that lifts for easy cleaning. Mince is "very fine" and unpeeled garlic was "no problem."

RECOMMENDED WITH RESERVATIONS

Rösle Garlic Press

$34.95

Solid, heavy press has a pop-up hopper for cleaning. Straight, cylindrical, shiny handles "didn't feel perfectly ergonomic."

RECOMMENDED WITH RESERVATIONS

Trudeau Garlic Press

$11.99

"Good press" with a "solid" feel produced garlic pieces that were "uniform but a little chunky." Press was "very easy to clean," with flip handles.

RECOMMENDED WITH RESERVATIONS

Messermeister Pro-Touch Jumbo Garlic Press with Santoprene Handles

$9.95

"Sturdy and easy to squeeze," except for unpeeled cloves, which required more muscle. Garlic came out slightly "chunky" and "coarse."

RECOMMENDED WITH RESERVATIONS

Zyliss Susi 2 Garlic Press

$14.99

Tapered holes shaped like tiny funnels gave "huge yield" of "fine-textured garlic" that was "super-easy" to press. "Effortless" with unpeeled cloves. However, the nonstick finish began to peel around the hopper.

RECOMMENDED WITH RESERVATIONS

Zyliss Jumbo Garlic Press

$16.99

"Jumbo" press held four to five cloves; handled unpeeled cloves well, producing a "very good mince." Nonstick finish began to peel.

NOT RECOMMENDED

OXO Steel 58181 Garlic Press

$16.99

Plunger couldn't be fully depressed to bottom of hopper. Testers deemed the sieve holes too large, producing "coarse," "chunky" pieces.

NOT RECOMMENDED

OXO Good Grips 28181 Garlic Press

$14.50

Plunger couldn't quite get to the bottom of the hopper, leaving some garlic unprocessed. Couldn't handle unpeeled cloves. Handles were comfortable and easy to press.

NOT RECOMMENDED

Giant Garlic Press

$14

Shaped like a potato ricer, this press struck testers as "flimsy." Hopper is "huge" but could press only three cloves, because the plunger couldn't get into position with more.

NOT RECOMMENDED

Cuisinart Red Garlic Press

$14.95

Testers disliked the "tiny hopper," which removes for cleaning. "I'd lose this in a second," complained one. Unpeeled garlic "spattered and squished up the sides."

NOT RECOMMENDED

Amco Houseworks Garlic Press

(also sold as the Crate and Barrel Garlic Slicer and Press)

$19.95

Fell completely apart in dishwasher after six washes. Press "left a lot behind," and pieces were somewhat uneven. Slices were "too thick."

NOT RECOMMENDED

Eva Solo Stainless Steel Garlic Press with Glass Container

$64.95

"Too cool for its own good" and "very uncomfortable." "I used my whole body weight to press it," complained one tester. Unpeeled cloves were "almost impossible."

TIME LEFT

755

LOW

The slow, steady heat of a slow
cooker is perfect for turning tough
cuts of meat, like chuck meat or
short ribs, tender and flavorful.

FAVORITE SLOW
CHAPTER 8   *cooker classics*

Most of us think of the slow cooker as a kitchen workhorse best reserved for use during the week for simple stews, hearty soups, and the like. But what about pulling the slow cooker out for entertaining? Between readying the house for company, setting the table, and getting all the other elements of the meal together, a slow cooker makes perfect sense. The test kitchen set out to adapt two company-worthy recipes for the slow cooker, Beef Burgundy and Beer-Braised Short Ribs.

Unlike American-style beef stews, Beef Burgundy is a bit more refined and delicate in flavor. Our challenge would be to develop a stew where the flavors wouldn't become dulled during the long, slow simmer in the slow cooker. And because the stew contains red wine, we'd need to work to ensure that the wine flavors turned out rich and complex, not boozy or harsh, in the finished dish.

Meaty, rich short ribs are perfect for the slow cooker, but we needed to find a way to produce beer-braised short ribs that weren't swimming in fat. And we wanted our beer-accented gravy to taste bold and rich, not washed out and heavy.

Come the weekend, don't put away the slow cooker, company's coming.

SLOW-COOKER BEEF BURGUNDY

WHAT WE WANTED: A slow-cooker method for producing tender chunks of beef in an earthy but refined sauce rich with red wine, garlic, onions, and mushrooms.

American-style beef stew is a perfect recipe for the slow cooker: The long, slow cooking tenderizes tough cuts of meat and creates a beefy sauce studded with soft vegetables. But beef Burgundy, a more refined beef stew built on a foundation of wine, usually doesn't fare so well in the slow cooker; the long hours in a covered cooker (with no evaporation or concentration of flavors) turn wine into sour, hot alcohol—not what we were looking for in this recipe.

What we did want was a rich, savory stew that was beefy, pleasantly winy, and a bit more sophisticated than regular beef stew. Starting with the beef, we knew from experience (and many prior tests) that chuck stew meat is best for long braises like beef Burgundy and that we needed to brown it first to develop a flavorful base for the dish. To save time, we used precut meat (instead of cutting up a whole roast) and browned it—along with carrots, onion, and garlic—in bacon drippings (the traditional fat in this recipe) before adding it to the slow cooker. Wanting to cut back on prep time, we made a batch where we browned only half the meat, and tasters couldn't tell the difference; half the work sounded good to us. To thicken the stew, we relied on tapioca—a surprising ingredient, but one that has worked well in past test kitchen recipes.

The slow cooker has a tendency to wash out the flavor of a stew. This led us to be aggressive with flavorful additions—tasters preferred a lot of garlic and fresh thyme, half a can of tomato paste for sweetness and satiny texture, and a big hit of soy sauce to boost both flavor and color.

Now it was time to move on to the big challenge: the wine flavor. When we marinated the beef in wine, the resulting stew tasted (and smelled) sour. Adding all the wine at the outset produced an acrid and boozy sauce. We tried cutting the wine with chicken broth (the test kitchen generally prefers chicken broth to beef broth, even in beef recipes), and it was a step in the right direction—but the wine flavor was still underdeveloped and flat. We tried adding a few splashes of wine to the finished dish to reawaken the flavors, and although it did add brightness, tasters found it too sharp and astringent. We were running out of options.

Most recipes that feature wine are cooked uncovered, allowing the alcohol time to cook out and giving the flavors a chance to reduce. Since our beef Burgundy was being slow-cooked under cover, we tried reducing the wine before adding it to the pot, but that made the sauce too winy. We had better luck adding part of the wine at the beginning and reducing the remaining wine before adding it at the end. This time, the reduced wine, stirred in just before serving, brought the tired stew back to life. Our humble slow cooker had finally produced a refined, full-bodied stew worthy of the best French restaurant.

WHAT WE LEARNED: Chuck roast, cut into pieces (often labeled chuck stew meat), is the best choice for long braises like beef Burgundy. It's only necessary to brown half the meat before adding it to the slow cooker for a great base of meaty flavor. Soy sauce reinforces the meaty flavor of this stew and also lends some color to a dish that can sometimes look washed out. Use generous amounts of garlic, thyme, and tomato paste for a robust sauce that won't dull over the long cooking time. And for fuller flavor, without a sour alcohol taste, stir in some reduced wine toward the end of cooking.

BEEF BURGUNDY

serves 6 to 8

Make sure to use the low setting on your slow cooker; the stew will burn on the high setting. Don't spend a lot of money for the wine in this recipe—in testing, we found that California Pinot Noir wines in the $6 to $20 price range worked just fine. Serve with boiled potatoes (the traditional accompaniment), mashed potatoes, or buttered egg noodles.

stew

8	ounces (8 slices) bacon, chopped
4	pounds stew beef (preferably chuck)
	Salt and ground black pepper
1	large onion, chopped fine
2	carrots, peeled and chopped fine
8	medium garlic cloves, minced or pressed through a garlic press (about 2 tablespoons plus 2 teaspoons)
2	teaspoons chopped fresh thyme leaves
4	tablespoons tomato paste
2½	cups Pinot Noir (see note)
1½	cups low-sodium chicken broth
⅓	cup soy sauce
3	bay leaves
3	tablespoons Minute tapioca
3	tablespoons minced fresh parsley leaves

onion and mushroom garnish

2	cups frozen pearl onions
½	cup water
5	tablespoons unsalted butter
1	tablespoon sugar
10	ounces white button mushrooms, wiped clean and quartered
	Salt

1. FOR THE STEW: Cook the bacon in a large skillet over medium-high heat until crisp. Using a slotted spoon, transfer the bacon to a paper towel–lined plate and refrigerate. Pour half of the bacon fat into a small bowl; set the skillet with the remaining bacon fat aside.

2. Dry the beef thoroughly with paper towels. Season the beef with salt and pepper; place half of the beef in a slow-cooker insert. Heat the skillet containing the remaining bacon fat over medium-high heat until just smoking. Cook the remaining beef in a single layer until deep brown on all sides, about 8 minutes. Transfer the browned beef to the slow-cooker insert.

3. Add the reserved bacon fat to the now-empty skillet and heat over medium-high heat until shimmering. Add the onion, carrots, and ¼ teaspoon salt and cook until the vegetables begin to brown, about 5 minutes. Add the garlic

and thyme and cook until fragrant, about 30 seconds. Add the tomato paste and stir until beginning to brown, about 45 seconds. Transfer the mixture to the slow-cooker insert.

4. Return the now-empty skillet to high heat and add 1½ cups of the wine, the chicken broth, and soy sauce. Simmer, scraping up any browned bits, until the pan bottom is clean, about 1 minute. Transfer the wine mixture to the slow-cooker insert.

5. Stir the bay leaves and tapioca into the slow-cooker insert. Set the slow cooker on low, cover, and cook until the meat is fork-tender, about 9 hours.

6. FOR THE ONION AND MUSHROOM GARNISH: Bring the pearl onions, water, butter, and sugar to a boil in a large skillet over high heat. Cover and simmer over medium-low heat until the onions are tender, about 5 minutes. Uncover, increase the heat to high, and cook until the

liquid evaporates, about 3 minutes. Add the mushrooms and ¼ teaspoon salt and cook until the vegetables are browned and glazed, about 5 minutes.

7. When ready to serve, discard the bay leaves and stir in the onion and mushroom garnish and the reserved bacon. Bring the remaining 1 cup wine to a boil in a large skillet over high heat and simmer until reduced by half, about 5 minutes. Stir the reduced wine and parsley into the stew and season with salt and pepper to taste. Serve.

VARIATION
MAKE-AHEAD BEEF BURGUNDY
Follow the recipe for Beef Burgundy through step 4 (without transferring the components to the slow-cooker insert) up to 2 days in advance. Refrigerate the bacon, browned beef, raw beef, vegetable mixture, and wine mixture separately. When ready to cook the stew, transfer these ingredients (except the bacon) to the slow-cooker insert and proceed with step 5.

EQUIPMENT CORNER: Slow Cookers

PART OF THE APPEAL OF A SLOW COOKER HAS ALWAYS been the modest price. But as slow cookers have gained popularity in recent years, manufacturers have added new features—and larger price tags. Does more money buy a better slow cooker? To find out, we rounded up seven models priced between $40 and $150. We chose slow cookers with oval inserts and capacities of 6 quarts or greater—features we found important when we looked at more basic models back in 2005. Here's what we found.

The stovetop-safe inserts in the Rival VersaWare and the West Bend Versatility didn't brown meat very well—the recommended medium heat simply doesn't get the job done. A programmable timer was deemed a real asset, especially because all the machines with timers automatically switch to a warming mode when the timed cooking is done. This means that even if you're late coming home from work, your dinner won't be overcooked (or cold). The models without timers were downgraded. Other features we found beneficial include an "on" light (so you don't accidentally leave it on overnight), insert handles (which make it easy to remove the insert), and a clear lid that allows you to see the food as it cooks.

Another important factor to consider is cooking speed. From a safety standpoint, it's important that slow cookers don't cook too slowly. The U.S. Department of Agriculture recommends that meat be brought out of the "danger zone" (that is, above 140 degrees) within four hours. We used remote temperature probes to monitor the internal temperature of large chuck roasts, and every machine was able to bring the meat up to temperature in the allotted time—even on "low." And none of the machines had trouble bringing the interior of the roasts up to about 200 degrees, the temperature at which collagen and connective tissue most efficiently melt away to make tough cuts tender.

Excess moisture tends to build up in slow cookers, because the covered vessel allows for little or no evaporation—and most, but not all recipes are written to reflect this issue. We filled all of our test models with 3 quarts of 42-degree water and noted that the All-Clad, Hamilton Beach Stay or Go, Hamilton Beach Probe, Rival, and West Bend machines allowed only about 2 percent of the water to evaporate after three hours of covered cooking on "high." The two cookers that fared worst in this test, the KitchenAid and the Cuisinart, lost about 6 percent and 4 percent of their water, respectively.

So where did we end up? All the slow cookers we tested did a good job with slow-cooking pot roast on both "high" and "low" and cooking chili and beans on "high." But more important than the cooking tests were the features we deemed essential: timers that automatically shift to a "keep warm" setting at the end of cooking; a clear lid; an "on" indicator light; and handles on the insert.

Rating Slow Cookers

WE TESTED SEVEN SLOW COOKERS ON PERFORMANCE AND EASE IN COOKING POT ROAST, CHILI, AND BEANS. The slow cookers are listed in order of preference. See www.americastestkitchen.com for up-to-date prices and mail-order sources for top-rated products.

HIGHLY RECOMMENDED
All-Clad Stainless Steel Slow Cooker with Ceramic Insert

$149.95; 6.5-quart capacity

This cooker aced the evaporation test and all the cooking tests, and it has every feature we want, including insert handles and a clear lid. Provided a steady, slow heat that is ideal for tough cuts of meat.

RECOMMENDED
KitchenAid Stainless Steel Slow Cooker

$129.95; 7-quart capacity

This model cooked slightly hotter than the other contenders, but none of the finished food suffered as a result. The slightly squared insert shape was praised for being "easy to pour out of."

RECOMMENDED
Cuisinart Slow Cooker

$99.95; 6.5-quart capacity

This machine did very well in all cooking tests. Several testers were surprised that the bulky, boxy exterior of this cooker got very hot during long cooking. "It looks like it should be insulated," said one.

RECOMMENDED
Hamilton Beach Programmable Slow Cooker with Temperature Probe

$59.95; 6-quart capacity

This model passed the evaporation test and performed well in the cooking tests. This cooker was downgraded for being the only one without handles on the insert, which made removing it difficult—especially when hot.

RECOMMENDED WITH RESERVATIONS
Hamilton Beach Oval Stay or Go Slow Cooker

$39.95; 6-quart capacity

The gimmicky travel clips and recipe name tag were not part of this model's appeal, but testers did appreciate its solid performance in the kitchen and the "straightforward, no frills" ease of operation. This inexpensive cooker does not have a timer, which is a serious drawback.

RECOMMENDED WITH RESERVATIONS
Rival Oval VersaWare Crock Pot

$54.95; 6-quart capacity

"No timer?" asked testers. "No 'on' light?" The opaque lid was another strike against this cooker, but it did perform well in the cooking tests.

NOT RECOMMENDED
West Bend Oval Versatility Slow Cooker

$64.95; 6-quart capacity

Testers complained about the lack of an "on" light, especially since this machine begins heating as soon as it's plugged in—there is no "off" setting. This model was also downgraded for heating faster on "low" than "high" and for having an awkward-fitting lid that "falls into the pot easily."

SLOW-COOKER BEEF SHORT RIBS

WHAT WE WANTED: A slow-cooker method for producing robust, meaty short ribs in a rich, oniony sauce.

Meaty short ribs are slow food; time and gentle heat turn this tough cut into a blue-ribbon dinner. So why not use a slow cooker? Short ribs are just what their name says—short pieces cut from any part of the beef ribs. Because they are rich with fat and connective tissue, they are perfect for slow cooking—a process that turns tough meat soft and also melts excess fat, which can be easily discarded. The problem is that we rarely have hours to tend a simmering pot. That's where we thought a slow cooker might come in handy. Armed with 50 pounds of short ribs (those bones weigh a lot), we marched into the test kitchen.

For our first test, we simply tossed the ribs into the slow cooker, added onions and beer for flavor, turned on the cooker, and turned to other tasks. After 10 hours in the slow cooker, these ribs were pretty much a disaster. The sauce was bland and watery, an inch of fat floated on top, and the meat was gray.

Our next efforts were all aimed at adding flavor to this dish. First we browned the short ribs in a skillet, and this helped to develop a beefy flavor (it also rendered quite a bit of fat). Next we tested combinations of beef and chicken broth with varying amounts of beer (both light and dark) and were continually disappointed. The sauce had no personality and little beer flavor. But when we used dark beer only—and no broth—the sauce was nicely enriched with its hearty flavor. Wanting an even more complex flavor, we tried an unlikely ingredient that we'd seen in another recipe: prunes. Melting into the sauce, they were detected by no one in the finished dish (not even by those who don't like prunes) yet magically sweetened it, adding deep color and flavor.

The onions were of course also crucial to flavor, and we found that we had to use a hefty 3 pounds, browning them in the skillet after browning and removing the ribs. A little tomato paste and soy sauce further punched up the flavor and color of the sauce, and tapioca worked like a charm to thicken the liquid as it cooked. (Flour and cornstarch imparted raw, starchy flavors that no one liked.)

The only remaining problem was the fat. Even after meticulous skimming, each dinner plate ended up with a slick of orange grease that challenged even the strongest dishwashing liquid. There was just one way to solve this problem: Make the ribs the night before we wanted to serve them, letting the slow cooker work while we slept. In the morning, we refrigerated the ribs and sauce separately and then, just before serving, we removed the fat that had solidified on top of the sauce. We then reheated the meat in the defatted sauce, adding a little Dijon mustard and fresh thyme to brighten the flavor. Perfect! These were short ribs that were rich and meaty, but not greasy.

WHAT WE LEARNED: For deep meaty flavor, brown the short ribs in a skillet before adding to the slow cooker. Sauté a generous 3 pounds of sliced onions in the same skillet used to brown the ribs. For a sauce with deep flavor and color, add a bit of tomato paste, soy sauce, and a surprise ingredient—prunes. To prevent the dish from being too greasy, cook the night before you plan to serve, so that you can simply skim the hardened fat off the top of the braising liquid and reheat in the defatted liquid. And, to enliven the finished sauce, stir in Dijon mustard and additional fresh thyme just before serving.

TECHNIQUE:

Getting the Most Flavor from Short Ribs

1. Brown First

Brown the meaty side of the ribs, then turn them on each side to finish browning (you can lean the ribs against each other if they won't stand on their own).

2. Then Slow-cook

Place the browned ribs in the slow cooker with the meaty side facing down and the bones facing up. This ensures that the meat stays submerged throughout the long cooking time.

BEER-BRAISED SHORT RIBS

serves 4 to 6

The only way to remove fat from the braising liquid is to prepare this recipe a day or two before you want to serve it. Luckily, the short ribs actually taste better if cooked in advance and then reheated in the defatted braising liquid.

5	pounds English-style beef short ribs (6 to 8 ribs), trimmed of excess fat
	Salt and ground black pepper
2	tablespoons vegetable oil
2	tablespoons unsalted butter
3	pounds yellow onions, halved and sliced thin
2	tablespoons tomato paste
2	(12-ounce) bottles dark beer (see at left)
12	pitted prunes
2	tablespoons soy sauce
2	tablespoons Minute tapioca
2	bay leaves
2	teaspoons minced fresh thyme leaves
3	tablespoons Dijon mustard
2	tablespoons minced fresh parsley leaves

1. Season the ribs with salt and pepper. Heat the oil in a 12-inch skillet over medium-high heat until just smoking. Add half of the ribs, meaty side down, and cook until well browned, about 5 minutes. Following the photo at left, turn each rib on one side and cook until well browned, about 1 minute. Repeat with the remaining sides. Transfer the ribs to a slow-cooker insert, arranging them meaty side down as shown in the photo at left. Repeat with the remaining ribs.

2. Pour off all but 1 teaspoon fat from the skillet. Add the butter and reduce the heat to medium. When the butter has melted, add the onions and cook, stirring occasionally, until well browned, 25 to 30 minutes. Stir in the tomato paste and cook, coating the onions with the tomato paste,

until the paste begins to brown, about 5 minutes. Stir in the beer, bring to a simmer, and cook, scraping the browned bits from the pan bottom with a wooden spoon, until the foaming subsides, about 5 minutes. Remove the skillet from the heat and stir in the prunes, soy sauce, tapioca, bay leaves, and 1 teaspoon of the thyme. Transfer to the slow-cooker insert.

3. Set the slow cooker on low, cover, and cook until the ribs are fork-tender, 10 to 11 hours. (Alternately, cook on high for 4 to 5 hours.) Transfer the ribs to a baking dish and strain the liquid into a bowl. Cover and refrigerate for at least 8 hours or up to 2 days.

4. When ready to serve, use a spoon to skim off the hardened fat from the liquid. Place the short ribs, meaty side down, and the liquid in a Dutch oven and reheat over medium heat until warmed through, about 20 minutes. Transfer the ribs to a serving platter. Whisk the mustard and remaining teaspoon

thyme into the sauce and season with salt and pepper to taste. Pour 1 cup of the sauce over the ribs. Sprinkle with the parsley and serve, passing the remaining sauce separately.

GETTING IT RIGHT:
Short Ribs for Braising

When it comes to choosing a cut of meat for our Beer-Braised Short Ribs, you have two options, both of which will deliver good results. English-style short ribs are cut from a single rib bone and feature a long flat bone with a rectangle of meat attached. Flanken-style ribs are cut across several bones and contain two or three small pieces of bone surrounded by pieces of meat. Because flanken-style ribs are more expensive and less widely available, we prefer English style.

English-Style Ribs

Flanken-Style Ribs

For our Double-Corn Cornbread we found that preheating an oiled cast-iron skillet before pouring in the batter produces a cornbread with a deeply brown, crunchy crust— and this method also ensures a clean release from the pan.

WHITE CHICKEN
chili supper

Chicken chili might sound like heresy—after all, isn't chili supposed to be made with beef? But this Southwestern dish is a light, bright alternative to tomato-rich beef chili. And by light, we don't mean low-cal or lean. This chili is rich in its own right, chock-full of juicy chicken and tender white beans. In chicken chili, green chiles figure prominently, adding not only heat but vibrant fresh chile flavor as well. The key to chicken chili is to find the right cooking method so that the chicken doesn't dry out and turn rubbery. We'd also need to find the right balance of chiles and other seasonings for a chili with zesty, not dull, flavor.

Cornbread is terrific partnered with any variety of chili, soup, or stew. We also like cornbread served simply—warm, with a pat of butter and a drizzle of honey at breakfast. In developing a cornbread recipe, we decided to put Northern and Southern biases aside (cakey and sweet versus savory and crumbly) to focus on developing a cornbread with strong corn flavor, which is often lacking in both styles. This would be a cornbread to please everyone.

WHITE CHICKEN CHILI

WHAT WE WANTED: A rich, stew-like chicken chili with moist meat, perfectly cooked beans, and a complex flavor profile.

White chicken chili is a fresher, lighter cousin of the thick red chili most Americans know and love. While its origins date back to the health and Southwestern crazes of the 1980s, white chicken chili has since shown up in a number of Midwestern family cookbooks and has become a regular on the chili cook-off circuit. Its appeal is not surprising. First, because the recipe uses chicken rather than beef, many folks appreciate it for being healthier. Next, because there are no tomatoes to mask the other flavors, the chiles, herbs, and spices take center stage. Unlike red chili, which uses any combination of dried chiles, chili powders, and cayenne pepper, white chicken chili gets its backbone from fresh green chiles. So much so, in fact, that the recipe is sometimes called chili verde, or green chili.

The ingredients in white chicken chili are fairly consistent: diced or ground chicken, green chiles (usually fresh but sometimes canned or pickled), onions, white beans, garlic, spices, and chicken broth. But most of the recipes we tried were too watery and bland, bearing a closer resemblance to chicken and bean soup than to actual chili. While the floating bits of mushy beans and overcooked chicken were hard to overlook, the chiles themselves were often barely noticeable. But amid all these bad recipes, we saw the possibility of creating something great—a hearty, satisfying chicken chili, rich with tender chunks of meat, hearty beans, and a bold, bracing green chile flavor.

The basic procedure for making white chicken chili is fairly simple. Most recipes start by browning the chicken. Next, the browned chicken is set aside and the chiles, onion, garlic, and spices are sautéed in the same pot. Finally, the chicken is added back in along with chicken broth and white beans and simmered until the chicken has cooked through.

Ground chicken was moist but had a chewy, spongy texture and an unattractive crumbly appearance. The choice between white and dark meat was a close call. Chicken thighs tasted richer and meatier, but they took twice as long to cook as the milder-flavored breasts and tended to compete with the fresh flavors of the chiles and seasonings. Boneless, skinless chicken breasts were attractive but lent little flavor to the broth. We had better luck with bone-in, skin-on breasts (later we would remove the bones and shred the chicken). We browned the pieces first to help develop fond (the flavorful bits on the bottom of the pot) and render out fat, which we saved to cook with the aromatics.

We were ready to move on to the main order of business: the chiles. Some recipes rely solely on canned or jarred green chiles. While offering convenience, they were also too vinegary and pickled. That left us with six widely available fresh chiles to choose from: poblanos, Anaheims, banana peppers, Italian peppers, jalapeños, and serranos. Banana peppers and Italian peppers were uninspiring. Extremely hot serranos were also out. We hoped to find a one-size-fits-all chile but discovered that more than one variety was necessary to provide the complexity and modest heat we were looking for. A trio of poblanos, Anaheims, and jalapeños did just that, with each chile bringing its own inimitable characteristics (see "Balancing Heat and Flavor" at right) to the table.

Following the lead of other recipe writers, we briefly sautéed the chopped chiles along with diced onions, garlic, and spices over relatively high heat before adding the broth, beans, and chicken. This technique often yielded chiles that retained too much texture and had a flat, vegetal flavor. Roasting softened the chiles but provided an unwanted smokiness that muddied the dish. We found our solution back on the stovetop by lowering the heat and covering the pot to help soften the chiles and other vegetables. In 10 minutes, the chiles and onions were softened, and the flavors of the garlic and spices were nicely bloomed. As for the spices, tasters liked the standard cumin but preferred aromatic coriander to the more commonly used dried oregano.

At this point, we were ready to deal with the chicken. After removing the skin, we poached the breasts until they were just done (about 20 minutes) and set them aside while the base continued to cook. Canned beans were our go-to choice, as dried beans were unnecessarily time-consuming. We favored larger cannellini beans over navy beans, which were too reminiscent of minestrone.

To fix the wateriness problem that had plagued so many of our test recipes, we tried adding a small amount of masa harina (a corn flour product), which we've used to thicken a red chili recipe in the past. While it technically worked, the masa also imparted a gelatinous texture and strong "corny" flavor. We were back to the drawing board. Most white chili recipes don't call for pureeing any of the ingredients, but we decided to try anyway. If it worked in vegetable soups, then why not in chili? Pureeing a cup each of the sautéed chile-onion mixture, beans, and broth not only gave our chili a nicely thickened consistency but also ensured that chile flavor was present in every drop. And to further sharpen the chiles' flavors, we stirred in a minced raw jalapeño just before serving.

With a host of complex Southwestern flavors, interesting textures, and filling but not heavy ingredients, this white chicken chili had come full circle. While we could never imagine ourselves eating a big bowl of thick, meaty red chili outside of the cold winter months, we would definitely make this light and flavorful white chili all year round. Starting now.

WHAT WE LEARNED: Bone-in, skin-on breasts give the chili deep, meaty flavor in a reasonable amount of time. Searing the breasts and then cooking the aromatics in the rendered fat add a further layer of flavor. A trio of chiles gives the chili just the right blend of flavor and heat. And to bloom the chiles' flavor, we cook them in a covered pot. Convenient canned cannellini beans were preferred to dried white beans, which simply weren't worth the trouble. Pureeing a portion of the chili mixture, beans, and broth helps thicken the chili without diluting its flavors. And stirring in a minced raw jalapeño just before serving gives the dish a hit of fresh chile flavor.

GETTING IT RIGHT: Balancing Heat and Flavor

We found that using a combination of jalapeños, Anaheims, and poblanos was the key to achieving vibrant chile flavor. Here's what each chile brings to the table.

Jalapeño
This small, smooth-skinned, forest green chile provides heat and a bitter, green bell pepper–like flavor.

Anaheim
This long, medium-green, mildly spicy chile has an acidic, lemony bitterness.

Poblano
This large, heart-shaped, blackish-green chile is mild to medium-hot and packs a rich, vegetal, slightly sweet flavor.

WHITE CHICKEN CHILI

serves 6 to 8

Adjust the heat in this dish by adding the minced ribs and seeds from the jalapeño as directed in step 6. If Anaheim chiles cannot be found, add an additional poblano and jalapeño to the chili. This dish can also be successfully made by substituting chicken thighs for the chicken breasts. If using thighs, increase the cooking time in step 4 to about 40 minutes. Serve the chili with sour cream, tortilla chips, and lime wedges.

- 3 pounds bone-in, skin-on chicken breast halves, trimmed of excess fat and skin
  Salt and ground black pepper
- 1 tablespoon vegetable oil
- 3 medium jalapeño chiles
- 3 medium poblano chiles, stemmed, seeded, and cut into large pieces
- 3 medium Anaheim chiles, stemmed, seeded, and cut into large pieces
- 2 medium onions, cut into large pieces (2 cups)
- 6 medium garlic cloves, minced or pressed through a garlic press (about 2 tablespoons)
- 1 tablespoon ground cumin
- 1½ teaspoons ground coriander
- 2 (15-ounce) cans cannellini beans, drained and rinsed
- 3 cups low-sodium chicken broth
- 3 tablespoons juice from 2 to 3 limes
- ¼ cup minced fresh cilantro leaves
- 4 scallions, white and light green parts sliced thin

1. Season the chicken liberally with salt and pepper. Heat the oil in a large Dutch oven over medium-high heat until just smoking. Add the chicken, skin side down, and cook without moving until the skin is golden brown, about 4 minutes. Using tongs, turn the chicken and lightly brown the other side, about 2 minutes. Transfer the chicken to a plate; remove and discard the skin.

TESTING NOTES: Chicken Chili Shortfalls and Solutions

We tried a variety of white chicken chili recipes from cookbooks and Internet sites. Here are three common problems we encountered and our solutions.

Problem: BLAND, WATERY SAUCE
Solution: PUREE VEGETABLES Process part of the chile-onion mixture and beans with broth to thicken the base.

Problem: FLOATING BITS OF RUBBERY CHICKEN
Solution: SHREDDED CHICKEN BREAST Brown, poach, and shred bone-in, skin-on chicken breasts for hearty texture and full chicken flavor.

Problem: NOT ENOUGH CHILE FLAVOR
Solution: TRIO OF FRESH CHILES Use a combination of fresh jalapeño, poblano, and Anaheim chiles.

2. While the chicken is browning, remove and discard the ribs and seeds from 2 of the jalapeños; mince the flesh. In a food processor, process half of the poblanos, Anaheims, and onions until the consistency of chunky salsa, 10 to 12 pulses, scraping down the sides of the workbowl halfway through. Transfer the mixture to a medium bowl. Repeat with the remaining poblanos, Anaheims, and onions; combine with the first batch (do not wash the food processor blade or workbowl).

3. Pour off all but 1 tablespoon of the fat from the Dutch oven (adding additional vegetable oil if necessary) and reduce the heat to medium. Add the minced jalapeños, chile-onion mixture, garlic, cumin, coriander, and ¼ teaspoon salt. Cover and cook, stirring occasionally, until the vegetables soften, about 10 minutes. Remove the pot from the heat.

4. Transfer 1 cup of the cooked vegetable mixture to the now-empty food processor workbowl. Add 1 cup of the beans and 1 cup of the broth and process until smooth, about 20 seconds. Add the vegetable-bean mixture, remaining 2 cups broth, and chicken breasts to the Dutch oven and bring to a boil over medium-high heat. Reduce the heat to medium-low and simmer, covered, stirring occasionally, until the chicken registers 160 degrees (175 degrees if using thighs) on an instant-read thermometer, 15 to 20 minutes (40 minutes if using thighs).

5. Using tongs, transfer the chicken to a large plate. Stir in the remaining beans and continue to simmer, uncovered, until the beans are heated through and the chili has thickened slightly, about 10 minutes.

6. Mince the remaining jalapeño, reserving and mincing the ribs and seeds (see note), and set aside. When cool enough to handle, shred the chicken into bite-sized pieces, discarding the bones. Stir the shredded chicken, lime juice, cilantro, scallions, and minced jalapeño (with seeds if desired) into the chili and return to a simmer. Season with salt and pepper to taste and serve.

TECHNIQUE: Key Steps to Building Flavor

1. Brown Chicken
Brown the bone-in, skin-on chicken breasts before poaching them to achieve deep chicken flavor.

2. Sauté Vegetables
To create a flavorful chile-centered base, sauté the trio of chiles and onion along with the spices and garlic.

3. Puree Vegetables
To thicken the chili, process 1 cup each of the sautéed chile mixture, beans, and broth in the food processor.

4. Stir In Fresh Chile
Add one minced raw jalapeño to the finished dish for a last-minute burst of chile flavor.

EQUIPMENT CORNER:
Cast-Iron Skillets

CENTURIES BEFORE DUPONT INVENTED TEFLON IN 1938, people were cooking with cast iron. Over the past 30 years, nonstick skillets have taken the place of cast iron in most homes. But with disturbing reports about the effects of nonstick coatings on the environment and our health, we decided to take another look at cast iron to see if it is worth bringing back into the kitchen.

Cast iron has always been known to have a few advantages over other types of cookware. Its material and weight give it excellent heat retention for high-heat cooking like frying and searing. You can use it on the stovetop or bake with it in the oven. Its durability is legendary—many people are still cooking with cast-iron pans handed down for generations. Unlike most consumer products, cast-iron pans actually improve with time and heavy use.

Cast iron also has disadvantages. It's heavy and needs special care. It must be seasoned by heating it with oil to prevent it from rusting or reacting with the foods you cook. Until its seasoning is well established, food will stick to it. You shouldn't use soap or steel wool on it, lest you strip off the seasoning. Compared to nonstick cookware, which works right out of the box and requires little maintenance, these are serious disadvantages.

When we went shopping for cast-iron pans to test, we noticed that although you can still find traditional cast iron, manufacturers have been tweaking the design and materials to maintain its principal benefits while diminishing some of the downside. They have begun coating the surface with a variety of materials to either begin the seasoning process for you or render it unnecessary. In some cases, new coatings bonded onto the cast iron make soap and even the dishwasher no longer off-limits.

One thing that didn't always get better with innovation

is price: Traditional unseasoned cast-iron skillets are a true bargain, costing between $11 and $20. Most preseasoned pans are also fairly cheap, at $15 to $30, but we found fancier pans that hovered around the $100 mark.

"Seasoning" is a word you hear a lot around cast iron. It might sound mysterious, but it's just oil and carbon residue from cooking that polymerize when heated and bond to the cast iron, forming a smooth surface. You build up seasoning over time simply by cooking in the pan and doing routine maintenance (see "Taking Care of Cast Iron," at right). Until recently, all cast-iron pans were purchased unseasoned. For our testing, we bought eight skillets, all about 12 inches in diameter: three factory-seasoned pans, three traditional unseasoned pans, and two with innovative finishes that required no seasoning. Le Creuset's skillet has a matte-textured black enamel inside, rather than the glossy cream-colored finish found inside the company's Dutch ovens. Newcomer Olvida offered the most unusual finish of all: nickel plating that made the pan shiny silver. The nickel finish is designed to be nonreactive and safe with metal utensils, soap, and the dishwasher. We followed manufacturer directions to prepare the unseasoned pans for cooking.

Our first goal was to see how the cast-iron pans stacked up against our favorite nonstick skillet, the All-Clad Nonstick 12-Inch Skillet ($159.95), and our favorite stainless steel skillet, the All-Clad Stainless 12-Inch Skillet ($134.95), in a battery of cooking tasks.

The primary reason to own a nonstick skillet is to cook eggs, so we started by rating each pan for sticking and ease of cleaning when cooking scrambled eggs. Next we baked cornbread to test evenness of browning and oven performance. We pan-seared steak to test searing ability and made tomato-caper pan sauce with the resulting fond to see whether the cast iron would react with the acid in the sauce. We also shallow-fried breaded chicken cutlets while wiring the pans with a thermocouple to measure their responsiveness, conductivity, and heat retention—all reflecting their ability to evenly and crisply fry chicken.

In the egg test, the nonstick skillet was the runaway winner; the performance of the cast-iron pans ranged from mediocre to poor. The cast-iron pans were clearly superior in the cornbread tests, producing the brownest, crispest crust. They were on par with the stainless steel pan in the

---

GETTING IT RIGHT:
Taking Care of Cast Iron

If you buy a preseasoned pan (and you should), you can use the pan with little fuss. The surface will become more nonstick with time, as long as you take care of it. Here's what you need to know.

Routine Maintenance

• Don't wash the pan with soap or leave it in the sink to soak. Rinse it out under hot running water, scrubbing with a brush to remove traces of food. (This is easiest if done promptly, while the pan is still warm.)

• Dry the pan thoroughly and put it back on the burner on low heat until all traces of moisture disappear (this keeps rusting at bay). Put a few drops of vegetable oil in the warm, dry pan and wipe the interior with paper towels until it is lightly covered with oil. Then get fresh paper towels and rub more firmly to burnish the surface and remove all excess oil. The pan shouldn't look or feel oily to the touch. Turn off the heat and allow the pan to cool before putting it away.

Heavy-duty Cleaning

If you have stuck-on food or you've inherited a pan that is rusty or gummy, you can get excellent scrubbing power with kosher salt.

• Pour in vegetable oil to a depth of ¼ inch, then place the pan on a burner set to medium-low for about five minutes. Remove the pan from the heat and add ½ cup of kosher salt. Using a potholder to grip the hot handle, make a thick cushion of paper towels and scrub the pan. The warm oil will loosen the food or rust, and the kosher salt will have an abrading effect. Rinse the pan under hot running water, dry well, and repeat, if necessary.

Reseasoning

If acidic foods or improper cleaning have removed the seasoning from your pan, it will look dull and dry instead of a smooth, rich black, in which case you need to restore the seasoning. We have found this stovetop method (rather than the usual oven method) to be the most effective way to season a cast-iron pan.

• Heat the pan on top of the stove on medium-high heat until a bead of water evaporates on contact. Wipe the inside with a wad of paper towels dipped in vegetable oil (hold the towels with tongs to protect yourself). Wipe out excess oil and repeat as needed until the pan is slick.

GETTING IT RIGHT:
A Nonstick Surface Comes with Time

All cast-iron pans will become more nonstick with time. While you might think this will take years, we found a significant difference after just a few weeks in the test kitchen.

Sticky Mess
Scrambled eggs stick to the surface of a new preseasoned cast-iron skillet just out of the box.

Seasoned Pro
After a few weeks the same pan became more seasoned and released all but a few wisps of egg.

cookware: You could make eggs and sear steak in the same pan. However, this endorsement comes with two important caveats—you must choose the right pan, and you must be willing to care for it.

So which of these eight cast-iron pans is our favorite? There were several factors that distinguished the high-ranked models. First, they were seasoned by the manufacturer. Seasoning new pans in the oven creates oily fumes and a mess as shortening drips off the pan. What's more, the unseasoned pans lagged behind the factory-seasoned pans in nonstick performance throughout our testing. Their lighter hue also produced lighter browning on the cornbread than the solidly black preseasoned pans. When we made our acidic tomato-caper pan sauce, the only pan to produce a metallic taste from a reaction with the acid was the Cajun Cast Iron, a pan we purchased unseasoned. This year, Lodge discontinued selling unseasoned cast iron, stating that customers preferred the preseasoned pans by a wide margin. According to Lodge spokesperson Mark Kelly, the factory seasoning is "equivalent to seasoning it yourself twenty times." We think this leg up is well worth a few extra dollars.

Second, evenness of cooking without hot spots or heat surges was very important. We wanted a pan that wouldn't cool off too much when food was added and would quickly climb back to the desired temperature. The Bayou Classic skillet had trouble maintaining steady heat, a major flaw for this type of pan. When we weighed the pans and measured the thickness of their bottoms, we discovered that the Bayou was the thinnest, with its weight distributed more heavily in its sides than on the cooking surface. Our top-ranked pans were significantly thicker—up to twice as thick—and all demonstrated more even distribution and retention of heat. Coatings of nickel and enamel appeared to slow conductivity slightly, but this was less of a factor in cooking performance than was the thickness of the pan bottom.

A third key factor was the diameter of the interior cooking surface, which made a difference when trying to accommodate multiple chicken breasts or steaks without

steak and chicken tests. Though not unexpected, the results were somewhat disappointing.

However, we noticed that most of the cast-iron pans improved their ability to release food as our testing progressed. The seasoning (whether done by the manufacturer or us) was becoming thicker and more reliable. We decided to try the egg test again and were surprised by the dramatic improvement. Pans that had performed poorly in the first egg test did a decent job, and the preseasoned pans were now nearly as good as the nonstick pan in this test. Given such dramatic improvement over just a few weeks, we were not surprised when the cast-iron pans continued to become more "nonstick" with time.

At this point, we concluded that a cast-iron pan can combine the best traits of both nonstick and traditional

crowding or steaming. Despite averaging 12 inches from rim to rim, the interior cooking surfaces of the pans ranged from 9¼ inches to 10¾ inches. We have a strong preference for the larger pans.

Weight was a thorny issue. While we preferred the bigger pans, they tended to be heavy and difficult for a smaller cook to manipulate in tasks such as swirling melting butter, pouring off a pan sauce, and flipping to release cornbread. Good handle design can help offset the problem. Our top-ranked pans all featured helper handles opposite the main handle. Two pans (Le Creuset and Lodge Pro-Logic) also featured larger main handles, which made the pans easier for a small cook to use.

Durability is one of the biggest virtues of cast iron. And while the Le Creuset pan performed very well, the enameled bottom of the pan also became chipped and scratched with routine use during testing. (You also can't use metal utensils with this pan or stack other pans inside it.) If you want a kitchen workhorse, this isn't it. The nickel finish on the Olvida pan was durable and worked as described, but didn't offer significant enough advantage over preseasoned cast iron to warrant spending nearly $100. While we often find that you get what you pay for, in the case of cast iron, you don't need to spend more to get more.

In the end, we preferred the classic design—with straight (rather than sloped) sides—and roomy interior of the preseasoned Lodge Logic Skillet ($26.95). It performed well in all our cooking tests, its surface gained seasoning in the course of testing, and it will last for generations. If you are strong and don't mind a truly big and heavy pan, the preseasoned Camp Chef skillet is a solid performer for only $15.20.

GETTING IT RIGHT:
Older Is Not Always Better

We tested several heirloom cast-iron skillets, including this 100-year-old Wagner pan we purchased from a collector for $110. While these pans had developed a nice patina and aced the scrambled egg test, they were lighter than the modern cast-iron pans in our lineup and didn't perform as well in the searing and frying tests.

Heirloom Cast-Iron Skillet

Rating Cast-Iron Skillets

WE TESTED EIGHT CAST-IRON SKILLETS, EACH APPROXIMATELY 12 INCHES IN DIAMETER, ALONG WITH OUR TOP-RATED nonstick and stainless steel skillets. We compared the performance of these pans in a number of cooking tests, which included cooking scrambled eggs, pan-searing steak, shallow-frying chicken, and baking cornbread. The skillets are listed in order of preference. See www.americastestkitchen.com for up-to-date prices and mail-order sources for top-rated products.

HIGHLY RECOMMENDED
Lodge Logic 12-Inch Skillet
$26.95; Cast iron, preseasoned
Eggs stuck "considerably" and took "tons of scrubbing" to clean the first time around but barely stuck and cleaned up easily the second time. Cornbread was very golden and crusty, with perfect release.

HIGHLY RECOMMENDED
The Camp Chef SK-12 Cast Iron Skillet
$15.20; Cast iron, preseasoned
Heaviest and thickest pan in the lineup was "a beast" to handle, but its heft made it shine in our cooking tests, where a consistent heat and deep sear were desirable. Right out of the box, we made scrambled eggs that didn't stick and cornbread that browned well and released perfectly.

RECOMMENDED
Lodge Pro-Logic 12-Inch Skillet
$29.95; Cast iron, preseasoned
"Gorgeous" browning on the fried chicken and steak. Eggs improved dramatically, from "horrible sticking" to "very easy to clean" by the end of testing. Curved (rather than angled) sides make sauces easier to scrape up but shrinks cooking surface.

RECOMMENDED
Le Creuset Round Skillet, 11-Inch
$109.95; Enameled cast iron with matte-finish black enamel interior
Sloping sides made eggs and sauce easier to scrape up. Achieved a "beautiful crust" on steak and cornbread. On first test, eggs stuck ferociously, but results improved dramatically in the second round, with minimal sticking and easy cleanup. The enamel finish makes it less durable than other cast-iron pans.

RECOMMENDED
Olvida 13-Inch Skillet
$98.95; Cast iron covered with nickel plate
Chicken and steak came out beautifully in this heavy, roomy, silver-colored pan with "steady heating." Eggs stuck a moderate amount, without much change as testing progressed. Dishwasher-safe.

RECOMMENDED WITH RESERVATIONS
Wagner Collection Skillet, 11¾-Inch
$19; Cast iron, unseasoned
Slightly less steady heating than higher-ranked pans, but good results shallow-frying chicken and searing steak. Eggs stuck moderately, even as testing progressed. Cornbread browned well but stuck to the pan.

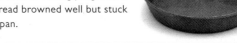

RECOMMENDED WITH RESERVATIONS
Cajun Classic 12-Inch Cast Iron Skillet
$16; Cast iron, unseasoned
Pan was crowded while shallow-frying two chicken breasts and when searing a pair of steaks. Steak pan sauce had a slight oily, metallic taste, indicating the acid had reacted with the pan. Eggs continued to stick over most of the pan in the second round but cleaned up easily. Cornbread came out well, but browned less than others.

RECOMMENDED WITH RESERVATIONS
Bayou Classic Heavy Duty Cast Iron Skillet, 12 Inches
$11; Cast iron, unseasoned
Thin bottom caused steep temperature drop when chicken was added to hot oil. Steaks cooked unevenly and with some difficulty, with unsteady temperatures (too hot, then too cool). Scrambled eggs stuck considerably throughout testing.

DOUBLE-CORN CORNBREAD

WHAT WE WANTED: A cornbread bursting with full corn flavor and one with a texture to please everyone—not too cakey, nor too crumbly.

Can North and South unite over cornbread? It's funny that something as humble as cornbread can be so polarizing. In the North, cornbread is cakey and sweet, while Southerners demand theirs thin, crusty, and utterly savory. For us, cornbread should offer the best of both worlds—neither too muffin-like nor too austere. Ideally, cornbread would fall politely between the extremes: it should be tender and slightly sweet, yet dark and crunchy. We also wanted it bursting with bold corn flavor. The question, then, was how best to marry the two regional styles without inciting civil war in the test kitchen.

We started with the cornmeal. Most self-respecting Southerners insist on white cornmeal, while Northerners prefer yellow. But in tests pitting white against yellow, blindfolded tasters (from both sides of the Mason-Dixon line) were hard-pressed to detect significant differences. In short: Either one works fine. Now the question was,

how much? Southern recipes call for more cornmeal than flour (typically 1½ cups cornmeal to a mere ½ cup flour), while Northern cornbread usually reverses the ratio. For cornbread that was neither too crumbly nor too cake-like, we had the best luck using equal amounts of each.

In search of more corn flavor, we found several recipes that swapped the buttermilk we had been using for a combination of sour cream (for tang) and a can of creamed corn. Tasters loved the added richness imparted by the sour cream but found the canned corn tinny. Not wanting to give up on creamed corn just yet, we made a quick homemade version by pureeing defrosted frozen kernels with the sour cream. This mixture, along with two eggs for moisture and structure and a shot of hot sauce for kick, gave our cornbread great flavor. Some recipes use bacon fat to enrich the cornbread, while others rely on melted butter. The bacon fat imparted good flavor, but having to cook bacon was an extra step we wanted to avoid. Melted butter was the easier choice, and it created a nice golden brown crust.

The most controversial ingredient was the sugar. It is taboo in Southern recipes, while Northern recipes often call for as much as ½ cup. To enhance the natural sweetness of the corn without making sweet corn muffins, we settled on 2 tablespoons.

Regardless of region, cornbread fares best in a super-hot oven, and 450 degrees proved the best temperature to form a craggy crust. This blast of heat also got the most from the leaveners. For the crunchiest, brownest bottom crust, a preheated pan (preferably cast iron, the traditional Southern choice) is a must. The key is to preheat the pan until it's ripping hot. The batter should sizzle as it hits the pan.

WHAT WE LEARNED: For a balanced texture use equal amounts of cornmeal and flour. For full corn flavor and tang, enrich the batter with frozen corn pureed with sour cream. And for a browned, crunchy crust, pour the batter into a preheated cast-iron skillet.

DOUBLE-CORN CORNBREAD

serves 8 to 10

A cast-iron skillet (or any ovensafe pan) is our first choice for this recipe, but a 9-inch cake pan will also work. Instead of heating it on the stovetop, place the cake pan with the oil in the preheated oven for 5 minutes before adding the batter.

1   cup (about 5 ounces) cornmeal (yellow or white)
1   cup (5 ounces) unbleached all-purpose flour
2   tablespoons sugar
2   teaspoons baking powder
¼   teaspoon baking soda
¾   teaspoon salt
1   cup frozen corn, thawed
1   cup sour cream
2   large eggs
½   teaspoon hot sauce
4   tablespoons (½ stick) unsalted butter, melted
2   teaspoons vegetable oil

1. Adjust an oven rack to the middle position and heat the oven to 450 degrees. Whisk the cornmeal, flour, sugar, baking powder, baking soda, and salt in a large bowl. Pulse the corn, sour cream, eggs, and hot sauce in a food processor until the corn is coarsely chopped and the mixture is combined. Fold the corn mixture into the cornmeal mixture, then stir in the melted butter.

2. Heat the oil in a 10-inch skillet over medium-high heat until just beginning to smoke. Take the skillet off the heat; quickly add the batter and place the skillet in the oven. Bake until a toothpick inserted in the center comes out clean, about 25 minutes. Cool the cornbread in the skillet on a wire rack for 20 minutes (the handle will be hot). Serve warm.

TASTING LAB: Tortilla Chips

WE LIKE TORTILLA CHIPS THAT ARE THICK, CRUNCHY, and terrifically "corny"; just as good eaten alone as they are dunked into salsa. It used to be that you had to go out to find chips like this. But now several "upscale" brands sold in supermarkets promise authentic Mexican-style chips. How does this new style of tortilla chip compare with traditional supermarket offerings?

To find out, we held a blind tasting of nine brands of tortilla chips. As a group, the boutique brands lived up to their promise of good flavor: Tasters commented on the "authentic" taste: "Like chips I've had in Mexico," said one. These chips—Green Mountain Gringo, Bearitos, Nana's Cocina, Kettle, and Cape Cod—were consistently rated as having the most corn flavor. Each is made with stone-ground corn, resulting in a coarser-textured chip.

Despite their corny flavor, most of the boutique chips were ultimately rejected by tasters as being "too thick" and "stale." In contrast, the finer-textured chips (several of which are made with corn flour, not stone-ground corn) were described as "thin and crispy" and were perceived as being fresher.

Coarse-textured, super-corny chips might be fine in a Mexican restaurant (where they can be freshly fried), but when bagged for sale at the supermarket this style of chip can come off as stale, especially when compared with thinner chips.

Rating Tortilla Chips

TWENTY-FOUR STAFF MEMBERS TASTED NINE BRANDS OF TORTILLA CHIPS PLAIN AND WITH SALSA AND RATED THEM on corn flavor, freshness, and how well they stood up to dipping. The chips are listed in order of preference and are available in supermarkets.

RECOMMENDED

Santitas Authentic Mexican Style White Corn Tortilla Chips

$1.99 for 18 ounces

Tasters liked the "mild and salty" flavor and "sturdy" texture of these winning chips, whose "great crunch" topped the crispness charts.

RECOMMENDED

Tostitos Brand Tortilla Chips 100% White Corn Restaurant Style

$3.49 for 13.5 ounces

Though some tasters found these chips "bland, blond, and boring," others praised the "delicately crisp" texture and "fresh" flavor. Most found them "scoop worthy."

RECOMMENDED

Green Mountain Gringo Tortilla Strips All Natural

$2.69 for 8 ounces

Tasters liked the "toasted" flavor of these "crunchy," "sturdy" chips, whose long shape made them "good scoopers." Wrote one fan, "Reminds me of chips you get at an authentic Mexican restaurant."

RECOMMENDED

Natural Tostitos Brand Yellow Corn Restaurant Style Tortilla Chips

$2.99 for 9 ounces

Fans praised their "great flavor and texture," though some complained that these large chips "need to be broken prior to dipping."

RECOMMENDED WITH RESERVATIONS

Snyder's of Hanover White Corn Tortilla Chips

$2.49 for 16 ounces

"Taste stale and dusty," wrote one taster of these "overly salty and slightly artificial" chips from the famous pretzel maker.

RECOMMENDED WITH RESERVATIONS

Bearitos All Natural Organic Tortilla Chips

$3.69 for 16 ounces

Although these were "very crisp," with "nice corn flavor," most tasters panned their "gritty," "cardboard" texture, which one person likened to "stale Fritos."

RECOMMENDED WITH RESERVATIONS

Nana's Cocina Traditional Tortilla Chips

$3.19 for 16 ounces

Despite their "very corny," "homemade" flavor, these chips were criticized for their "brittle," "stale" texture.

NOT RECOMMENDED

Kettle Tortilla Chips Little Dippers Organic

$2.47 for 8 ounces

"My thumb is bigger than this," wrote one taster of these petite chips. Others liked the "fun shape," but most agreed that these chips tasted "burnt," "stale," and "rancid," though they did have "good crunch."

NOT RECOMMENDED

Cape Cod All Natural White Corn Tortilla Chips

$2.99 for 8.5 ounces

Tasters described these chips as "overwhelmingly stale," "tough," and "artificial."

Salting a turkey is a space-saving alternative to brining
(no big bucket required). And icing down the breast
before roasting ensures it will cook at a slower rate,
along with the legs and thighs, so that the meat doesn't
dry out, as it does on so many birds.

A NEW WAY

CHAPTER 10

with turkey

Finding a way to roast a moist, juicy turkey is a goal
that has plagued many a Thanksgiving cook. For years America's Test
Kitchen has touted brining (soaking the turkey in a salt water solution) not only to season the meat, but also to prevent it from drying
out. But to properly brine a turkey, you need space—and lots of it. But
fridge space around the holidays (when most of us are cooking turkey)
is tight—crammed with all the other dinner fixings. Is there an easier,
space-saving alternative to brining? In the past, the test kitchen has had
success in salting poultry, a sort of shallow brine minus the bucket and
water. But would this method work with turkey? We were ready to
find out.

By the time Thanksgiving rolls around, the green beans at the
market are looking a little weary. Throwing them in a green bean casserole is one option, but we wanted to find a way to cook over-the-hill
beans that brought back some of their summertime sweetness. The high
heat of roasting intensifies the flavor of many vegetables. Could roasting
do the same for string beans? After all, when we think of roasted vegetables, hardy root vegetables like potatoes and carrots come to mind. In
comparison, green beans are delicate. If we could pull off roasting green
beans, we'd be able to enjoy them far into the winter.

SALTED ROAST TURKEY

WHAT WE WANTED: An easier alternative to brining—one that would produce a well-seasoned moist turkey with minimal fuss.

We've been advocating brining here at America's Test Kitchen for 13 years. During that time, what was once an obscure technique has become mainstream. Pick up almost any recent cookbook and you can read about the virtues of brining, which will keep turkey (as well as chicken and pork) tender and juicy by pumping it up with water and salt. But let's face it, refrigerating a big turkey in a bigger bucket filled with cold water and salt isn't always feasible, especially around the holidays, when most refrigerators are packed. A large beer cooler filled with ice packs is one way to get around the space issue, but many readers can't lift a cooler loaded down with gallons of water and a big turkey—and disinfecting the cooler afterward is no easy matter. We were stuck. Brining is the best way to guarantee a moist turkey, but it isn't always practical.

We seriously began to rethink our brine-at-all-costs philosophy while developing a recipe for spice-rubbed chicken. We found that salting, a kind of "dry-brining" in which we rubbed the chicken with salt and let it rest in the refrigerator for several hours, not only seasoned the meat but also helped keep it moist. How does salting do its work? Initially, the salt draws out moisture from the meat, and this moisture mixes with the salt to form a shallow brine. Over time, the salt migrates from the shallow brine into the meat, just as it does in our usual brining technique. Once inside the meat, the salt changes the structure of the muscle fibers so that the meat is able to hold on to more water—even in a hot oven. But we had taken our first stab at salting with pieces of cut-up chicken. Would it work with a whole turkey? If it did, would the salted turkey taste as good as a brined one?

Heading into the test kitchen, we already knew a few things about salting poultry: It is more effective when the salt is applied directly to the meat, not the skin, and, just as in brining, the amount of time the bird is exposed to the salt is important. Getting the salt under the skin was easy. After using a chopstick or the handle of a wooden spoon to separate the skin from the meat (this worked better than our fingers, which tended to tear the skin), we had ample room to give the turkey a proper salt rubdown. Starting with ¼ cup, we proceeded to rub table salt on the meat under the skin and in the cavity, then wrapped the bird up and refrigerated it for 12 hours. Using our much-tested single-flip roasting technique, we cooked the turkey at 425 degrees with the breast down for 45 minutes, then flipped the breast up, lowered the temperature to 325 degrees, and continued roasting until the meat was done. The results? The outer layers of meat were well seasoned, but there was little salt flavor much beyond that.

Switching to larger-grained kosher salt (which is easier to rub over the meat without leaving salty pockets), we began to increase the amount of salt, but quickly found that more salt just made the problem worse. We then scaled back the kosher salt to ⅓ cup and tried gradually increasing the salting time instead. Because 12 hours had yielded ho-hum results, we tried leaving the salt on for 24, 48, and 72 hours. Whereas the birds that were salted for only 12 hours had a salty crust with a moderately moist and slightly flavored interior, the turkeys salted for 72 hours were overly salty, with a jerky-like appearance. The turkeys salted for 24 and 48 hours were the perfect compromise: Most of the meat was nicely seasoned, and it was pretty moist.

There were, however, some salty pockets, especially in the deep valleys between the thighs and breast. Rinsing away excess salt before roasting solved this problem but left the skin flabby. Blotting up the excess moisture ensured that the roasted bird would emerge from the oven crisp and brown.

Now for the moment of truth: comparing the salted bird with one that had been brined. First the bad news.

Tasters found the brined turkey to be moister, and the numbers confirmed their impression. While a brined bird shed 19 percent of its initial weight in the oven, a salted bird shed 22 percent of its out-of-the-package weight. (A bird that is neither brined nor salted will shed 28 percent of its initial weight in the oven.)

Although salting couldn't quite compete with brining as a way to pump moisture into a turkey, it more than held its own in terms of flavor. In fact, most tasters chose the salted turkey over the brined for its "fuller turkey flavor." It "actually tastes like turkey," said one. Several tasters also preferred the more "natural" texture of the salted bird, even if the meat was a bit dry. If only we could find a way to make a salted bird retain a bit more moisture without pumping it up with water or slathering on extra gravy, we knew we would have a winning formula.

We had one more trick to try out. The dryness problem in the salted turkey was confined to the breast meat. (The fat in dark thigh and leg meat makes dryness a minimal concern.) Ideally, the breast should be cooked to 160 degrees and the thigh to 175 degrees, but these two temperatures are hard to achieve simultaneously, even when the bird is roasted breast side down (which gives it some protection from the direct heat of the oven). Some time ago, we heard a radio interview with food scientist Harold McGee, who said he dealt with the temperature differential between breast and thighs by chilling the breast on ice. He explained that if the temperature of the breast was lower than the temperature of the thighs before the turkey went into the oven, that differential would be easier to maintain as the turkey roasted. McGee's idea sounded great, but how would we ice just the breast?

We tried to attach ice packs to the breast with masking tape, but they slid down onto the legs and thighs, parts of the bird that we did not want to cool down. Attaching the ice bags with duct tape and an athletic bandage (what were we thinking?) was more effective, but colleagues joked that it looked like we were holding the bird hostage. Snickers aside, one thing was sure: Icing the breast was having an effect.

The breast meat on this bandaged bird cooked up moist and juicy. If only we could ice the bird with less fuss.

One day, after filling several gallon-sized zipper-lock bags with ice, two bags were left in the bottom of a bowl. And then we realized—we could have simply placed the turkey, breast side down, on top of two ice bags. No wrapping, no fuss. After the first try, we knew this method was a keeper. It also allowed the thighs and legs to warm up faster, since they were now facing up. Wanting to chill the breast more thoroughly, we stuffed one small bag of ice in the cavity and placed another against the breast under the skin of the neck. The effect of all this icing was pretty dramatic. While the breast and legs were the same temperature (41 degrees) when the turkey first came out of the refrigerator, the breast, after an hour on ice, dropped to 36 degrees, while the un-iced legs had risen to 43 degrees. That 7-degree head start for the legs meant the turkey could stay in the oven long enough to fully cook the dark meat without drying out the white meat.

But had we convinced the test kitchen that salting could rival brining? When tasted head-to-head one last time, both turkeys were well liked. Tasters who wanted more moisture still favored the brined bird (which was still ever so slightly juicier), while those wanting a more natural turkey texture and flavor picked the salted and iced version. One thing, however, was perfectly clear: Brining now had a strong rival, which also happened to take up much less space in the refrigerator.

WHAT WE LEARNED: Salt the turkey by applying kosher salt directly onto the meat, not the skin. To do so without tearing the skin, use chopsticks or the handle of a wooden spoon to gently separate the skin from the meat. To ensure moist, not dry, breast meat, chill the breast by placing a small bag of ice inside the cavity against the breast and setting the turkey breast side down on ice. This trick brings down the temperature of the breast, thus allowing it to cook through over a longer period in the oven (more in line with the cooking time of the dark meat) without drying out.

ROAST SALTED TURKEY

serves 10 to 12

This recipe was developed and tested using Diamond Crystal Kosher Salt. If you have Morton's Kosher Salt, which is denser than Diamond Crystal, use only 4½ teaspoons of salt in the cavity, 2¼ teaspoons of salt per each half of the breast, and 1 teaspoon of salt per leg. Table salt is too fine and not recommended for this recipe. If you are roasting a kosher or self-basting turkey (such as a frozen Butterball), do not salt it; it already contains a good amount of sodium.

- 1 turkey (12 to 14 pounds), giblets and neck reserved for gravy, if making
- 5 tablespoons kosher salt (see note)
- 1 (5-pound) bag ice cubes
- 4 tablespoons (½ stick) unsalted butter, melted

1. Following illustration 1 at right, carefully separate the turkey skin from the meat on the breast, legs, thighs, and back; avoid breaking the skin. Following illustrations 2 through 4,

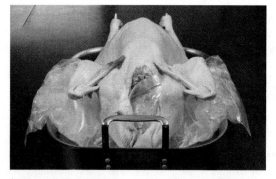

TECHNIQUE: Icing the Turkey Breast

Cooling the breast down with ice ensures that it will cook more slowly than the legs and thighs, preventing the meat from drying out. Place bags of ice underneath the breast and inside both the large cavity and the neck area.

rub 2 tablespoons salt evenly inside the cavity of the turkey, 1 tablespoon salt under the skin of each breast half, and 1½ teaspoons salt under the skin of each leg. Wrap the turkey tightly with plastic wrap; refrigerate 24 to 48 hours.

2. Remove the turkey from the refrigerator. Following illustrations 5 and 6, rinse off any excess salt between the meat and skin and in the cavity, then pat dry inside and out with paper towels. Add ice to two 1-gallon zipper-lock bags until each is half full. Place the bags in a large roasting pan and lay the turkey, breast side down, on top of the ice. Add the ice to two 1-quart zipper-lock bags until each is one-third full; place one bag of ice in the large cavity of the turkey and the other bag in the neck cavity. (Make sure that the ice touches the breast only, not the thighs or legs; see the photo at below left.) Keep the turkey on ice for 1 hour (the roasting pan should remain on the counter).

3. Meanwhile, adjust an oven rack to the lowest position and heat the oven to 425 degrees. Line a large V-rack with heavy-duty foil and use a paring knife or skewer to poke 20 to 30 holes in the foil.

4. Remove the turkey from the ice and pat dry with paper towels (discard the ice). Tuck the tips of the drumsticks into the skin at the tail to secure and tuck the wingtips behind the back. Brush the turkey breast with 2 table-spoons of the butter. Set the prepared V-rack in the roasting pan; set the turkey, breast side down, on the V-rack; brush the back and legs with the remaining 2 tablespoons butter. Roast for 45 minutes.

5. Remove the roasting pan with the turkey from the oven (close the oven door to retain the oven heat) and reduce the oven temperature to 325 degrees. Using clean potholders or kitchen towels, rotate the turkey breast side up; continue to roast until the thickest part of the breast registers 160 degrees and the thickest part of the thighs

TECHNIQUE: How to Salt a Turkey

Rubbing the meat with salt 24 to 48 hours prior to cooking flavors the turkey and breaks down some of the proteins, allowing them to retain more moisture. It's imperative that you massage the salt evenly inside the cavity and directly onto the meat.

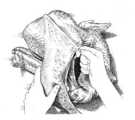

1. Lift Skin: Use chopsticks or a thin wooden spoon handle to separate the skin from the meat over the breast, legs, thighs, and back.

2. Salt Cavity: Rub 2 tablespoons kosher salt inside the main cavity.

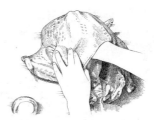

3. Salt Breast: Lift the skin and apply 1 tablespoon kosher salt over each breast half, placing half of the salt on each end of each breast, then massaging the salt evenly over the meat.

4. Salt Each Leg: Apply 1½ teaspoons kosher salt over the top and bottom of each leg.

5. Rinse: After 24 to 48 hours, rinse the bird well to remove excess salt trapped under the skin.

6. Dry: Use paper towels to blot excess moisture from the skin so it can crisp and brown in the oven.

---

registers 170 to 175 degrees on an instant-read thermometer, 1 to 1½ hours longer. Transfer the turkey to a carving board; let rest 30 minutes. Carve and serve.

VARIATION

ROAST SALTED TURKEY FOR A CROWD

serves 14 to 16

To roast a 15- to 18-pound turkey, follow the recipe for Roast Salted Turkey, increasing the salt rubbed into the cavity to 3 tablespoons (6¾ teaspoons if using Morton's salt) and into each breast half to 1½ tablespoons (3½ if using Morton's). Increase the roasting time in step 4 to 1 hour; reduce the oven temperature to 325 degrees, flip the turkey, and continue roasting until it reaches the proper internal temperature, 1½ to 2 hours longer.

SCIENCE DESK:
The Effects of Salting Turkey

WEIGHING SALTED AND UNSALTED BIRDS BOTH BEFORE and after roasting convinced us that salting could indeed help turkey retain moisture and produce a juicier bird. But a few naysayers wanted visual proof that the salt was worth the effort. Our first thought was to mix either food coloring or turmeric with the salt, but the color compounds in both were too large to pass through muscle cells in the meat. Next we attached an electric meter to the turkey and ran electricity through the breast to determine where the salt had penetrated, but the tests produced inconsistent results. We needed a compound that, once dissolved, would travel

EQUIPMENT CORNER:
Inexpensive Roasting Pans

HOW OFTEN DO YOU USE A ROASTING PAN—ONCE OR twice a year for a big holiday roast? A really nice roasting pan can easily retail for $200, and it doesn't make sense to spend so much money on a flashy pan that will sit in a cabinet most of the year. Could we find a more utilitarian pan?

Selecting which pans to test was easy. Since, to develop flavor, we often sear meat before roasting it, we chose pans that were flameproof and could be used on the stovetop; aluminum disposables, Pyrex, stoneware, and ceramic pans were out. We also wanted a pan that could accommodate a big holiday turkey with ease, so 15 by 11 inches was our minimum size. We wanted to be able to broil and roast at high heat, so we eliminated pans with nonstick finishes.

We found seven pans in the $20 to $80 range and headed into the test kitchen to put them through their paces. We also added the $100 Calphalon Contemporary Stainless roasting pan to the mix; this pan won a prior kitchen test and has since become a favorite among our cooks. We used each pan to roast a 15-pound turkey and deglaze the drippings to make gravy, sear a 5-pound pork loin on the stovetop before roasting it, and roast 2 pounds of potatoes. Here's what we found.

The best handles are sturdy and easy to grip with thick potholders and don't protrude far enough upward or outward to become a hazard. Our testers preferred the upright, riveted handles of the Calphalon, Cuisinart, and KitchenAid pans. Thick handles on the Anolon pan and hinged handles on the rectangular Metro pan were hard to grasp. The handles on the two oval pans were too small—especially when the pan was loaded with a heavy turkey.

Buckling can be an issue with roasting pans. The last thing you want to hear when you're working with a hot roasting pan—and its sizzling contents—on the stovetop is the "pop" of the pan buckling, which can send scalding-hot projectiles of fat onto your arms. Buckling is also a telltale

the same path as the salt to the center of the meat. The two likely candidates were tinctures of iodine and copper sulfate, both vibrantly colored inorganic salts. The test with rust-colored iodine did not work, but the turkey coated with the blue copper sulfate lit up like a road map of salt penetration: The meat was dyed blue from the skin to the bone. Don't try this at home—copper sulfate is poisonous—but we finally convinced even the most stubborn kitchen skeptics that salting works.

GAUGING SALT PENETRATION
We rubbed a turkey with salt dyed blue, waited 24 hours, then removed pieces to track salt penetration.

Rating Inexpensive Roasting Pans

WE TESTED EIGHT ROASTING PANS, SEVEN OF THEM IN THE $20 TO $80 RANGE AND ONE $100 PAN, THE CALPHALON Contemporary Stainless Steel Roasting Pan, which was the winner of a previous roasting pan test. The pans were rated on performance, ease of use, and durability in a variety of tests including roasting a turkey, deglazing the pan to prepare gravy, roasting a pork loin, and roasting potatoes. The pans are listed in order of preference. See www.americastestkitchen.com for up-to-date prices and mail-order sources for top-rated products.

RECOMMENDED
Calphalon Contemporary Stainless Steel Roasting Pan
$99.99; 16" x 13"; Stainless steel with aluminum core

This heavy, sturdy pan features good handles and an efficient, gently flared interior shape, making it especially easy to stir and deglaze. It was also the best at browning. Comes with sturdy nonstick U-shaped rack.

RECOMMENDED
Cuisinart Chef's Classic Roasting Pan
$79.95; 16" x 13"; Stainless steel with aluminum core

Very good on the stovetop, but testers saw some uneven browning in the pork loin test. Excellent handles, good heft, and an overall solid feel were more than enough to overcome that small demerit. Comes with useful V-rack.

RECOMMENDED
KitchenAid Gourmet Distinctions Roasting Pan
$49.95; 15" x 12"; Stainless steel

This pan shined brightest in the potato test, but buckled a bit on the stovetop with both the turkey drippings and the pork loin. It has some of the winning attributes of the two pans above, but wasn't quite in their class for heft and performance. All things considered, a good buy for the price.

RECOMMENDED
Granite Ware Oval Roasting Pan
$21.95; 19" x 13.5"; Porcelain-enameled steel

Very fast, even, deep browning on the potatoes, but this pan's thin bottom made it highly temperamental on the stovetop. Also, testers found the raised, patterned bottom to be problematic when deglazing. No rack included. A good choice for infrequent roasters.

RECOMMENDED WITH RESERVATIONS
Farberware Classic Accessories Large Roasting Pan
$34.95; 20" x 13"; Stainless steel

This wide, shallow pan had acceptable performance, but felt flimsy and awkward. The rounded corners provided easy access for stirring and made pouring a breeze. Comes with a flat rack that sits too low to be effective.

NOT RECOMMENDED
Metro Roasting/Lasagna Pan
$19.95; 16" x 12"; Stainless steel

The hinged handles were a big drawback, as they were very difficult to grab with potholders and felt perilously close to snapping under the weight of the turkey. Comes with a flat rack that sits too low to be effective.

NOT RECOMMENDED
Anolon Accessories Stainless Steel Roasting Pan
$49.95; 16" x 12"; Stainless steel

This pan was noticeably hotter around the edges and cooler in the middle, resulting in very uneven browning, especially with the pork loin. Thick spots make handles hard to grip. Comes with a U-rack that has awkward hinged handles.

NOT RECOMMENDED
Metro Stainless Steel Oval Roasting Pan with Domed Lid
$29.95; 15.5" x 11"; Stainless steel

Deep sides on this oval pan make it hard to monitor browning, which was very uneven on both the potatoes and pork loin. Overall, its performance just wasn't up to par. Comes with a flat rack that sits too low to be effective.

symptom of uneven heating, which leads to uneven cooking and browning. Most of the lighter pans buckled on the stovetop and produced food with spotty browning. The heaviest pans didn't buckle and were better at browning.

One surprising exception: The comparatively flimsy Granite Ware did a beautiful job browning the potatoes, because its black surface was a magnet for the oven's moderate heat. This benefit didn't carry over to the stovetop, however, where this thin pan scorched easily.

Material makes a difference with roasting pans. Stainless steel is attractive, nonreactive, lightweight, and relatively durable. It's also a poor conductor of heat, making it no surprise that our two top-performing pans featured an aluminum core inside the stainless steel.

Aluminum is a superior metal for fast and even heat conductivity, which translates into no buckling and more responsive cooking—especially on the stovetop. The rest of the lineup was made of plain stainless steel or porcelain-enameled steel-fine materials for roasting a turkey in the oven (where the conductivity of the pan is not as important, as the food cooks mostly by radiant heat), but not well suited to the stovetop.

So where did we end up? For cooks who do a lot of roasting, we recommend the Calphalon ($100) and Cuisinart ($80) pans—they are sturdy and excellent performers both in the oven and on the stovetop. Neither option is cheap, but both are solid values if you use a roasting pan often. The KitchenAid pan ($50) is the best bet for the occasional roaster. The once-a-year turkey roaster should be fine with the $22 Granite Ware.

TASTING LAB: Turkey

OVER THE YEARS, WE'VE OFFERED A LOT OF ADVICE about the best way to cook your holiday turkey. But does roasting a better bird start before you even get into the kitchen? Does it depend on which bird you buy? And is it ever worthwhile to mail-order a fancier turkey, which can run as much as $100—before overnight shipping charges? To find out, we selected eight turkeys, including common supermarket brands as well as kosher, organic, pasture-raised, and heritage birds.

A great-tasting roast turkey is not just about turkey flavor; the texture and moisture of the meat are important, too, as anyone who has eaten a mouthful of dry, chewy turkey can attest. Wondering if fat was a factor, we sent the turkeys in our lineup to an independent laboratory to test samples from the skin, the white meat, and the dark meat; we also had the lab measure their salt content. As we awaited the results, we talked with turkey experts about the factors that contribute to a turkey's quality, which include its breed, how it's raised and fed, and how it's processed for sale.

In a sense, modern commercial turkeys have been bred to have very little flavor, said Michael Lilburn, a professor of animal sciences at Ohio State University. "In the United States, we're a white-meat market. This created a heavy emphasis on genetic selection for breast-muscle growth."

The most common commercial turkey, the Broad-Breasted White, has been selectively bred to grow bigger in less time and on less feed (to reduce costs), and to produce the maximum possible white meat, Lilburn said. Today's turkeys are up to 70 percent white meat, and they grow fast. "Twenty years ago, the average tom [male] turkey weighed 30 pounds at 18 weeks," Lilburn said. "Today, toms weigh 40 pounds at 20 weeks." Tom turkeys are used primarily for products like deli meat, sausage, ground turkey, and the like; most Americans eat a hen turkey on Thanksgiving. Much smaller than the toms, hens are ready for market in just 14 weeks, when they weigh 16 to 22 pounds, which yields processed birds in the 12- to 18-pound range. (By contrast, older breeds of turkey, called heritage birds, need seven to eight months to grow to full size—roughly twice as long as modern turkeys.)

That rapid growth may be good for the farmer, but it's not so great for the cook. Modern turkeys have less fat when fully grown, said Dong Ahn, a professor of animal science at

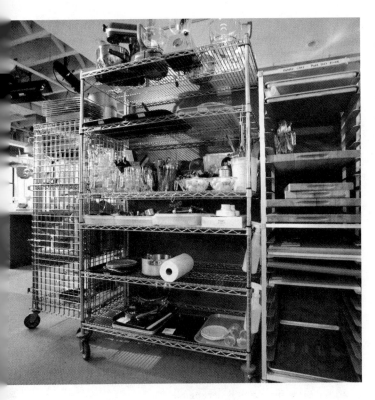

Iowa State University, and fat is what keeps meat moist and gives it flavor. "Fats contain more flavor compounds over time," Ahn said. "Commercial birds grow so fast, they don't have time to accumulate flavor."

Turkey growers have resorted to other means to return flavor—and fat—to the turkey, including injecting "basting" solutions during processing. These basting solutions can contain salt, turkey broth, oil, sugar, and sodium phosphate (which raises the meat's pH, binding water to the cells), all of which work to season the meat and keep it moist. Turkeys sold this way are often called "prebasted" and can be identified by the ingredient label. While our tasting panel generally liked Butterball and Jennie-O birds in this familiar style, some found them bland and "wet" rather than actually moist.

Another way turkey gains flavor is through koshering. Kosher birds start as the same breed of commercial large-breasted turkeys, but they are processed with salt according to Jewish dietary law and under rabbinical supervision. The carcasses are covered in kosher salt, then rinsed multiple times in cold water, all of which works to season the meat,

improve the texture, and help it retain moisture. Rubashkin's Aaron's Best and Empire Kosher were the two kosher birds in our lineup. While Aaron's Best ranked highly, tasters found the Empire to be decidedly mediocre. What made the difference? The lab tests were revealing. The Aaron's Best turkey had slightly more fat and nearly twice as much salt, which explains why tasters found the Empire turkey bland by comparison.

So what about the unconventional turkeys? The organic, pasture-raised bird from Good Earth Farms in Wisconsin (purchased online through the independent farm cooperative LocalHarvest) was the same breed as commercial turkeys, but it had been free to roam and eat foraged grass and insects. It also ate organic versions of the usual soy and cornmeal feed most turkeys consume.

While all this sounds great, our tasters didn't notice a big improvement in flavor. Indeed, Ahn noted that unless the bird was eating 100 percent foraged food, most consumers would not be able to taste a difference in the meat. The texture of this bird was slightly more stringy and tough than most tasters preferred, probably because it got more exercise. It also had among the lowest levels of fat, about half that of the top-ranked turkeys, and cost more than twice as much as a supermarket bird, at $45 (plus shipping) for a 12- to 14-pound bird. It finished second to last in our lineup.

Another unconventional turkey, from Diestel Family Turkey Ranch in Sonora, Calif., was raised on a vegetarian diet—meaning the bird ate none of the animal byproducts that can be part of commercial turkey diets—and was "range-grown," another term for pasture-raised. The company claims its birds are allowed to grow longer than average—in this case, about six months—for better flavor; however, tasters found that flavor "gamy" and "fishy," particularly in the dark meat. It finished last in the rankings.

Unlike the other two unconventional birds, the single heritage turkey in our lineup won favor, with tasters remarking on its "robust turkey flavor" that was "sweet" and "complex." Heritage turkeys are directly descended from wild turkeys and nearly disappeared in the mid–20th century as commercial Broad-Breasted Whites were created by the poultry industry. Heritage turkeys have colorful feathers, a more elongated frame, and a narrower breast, and they take nearly twice as long as commercial birds to reach a marketable weight. (They also mate naturally, unlike commercial birds, which must be artificially inseminated.)

The heritage turkey in our lineup, sold through Dean & Deluca for $100 plus shipping (we eventually figured out how to order the bird directly from the farm at half the cost), had the most fat by far of the turkeys we tasted—lab results showed it had nearly three times the fat of the leanest bird. A call to its grower, Mike Walters of Walters Hatchery in Stilwell, Okla., revealed his secret for a sweeter bird. While most turkeys eat a ration of corn and soybean meal throughout their lives, Walters eliminates soy from his turkeys' diet in the final weeks, feeding them sweet corn only. "It gives the birds a layer of fat under the skin, and it's extremely low in sodium, so they don't retain water, which means you get less water loss when you cook them," Walters said. He also tastes the feed himself before he gives it to the turkeys. "I figure whatever residual flavor is in my mouth is the residual flavor that you will have after eating my turkey," he said. "If you ever ate a plain soybean, you know it's bitter. Why feed your birds a flavor that is bitter?" Walters said that he believes any breed of turkey would benefit from this feeding system, though he admits to having no science to back up this assertion, and the food scientists we spoke to were a bit skeptical.

So what should you buy? It's hard to go wrong with the frozen kosher bird from Aaron's Best. It's moist, flavorful, and ready to cook, since no brining is needed. The prebasted birds from Butterball and Jennie-O finished a notch below our top choices, but they are consistent and also don't require brining. Although unremarkable, the frozen prebasted birds are certainly acceptable.

It's harder to give definitive advice about the less conventional choices. We didn't like the two pasture-raised birds we tasted, and heritage turkeys tend to be more variable in flavor than commercial options. Although the heritage bird from Walter's Hatchery finished in the top tier, in a previous tasting of several heritage turkeys we did a few years ago tasters complained that many of the birds were too gamy.

Finally, there's the cost issue. A 14-pound supermarket turkey sells for about $20. Order the same-size bird by mail and the price tag could top $100 once you pay for overnight shipping. You might end up with a superior turkey, but it's a gamble. What's more, the smaller producers can undergo some upheaval, as we found with our favored heritage bird. After our tasting, we learned that the Walters family was moving their turkey hatchery business to Missouri, and while they plan to use the same breeder stock, growing conditions, and feed, there is no guarantee that this Thanksgiving's birds will be the same as the ones we tasted. We will be tasting this brand again just before the holidays; look for the results at www.americastestkitchen.com.

SHOPPING NOTES: Fresh or Frozen?

When organizing our tasting, we decided to buy fresh turkeys wherever possible, assuming they would be better. But after the tasting we learned that most of our higher-ranked birds were, in fact, frozen. Our tasters consistently found the frozen birds to be moister than the fresh. This puzzled us until Professor Ahn explained that a "fresh" bird can actually be tougher and drier than a frozen one.

Turkeys may be labeled as "fresh" if they have never been chilled below 26 degrees. But at this temperature, tiny ice crystals can form in the meat. If the temperature fluctuates (during transport, at the supermarket, or on the way to your home), these crystals can melt, combine with neighboring crystals, and then refreeze. According to Ahn, "Eventually, irregularly shaped ice crystals will start to poke the cell membranes in the meat. They make holes and the cell tissues in the muscles will start to lose their internal contents. Then when they are cooked, those birds will be dry."

Rating Turkey

A PANEL OF 24 TASTERS FROM AMERICA'S TEST KITCHEN SAMPLED EIGHT TURKEYS, EACH WEIGHING 12 TO 14 POUNDS. Tasters rated the roasted birds on turkey flavor, texture, moistness, and overall appeal, taking into account both white and dark meat for each sample. The turkeys are listed below in order of preference. See www.americastestkitchen.com for up-to-date prices and mail-order sources for top-rated products.

HIGHLY RECOMMENDED
Rubashkin's Aaron's Best
$1.99 per pound; Frozen kosher

Lab tests revealed that this bird had the most salt and one of the highest levels of fat among the birds in our lineup; tasters noticed, finding this kosher turkey "very moist, with excellent texture" and boasting "both white and dark meat that are moist and flavorful."

HIGHLY RECOMMENDED
Walters Hatchery Heritage Breed
$4.06 per pound (plus shipping); Shipped frozen from Oklahoma

Virtually tied for first place, this heritage bird had nearly three times as much fat as the leanest turkeys. It offered "robust turkey flavor" and was "very tender." "What I expect a turkey to be: mild, sweet, flavorful." Both the light and dark meat were juicy.

RECOMMENDED
Butterball
$1.49 per pound; Frozen basted

Tasters generally liked this prebasted turkey, calling it "nice and moist, with fairly good, unremarkable flavor," though some found it "too salty," "almost wet rather than moist," and "rather bland." Lab tests showed it had the second-highest salt level in the lineup.

RECOMMENDED
Jennie-O
$1.49 per pound; Fresh basted

Tasters dubbed this prebasted turkey "middle-of-the-road," with "mild flavor, but it's good." A few described it as tasting "more like chicken," calling the white meat a bit "dry and chewy." Its salt level was quite low, closer to the natural birds than the pre-basted Butterball.

RECOMMENDED WITH RESERVATIONS
Empire
$2.69 per pound; Fresh kosher

"A good consistency, with good moisture and texture, but lacking flavor," was the consensus on this kosher turkey. "White meat tastes like nothing: What am I eating?" A few noted a "metallic," "almost bitter" aftertaste. Lab tests revealed that this kosher bird had just over half the salt of the top-rated Aaron's bird.

RECOMMENDED WITH RESERVATIONS
Shady Brook Farms
$1.29 per pound; Fresh

"Bland-o-rama" white meat, with a "chewy" texture that was "too dry." "Like my mother used to make, unfortunately." Tasters were divided on the dark meat, with some finding it good and others complaining of a "gamy" taste and "stringy" texture.

RECOMMENDED WITH RESERVATIONS
Good Earth Farms Organic Pasture-Raised
$3.21 per pound (plus shipping); Shipped frozen from Wisconsin

Tasters found this organic bird "tough," with a "dense, chewy quality." They noted its "clear turkey flavor," which was "very good," but felt it "needs gravy!" "Not a good stand-alone turkey." It had the lowest salt level in the lineup.

RECOMMENDED WITH RESERVATIONS
Diestel Family Turkey Ranch
$1.99 per pound; Frozen

"Even the dark is dry," tasters said of this California-raised bird, noting the dark meat was "rubbery, dark, and funky," with a "fishy flavor." The light meat fared better, with "great turkey flavor," but again, it was "too chewy."

ROASTING GREEN BEANS

WHAT WE WANTED: A method for cooking over-the-hill green beans that would give them a flavor comparable to sweet, fresh-picked beans.

Delicate and slender, garden-fresh haricots verts need only a few minutes of steaming, a pat of butter, and a sprinkle of salt and pepper to be ready for the table. In fact, they are so sweet, crisp, and tender that it's not uncommon to eat them raw. Take the same route with mature supermarket green beans, however, and you'll regret it. Unlike their lithe cousins, overgrown store-bought beans are often tough and dull, demanding special treatment.

Italians solve the problem with braising; gentle, moist cooking has a tenderizing effect. But the stovetop can get awfully crowded as dinnertime approaches—especially during the holidays. Roasting is commonplace for root vegetables like potatoes and carrots, and the technique is becoming popular for other vegetables, too. Would a stint in the oven have a positive effect on out-of-season green beans?

We had our answer when an embarrassingly simple test produced outstanding results. Roasted in a hot oven with only oil, salt, and pepper, an entire baking sheet of beans disappeared faster than french fries. Repeated tests confirmed that roasting green beans consistently transforms geriatric specimens into deeply caramelized, full-flavored beauties. Here's why: As green beans mature, their fibers toughen and their sugars are converted to starch. The hot, dry heat of the oven helps to reverse the aging process. Fibers break down and an enzymatic reaction causes the starch to turn back into sugar, restoring sweetness. Roasting also encourages the Maillard reaction (a chemical response that creates flavor through browning), a benefit lost with moist cooking methods.

The technique needed a few refinements. Those rare roasted-green-bean recipes that we found called for at least 2 tablespoons of oil per pound of beans, but we favored a more restrained approach. A single tablespoon of oil encouraged browning without making the beans slick and greasy. And after testing multiple time and temperature combinations, 20 minutes (with a quick stir at the halfway point) in a 450-degree oven proved optimal. Finally, when we tested the recipe using a dark nonstick baking sheet and encountered scorching, we began lining the sheet with aluminum foil. The foil warded off burning and made cleanup so easy that we made it part of the recipe, regardless of the pan.

We now had beans that tasted great straight up, and it was time to experiment with recipe variations. But their development was not without missteps: Aromatics (garlic and ginger) added at the outset scorched. The solution wasn't to lower the heat (the beans didn't brown well enough) but rather to add these ingredients halfway through cooking. And when liquid seasonings like vinegar and sesame oil slid right off the beans onto the baking sheet, we included a spoonful of sticky sweetener (honey or maple syrup) to create an appealing glaze, a move that incidentally encouraged even more caramelization. Last, a smattering of raw ingredients (toasted nuts or seeds, fresh herbs, or crumbled cheese) when the beans finished cooking provided complexity and textural interest.

WHAT WE LEARNED: The high heat used in roasting mature green beans helps reverse the aging process by converting the starches in the beans back to sugar. Just one tablespoon of oil is enough to lend flavor and moisture without making the beans greasy. Line the pan with foil to prevent scorching and for easy cleanup. If flavoring the green beans, it's best to add aromatics partway through cooking to avoid burning them.

ROASTED GREEN BEANS

serves 4

Aluminum foil prevents burning on dark nonstick baking sheets. When using baking sheets with a light finish, foil is not required, but we recommend it for easy cleanup.

1   pound green beans, stem ends snapped off
1   tablespoon olive oil
     Salt and ground black pepper

1. Adjust an oven rack to the middle position and heat the oven to 450 degrees. Line a rimmed baking sheet with aluminum foil; spread the beans on the baking sheet. Drizzle with the oil; using your hands, toss to coat evenly. Sprinkle with ½ teaspoon salt, toss to coat, and distribute in an even layer. Roast 10 minutes.

2. Remove the baking sheet from the oven. Using tongs, redistribute the beans. Continue roasting until the beans are dark golden brown in spots and have started to shrivel, 10 to 12 minutes longer.

3. Season with salt and pepper to taste, transfer to a serving bowl, and serve.

VARIATIONS

ROASTED GREEN BEANS WITH RED ONION AND WALNUTS

Onion gives these beans some savory sweetness and walnuts provide nutty crunch.

Combine 1 tablespoon balsamic vinegar, 1 teaspoon honey, 1 teaspoon minced fresh thyme leaves, and 2 medium thin-sliced garlic cloves in a small bowl; set aside. Follow the recipe for Roasted Green Beans through step 1, roasting ½ medium red onion, cut into ½-inch-thick wedges, along with the beans. Remove the baking sheet from the oven. Using tongs, coat the beans and onion evenly with the vinegar-honey mixture; redistribute in an even layer. Continue roasting until the onions and beans are dark golden brown in spots and the beans have started to shrivel, 10 to 12 minutes longer. Season with salt and pepper to taste and toss well to combine. Transfer to a serving dish, sprinkle with ⅓ cup toasted and chopped walnuts, and serve.

ROASTED SESAME GREEN BEANS

Using sesame oil in combination with sesame seeds gives these beans a pleasant nutty flavor.

Combine 1 tablespoon minced garlic (about 3 medium cloves), 1 teaspoon minced fresh ginger, 2 teaspoons honey, ½ teaspoon toasted sesame oil, and ¼ teaspoon hot red pepper flakes in a small bowl; set aside. Follow the recipe for Roasted Green Beans through step 1. Remove the baking sheet from the oven. Using tongs, coat the beans evenly with the garlic-ginger mixture; redistribute in an even layer. Continue roasting until dark golden brown in spots and starting to shrivel, 10 to 12 minutes longer. Season with salt to taste and toss well to combine. Transfer to a serving dish, sprinkle with 4 teaspoons toasted sesame seeds, and serve.

ROASTED GREEN BEANS WITH SUN-DRIED TOMATOES, GOAT CHEESE, AND OLIVES

The goat cheese melts slightly into a creamy coating for the beans in this boldly flavored variation.

Follow the recipe for Roasted Green Beans through step 2. While the beans roast, combine 1 teaspoon extra-virgin olive oil, 1 tablespoon lemon juice, ½ cup drained oil-packed sun-dried tomatoes (rinsed, patted dry, and chopped coarse), ½ cup pitted kalamata olives (quartered lengthwise), and 2 teaspoons minced fresh oregano leaves in a medium bowl. Add the beans, toss well to combine, and season with salt and pepper to taste. Transfer to a serving dish, top with ½ cup crumbled goat cheese (about 2 ounces), and serve.

The key to a stuffed tenderloin with a flavorful, browned crust is to sear it all over in a hot skillet before roasting it in the oven. And be sure to tie the roast snugly, so that it holds its shape, contains the stuffing, and cooks evenly.

HOLIDAY BEEF
CHAPTER 11 tenderloin dinner

Whether we like to admit it or not, turkey's appeal wanes a bit after Thanksgiving. Come December no cook wants to hear, "We're having turkey, again?" so when you're looking for a main course for the winter holidays that won't disappoint, look no further than beef tenderloin. Add a rich stuffing and you've got the ultimate main course—at least in theory. But cooking the tenderloin through can be a challenge—this is one big piece of meat and because it's expensive, you don't want to risk overcooking it. The stuffing can pose challenges too—what flavors will stand up to and complement the buttery beef? And just what is the best way to stuff a tenderloin without marring the meat or causing the stuffing to spill out during cooking? The test kitchen addressed these questions and more in developing a truly special main course—rich, tender beef with a bite of flavorful stuffing in every forkful.

Fluffy mashed potatoes are fine served with meatloaf during the week, or with roast chicken, drizzled with gravy, on the weekends. But come the holidays, we like to go the super creamy route—spuds so rich and decadent, not a drop of gravy is necessary to enjoy them. Of course, mashed potatoes in this style have a tendency to go from creamy to gluey in no time—and for special occasions, this wouldn't do. We wanted to develop a foolproof method for ultra-creamy mashed potatoes that delivers on its promise.

ULTIMATE BEEF TENDERLOIN

WHAT WE WANTED: A stuffed beef tenderloin that tastes as great as it looks—crusty on the outside, juicy on the inside, and stuffed with a filling seasoned to complement the roast's beefy flavor.

We have to admit, we thought we had it made when we started our research on developing a stuffed beef tenderloin. As we combed through stacks of recipes, we had visions of daily sessions spent carving into deeply charred crusts and tender, rosy-pink interiors to reveal generous caches of luxurious fillings—buttered lobster chunks, cognac-soaked chanterelles, truffled bread crumbs, and the like.

Once we stopped daydreaming and prepared these recipes, however, reality reared its ugly head. Much of the problem lay in the tenderloin's thin, tapered shape. By the time the thicker end reached medium-rare (about 30 minutes), the skinny end was overcooked. And forget about a nice crust—the exterior had hardly begun to brown at this point. The stuffing situation was even worse. The aforementioned "deluxe" fillings were either so chunky they fell out unceremoniously onto the platter upon carving or so absorbent they turned an unappealing blood red (literally). Clearly, we had our work cut out for us if we wanted to make a stuffed beef tenderloin worthy of its elegant reputation.

Our first decision involved the cut of meat. We could go with the whole tenderloin or the center-cut roast, also known as the Châteaubriand, a fancy name to match the fancy price tag (about $17 a pound). At $13 a pound, the whole tenderloin definitely had the price advantage, but was it worth the headaches?

We knew from past experience that to get a sufficient crust, the tenderloin would have to spend some time in a hot skillet. Although in previous recipes, the test kitchen has fit a whole tenderloin in a 12-inch skillet by coiling it tightly, that trick doesn't work so well when the tenderloin is bursting at the seams with stuffing. What's more, the tapered end of the tenderloin (called the tail) is too narrow to hold more than a few teaspoons of stuffing. By contrast, we found that the almost perfectly cylindrical Châteaubriand fits comfortably in a 12-inch skillet, roasts at an even rate, and accommodates just as much stuffing in one end as it does in the other. In this case, we decided, the higher per-pound price was worth it.

Starting with a basic sautéed-mushroom stuffing (a simplified version of the least disappointing filling from initial tests—but more on that later), we tried a basic butterflying procedure, making one cut down the length of the Châteaubriand, opening it up like a book, spreading the filling on the meat, then tying the flaps back together with twine. This method wasn't bad, but the amount of stuffing it could manage was pretty skimpy. One colleague suggested we try "double-butterflying" the roast, making two cuts so that it opened up into three parts (like a business letter) rather than two parts (like a book). Sure enough, this modified butterflying technique (see the illustrations on page 139) accommodated 50 percent more filling.

Searing the stuffed tenderloin in a skillet over medium-high heat for 10 minutes did a decent job of developing a crust, but tasters wanted more of a contrast between exterior and interior. Given the 15 or 20 additional minutes this long, narrow roast needed to cook up to temperature, the oven wasn't going to help much. Borrowing a trick the test kitchen has used for other beef roasts, we coated the exterior with kosher salt for a full hour before searing (along with olive oil and ground black pepper). Not only does the texture of the salt itself contribute to the crust, but an hour is enough time for the salt to begin breaking down the protein fibers of the outermost layer of meat, desiccating it to the point that it browns quickly.

Once seared, the tenderloin went into the oven on top of a rack-lined baking sheet (the elevation encourages uniform cooking). We found that a fairly hot oven (450 degrees) produced both a beautiful reddish-pink interior and a deep, dark crust in just 20 minutes.

Our initial round of tests had taught us a few things about how not to stuff a tenderloin. Lesson one: Don't stuff a beef roast with bread cubes; they turn into absorbent little

sponges saturated with bloodred juices. Lesson two: Avoid bulky ingredients (such as buttered lobster chunks), which fall out of the roast in a heap as soon as you start carving.

Despite the advances we'd made, the roast could accommodate only about a cup of filling. To get the most mileage from this relatively small amount, it was clear that we needed the most concentrated flavors possible. The mushroom stuffing we'd been using thus far needed some work.

Replacing the button mushrooms with earthy cremini deepened the flavor, while pulsing the mushrooms in the food processor reduced their bulk. Caramelized onions contributed sweetness and bound the mushrooms into a thick, slightly sticky jam that was easy to spread across the surface of the butterflied beef—and helped it stay put upon carving. Minced garlic and a splash of Madeira rounded out the flavors. To give the stuffing an aesthetic boost, we added a layer of baby spinach before rolling and tying the roast.

We wondered if we could pack in a little more flavor. As a finishing touch, we added a rich, herb-studded compound butter, a traditional accompaniment for lean beef tenderloin. With a swirl of intensely flavored stuffing in each bite, and a potent butter permeating the deeply charred crust, this royal entrée was finally worth its royal price.

WHAT WE LEARNED: For the best cut for stuffing, choose a center-cut beef tenderloin (the Châteaubriand). Its cylindrical shape fits into a skillet for searing and cooks evenly. In order to accommodate the stuffing, double-butterfly the roast, which involves making two cuts so that the roast opens up like a business letter. To encourage a well-seasoned crust, rub the exterior of the roast with salt, pepper, and olive oil one hour before cooking. Sear and then roast the tenderloin in a hot oven for a well-browned crust and juicy, rosy interior. Because the roast can hold just one cup of stuffing, choose an intensely flavored blend of caramelized onions and woodsy cremini mushrooms, seasoned with Madeira and garlic—and baby spinach for some welcome color and freshness.

ROAST BEEF TENDERLOIN WITH CARAMELIZED ONION AND MUSHROOM STUFFING

serves 4 to 6

The roast can be stuffed, rolled, and tied a day ahead, but don't season the exterior until you are ready to cook it. This recipe can be doubled to make two roasts. Sear the roasts one after the other, cleaning the pan and adding new oil after searing the first roast. Both pieces of meat can be roasted on the same rack.

stuffing

- 8   ounces cremini mushrooms, cleaned, stems trimmed, and broken into rough pieces
- 1½ teaspoons unsalted butter
- 1½ teaspoons olive oil
- 1   medium onion, halved and sliced ¼ inch thick
- ¼   teaspoon salt
- ⅛   teaspoon ground black pepper
- 1   medium garlic clove, minced or pressed through a garlic press (about 1 teaspoon)
- ½   cup Madeira or sweet Marsala wine

beef roast

- 1   beef tenderloin center-cut Châteaubriand (2 to 3 pounds), trimmed of fat and silver skin
     Kosher salt and ground black pepper
- ½   cup lightly packed baby spinach
- 3   tablespoons olive oil

herb butter

- 4   tablespoons (½ stick) unsalted butter, softened
- 1   tablespoon chopped fresh parsley leaves
- ¾   teaspoon chopped fresh thyme leaves
- 1   medium garlic clove, minced or pressed through a garlic press (about 1 teaspoon)

- 1   tablespoon whole grain mustard
- ⅛   teaspoon salt
- ⅛   teaspoon ground black pepper

1. FOR THE STUFFING: Process the mushrooms in a food processor until coarsely chopped, about 6 pulses. Heat the butter and oil in a 12-inch nonstick skillet over medium-high heat until foaming subsides. Add the onion, salt, and pepper; cook, stirring occasionally, until the onion begins to soften, about 5 minutes. Add the mushrooms and cook, stirring occasionally, until all the moisture has evaporated, 5 to 7 minutes. Reduce the heat to medium and continue to cook, stirring frequently, until the vegetables are deeply browned and sticky, about 10 minutes. Stir in the garlic and cook until fragrant, about 30 seconds. Slowly stir in the Madeira and cook, scraping the bottom of the skillet to loosen any browned bits, until the liquid has evaporated, 2 to 3 minutes. Transfer the onion-mushroom mixture to a plate and cool to room temperature.

2. FOR THE ROAST: Following illustrations 1 and 2 at right, butterfly the tenderloin. Season the cut side of the tenderloin liberally with kosher salt and pepper. Following illustration 3, spread the cooled stuffing mixture over the interior of the beef, leaving a ½-inch border on all sides; lay the spinach on top of the stuffing. Following illustrations 4 and 5, roll the roast lengthwise and tie.

3. In a small bowl, stir together 1 tablespoon of the olive oil, 1½ teaspoons kosher salt, and 1½ teaspoons pepper. Rub the roast with the oil mixture and let stand at room temperature for 1 hour.

4. Adjust an oven rack to the middle position and heat the oven to 450 degrees. Heat the remaining 2 tablespoons olive

TECHNIQUE:
Stuffing and Tying a Tenderloin

1. Insert a chef's knife about 1 inch from the bottom of the roast and cut horizontally, stopping just before the edge. Open the meat like a book.

2. Make another cut diagonally into the thicker portion of the roast. Open up this flap, smoothing out the butterflied rectangle of meat.

3. Spread the filling evenly over the entire surface, leaving a ½-inch border on all sides. Press the spinach leaves evenly on top of the filling.

4. Using both hands, gently but firmly roll up the stuffed tenderloin, making it as compact as possible without squeezing out any filling.

5. Evenly space 8 pieces of kitchen twine (each about 14 inches) beneath the roast. Tie each strand tightly around the roast, starting with the ends.

---

oil in a 12-inch skillet over medium-high heat until smoking. Add the beef to the pan and cook until well browned on all sides, 8 to 10 minutes total. Transfer the beef to a wire rack set in a rimmed baking sheet and place in the oven. Roast until an instant-read thermometer inserted into the thickest part of the roast registers 120 degrees for rare, 16 to 18 minutes, or 125 degrees for medium-rare, 20 to 22 minutes.

5. FOR THE BUTTER: While the meat roasts, combine the butter ingredients in a small bowl. Transfer the tenderloin to a cutting board; spread half of the butter evenly over the top of the roast. Loosely tent the roast with foil; let rest for 15 minutes. Cut the roast between the pieces of twine into thick slices. Remove the twine and serve, passing the remaining butter separately.

EQUIPMENT CORNER: Knife Sharpeners

WHAT'S THE BEST WAY TO MAINTAIN THAT SNAPPY edge that makes light work of chopping and slicing? First, it's important to note that there's a difference between tuning up a relatively sharp knife and sharpening a dull knife. A so-called sharpening steel, the metal rod sold with most knife sets, doesn't sharpen at all: It's a tune-up device. As you cut with a sharp knife, the thin cutting edge of the blade can actually turn to the side, making your blade seem duller than it is. Running the knife blade over the steel, as most professional chefs do each time they're about to use a knife, simply realigns that edge and makes it straight again. It can't reshape a truly dull blade that's rounded and worn down. That's when you need a sharpener that can cut away metal and restore the standard 20-degree angle of each side of the edge.

To reshape the edge of a dull knife, you have a few choices, depending on the amount of effort, skill, and money you want to invest. You can send it out (inconvenient, even if you can find someone to do it). You can use a whetstone (very difficult for anyone but a professional). But the best option for most home cooks is to buy a tool (either electric or manual) that does most of the work for you.

Based on previous kitchen tests, we've said that electric knife sharpeners are the most reliable choice for home cooks. Several years ago, we recommended the Chef'sChoice Model 110 for its easy, reliable sharpening of even the dullest knives. But since that time, new electric sharpeners have come on the market, both from EdgeCraft, maker of Chef'sChoice, and from other companies. Are any better than the trusty machine we've used in the test kitchen for nearly a decade? Given that most electric sharpeners cost around $100, we thought it was also time to revisit manual sharpeners, many of which are available for a fraction of the cost. Is there an inexpensive gem out there?

Most sharpeners, both electric and manual, start their work with a coarse material and progress through stages of finer material to polish the edge. In general, the hardest material is diamond, followed by tungsten carbide, followed by high-alumina ceramic, followed by steel. Hardness isn't everything, though; the material is only as good as the angle of the knife being swiped against it, so the design of the sharpener is important. Some models guarantee that even an inexperienced user will get the right angle; other models make this more a matter of chance.

To level the playing field for our testing, we wanted to start with knives of equal dullness. Looking to simulate the condition of knives that have been used for about a year without sharpening, we turned for advice to Stoddard's, a cutlery shop in Boston. Although the company has been in the business of sharpening knives since the early 1800s, owner David Marks good-naturedly agreed to "dull" dozens

of new knives over the course of our testing. On a 220-grit whetstone, he used a heel-to-tip rocking motion that mimics a chef's slicing, repeating this motion 45 times for each knife. Marks also used a diamond slipstone to cut 1/16-inch notches in each blade near the heel and near the tip, where he said he often sees nicks appearing in chef's knives that have been roughly used—the kind of damage that might occur if you use your knife to hack through chicken bones or frozen foods.

Back in the test kitchen, we confirmed the knives' dullness by attempting to slice through a sheet of paper—without success. Following the manufacturers' instructions, we sharpened one knife on each sharpener and tried again to slice paper—with decidedly better results. We used the sharp knives to cut paper-thin slices of ripe tomato and chiffonade fresh basil leaves. In the final test, we measured how long it took to regrind the blades and smooth out those notches—a measure of how well the sharpeners could repair severe damage.

As in our earlier tests, most of the electric sharpeners were up to the job (see the chart on page 142). Only one, the Kershaw Electric Knife Sharpener ($59.95), failed to restore a good cutting edge. The Waring PRO KS80 ($99.95) aced the paper, tomato, and basil tests, but it also cut a quarter-inch scoop, or swale, out of the heel because the knife dropped down onto the grinding wheel each time it was inserted. The heel of the blade thus no longer made contact with the cutting board, making it unusable. The Presto EverSharp 8800, the least expensive electric at $39.95, restored a sharp but "moderately rough" edge to the knife that one tester described as "chewed up." Its loud motor stalled frequently and alarmingly, halfway up the blade, whenever we failed to keep a very light touch on the knife.

As for Chef'sChoice, our old model 110 ($79.95) performed well, but improvements on its newer siblings made them quicker and easier to use. In addition to taking less time and trouble to reach a fine edge, the new models feature spring-loaded blade guides that allow no ambiguous wiggle room as they hold the blade against the sharpening wheels at the proper angle, replacing the trickier magnetic guides on the 110. The sharpening wheels on newer models also reach closer to the edge of the machine, ensuring that the sharpening extends all the way to the end of the knife.

Overall, we preferred the sharper, finer, more polished edge we got with the Chef'sChoice 130 ($139), the quietest and smoothest of the six electric sharpeners we tested. It sharpened dulled knives quickly. We also liked its nonmotorized slot, which operates like a sharpening steel. Because many people have a hard time mastering the motion needed to use a traditional steel, this is an easy way to get the benefit of steeling. To keep your knives in prime condition, you would keep this sharpener on the counter and use the built-in steel just as professional chefs do, right before—and every time—you use your knives. If money is no object, the Chef'sChoice Model 130 is our new electric sharpener of choice. If your budget is more modest, the 110 is still worth buying and will keep your knives in top condition.

Manual sharpeners share some similarities: In size, most are a little bigger than a desktop stapler, and the sharpening material used may be diamond, steel, ceramic, tungsten carbide, or a combination of these. In most manual sharpeners, the sharpening material is enclosed in a plastic or metal body, with one, two, or three angled openings for the knife to be drawn through. In a few models, the sharpener consists of a base that holds the exposed honing material, such as ceramic sticks, in a V-shape that the knife is drawn against.

Could manual sharpeners hold a candle to the electric models we tested? In a word, yes. A few made admirably quick and thorough work of basic sharpening tasks and did so for a fraction of the price of an electric sharpener.

Coming out on top in our testing was the AccuSharp Knife and Tool Sharpener ($11.71), a simple plastic handheld device with a single tungsten carbide V-shaped blade. The AccuSharp produces metal shavings as you draw it over the knife, which you hold against the countertop with the cutting edge up. Once testers got over the strangeness of "straddling" the blade with the sharpener, they found themselves "surprised at how quickly this works," noting that it was "really easy to use. . . . I'm impressed."

The second-place model, Anolon's Universal Sharpener ($29.95), has three sets of ceramic stones, from coarse to fine, in a plastic housing that you fill with water to keep the stones from clogging with metal filings, a common problem with ceramic. Testers remarked that it was "very easy, no pressure required," to make the knife cut through paper ("like butter") and that it was "no effort" to slice through tomatoes.

Another single-slot device, the Chantry Knife Sharpener ($39.95), took third place. Inside a sturdy metal casing, two spring-loaded steel rods are crossed at a 40-degree angle; the knife is pressed down as you saw it back and forth, as if cutting a loaf of bread. Its simplicity and sharp edge appealed to testers.

Clearly the sharpening material was not what set these sharpeners ahead of the others. In each case they won over testers with a combination of good results and ease of use—not always a given with a manual sharpener. Some of

Rating Electric Knife Sharpeners

WE TESTED SIX ELECTRIC KNIFE SHARPENERS AND EVALUATED THEM ACCORDING TO PERFORMANCE AND EASE OF use. The sharpeners are listed in order of preference. See www.americastestkitchen.com for up-to-date prices and mail-order sources for top-rated products.

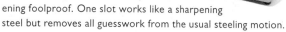

HIGHLY RECOMMENDED
Chef'sChoice Model 130
$139

This quiet model is the Rolls-Royce of sharpeners. Spring-loaded blade guides make sharpening foolproof. One slot works like a sharpening steel but removes all guesswork from the usual steeling motion.

RECOMMENDED
Chef'sChoice Model 120
$129.95

Very easy to operate; spring-loaded blade guides make sharpening foolproof. Knives seem to "fall" somewhat jarringly into the first slot.

RECOMMENDED WITH RESERVATIONS
Chef'sChoice Model 110
$79.95

Does the job at a reasonable price, although somewhat noisily. Instructions are a bit confusing and magnetic guides could control blade angle more easily. Grinding elements are set in from edge of machine and miss the heel on knives.

RECOMMENDED WITH RESERVATIONS
Presto EverSharp 8800
$39.95

Very loud, and stalled when testers applied any pressure. Appeared to scuff blades.

NOT RECOMMENDED
Waring PRO KS80
$99.95

Grinding wheels on this large, quiet machine are set in too far from end of slot, so user can't hone entire blade edge. One knife dropped onto wheel, causing "scoop" to develop near heel end.

NOT RECOMMENDED
Kershaw Electric Knife Sharpener
$59.95

Loud, "nerve-wracking" metallic noise. The grinding action sharpened at tip and heel of knives but not in middle, eventually ruining our knives. Crucial operation instructions found only on DVD. Can operate for only two minutes at a time.

---

the low-rated models were nearly as expensive as an electric but took a lot more work and time to do the job. Other low-rated models were squeaky, jerky, awkward, or even useless.

Now for the bad news: While some of the manual sharpeners could restore a respectable edge to the knives, not one removed the notches. We put the knives through each device 300 times, with no visible effect. What does this mean? Manual sharpeners take off a good deal less metal than electric sharpeners and simply cannot remove enough, in a reasonable amount of time, to restore a nicked or damaged knife. For these knives (and undoubtedly you have

several), an electric sharpener is the only choice.

Should you bother buying a manual knife sharpener? The better options will help you maintain new knives and are fine with moderately dull blades. At $11.71, the appeal of the easy-to-operate AccuSharp is clear. But be prepared to pay a professional to handle your more challenging sharpening needs. In the long run, an electric sharpener is a good investment, if you can make the initial cash outlay. If not, pick up a cheap manual sharpener. The best ones are far superior to steeling rods and will keep many of your knives in decent shape.

Rating Manual Knife Sharpeners

WE TESTED 12 MANUAL KNIFE SHARPENERS AND EVALUATED THEM ACCORDING TO PERFORMANCE AND EASE OF USE. The sharpeners are listed in order of preference. See www.americastestkitchen.com for up-to-date prices and mail-order sources for top-rated products.

RECOMMENDED

AccuSharp Knife and Tool Sharpener
$11.71

Establishes a sharp edge quickly and easily. This compact sharpener must be drawn over the exposed knife blade, which gave users some pause, at least initially.

RECOMMENDED

Anolon Universal Knife Sharpener 3-Stage Wet Stone
$29.95

Smooth, easy motion yields very sharp, polished blade. Handle is especially comfortable. Must fill with water before each use.

RECOMMENDED

Chantry Knife Sharpener
$39.95

Heavy metal casing on this fast, simple sharpener is durable and stays put. Instructions are vague.

RECOMMENDED WITH RESERVATIONS

Chef'sChoice 460 Multi-Edge Diamond Hone Sharpener
$29.95

This lightweight model must be held down, but it did yield a sharp edge. Wheels indicating correct blade angle never turned as described, and knives didn't move smoothly.

RECOMMENDED WITH RESERVATIONS

Spyderco Tri-Angle Sharpmaker
$47.20

Although overly complex (the instruction booklet has 28 pages!), slow to operate, and difficult to control, this model did produce a sharp edge— eventually.

RECOMMENDED WITH RESERVATIONS

Wüsthof Knife-Life 3-Stage Knife and Scissor Sharpener
$19.95

Quick to operate, but performance is a notch below the better options. Knives sharpened with this tool tore, rather than sliced, tomatoes.

NOT RECOMMENDED

Füri Tech Edge Professional Sharpening System
$89.95

Although this model put a fairly sharp edge on knives, the jumpy, jerky motion of the tungsten tool damaged the blade edge.

NOT RECOMMENDED

Global MinoSharp Plus Knife Sharpener, Model 440
$48.95

Uncomplicated, but sharpening motion is jerky and produces blade that's not sharp enough. Must fill with water before each use.

NOT RECOMMENDED

Henckels TwinSharp Select Knife Sharpener
$39.95

Knife squeaks unpleasantly as it goes through steel slot. Easy to use, but results are so-so.

NOT RECOMMENDED

Meyerco Sharpen-It
$29.99

This pocket-size sharpener was hard to manipulate, and instructions were poorly written. Blade drags in tungsten slot.

NOT RECOMMENDED

Lansky Crock Stick Two-Stage Professional Knife Sharpener
$39.99

Complicated hand motion feels unnatural. Sharpening rods quickly became smooth, and cleaning didn't restore their abrasive feel.

NOT RECOMMENDED

Chicago Cutlery MagnaSharp Mouse Knife Sharpener
$7.99

This compact unit emitted a terrible squeaking noise. One sample didn't work; others were not much better.

ULTIMATE CREAMY MASHED POTATOES

WHAT WE WANTED: Lush, creamy mashed potatoes, with so much richness and flavor they can stand on their own—no gravy necessary.

During the holiday season, we shelve our tried-and-true recipe for mashed potatoes in favor of a much more luxurious mash, one that is silky smooth and loaded with cream and butter. But there's a fine line between creamy and gluey. Sometimes the potatoes are as good as any you might get in the finest restaurant. Other times, they closely resemble paste or Spackle. Why is this simple recipe (with just potatoes, cream, butter, and salt) so fickle?

The problem is the starch. When the cooked potatoes are mashed, some starch is released, which helps to make the potatoes incredibly smooth and creamy. But if you've ever mashed potatoes with an electric mixer, you've seen what happens when you get too much of a good thing: The mixer releases too much starch from the potatoes and turns them into a gluey mess.

Finding the right type of potato was our first challenge. Russets yielded a fluffy, relatively light mash. We wanted something a bit creamier and more substantial. Red potatoes were too dense and gluey. Yukon Golds were the perfect compromise—creamier than russets but not sticky and heavy, like the red potatoes.

Preparing potatoes for mashing is pretty straightforward. The potatoes are peeled, cut into chunks, boiled, drained, and mashed. Could we improve upon this method? We found a few recipes that suggested microwaving or baking the potatoes, but the results were grainy. We finally hit upon a simple refinement borrowed from classic french fry recipes, which call for rinsing the cut potatoes to wash away excess starch. What if we adapted this idea for mashed potatoes? Cutting the potatoes into round slices (rather than the usual chunks) would expose more surface area, so we ran a test with rinsed versus unrinsed rounds of potatoes. The differences were significant. The rinsed potatoes were much creamier (and not at all gluey) when mashed.

To remove any water still clinging to the potatoes, we returned them to the empty pot and set it over low heat (excess water reduces the amount of butter and cream the potatoes can hold).

As for the butter and cream, we've never understood cooks who add these ingredients cold to hot potatoes. Melting the butter and heating the cream ensure that the potatoes will arrive at the table hot.

Creamy potatoes demand a fair amount of butter and cream, but too much will turn them soupy. After testing various amounts of each, tasters decided that 1½ sticks of butter and 1½ cups of cream gave 4 pounds of potatoes the best flavor and texture.

These rich potatoes are an indulgence, and we would never douse them with gravy (use a leaner recipe if that's your goal). Eat these mashed potatoes just as they are, so you can appreciate every drop of cream.

WHAT WE LEARNED: Choose Yukon Gold potatoes for creamy mashed potatoes that aren't heavy. Slicing the potatoes into rounds and then rinsing away the surface starch before boiling helps intensify their creamy texture. Set the boiled and drained potatoes in their pot over a low flame to further evaporate any excess moisture. Using 1½ sticks of butter and 1½ cups of heavy cream gives these potatoes luxurious flavor and richness without making the mash too thin. Be sure to melt the butter and warm the cream before adding them to the potatoes, so that the finished dish arrives at the table piping hot.

CREAMY MASHED POTATOES

serves 8 to 10

This recipe can be cut in half, if desired.

4	pounds Yukon Gold potatoes, scrubbed and peeled
12	tablespoons (1½ sticks) unsalted butter, cut into 6 pieces
1½	cups heavy cream
2	teaspoons salt

1. Cut the potatoes into ¾-inch slices. Place the potatoes in a colander and rinse under cool running water, tossing with your hands, for 30 seconds. Transfer the potatoes to a Dutch oven, add water to cover by 1 inch, and bring to a boil over high heat. Reduce the heat to medium and boil until the potatoes are tender, 20 to 25 minutes.

2. Meanwhile, heat the butter and heavy cream in a small saucepan over medium heat until the butter is melted, about 5 minutes. Keep warm.

3. Drain the potatoes and return to the Dutch oven. Stir over low heat until the potatoes are thoroughly dried, 1 to 2 minutes. Set a ricer or food mill over a large bowl and press or mill the potatoes into the bowl. Gently fold in the warm cream mixture and salt with a rubber spatula until the cream is absorbed and the potatoes are thick and creamy. Serve.

Bridget may look like she's about to cast a spell, but no hocus-pocus is required to replicate Missouri's Kansas City Sticky Ribs.

KANSAS CITY bbq

For serious barbecue lovers, it's hard to choose a best-loved style of ribs, but we'd be willing to bet that smoky, sweet Kansas City ribs would be a top contender. These meaty ribs are slow-smoked for their trademark flavor—and traditional recipes truly do take all day to barbecue. Is there a faster way to barbecue ribs with authentic Kansas City flavor? From a practical point of view, standing over a hot grill all day is no fun for the cook, no matter how dedicated. In addition to speeding up the barbecuing process, we wanted to determine the best type of ribs for this dish—there are many to choose from—and we wanted to develop a KC-style barbecue sauce. It should be sticky enough to cling to the ribs, but not overly sweet or cloying, and have the slightly spicy, warm flavors of the real thing.

Just what are Kansas City barbecued beans? Traditionally, these saucy beans contain the "burnt ends" of smoked brisket—a typical leftover in KC barbecue joints—the smoky meat adds remarkable flavor and richness. But at home, who has leftovers like burnt ends on hand? We wanted to develop a more practical approach to Kansas City–style beans for the home cook. And we wanted to be able to serve these beans alongside our ribs, so we'd also need to coordinate their cooking so both would be finished simultaneously. A tall order, but, for true barbecue fans, one worth seeking out.

KANSAS CITY RIBS

WHAT WE WANTED: A faster method for Kansas City ribs—one that would produce the same fall-off-the-bone, tender smoky meat of the long-cooked original recipe.

Kansas City ribs are slow-smoked pork ribs slathered in a sauce so thick, sweet, and sticky that you need a case of wet naps to get your hands clean after eating them. But authentic ribs can take all day to prepare. Could we come up with a more reasonable recipe for the home cook?

Aside from the sauce and the smoke, the defining characteristic of KC ribs is their "finger tender" texture: The meat should pull off the bone with very little resistance, and this starts with the right cut. Spareribs are well marbled with fat, which makes them cook up moist and tender. (Baby back ribs are too lean for this recipe.)

Barbecuing is all about utilizing low, indirect heat to turn the ribs smoky and tender. However, keeping a grill at an average temperature of 275 to 300 degrees requires diligence, and adding charcoal every hour tried our patience. Was there an easier way? Well, yes and no. You can build the charcoal fire hotter at the outset, but you will still need to add charcoal once during the four-hour cooking time. Some things just can't be rushed. (For folks who really don't want to add charcoal, we developed a variation that spends two hours on the grill and then goes into the oven.)

Our four-hour ribs were nice and smoky, but they were not as tender as we wanted. They were also too dry. We tried wrapping the ribs with foil (cutting holes in the foil to let smoke in), but this caused them to take on a squishy texture and boiled flavor. What if we just placed the foil on top of the ribs rather than wrapping them? Somewhat to our surprise, this worked nicely. The foil held in some of the steam, helping to make the ribs tender and moist. Because they were still exposed to the fire, they also developed a nice crusty exterior. A simple spice rub helped to further develop the crust.

From here all we had to do was give the ribs a double coating of sauce, once during the last hour on the grill (so that the sauce wouldn't char) and once just before serving. We can make these ribs in much less time than it takes to get to Kansas City—and they taste just as good.

WHAT WE LEARNED: Spareribs, because they are well marbled with fat, will produce moist, tender KC ribs. Apply a spice rub for flavor and to encourage a savory crust on the meat. Barbecue the ribs, covered with foil (for tender, not dry, meat), over indirect heat for four hours. The foil traps some of the steam over the meat, so that it cooks up tender, not dry. Using wood chips on the grill imparts the meat with great smoky flavor. For sticky, saucy ribs, brush the ribs all over with barbecue sauce during the last hour of cooking, then wrap them in foil and cook until tender.

KANSAS CITY STICKY RIBS

serves 4 to 6

Buy St. Louis–style racks (see page 150), which are more manageable than untrimmed pork ribs. We prefer our sauce recipe but store-bought works, too.

- 3 tablespoons paprika
- 2 tablespoons light brown sugar
- 1 tablespoon ground black pepper
- 1 tablespoon salt
- ¼ teaspoon cayenne pepper
- 2 full racks pork spareribs, preferably St. Louis cut, trimmed of any large pieces of excess fat, membrane removed (see photo 1 at right), and patted dry
- 2 cups wood chips
- 2 cups Kansas City Barbecue Sauce (page 151)

1. Combine the paprika, sugar, pepper, salt, and cayenne in a small bowl. Massage the spice rub into both sides of the rib racks.

2. Soak the wood chips in a bowl of water for 15 minutes. Open the bottom grill vents of a charcoal grill completely. Light a large chimney starter filled two–thirds with charcoal briquettes (about 65 briquettes) and burn until covered with a fine gray ash, about 20 minutes. Use a grill brush to scrape the cooking grate clean. Arrange a 13 by 9-inch disposable aluminum pan on one side of the grill and pour the hot coals into a pile on the opposite side. Sprinkle 1 cup of the wood chips over the coals, set the cooking grate in place, and position the ribs over the pan.

3. Place a sheet of aluminum foil directly on top of the ribs (see photo 2 at right) and cover the grill, positioning the lid vents (three-quarters open) directly over the ribs. Barbecue, turning and rotating the ribs after 1 hour, until the coals are almost spent, about 2 hours.

TECHNIQUE:
How to Make Tender Ribs

Making tender ribs can be tough work, but we've found a few tips to get that fall-off-the-bone texture every time.

1. Remove the membrane: Ribs have a papery membrane on the underside. Before cooking, loosen this membrane with the tip of a paring knife and, with the aid of a paper towel, pull it off slowly, all in one piece.

2. Cover with foil: Barbecuing the ribs for hours on end won't guarantee super-tender meat. Fortunately, you can trap steam and make the ribs tender by covering them with sheets of aluminum foil.

3. Wrap it up: During the last hour of barbecuing, wrap the ribs tightly in the foil to keep them from drying out. After removing the ribs from the grill, let them rest for 30 minutes, still wrapped.

Choosing the Right Rack

When developing our recipe for Kansas City Sticky Ribs, we found that some racks of spareribs were so big they would barely fit on the grill. Because whole spareribs contain the brisket bone and surrounding meat, each rack can weigh upward of 5 pounds. For a more manageable cut, we looked 250 miles east of Kansas City. With "St. Louis" ribs, the brisket bone and surrounding meat are trimmed off to produce a narrower, rectangular rack that usually weighs in at a relatively svelte 3 pounds. In our opinion, St. Louis ribs offer all the taste of whole spareribs without any of the trouble. If you can find only whole spareribs, use the biggest grill possible and be prepared to increase the cooking time significantly.

Whole Spareribs
Bulky and hard to handle on the grill.

St. Louis Ribs
Same great flavor but in a smaller package.

4. About 20 minutes before the coals are spent, light another 65 briquettes in the chimney starter and burn until covered with a fine gray ash. Place the hot coals from the chimney on top of the spent coals and sprinkle the remaining cup of wood chips over the coals. Turn and rotate the ribs and barbecue, covered, for 1 hour. Brush the ribs liberally on both sides with the sauce, wrap tightly with foil (see photo 3 on page 149), and barbecue until very tender, about 1 hour longer.

5. Transfer the ribs (still in the foil) to a cutting board and let rest 30 minutes. Unwrap the ribs and brush with additional barbecue sauce. Slice the ribs between the bones and serve with the remaining sauce.

VARIATIONS

KANSAS CITY STICKY RIBS ON A GAS GRILL

Note that a 13 by 9-inch disposable aluminum pan will not fit under the grill grate of a gas grill, so choose a shallower aluminum pan.

Follow step 1 of Kansas City Sticky Ribs then place 2 cups soaked wood chips in a small disposable aluminum pan. Place the pan directly on the primary burner of a gas grill, turn all the burners to high, and preheat with the lid down until the chips are smoking heavily, about 15 minutes. Use a grill brush to scrape the cooking grate clean. Turn the primary burner to medium and shut off the other burners, adjusting the temperature of the primary burner as needed to maintain an average temperature of 275 degrees. Position the ribs over the cool part of the grill. Barbecue the ribs as directed.

EASIEST KANSAS CITY STICKY RIBS

Not keen on tending a grill for 4 hours? Our ribs will taste good even if they spend the last 2 hours of cooking in your oven.

In step 4, instead of adding more charcoal to the grill, wrap the ribs tightly in foil, place on a baking sheet, and bake in a 250-degree oven for 1 hour. Remove from the oven, brush both sides with the barbecue sauce, rewrap with foil, and bake until very tender, about 1 hour longer. Proceed as directed in step 5.

KANSAS CITY BARBECUE SAUCE

makes about 4 cups

Kansas City barbecue sauce is a sweet, smoky, sticky, and thick tomato-based sauce. This style of sauce is the model for most bottled brands, including KC Masterpiece. We like our barbecue sauce extra-thick. If you like a thinner, smoother texture, the sauce can be strained after it has finished cooking.

    2   teaspoons vegetable oil
    1   onion, minced
    4   cups low-sodium chicken broth
    1   cup root beer
    1   cup cider vinegar
    1   cup dark corn syrup
    ½   cup molasses
    ½   cup tomato paste
    ½   cup ketchup
    2   tablespoons brown mustard
    1   tablespoon hot sauce
    ½   teaspoon garlic powder
    ¼   teaspoon liquid smoke (optional)

Heat the oil in a saucepan over medium–high heat until shimmering. Add the onion and cook until softened, about 5 minutes. Whisk in the remaining ingredients, except for the liquid smoke, and bring to a boil. Reduce the heat to medium and simmer until the mixture is thick and has reduced to 4 cups, about 1 hour. Stir in the liquid smoke, if using. (The sauce can be refrigerated in an airtight container for up to 1 week.)

GETTING IT RIGHT: Key Ingredient to KC Barbecue Sauce

Our Kansas City Barbecue Sauce is flavored by an unlikely ingredient: root beer. We wondered how other types of soda might fare in the recipe. Birch beer, cream soda, and cola were fine but couldn't top root beer. Other sodas, especially Dr Pepper and Mountain Dew, gave the sauce a medicinal flavor.

Spicy and Sweet
Root beer is the secret ingredient in our barbecue sauce.

SMOKY BARBECUED BEANS

WHAT WE WANTED: The perfect partner to our Kansas City Sticky Ribs—smoky tender beans, rich with the flavor of barbecue.

Whether it's salt pork, bacon, or lard, no recipe for barbecued baked beans is complete without some kind of pork. In Kansas City, many barbecue joints stir "burnt ends"—tough, overcooked bits of smoked brisket (the most common option), ribs, or pulled pork—into their barbecued beans. What likely began as a way to recycle leftovers has become a Kansas City classic, with local restaurants offering burnt-ends sandwiches and burnt-ends platters. We even found several companies that will accept mail orders for burnt ends.

Beans with smoky bits of barbecued meat sound incredibly appealing, but we weren't sure how to translate this recipe for the home kitchen. Who has burnt ends in the fridge? We gave up on this idea until a kitchen colleague told us about a recipe from Fiorella's Jack Stack Barbecue,

a Kansas City restaurant that suggests cooking the beans on the bottom of the grill—right under the ribs. As the beans simmer in the smoky heat, they catch drippings from the ribs and become unbelievably flavorful—or so our colleague promised. Now this was something we could try at home.

We quickly learned that the beans have to be almost fully cooked when they go into the grill, where they pick up flavor but don't really soften much. Besides, if the beans go into the grill at the outset (when the ribs are rendering most of their fat), they become too greasy. This meant we needed to start them on the stovetop at the same time the ribs went on the grill.

We began by cooking bacon in a Dutch oven until crisp. True, we would be picking up some of the smoky, salty fat of the ribs in our beans, but bacon would add a base layer of smoky flavor. We cooked onion and garlic in the rendered bacon fat and then added dried pinto beans (which had been soaked overnight) and water. After cooking the beans for an hour, we added further seasonings to build the sauce for the beans. We kept things simple and chose traditional ingredients—barbecue sauce, brown sugar, mustard, and hot sauce—and simmered them for another hour. By this time, the ribs had been on the grill two hours, so we could now add the pan of beans. (We had to open the grill anyway to add more charcoal.) And two hours later the ribs and beans were done at the same time.

So how do these beans taste? The combination of smoke and pork flavor makes this Kansas City recipe hard to beat.

WHAT WE LEARNED: Start the beans on the stovetop, then transfer them to the grill, underneath the ribs, where they can catch the ribs' flavorful smoky fat. Bacon, onions, and garlic give the beans a meaty, savory base of flavor. Use restraint in seasoning the beans' sauce, sticking to traditional ingredients like barbecue sauce, brown sugar, mustard, and hot sauce.

SMOKY KANSAS CITY BARBECUE BEANS

serves 4 to 6

This recipe is meant for a charcoal grill. If you're cooking on a gas grill, omit step 3 and finish cooking the beans in a 300-degree oven for 2 to 2½ hours. We prefer our sauce recipe but store-bought works, too. (Bull's-Eye is our favorite.)

4	slices (4 ounces) bacon, chopped fine
1	onion, minced
4	garlic cloves, minced or pressed through a garlic press (about 4 teaspoons)
1	pound pinto beans, soaked overnight
6	cups water
1	cup Kansas City Barbecue Sauce (page 151)
⅓	cup packed light brown sugar
2	tablespoons brown mustard
1	teaspoon hot sauce
	Salt

1. Cook the bacon in a Dutch oven over medium heat until beginning to crisp, about 5 minutes. Stir in the onion and cook until softened, about 5 minutes. Stir in the garlic and cook until fragrant, about 30 seconds. Add the beans and water and bring to a simmer. Reduce the heat to medium-low, cover, and cook until the beans are just soft, about 1 hour.

2. Stir in ½ cup of the barbecue sauce, the brown sugar, mustard, hot sauce, and 2 teaspoons salt and simmer, uncovered, over medium-low heat until the beans are tender and the sauce is slightly thickened, about 1 hour. (If the mixture becomes too thick, add water.) Transfer the beans to a 13 by 9-inch disposable aluminum pan and wrap tightly with aluminum foil. Using a paring knife or skewer, poke holes in the foil.

TECHNIQUE:

Making Beans on the Grill

Our barbecue beans finish cooking on the grill, where they pick up smoke and pork flavors. Here's how to let the flavors in and keep the grease out.

1. Transfer the parcooked beans to a 13 by 9-inch disposable aluminum pan. Wrap tightly in foil and poke several holes in the foil so that the juices from the ribs can flavor the beans.

2. When you're ready to add more coals, nestle the beans in the pan already on the bottom of the grill. Replace the cooking grate, making sure to position the ribs directly above the beans.

3. In step 4 of Kansas City Sticky Ribs on page 150 (when new coals are added), nestle the pan with the beans inside the disposable pan already in the grill. Replace the cooking grate and position the ribs directly above the beans. Cover the grill and cook until the beans are smoky and completely tender, about 2 hours. Discard the foil, stir in the remaining ½ cup barbecue sauce, and season with salt. Serve.

Rating Bread-and-Butter Pickles

TEN TASTERS RATED SEVEN NATIONALLY AVAILABLE brands of bread-and-butter pickles, rating them on flavor and crunch. The pickles are listed in order of preference and are available in supermarkets.

HIGHLY RECOMMENDED
Cascadian Farm Bread & Butter Chips
$3.99 for 24 ounces

Tasters praised these organic cukes for their natural sweet-and-tangy flavor and pleasant crunch.

RECOMMENDED
Bubbies Bread & Butter Chips
$4.69 for 33 ounces

These small-producer slices picked up a subtle, briny tang from their all-natural solution.

RECOMMENDED WITH RESERVATIONS
Vlasic Bread & Butter Chips
$2.50 for 24 ounces

Your basic, well-balanced sweet-sour-salty pickle, but many tasters deemed them "boring."

RECOMMENDED WITH RESERVATIONS
Mt. Olive Bread & Butter Chips
$2.69 for 16 ounces

These petite chips were especially crunchy, but their "fake," "saccharine" flavor was overwhelming.

NOT RECOMMENDED
Mrs. Fanning's Bread 'n Butter Pickles
$1.99 for 14 ounces

Their strange tawny hue, "mushy" texture, and "soapy" flavor made tasters' faces scrunch up.

NOT RECOMMENDED
Vlasic Zesty Bread & Butter Chips
$2.50 for 24 ounces

These pickles' extra "zing" is a distraction from true bread-and-butter pickle flavor.

NOT RECOMMENDED
Claussen Bread 'N Butter Sandwich Slices
$3.49 for 20 ounces

These sandwich stackers live in the refrigerated section of the supermarket but taste no better than the other shelf-stable samples packed in corn syrup.

TASTING LAB: Bread-and-Butter Pickles

MANY BARBECUE AFICIONADOS ARE QUICK TO POINT out that a plate of smoky barbecue or a grilled burger isn't complete without the sweet and sour tang and snappy crunch of bread-and-butter pickles. After crunching our way through several brands, we learned that not just any crispy cuke will do. Though some form of sweetener is essential for preserving and flavoring a bread-and-butter chip, many brands have opted to replace real sugar with cheaper high-fructose corn syrup. Five of the seven pickle brands we sampled list this shelf-stable syrup as their second ingredient, which led to complaints about "artificial sweetness" and "syrupy" flavors. Our two favorites—Cascadian Farm and Bubbies—are made with real sugar, and our tasters could tell the difference.

EQUIPMENT CORNER:
Barbecue Thermometers

WITH SLOW AND LOW BARBECUING, IT'S ESPECIALLY important to monitor the temperature of the fire without opening the grill lid. If your grill doesn't have a built-in thermometer, it's a good idea to buy one that will fit through the vent holes of your grill lid. We tested eight oven and barbecue thermometers, digital and dial-faced, all of which could slip through the grill lid's vent holes. We found a surprising range of features and prices—from $7.99 to $99. Our two favorites turned out to be the cheapest models tested: the Polder Dual Sensor Thermometer ($10) and the Weber 9815 Replacement Food Thermometer ($7.99). For a couple dollars more than the Weber, the Polder gives you simultaneous meat and oven temperature readings. On the grill, a heatproof silicone finger-grip under the dial allows you to take the thermometer out of the lid vents and check the temperature of the meat.

Rating Barbecue Thermometers

WE TESTED EIGHT OVEN AND BARBECUE THERMOMETERS (ALL OF WHICH COULD SLIP THROUGH THE GRILL LID'S vent holes), rating them on accuracy, speed at registering temperatures, and clear, user-friendly design. The thermometers are listed in order of preference. See www.americastestkitchen.com for up-to-date prices and mail-order sources for top-rated products.

HIGHLY RECOMMENDED
Polder Dual Sensor Thermometer
$10
We loved that this well-priced meat and oven thermometer easily doubled for use at the barbecue.

RECOMMENDED
Weber 9815 Replacement Food Thermometer
$7.99
The 1¾-inch dial face was a bit hard to read, but this bargain probe gets the job done.

RECOMMENDED WITH RESERVATIONS
Polder Dual Sensor Thermometer/Timer
$24.99
The screen is easy to read and the probe's wire extends nearly three feet for easy maneuverability, but an accurate temperature reading took far too long—roughly 45 minutes—to register. Plus, a kickstand for the screen would have been a helpful accessory.

RECOMMENDED WITH RESERVATIONS
Tel-Tru BQ250 BBQ Thermometer
$28
Your basic dial-faced probe, with a hefty price tag and a longer-than-average time to register the temperature.

RECOMMENDED WITH RESERVATIONS
Tel-Tru BQ300 BBQ Thermometer
$49
This larger version of their BQ250 includes a range chart for "smoke," "barbecue," and "grill," but takes too long to register the temperature.

RECOMMENDED WITH RESERVATIONS
Maverick RediChek Remote Wireless Smoker Thermometer
$49.99
If the on/off switches on the transmitter and the receiver weren't so inaccessible and the remote range was truly 100 feet, this digital instrument would be as convenient as it advertises.

NOT RECOMMENDED
Old Smokey 2" Smoker Thermometer
$24.99
Not only was this thermometer's probe far too short, but its registering temperature was roughly 60 degrees off.

NOT RECOMMENDED
Tel-Tru BQ575 BBQ Thermometer
$99
One tester commented that this enormous model—five inches in diameter with oversized numbers—would be "perfect for people wearing beer goggles." Otherwise, the dial's advertised adjustable head requires several minutes with a screwdriver, and the model takes more time than that to gauge the temperature. Besides, nobody needs a thermometer that weighs more than 1 pound.

Scoring the fish's skin helps ensure that our blackened fillets cook evenly and remain flat, rather than curled and buckled. And blooming the spices in melted butter gives our spice rub a deep, rich flavor.

FISH ON THE grill

CHAPTER 13

Generally, those who grill consider themselves a fearless lot. They're delighted by wacky recipes like beer can chicken and will tackle behemoth cuts of meat like beef tenderloin or racks of ribs without breaking a sweat. But present them with simple fish fillets and they drop their grill tongs and run. We understand because we've been there. Fish fillets might look innocent, but once their delicate flesh hits the grill, there's no getting them off without a fight. Simply put, fish sticks. And because fish is delicate, in comparison to meat, the flesh easily dries out. We decided to take the fear out of grilling fish and in doing so we chose two recipes: blackened grilled snapper and glazed salmon.

Blackening fish is a popular Cajun technique that results in moist, smoky fish in a complex-flavored, spicy crust. But getting the spices to adhere to the fish can be tricky, and preventing the spice rub from burning on the grill is also a challenge. We'd have these issues, along with preventing the fish from sticking to the grill, to contend with.

Glazed salmon is a treat. Spicy sweet glazes are a perfect match to rich, meaty salmon. But adding a glaze to a fish that's already prone to sticking might be asking for trouble. Undeterred, the test kitchen was still determined to find a fuss-free foolproof method for this dish.

BLACKENED SNAPPER

WHAT WE WANTED: Blackened, not burnt, fish, with a spicy, well-seasoned crust and moist interior.

Ever since Paul Prudhomme popularized his signature dish of blackened redfish in the 1980s, blackened anything has become synonymous with nouvelle Cajun cookery. Creating the recipe's namesake crust required ¾ pound of melted butter in two applications: first to coat the fish before it was dredged in a mixture of spices, and again to drizzle over both sides of the fish as it seared in a white-hot cast-iron skillet. The result was a dark brown, crusty, sweet-smoky, toasted spice exterior that provided a rich contrast to the moist, mild-flavored fish inside. But achieving this meant cooking in a well-ventilated kitchen. In *The Prudhomme Family Cookbook,* the author recommends the recipe be made either outdoors or in a commercial kitchen, since the process creates "an incredible amount of smoke that will set off your own and your neighbors' smoke alarms."

We wanted to make this dish at home, but not if it necessitated a visit from the fire department. That left us with no choice but to take the entire project outdoors onto the grill. Our first attempts revealed several challenges. The fish almost always stuck to the grate, leaving us with a pile of shredded fillets. They either burned on the outside by the time the flesh cooked through or failed to get dark and crusty enough. Complicating matters, the fillets often curled midway through cooking, resulting in burnt edges and an arched, barely blackened center. Because redfish is found primarily near the Gulf Coast, we used nationally available red snapper—another mild fish with firm, white flesh. Red snapper's pinkish-red skin is delicious when cooked to a thin, crisp state. But like the redfish, whenever the snapper

was placed skin side down over the high heat of the grates, it would buckle. By simply scoring the skin, we got the fillets to stay flat—an easy fix.

A cast-iron pan is another of the recipe's defining elements. We quickly cast it aside, however, as it couldn't comfortably hold two fillets and failed to deliver a full grilled flavor. Cooking directly on the grate eliminated the need to cook in batches. After some experimentation, we decided to use a modified two-level fire (see "The Right Fire," page 161). But even once we had our grilling technique down, the fillets had an annoying habit of sticking to the grate, and efforts to dislodge them resulted in the type of shredded fillets only a feline could love (see "Preventing Stuck Fish," page 160). The solution was right in front of us: the aluminum pan that was serving as a holding tray for our

grilling utensils. By inverting the pan over the grate while it preheated, we were able to get the grill super-hot—almost 200 degrees hotter than normal—and incinerate any nasty gunk. We now had a really clean surface on which to cook the fish.

The basic dry rub we'd been experimenting with remained unexciting, since so many spices burned on the grill. Our blackened spirits were lifted when we added coriander, which could take the heat and gave the spice rub a bright floral note. Prudhomme's recipe calls for garlic powder and onion powder (fresh equivalents would burn), items not usually stocked in our test kitchen. We found the powders gave the rub a robust flavor boost that tasters enjoyed.

Although our rub was improving, we wanted still more flavor, so we tried blooming the spices—that is, releasing their trapped flavors—by sautéing them in melted butter until they turned several shades darker (from bright red to dark, rusty brown) and emitted a deep, fragrant aroma. Once the spice mixture cooled to room temperature, we broke up any large clumps with a fork and applied it to the fish in a thin layer: no extra melted butter necessary. By the time the fillets were fully cooked, they were also well blackened on all sides, and—most important—the spice crust had finally acquired the proper depth and richness. At last, we had blackened fish that looked and tasted like it had come out of a bona fide New Orleans establishment, with no indoor smell to mask, mess to clean up, or walls to repaint.

WHAT WE LEARNED: To prevent fish from sticking to the cooking grate and burning, begin with a spotless grill. Heat the grill, then place a disposable aluminum pan over the grate—this increases the heat on the grate, incinerating any remaining residue. To prevent the fish from buckling on the grill, score the fish's skin, which will encourage them to lie flat. And for the spice rub, bloom the spices in melted butter on the stovetop before applying the rub to the fish—blooming intensifies the spices' flavor for blackened fish with deep, well-rounded flavor.

CHARCOAL-GRILLED BLACKENED RED SNAPPER

serves 4

If using fillets that are ½ inch or thinner, reduce the cooking time to 3 minutes per side. If using fillets that are 1 inch or thicker, increase the cooking time on the second side by 2 minutes, moving the fish to the cooler side of the grill after the second side has browned. If you cannot find red snapper, substitute striped bass, halibut, or catfish. Making the slashes in the skin requires a sharp knife. If your knife isn't sharp enough, try cutting through the skin with a serrated knife. However, cut in one direction (don't saw) and be careful to not cut into the flesh. If you choose not to eat the skin, be sure to remove it after cooking rather than beforehand. Serve the fish with lemon wedges and Rémoulade on page 161 or Pineapple and Cucumber Salsa with Mint on page 162.

- 2 tablespoons sweet paprika
- 2 teaspoons onion powder
- 2 teaspoons garlic powder
- ¾ teaspoon ground coriander
- ¾ teaspoon salt
- ¼ teaspoon cayenne pepper
- ¼ teaspoon ground black pepper
- ¼ teaspoon ground white pepper
- 3 tablespoons unsalted butter
  13 by 9-inch disposable aluminum roasting pan
- 4 red snapper fillets, 6 to 8 ounces each, ¾ inch thick
  Vegetable oil for cooking grate

1. Combine the paprika, onion powder, garlic powder, coriander, salt, and peppers in a small bowl. Melt the butter in a 10-inch skillet over medium heat. When the foaming subsides, stir in the spice mixture. Cook, stirring frequently, until fragrant and the spices turn a dark rust color, 2 to 3 minutes. Transfer the mixture to a pie plate and cool, stirring occasionally, to room temperature, about 10 minutes. Once cooled, use a fork to break up any large clumps.

TECHNIQUE: Preventing Stuck Fish

We knew from past grill testing that preheating the grate before scraping it with a grill brush was the most effective way to keep food from sticking. When it came to delicate fish, the grates had to be spotless. Thinking how the self-cleaning cycle in an oven transforms caked-on gunk into fine gray ash by superheating the interior, we decided to replicate the process with an inverted aluminum pan. This boosted the grill temperature to 818 degrees: Residue and stuck-on bits didn't stand a chance. This trick, along with a few others, will allow you to grill any fish without it sticking.

1. Chilling
Keep the fish refrigerated until ready to grill. At room temperature, fillets become floppy.

2. Superheating
Place a disposable aluminum pan upside down over the hot side of the grill. Cover and heat for 5 minutes.

3. Scraping/Oiling
Scrape the grate clean with a grill brush. Then wipe the grate with oil-dipped paper towels.

4. Positioning
Place the fish lengthwise at a right angle to the grill grate bars with the skin side facing down.

5. Flipping
Slide one spatula underneath the fillet to lift; use another to support the fish while it is being flipped.

2. Light a large chimney starter filled two-thirds with charcoal (4 quarts, or about 65 briquettes) and burn until the coals are fully ignited and partially covered with a thin layer of ash, 15 to 20 minutes. Build a modified two-level fire by arranging the coals to cover one half of the grill. Position a cooking grate over the coals, place a disposable roasting pan upside down on the grate directly over the coals, cover the grill, and heat the grate until hot, about 5 minutes. Remove the roasting pan and scrape the grate clean with a grill brush. The grill is ready when the coals are hot (you can hold your hand 5 inches above the grate for 2 to 3 seconds).

3. Meanwhile, pat the fillets dry on both sides with paper towels. Using a sharp knife, make shallow diagonal slashes every inch along the skin side of the fish, being careful not to cut into the flesh. Place the fillets skin side up on a rimmed baking sheet or a large plate. Using your fingers, rub the spice mixture in a thin, even layer on the top and sides of the fish. Flip the fillets over and repeat on the other side (you should use all of the spice mixture). Refrigerate until needed.

4. Lightly dip a wad of paper towels in the oil; holding the wad with tongs, wipe the cooking grate. Place the fish

TECHNIQUE: The Right Fire

To concentrate heat and promote better blackening, we piled all the lit coals onto one side of the grill. The cooler side can be used to finish cooking fillets that are slightly thicker.

RÉMOULADE

makes about ½ cup

The rémoulade can be refrigerated for up to three days.

- ½   cup mayonnaise
- 1½ teaspoons sweet pickle relish
- 1   teaspoon hot sauce
- 1   teaspoon juice from 1 lemon
- 1   teaspoon minced fresh parsley leaves
- ½   teaspoon capers, drained and rinsed
- ½   teaspoon Dijon mustard
- 1   small garlic clove, chopped coarse (about ½ teaspoon)
    Salt and ground black pepper

Pulse all the ingredients except the salt and pepper in a food processor until well combined but not smooth, about 10 pulses. Season with salt and pepper to taste. Transfer to a serving bowl.

lengthwise at a right angle to the direction of the bars on the cooking grate, skin side down, on the hot side of the grill. Grill, uncovered, until the skin is very dark brown and crisp, 3 to 4 minutes. Using a thin metal spatula, carefully flip the fish and continue to grill until dark brown and beginning to flake and the center is opaque but still moist, about 5 minutes longer. Serve immediately.

VARIATION
GAS-GRILLED BLACKENED RED SNAPPER
Follow the recipe for Charcoal-Grilled Blackened Red Snapper, skipping step 2. Turn all the burners to high, cover, and heat the grill until very hot, about 15 minutes. Use a grill brush to scrape the grate clean. Proceed with the recipe from step 3, leaving the burners on high and cooking with the lid up.

GETTING IT RIGHT:
Preventing Buckling Fish
Skin-on fillets will buckle when grilled because the skin will shrink back, pulling the flesh along with it (top). They remain flat if the skin is scored first (bottom), which prevents it from contracting more quickly than the flesh.

A Fishy Mess
Cooked fillet with unscored skin, buckled

A Flat Fillet
Cooked fillet with scored skin, perfectly flat

PINEAPPLE AND CUCUMBER SALSA WITH MINT

makes about 3 cups

This salsa can be made spicier by mincing and adding the chile's seeds and ribs.

½   large pineapple, peeled, cored, and cut into ¼-inch dice (about 2 cups)
½   medium cucumber, peeled, seeded, and cut into ¼-inch dice (about 1 cup)
1   small shallot, minced (about 2 tablespoons)
1   medium serrano chile, seeds and ribs removed, then minced (about 2 tablespoons)
2   tablespoons chopped fresh mint leaves
½   teaspoon grated fresh ginger
1–2 tablespoons juice from 1 lime
     Salt
     Sugar

In a medium bowl, toss together the pineapple, cucumber, shallot, chile, mint, ginger, 1 tablespoon lime juice, and ½ teaspoon salt; let stand at room temperature to blend the flavors, 15 to 30 minutes. Adjust the seasoning with additional lime juice and salt, and add sugar as needed if the pineapple is tart; serve.

TASTING LAB: Blackening Spice Rubs

AFTER SAMPLING SIX STORE-BOUGHT Cajun spice rubs, we found that mixing your own delivers superior results. But if you really want to buy a rub, Paul Prudhomme's Blackened Redfish Magic has the best blend of flavors.

THE BEST SPICE RUB
Paul Prudhomme's Blackened Redfish Magic fared best among the spice rubs we tested.

TECHNIQUE: Preparing Pineapple

1. Start by trimming the ends of the pineapple so it will sit flat on a work surface. Cut the pineapple through the ends into four quarters.

2. Place each quarter, cut-side up, on a work surface and slide a knife between the skin and the flesh to remove the skin.

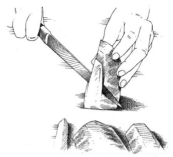

3. Stand each peeled quarter on end and slice off the portion of the tough, light-colored core attached to the inside of the piece. The peeled and cored pineapple can be sliced as desired.

GRILLED GLAZED SALMON

WHAT WE WANTED: Sweet and saucy glazed salmon, complete with a moist interior and caramelized crust—and we wanted the fish to come off the grill in one piece.

Salmon is perfect for glazing and for grilling, but try to do both things at once and the fish desperately wants to stick to the grate. The sweet, smoky flavor of glazed grilled salmon makes this recipe very appealing, as does the fact that the mess and dreaded fishy odors stay outside. But how could we make this recipe less frustrating?

Salmon sticks to the grill all by itself. A glaze just compounds the problem, so the glaze had better be good. We tried recipes with maple syrup, honey, brown sugar, jellies, or jams as the base ingredient. Tasters preferred the concentrated sweetness of the jelly-based glazes, which also had just the right consistency to coat and cling to the salmon. Tasters especially appreciated the sweet heat of jalapeño jelly.

But no matter how much we scrubbed the grill grate or how well we oiled it, time after time the sticky, sweet glaze adhered to the grill and wouldn't let go, causing the salmon to tear when we tried to get a spatula under it. Our recipe was literally going up in smoke. We tried cooking the salmon skin side down and not flipping it, sacrificing the skin to the grill when we removed the flesh above it. This worked, but tasters rightfully complained that this salmon didn't have grill marks—or much grill flavor. We needed a better solution.

At home, we regard the grill as an outdoor stove, often putting saucepans right on the grate next to whatever we're grilling. We wondered if we could use a disposable aluminum pie plate as a mini-skillet, so we threw one on the hot grill and tossed a piece of salmon in it. We got some encouraging results: partial browning, some smoke flavor, and no sticking when we flipped the salmon. To get more browning and grill flavor, we downgraded from a thick pie plate to individual pieces of aluminum foil, and this worked like a charm. Now we were getting great grill marks, full

smoke flavor, no sticking, and, if we removed the skin (which most people discard anyway), we could glaze both sides of the salmon. The extra glaze, enriched with butter, even caramelized in the foil "boat," adding another great dimension of flavor.

WHAT WE LEARNED: Grill the salmon fillets in aluminum foil trays set over the grill—the fish will still pick up great smoky flavor, but won't stick to the cooking grate. Jelly is the best base ingredient for a sweet and sticky glaze. For the deepest flavor, brush some glaze over the fish toward the end of grilling, so it caramelizes, and spoon the remaining glaze, enriched with butter, over the fish just before serving.

CHARCOAL-GRILLED GLAZED SALMON

serves 4

Use any brand of heavy-duty aluminum foil to make the grill trays, but be sure to spray the foil with nonstick cooking spray. Alternatively, you can use Reynolds Wrap nonstick aluminum foil and skip the cooking spray.

½   cup jalapeño jelly
½   cup packed fresh cilantro leaves and stems
1   teaspoon grated zest and 2 tablespoons juice from 1 large lime
2   medium garlic cloves, minced or pressed through a garlic press (about 2 teaspoons)
2   scallions, chopped rough
2   tablespoons unsalted butter
4   salmon fillets (each 6 to 8 ounces and 1¼ inches thick), skin removed (see page 165)
    Salt and pepper

1. Process the jelly, cilantro, lime zest, lime juice, garlic, and scallions in a food processor or blender until smooth. Heat the glaze in a small saucepan over medium heat until just bubbling, 2 to 3 minutes. Remove from the heat and transfer ¼ cup of the glaze to a small bowl to cool slightly. Stir the butter into the glaze remaining in the saucepan, cover, and set aside.

2. Light a large chimney starter filled with charcoal (6 quarts, or about 100 briquettes) and burn until the coals are covered with a fine gray ash, about 20 to 25 minutes. Pour the coals over three-quarters of the grill; set the cooking grate in place, cover, and let the grill heat up for 5 minutes.

3. Following the photo above, use heavy-duty foil to make four 7 by 5-inch trays. Coat the trays with cooking spray. Season the salmon with salt and pepper, brush each side of each fillet with ½ tablespoon reserved glaze (without the butter), and place skinned side up on the trays.

TECHNIQUE: Making a Foil Tray

Cut out four rectangles of heavy-duty aluminum foil and crimp the edges until each tray measures 7 by 5 inches.

---

4. Place the trays with the salmon over the hot side of the grill and grill until the glaze forms a golden brown crust, 6 to 8 minutes. (Move the fillets to a cooler part of the grill if they darken too soon.) Using tongs, flip the salmon and cook 1 minute. Spoon half of the buttered glaze on the salmon and cook until the center of each fillet is still just translucent, about 1 minute. Transfer the salmon to a platter and spoon the remaining buttered glaze over it. Serve.

GAS-GRILLED GLAZED SALMON

Follow the recipe for Charcoal-Grilled Glazed Salmon through step 1. Turn on all the burners to high, cover, and heat the grill until very hot, about 15 minutes. Use a grill brush to scrape the grate clean. Proceed with the recipe from step 3, leaving the burners on high and cooking with the lid down.

ORANGE-SESAME GLAZE

Replace the lime zest and juice with lemon zest and juice, and replace the jalapeño jelly with orange marmalade. Puree 2 tablespoons oyster-flavored sauce and 1 teaspoon toasted sesame oil with the other glaze ingredients. Add 1 teaspoon toasted sesame seeds along with the butter.

SPICY APPLE GLAZE

Replace the lime zest and juice with 2 tablespoons cider vinegar and replace the jalapeño jelly with apple jelly. Puree ½ teaspoon red pepper flakes with the other glaze ingredients.

TECHNIQUE:

Removing Skin from Salmon

Many grilled salmon recipes use skin-on fillets, but we prefer to trim off the skin for our Charcoal-Grilled Glazed Salmon, making a flavorful, glazed crust possible on both sides of the fish. In case the fishmonger doesn't remove the skin for you, here's how to do it yourself. If you don't have a flexible boning knife, a sharp chef's knife can be used.

1. Using a sharp boning knife, insert the blade just above the skin about 1 inch from one end of the fillet. Cut through the nearest end, keeping the blade just above the skin.

2. Rotate the fish and grab the loose piece of skin. Run the knife between the flesh and the skin, making sure the knife is just above the skin, until the skin is completely removed.

EQUIPMENT CORNER: Barbecue Mitts

YOU CAN PAY ANYWHERE FROM $5 FOR A SIMPLE cotton barbecue mitt to $33 for a high-tech model. Does advanced technology equal advanced performance? For a dedicated outdoor cook, a good barbecue mitt is an invaluable grilling accessory. After all, if you can't pick up a hot cooking grate or reach over the coals to tend to the food, you might as well stay indoors. But choosing a barbecue mitt isn't as easy as you might think. Models have lately turned high-tech, offering a confusing array of materials and features, including leather, rawhide, treated cotton, neoprene (the same rubber used to make wet suits), Kevlar (a fiber used in bulletproof vests), Nomex (a plastic used in uniforms for race-car drivers, firefighters, and military pilots), and silicone (a rubber-like injected polymer). These modern mitts are expensive, selling for up to $33 apiece. We wondered if these innovations are really worth the extra money.

Fancy features aside, a barbecue mitt must meet two core requirements: enough heat resistance to keep hands from burning and enough pliability to keep cooks from inadvertently dropping grill grates or smashing food. Because impressive dexterity is of zero importance if you can't pick up the cooking grate in the first place, initial testing focused on heat resistance. Our lineup consisted of eight mitts, including the winner of a previous oven mitt testing, a Nomex/Kevlar model from Kool-Tek. Once outdoors, testers were asked to hold mitt-clad hands three inches over a 600-degree grill. As the seconds ticked by, testers were questioned about their comfort level. The Leather Grill Glove showed the best performance in this exercise; its thick leather provided superior protection during a minute-long stint over hot coals. Following the success of this leather model, we were optimistic about the Mr. Bar-B-Q Rawhide Barbecue Mitt. But our hopes were dashed when our hands quickly became uncomfortable: This mitt was far too thin to offer much protection at all. Cotton mitts—the Charcoal Companion BBQ Mitt, the Weber Barbecue Mitt (a cotton model treated with flame retardants, like children's pajamas), and the Ducane Barbecue Mitt—all did a fine job of protecting hands from the scorching heat of the grill.

When it came to the silicone mitt, protection was less than stellar. Testers flatly rejected the silicone OXO. While this mitt initially stayed cool when held over the grill and protected very well when in direct contact with the hot grate, we were surprised at how warm (and sweaty) our hands got while using the mitt for just 30 seconds, as its outside surfaces became almost too hot to touch.

Until this point, we had been careful to keep the mitts dry, as per manufacturer warnings. But such a caveat seemed a cop-out for a product meant for settings in which rain might be in the forecast. So we dunked each mitt briefly in water, let it dry overnight, then repeated the heat-resistance test. The silicone and rubber models were waterproof, as advertised, while the leather gloves initially resisted moisture but then soaked through and stayed that way. The damp gloves still protected us from the heat of the grill, however. The cotton mitts got soaked and took a long time to dry, though they also protected our hands while wet. Next, we evaluated the mitts' effect on testers' dexterity when flipping zucchini slices with tongs and reaching to the back of the grill to turn potatoes with our hands. In most cases, we found that heavy, thick fabrics significantly impaired agility. Models that reduced dexterity slipped in our hands, allowed zucchini to escape from tongs during flipping, and made picking up hot potatoes nearly impossible. In fact, some models were so thick that we couldn't comfortably grasp a pair of tongs.

The exception among thick gloves was the Grill Life Leather Grill Glove, whose five-fingered shape was surprisingly comfortable and nimble. We also had decent luck with advanced synthetic models, namely the Kool-Tek and the Duncan's Bar-B-Que Grips. These mitts had thin layers of fabric, allowing the grill cook to feel very much in control of the tongs and potatoes. As for the silicone mitt, it was thick and slippery, making it extremely difficult and frustrating to maneuver.

Last, we briefly (and carefully) inserted each mitt directly into a flame to simulate a flare-up, a common occurrence in the outdoor kitchen. The Grill Life Leather Grill Glove aced the test, braving the fire unscathed. The cotton mitts, on the other hand, scorched and charred. And since neither the Kool-Tek nor the Duncan mitt is made entirely of flameproof material, both emerged from the tests with char marks in certain sections, with the seam on the Duncan's mitt briefly catching fire.

Having analyzed fabric choices, we turned to the question of length. Testers discounted the shortest mitt tested, the 12-inch Mr. Bar-B-Q Rawhide Mitt, which left much of the arm uncomfortably exposed. While 15 inches is the optimal length for indoor oven mitts, testers wanted more security over the grill, especially with large gas grills, which can be as deep as 35 inches. We found that 17- or 18-inch models were long enough to protect our arms while still allowing good maneuverability. In the end, the highest rating went to the Grill Life Leather Grill Glove: Its heavy leather and 18-inch length kept hands and arms cool, and the glove

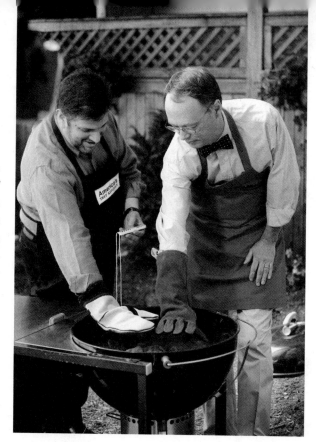

shape provided a surprising amount of control. The Charcoal Companion BBQ Mitt is also a good bet. It is comfortable, keeps hands cool, and doesn't cut down on a cook's dexterity. However, as with all of the cotton mitts, it took a long time to dry out after being soaked in water (though heat resistance was not affected) and scorched in a direct flame.

And what about our favorite kitchen oven mitt, the Kool-Tek? If you are an occasional griller and want a dual-purpose accessory, you may want to consider this mitt, which didn't restrict dexterity, repelled water nicely, and provided good protection against brief direct flame contact. Keep in mind, however, that while an oven mitt needs to protect a cook's hand for only the short time it takes to transport a hot dish from the oven to the counter, a barbecue mitt must protect for longer periods—while extended over a hot grill flipping numerous shrimp or reaching to the back of the grill to turn corncobs or potatoes. The thicker Grill Life and Charcoal Companion gloves might sacrifice some flexibility (which makes them unsuitable for pulling a pie plate out of a hot oven), but these top-rated, reasonably priced gloves do offer increased protection from heat—which is exactly what you need when cooking outdoors.

Rating Barbecue Mitts

WE TESTED EIGHT BARBECUE MITTS, EVALUATING THEM ON HEAT RESISTANCE, DEXTERITY, AND DURABILITY. THE MITTS are listed in order of preference. See www.americastestkitchen.com for up-to-date prices and mail-order sources for top-rated products.

HIGHLY RECOMMENDED
Grill Life Leather Grill Gloves
$13.99 (for pair); leather
These gloves won us over by keeping our hands and arms cool and well protected. Offered nice control when picking up food with either tongs or hands. No flare-up could hurt them.

RECOMMENDED
Charcoal Companion BBQ Mitt
$8.95; treated cotton
This mitt kept our hands as cool as any other and performed well in dexterity testing. Flare-ups caused a scorch mark, but the mitt did not burn. As with all cotton models, once wet, this mitt stayed wet. Some testers felt the thumb section was a bit short.

RECOMMENDED WITH RESERVATIONS
Kool-Tek Protective Apparel
$32.95; Nomex, Kevlar, and treated cotton
Testers liked this relatively thin mitt's flexibility, and wetness didn't bother it one bit. Because the fabric is not especially breathable, our hands began to sweat after 30 seconds of use and the exterior of the mitt became hot to the touch.

RECOMMENDED WITH RESERVATIONS
Weber Barbecue Mitt
$5.95; treated cotton
Although it's similar in appearance to the Charcoal Companion BBQ Mitt, testers felt this model wasn't as agile, nor did it fit as well: Dexterity was moderately limited. Otherwise, like its near twin, this inexpensive cotton mitt kept hands cool, scorched but didn't burn, and provided effective protection even when very wet.

RECOMMENDED WITH RESERVATIONS
Duncan's Bar-B-Que Grips
$19.99; synthetic rubber
While this mitt offered a high degree of maneuverability, hands soon became hot and sweaty, with the somewhat slippery outside surface becoming very hot. While flare-ups didn't damage the rubber, the seam stitching burned when exposed to flame.

NOT RECOMMENDED
Ducane Barbecue Mitt
$4.99; treated cotton
This basic mitt kept our hands cool, but at the expense of dexterity—the tongs kept slipping from our grasp. It also caught fire when inserted into a flame.

NOT RECOMMENDED
OXO Good Grips Silicone Barbecue Mitt with Magnet
$24.95; treated cotton and silicone
Our hands quickly became uncomfortably warm as the outside surface of this mitt heated up. Every tester complained about the thumb angle, which pinched the area between the thumb and forefinger.

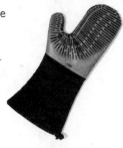

NOT RECOMMENDED
Mr. Bar-B-Q Rawhide Barbecue Mitt
$9.99; rawhide
The rawhide was too thin to keep our hands cool, the mitt was too short to protect our arms, and there was so much excess fabric on this "one-size-fits-all" mitt that dexterity was limited.

Julia shows Chris that skewered and butterflied Cornish hens stay flat on the grill and thus cook more evenly.

GRILLED CORNISH
hens

CHAPTER 14

Elegant entertaining and the grill don't always seem
to go hand in hand—ribs, burgers, and sticky barbecue chicken served
with lots of napkins come to mind more often. But consider Cornish
game hens—each hen makes a serving, giving each person white and
dark meat. And these small birds are a cinch to serve—the host needn't
worry about fussy last-minute carving. We've always enjoyed roasting
game hens and thought the grill might deliver even more flavor to
the tender meat and produce wonderfully burnished, ultra-crispy skin.
But the test kitchen is well aware of the challenges in grilling poultry
and especially whole birds, with their uneven shape, which can cook
through at varying rates, resulting in dry, overcooked meat. We'd need
to find a way to deliver moist meat all around and a crust that was crisp
and golden brown, not burned.

Rice salad is a lighter, more elegant alternative to other warm
weather salads like potato salad and pasta salad. But chilling rice can
turn the grains hard and chewy. And sometimes the rice can soak up
the dressing, turning the salad heavy and dull. We developed a method
for preparing rice salad that overcomes these pitfalls to deliver tender
rice, crunchy bits of vegetables, and a light, bright dressing to bring it
all together.

IN THIS CHAPTER

THE RECIPES
Grill-Roasted Cornish Game
    Hens
Grill-Roasted Cornish Game
    Hens on a Gas Grill

Boiled Rice for Rice Salad
Rice Salad with Oranges, Olives,
    and Almonds
Rice Salad with Cherry Tomatoes,
    Parmesan, Peas, and Ham

EQUIPMENT CORNER
Charcoal Chimney Starters

SCIENCE DESK
Starch and Rice

TASTING LAB
Basmati Rice

GRILLED CORNISH GAME HENS

WHAT WE WANTED: An elegant alternative to grilled chicken—crisp-skinned Cornish hens with moist, juicy meat infused with great grilled flavor.

Cornish game hens look good on the plate, and since one hen makes a single serving, everyone gets tender portions of both white and dark meat. Most home cooks roast these elegant birds, but grilling has the potential to add smoky flavor and deliver really crisp skin. We started our testing by trying to adapt the test kitchen's method for grilling whole chickens. After the chicken is treated to a short brine and spice rub, it's placed in the middle of a hot grill with coals and soaked wood chunks banked to either side. An hour later, the chicken emerges beautifully bronzed. We thought we could easily translate this method to game hens. Not quite.

Our first modification was to put a drip pan under the hens to catch the rendered fat while also creating defined banks for the charcoal. Getting crisp skin without overcooking the delicate breast meat was trickier. The closest our initial testing came was spotty patches of browned and flabby skin. This was a hurdle we'd have to clear before we could begin worrying about a spice rub and finishing glaze.

Whereas grill-roasting large birds for an hour produces mahogany skin and a juicy interior, keeping game hens on the grill for an hour made for bone-dry meat. Many recipes called for removing the backbone (a process called butterflying). This would put all of the skin on one side, which could face the coals and crisp more quickly. Butterflying also makes each bird a uniform thickness, which promotes even cooking. We used scissors to remove the delicate backbone and to cut the bone dividing the breast halves.

Although these splayed-open birds browned evenly and cooked uniformly, presentation was another matter. Turning backbone-less birds resulted in the legs flipping over the breast and the scant piece of skin holding the breast to the thighs tearing. Securing the legs to the body seemed like our best option. We used metal skewers to poke and stick a dozen hens into various contortionist positions before we landed on a method that worked (see "Butterflying and Skewering Game Hens for the Grill," on page 172). This kebab-like presentation also made it easier to fit the birds on the cooking grate.

In flavor, texture, and appearance, tasters agreed these Cornish game hens were finally in a class by themselves. But we still thought they could benefit from a last blast of intense heat to make the skin crispier. To avoid charred birds, we found it best to sear them last, not first, as is traditionally the case with meats. Grill-roasting the birds with the lid down to an internal temperature of 160 to 165 degrees before finishing them over the now-cooler coals gave them just the right amount of browning and crispy skin. All we had left to do was build upon the grilled, smoky flavor via a rub and a glaze. After trying rubs with up to 20 ingredients, we settled on a seven-ingredient version that gave the hens a sweet and savory complexity. The rub helped crisp the skin even further, giving it a gorgeous mahogany hue. Finishing the birds with a quick glaze of ketchup, brown sugar, and soy sauce provided the crowning touch.

WHAT WE LEARNED: Brine the hens for well-seasoned, juicy meat and butterfly them (remove the backbone), so that they lie flat and are of uniform thickness throughout—this ensures that the meat cooks evenly. To keep the hens intact throughout grilling (and make them easier to turn on the hot grill), run a skewer through the hens to secure the legs to the body. A spice rub, applied to the hens at the outset, adds flavor and promotes browning. A combination of grill-roasting (grilling, covered, over indirect, gentle heat) until the hens are cooked through and then a final blast of direct heat browns and crisps the skin. And a sweet and tangy glaze, brushed on the hens toward the end of grilling, gives their crisp skin deep flavor and a mahogany luster.

GRILL-ROASTED CORNISH GAME HENS

serves 4

If your hens weigh 1½ to 2 pounds, cook three instead of four, brine them for an extra 15 minutes, and extend the cooking time in step 5 by 10 to 15 minutes. Thaw frozen game hens in the refrigerator for 24 to 36 hours before brining. To add smoke flavor to the hens, use the optional wood chunks. Note that you will need four 8- to 10-inch flat metal skewers to secure the hens. If you want to use kosher salt in place of table salt, use 2 cups Diamond Crystal kosher salt or 1½ cups Morton's kosher salt.

hens

- 1 cup table salt (see note)
- 4 Cornish game hens (1¼ to 1½ pounds each), butterflied according to illustrations 1 through 4 on page 172
- 2 tablespoons brown sugar
- 1 tablespoon paprika
- 2 teaspoons garlic powder
- 2 teaspoons chili powder
- 1 teaspoon ground black pepper
- 1 teaspoon ground coriander
- ⅛ teaspoon cayenne pepper
- 4 (3-inch) wood chunks (optional)
  Disposable 16 by 12-inch aluminum roasting pan
  Vegetable oil for the cooking grate

barbecue glaze

- ½ cup ketchup
- 2 tablespoons brown sugar
- 1 tablespoon soy sauce
- 1 tablespoon distilled white vinegar
- 1 tablespoon prepared yellow mustard
- 1 medium garlic clove, minced or pressed through a garlic press (about 1 teaspoon)

1. FOR THE HENS: Dissolve the salt in 4 quarts cold water in a large container. Submerge the hens in brine, cover with plastic wrap, and refrigerate 1 hour.

2. While the hens brine, combine the sugar and spices in a small bowl. If using the wood chunks, soak them in water for 1 hour; drain. Remove the birds from the brine and rinse inside and out with cold running water; pat dry with paper towels. Following illustrations 5 through 8, use an 8- to 10-inch flat metal skewer to secure each hen. Rub the hens evenly with the spice mixture and refrigerate while preparing the grill.

3. TO MAKE THE GLAZE: Cook all the ingredients in a small saucepan over medium heat, stirring occasionally, until thick and slightly reduced, about 5 minutes. Set aside.

4. TO GRILL THE HENS: Light a large chimney starter filled with charcoal (6 quarts, or about 100 briquettes) and burn until the coals are fully ignited and partially covered with a thin layer of ash, about 20 minutes. Place a disposable aluminum roasting pan in the center of the grill. Empty the coals into the grill, creating equal-sized piles on each side of the pan. Place 2 soaked wood chunks on each pile of coals, if using. Position the cooking grate over the coals, cover the grill, and heat the grate until hot, about 5 minutes; scrape the grate clean with a grill brush. Lightly dip a wad of paper towels in the oil; holding the wad with tongs, wipe the cooking grate.

5. Place the hens, skin side down, on the center of the grill over the aluminum pan. Open the grill lid vents completely and cover, positioning the vents over the hens. Grill-roast the hens until an instant-read thermometer inserted in the thickest part of the thighs registers 160 to 165 degrees and the skin has started to turn golden brown, 20 to 30 minutes.

6. Using tongs, move the birds to the hot sides of the grill (2 hens per side). Cover and continue to cook until browned, about 5 minutes. Brush the birds with half of the glaze; flip and cook for 2 minutes. Brush the remaining glaze over the hens; flip and continue to cook until an instant-read thermometer inserted in the thickest part of the thighs registers 170 to 175 degrees, 1 to 3 minutes longer.

7. Transfer the hens to a cutting board and let rest 10 minutes. Cut in half through the breastbone and serve immediately.

VARIATION

GRILL-ROASTED CORNISH GAME HENS ON A GAS GRILL

1. Follow the recipe for Grill-Roasted Cornish Game Hens through step 3, soaking 1 cup wood chips for 30 minutes if a smoke flavor is desired. Drain the chips and place in a small disposable aluminum pan; set the pan on one burner and replace the cooking grate. Turn all the burners to high, cover, and heat until very hot and the chips are smoking, about 15 minutes (if the chips ignite, use a water-filled spray bottle to extinguish). Scrape the grate clean with a grill brush. Lightly dip a wad of paper towels in the oil; holding the wad with tongs, wipe the cooking grate. Turn all the burners to medium.

2. Place the hens, skin side down, on the grill grate. Cover and grill until the skin is deeply browned and shows grill marks, 10 to 15 minutes. (If the grill has hot spots, you might have to move the hens on the grill.) Using tongs, flip the birds; cover and continue to grill until the thickest part of the thighs registers 160 to 165 degrees on an instant-read thermometer, 10 to 15 minutes more.

TECHNIQUE: Butterflying and Skewering Game Hens for the Grill

1. Remove the Backbone
Use poultry shears to cut through the bones on either side of the backbone.

2. Cut the Breastbone
With the skin side down, make a ¼-inch cut into the bone separating the breast halves.

3. Flatten the Bird
Lightly press on the ribs with your fingers to flatten the game hen.

4. Tuck the Wings
With the skin facing up, fold the wingtips behind the bird to secure them. Brine the birds.

5. Insert the Skewer
Insert a flat metal skewer ½ inch from the end of a drumstick through the skin and meat and out the other side.

6. Skewer the Thigh
Turn the leg so that the end of the drumstick faces the wing, then insert the tip of the skewer into the meaty section of the thigh under the bone.

7. Skewer Across the Bird
Press the skewer all the way through the breast and second thigh. Fold the end of the drumstick toward the wing and insert the skewer ½ inch from the end.

8. Stretch the Skin
Press the skewer so that the blunt end rests against the bird and stretch the skin tight over the legs, thighs, and breast halves.

3. Brush the birds with half of the glaze. Using tongs, flip the birds and cook until deeply browned, 2 to 3 minutes. Brush the remaining glaze over the hens; flip and continue to cook until deeply browned and the thickest part of the thighs registers 170 to 175 degrees on an instant-read thermometer, 2 to 3 minutes more.

4. Transfer the hens to a cutting board and let rest 10 minutes. Cut in half through the breastbone and serve immediately.

EQUIPMENT CORNER:
Charcoal Chimney Starters

WE'VE LONG CONSIDERED A CHIMNEY STARTER TO BE the best way to light charcoal. Shaped like oversized coffee mugs, these metal contraptions are divided into two chambers, the lower of which holds a few sheets of crumpled newspaper that, once lit, ignite the charcoal in the upper chamber. Lately, we've been struck by how many chimney starters there are on the market—and how different they are from the Weber model we use. So we rounded up six chimneys to see which ones worked best.

A few of the chimneys were nonstarters, thanks to their small size. While our Weber holds just enough charcoal (6 quarts) to handle the frequent grilling applications that require high heat, four models held significantly less, at 4 quarts. That's fine for a medium-level fire, but not ideal for getting a deep, dark sear on a porterhouse steak. One model, the Steven Raichlen, had room to accommodate a whopping 7 quarts of charcoal. As far as we're concerned, the more capacity, the better (you can always fill the chimney partway).

Otherwise, the design differences were few. One model was designed with a "trap door"—the metal grate separating the two chambers automatically gives way as the chimney is lifted, depositing the coals in a pile. It's a novel design, but not ideal for building two-level fires. (Pouring the hot coals where you want them is much easier—and much less dangerous—than rearranging them with tongs after the fall.)

A design feature testers did appreciate was a second handle (found on the Weber and the Steven Raichlen), which made for easier-to-control coal distribution. In the end, the no-frills Weber was adequate for most grill sizes. If your behemoth requires more fuel, the Steven Raichlen's extra quart of charcoal may be worth the extra cash. Still not enough? Buy two Webers.

THE BEST CHIMNEY STARTERS
The Weber Rapid Fire Chimney Starter (left) ($16.99) is the right size and has a helpful second handle, and the Steven Raichlen Best of Barbecue Ultimate Chimney Starter (right) ($29.99) is pricey but holds enough coals for large grills.

RICE SALAD

WHAT WE WANTED: Tender grains of rice and vegetables in a light, bright vinaigrette.

Rice makes a light, bright salad when dressed properly and studded with vegetables and herbs. The concept of making rice salad seems quite simple, yet it presents two basic problems. For starters, this understated grain does not hold up to assertive flavors the way pasta can. It is readily bogged down by a vinaigrette that would be well suited to a green salad.

Even more troubling than the delicate dance of flavors is the texture of the rice. Long-grain rice normally just isn't good cold; it tends to turn hard, clumpy, and slightly crunchy. Short-grain rice holds up better as it cools, but it has a sticky heaviness that we didn't want in a rice salad. We needed to isolate a cooking method for long-grain rice that would preserve its fresh-from-the-pan characteristics once cooled.

We began with our favorite technique for cooking rice pilaf. This made for a nice pilaf dish, but its buttery flavor was ill suited to a rice salad; what's more, as the rice cooled, it lost its appealing fluffiness. We then began to test every method of cooking rice imaginable. While many methods cooked up great rice, inevitably the quality deteriorated upon cooling.

We finally realized that the source of these failures was also the source of its initial fluffiness after cooking: amylose, one of the two primary starches contained in rice. When long-grain rice cools, the long amylose molecules form rigid crystals that squeeze out liquid and turn the rice rock-hard. Technically speaking, this process is called retrogradation. We realized that if we were going to come up

with a palatable rice salad, we would need to apply some kind of sorcery to the starch.

In a last-ditch effort, we tried cooking the long-grain rice with the "abundant water" technique, whereby rice is boiled in a large volume of water, just like pasta, until it is tender but not mushy, and cooked through but has not yet begun to fray. At this point, the water is simply strained out. The drawback of this technique is that it tends to turn out rice that tastes waterlogged, but the light texture and separate grains held up so well after cooling that we did not dare to disregard it. Instead, we added a couple of steps

to the process to cope with the waterlogging problem.

Taking a cue from the pilaf recipe, we toasted the rice before boiling to tease out its nutty essence. Actually, its aroma might be better likened to popcorn. We did this, however, without the oil, as we found that oil made the rice heavy and greasy in salad form. (A bonus is that all that's needed to clean the pan is a swipe with a dry towel.)

After the rice was boiled, we spread it across a baking sheet to cool. This creates a great deal of surface area, which allows the excess moisture to evaporate. Spreading the rice to cool also prevents it from clumping, as it would if left to rest in a bowl. In addition, because the rice cools to room temperature in about 10 minutes, the salad can be assembled quickly.

Rice salads are not meant to be doused in oil and vinegar—just a small amount does the trick. This means you can use a dark-colored vinegar, such as balsamic, without discoloring the rice.

Rice salad is particularly suited to flavors that are politely understated, not especially bold or loud. It is a side dish that should taste light, not at all filling, yet every forkful should have character. Rice salads pair particularly well with grilled fish or chicken and are best served at room temperature. Toss the rice with the dressing about 20 minutes before serving so that the subtle flavors have time to develop. If you dress it too far ahead, the rice absorbs the flavor and mutes it. The rice in this salad does stand up to refrigeration. Simply let it rest at room temperature for 30 minutes before serving.

WHAT WE LEARNED: Toast the rice to intensify its flavor and then boil the rice in a large amount of water, as you would pasta. This method keeps the rice tender when cooled. Dry the rice by spreading it out on a large baking sheet—this ensures the rice doesn't become waterlogged and prevents clumping. Use restraint with the vinaigrette—small amounts of oil, vinegar, and seasonings are enough to complement, but not overshadow, the grains of rice.

BOILED RICE FOR RICE SALAD

makes about 6 cups cooked rice

Taste the rice as it nears the end of its cooking time; it should be cooked through and firm, but not crunchy. Be careful not to overcook the rice or the grains will "blow out" and fray. Aromatic basmati rice works well in any of the rice salads, but regular long-grain rice works fine, too.

- 1½ cups long-grain or basmati rice
- 1½ teaspoons salt

1. Bring 4 quarts water to a boil in a large stockpot. Meanwhile, heat a medium skillet over medium heat until hot, about 3 minutes; add the rice and toast, stirring frequently, until faintly fragrant and some grains turn opaque, about 5 minutes.

2. Add the salt to the boiling water and stir in the toasted rice. Return to a boil and cook, uncovered, until the rice is tender but not soft, 8 to 10 minutes for long-grain rice or about 15 minutes for basmati. Meanwhile, line a rimmed baking sheet with foil or parchment paper. Drain the rice in a large fine-mesh strainer or colander; spread on the prepared baking sheet. Cool while preparing the salad ingredients.

RICE SALAD WITH ORANGES, OLIVES, AND ALMONDS

serves 6 to 8

The Mediterranean flavors in this rice salad are a great match for Grill-Roasted Cornish Game Hens as well as most grilled meats and fish.

- 2 tablespoons olive oil
- 1 small garlic clove, minced or pressed through a garlic press (about ½ teaspoon)
- ¼ teaspoon grated zest plus 1 tablespoon juice from 1 small orange

2 teaspoons sherry vinegar

1 teaspoon salt

½ teaspoon ground black pepper

1 recipe Boiled Rice for Rice Salad

⅓ cup coarsely chopped pitted green olives

2 medium oranges, peeled and cut into segments

⅓ cup slivered almonds, toasted in small dry skillet over medium heat until fragrant and golden, about 2 minutes

2 tablespoons fresh oregano leaves, minced

Stir together the oil, garlic, orange zest and juice, vinegar, salt, and pepper in a small bowl. Combine the rice, olives, oranges, almonds, and oregano in a large bowl; drizzle the oil mixture over the salad and toss thoroughly to combine. Let stand 20 minutes to blend the flavors, and serve.

RICE SALAD WITH CHERRY TOMATOES, PARMESAN, PEAS, AND HAM

serves 6 to 8

This Italian-style rice salad makes a nice addition to an antipasto spread on a warm summer night.

2 tablespoons extra-virgin olive oil

1 tablespoon balsamic vinegar

1 small garlic clove, minced or pressed through a garlic press (about ½ teaspoon)

1 teaspoon salt

½ teaspoon ground black pepper

1 recipe Boiled Rice for Rice Salad

½ cup frozen peas, thawed

6 ounces cherry tomatoes, quartered and seeded (about 1 cup)

1 ounce thin-sliced cooked deli ham or prosciutto, chopped fine (about ¼ cup)

1 ounce Parmesan cheese, shredded (about ¼ cup)

¼ cup shredded fresh basil leaves

Stir together the oil, vinegar, garlic, salt, and pepper in a small bowl. Combine the rice, peas, tomatoes, ham, Parmesan, and basil in a large bowl; drizzle the oil mixture over the salad and toss thoroughly to combine. Let stand 20 minutes to blend the flavors, and serve.

SCIENCE DESK: Starch and Rice

LEARNING HOW RICE COOKS HELPS TO EXPLAIN WHY this unorthodox method of boiling rice works best for rice salad. Starch granules, which are the primary component of rice, tend not to absorb water. As you heat rice in water, however, the energy from the rapidly moving water molecules begins to loosen the bonds between the starch molecules so that water can seep in. This in turn causes the starch molecules to swell, softening the rice but also making it more sticky, or "starchy." If you use the "abundant water" method for cooking long-grain rice, some of this starch leaches into the water, which is ultimately drained off. The result is a pot of long-grain rice with less concentrated starch. This is what allows the grains to cook up so remarkably light and separate and to maintain that consistency as they cool to room temperature.

TECHNIQUE:
Prepping Rice for Salad

Start by toasting the rice in a hot skillet for about five minutes. Then, when the rice has been cooked, cool it on a baking sheet.

Rating Basmati Rice

TEN AMERICA'S TEST KITCHEN STAFF MEMBERS TASTED SEVEN BRANDS OF BASMATI RICE. WE COOKED THE RICE WITH water and salt and tasted the rice plain. The rices are listed in order of preference. See www.americastestkitchen.com for up-to-date prices and mail-order sources for top-rated products.

HIGHLY RECOMMENDED
Tilda Pure Basmati Rice
$7.99 for 4 pounds
This Indian-grown sample is our favorite basmati rice. Tasters called it "wonderfully textured," even "graceful."

RECOMMENDED
Goya Aged Basmati Rice
$11.49 for 10 pounds
Texture of these Indian grains was less of an issue than the "slight, chemical, off-flavors."

RECOMMENDED
Kohinoor Super Basmati Rice
$19.99 for 10 pounds
Tasters appreciated that these premium Indian grains "separated nicely" when cooked and had a "floral aroma."

NOT RECOMMENDED
Della Basmati White Rice
$4.99 for 2.5 pounds
"Is this regular rice?" one taster asked of this domestic sample. These "mushy" grains were "void of aroma" and more closely resembled medium-grain rice.

RECOMMENDED
Lal Qilla Basmati Rice
$19.99 for 10 pounds
Some tasters found this rice "nutty" and "fluffy," while others found it "dry."

NOT RECOMMENDED
Lundberg White Basmati Rice
$3.49 for 2 pounds
"A gummy mess," wrote one taster about this California grain. "Not much in the flavor department."

RECOMMENDED
Royal Basmati Rice
$20 for 10 pounds
"Toothsome" yet "fluffy," this Indian-grown rice was "pretty good," but its flavor was "plasticky" and "too mild" to some.

TASTING LAB: Basmati Rice

PRIZED FOR ITS NUTTY FLAVOR AND PERFUME-LIKE aroma, basmati rice is eaten worldwide in pilafs and biryanis and as an accompaniment to curries. Most Indian-grown rice comes from the Himalaya foothills, where the snow-flooded soil and humid climate offer ideal growing conditions. Choosing among the multitude of boxes, bags, and burlap sacks available today on supermarket shelves can be confusing. To find a truly great grain, we steamed seven brands, five from India and two domestic options. Matched against Indian imports, domestic brands Lundberg and Della suffered. They were less aromatic and the grains didn't elongate as much. Their overall texture was mushy, too. While all of the imported brands were acceptable, tasters overwhelmingly chose the longest sample, Tilda, as their favorite.

Most well-done burgers are so tough that you need to have the jaws of a Viking to eat one. The test kitchen found that a milk and bread paste, called a panade, helps keep burgers tender, moist, and juicy—even when well-done.

DRIVE-IN specials

In a perfect world, we'd grill our burgers until crusty on the outside and pink and juicy on the inside. But because of food safety concerns (bacteria on the exterior of a cut of beef often get mixed in during grinding), many of us now grill burgers to medium-well and beyond. Unfortunately, grilling burgers for so long results in disappointingly dense, dry meat. We weren't yet ready to omit burgers from our backyard menu, so we set out to develop a method for turning out juicy, well-done burgers that we'd be proud to serve—and happy to eat.

Onion rings are a terrific accompaniment to burgers. But deep-frying these treats is a messy, bothersome chore. What about oven-frying? Could our oven produce onion rings with deep-fried flavor? With flavor and crunch foremost in our minds (our goal was not low-fat rings), we headed into the test kitchen ready to find out.

WELL-DONE BURGERS

WHAT WE WANTED: A hamburger grilled to medium-well (or well), but one that still manages to be juicy with great beef flavor.

As much as the test kitchen respects the U.S. Department of Agriculture, you won't catch us buying their cookbooks. While recipes like Parchingly Dry Pork Chops (cooked to the USDA's suggested 170 degrees) and No-Pink Porterhouse (also 170 degrees) may be appealing options for the squeamish, the test kitchen generally errs on the side of great taste, great texture, and common sense.

When it comes to hamburgers, however, we've become a little less cavalier. Given the real food safety issues surrounding ground beef (bacteria on the exterior of a cut of beef get mixed in during grinding), we recognize that many backyard cooks (and test cooks) grill their burgers to medium-well and beyond—especially when kids are around. At the very least, it's a recipe one needs in the repertoire. What we weren't willing to accept was the usual outcome of cooking ground beef beyond medium: tough, desiccated hockey pucks with diminished beefy flavor. Could we make them better?

From the outset, we decided that this recipe should work with supermarket ground beef—nothing fancy. But which type was best? Supermarkets sell beef according to the ratio of lean meat to fat, the three most common categories being 80 percent lean (usually from the chuck, or front shoulder), 85 percent (usually from the round, or hind legs), and 90 percent (usually from the sirloin). We assumed that the fattier 80 percent lean chuck would be the tasters' favorite, and a quick test confirmed it. The well-done chuck burgers were noticeably moister than the inedible versions made from the leaner sirloin.

Well, an "edible" well-done burger was a start. We wondered if adding more fat to the mix might help matters, so we prepared patties with chunks of butter, bacon fat, whole milk ricotta, and Boursin cheese added in. While each ingredient proved interesting, most of the burgers tasted too rich or distinctly flavored—and the moisture factor was hardly affected. (However, the one made with bacon fat was such a hit that we kept it as a variation.)

We had always grilled medium-rare burgers over the hottest fire we could muster, the goal being to sear the exterior quickly before the interior overcooked. Did a well-done burger call for a different strategy? Several tests later, we had mixed results. A moderate fire rendered a slightly juicier, more tender burger, but it lacked a flavorful sear. We might as well have baked it in the oven.

We tried various multistep methods and multilevel fires, but no combination yielded a well-done burger that was both grill-marked and juicy. We were unwilling to surrender either one.

Back at the drawing board, we decided to bone up on burger physics. Turns out the reason a medium-well or well-done hamburger becomes dry and tough is fairly simple. Collagen, a protein in muscle fiber, seizes when heated beyond 130 degrees (about medium-rare) and squeezes the meat tissue, causing it to expel its juices. (Think of wringing the water out of a wet towel.) By the time the burger is well-done (about 160 degrees), it's as dry as the bun on which it's served.

Was there any way to stem this moisture loss? With

poultry and pork, the solution is brining (soaking the meat in salted water), which adds both moisture and moisture-retaining salt to the interior. But that trick doesn't work well with beef: The muscle fibers turn to mush—an effect that's multiplied with already-ground beef.

If we couldn't force the meat to retain moisture, perhaps we could pack the patties with something better suited to the task. That's when we (finally) began to think outside the box. After all, there were recipes in the test kitchen's archives that had already solved this very problem: meat loaf and meatballs, both of which include a panade, a paste made from bread and milk, to keep the ground beef from drying out. We tried mashing a slice of bread in a little milk to a stiff paste and folded it into the beef. Once grilled, these burgers were the best yet.

In our research, we'd seen all manner of flavorings added to burgers: mustard, Worcestershire sauce, garlic, onion soup mix, steak sauce, even applesauce. After sampling most of the possibilities (leaving the applesauce an unknown), tasters most liked the punch of minced garlic and the subtle tang of steak sauce, which contributed a deep, meaty flavor.

Our last problem, more cosmetic than functional, was the burger's shape. As it cooked, it went through a transformation from flat puck to puffed-out burger ball. The fix was easy. Previous test kitchen efforts had found that if you make a depression in the center of the patty, it will puff slightly as it cooks and level out to form a flat top. Nicely grill-marked and moist as could be, this well-done burger was finally well done.

WHAT WE LEARNED: A panade (milk and bread mashed to a paste) added to 80 percent lean ground beef gives the meat enough moisture and richness so that the burgers won't dry out on the grill. Minced garlic and steak sauce help highlight the meatiness of the burgers. And to prevent the burgers from ballooning on the grill, make a slight depression in the center of each patty—during cooking the meat will expand to be evenly thick across the burger.

WELL-DONE HAMBURGERS ON A CHARCOAL GRILL

serves 4

Adding bread and milk to the beef creates burgers that are juicy and tender even when well-done. For cheeseburgers, follow the optional instructions below. (See our tasting of presliced cheddar cheese on page 183.)

1	large slice good-quality white sandwich bread, crust removed and discarded, bread chopped into ¼-inch pieces (about ½ cup)
2	tablespoons whole milk
¾	teaspoon salt
¾	teaspoon ground black pepper
1	medium garlic clove, minced or pressed through a garlic press (about 1 teaspoon)
2	teaspoons steak sauce, such as A-1
1½	pounds 80 percent lean ground chuck
	Vegetable oil for cooking grate
6	ounces sliced cheese, optional (see note)
4	rolls or buns

1. Light a large chimney starter filled with charcoal (6 quarts, or about 100 briquettes) and burn until covered with a fine gray ash, 20 to 25 minutes. Empty the coals into the grill; build a modified two-level fire by arranging the coals to cover half of the grill. Position the cooking grate over the coals, cover the grill, and heat the grate for 5 minutes; scrape the grate clean with a grill brush. The grill is ready when the coals are medium-hot (you can hold your hand 2 inches above the grate for 3 to 4 seconds).

2. Meanwhile, mash the bread and milk in a large bowl with a fork until homogeneous (you should have about ¼ cup). Stir in the salt, pepper, garlic, and steak sauce.

3. Break up the beef into small pieces over the bread mixture. Using a fork or your hands, lightly mix together until the mixture forms a cohesive mass. Divide the meat into 4 equal portions. Gently toss one portion of meat back and forth between your hands to form a loose ball. Gently flatten into a ¾-inch-thick patty that measures about 4½ inches in diameter. Press the center of the patty down with your fingertips until it is about ½ inch thick, creating a slight depression in each patty. Repeat with the remaining portions of meat.

4. Lightly dip a wad of paper towels in the oil; holding the wad with tongs, wipe the cooking grate. Grill the burgers on the hot side of the grill, uncovered, until well seared on the first side, 2 to 4 minutes. Using a wide metal spatula, flip the burgers and continue grilling, about 3 minutes for medium-well or 4 minutes for well-done. (Add the cheese, if using, about 2 minutes before reaching desired doneness, covering the burgers with a disposable aluminum pan to melt the cheese.) While the burgers grill, toast the buns on the cooler side of the grill. Serve on buns with desired toppings.

VARIATIONS
WELL-DONE HAMBURGERS ON A GAS GRILL
Turn all the burners on a gas grill to high, close the lid, and heat until very hot, about 15 minutes. Use a grill brush to scrape the cooking grate clean. Lightly dip a wad of paper towels in the oil; holding the wad with tongs, wipe the cooking grate. Leave the primary burner on high, turn the other burners to low. Follow the recipe for Well-Done Hamburgers on a Charcoal Grill from step 2, grilling the patties with the lid down.

WELL-DONE GRILLED BACON CHEESEBURGERS
Most bacon burgers simply top the burgers with bacon. The test kitchen goes a step further, adding bacon fat to the ground beef flavors, which adds juiciness and unmistakable flavor throughout the meat.

Cook 8 strips bacon (about ½ pound) in a medium skillet over medium heat until crisp, 7 to 9 minutes. Transfer the bacon to a paper towel–lined plate; set aside. Measure 2 tablespoons bacon fat into a heatproof bowl; refrigerate until just warm. Follow the recipe for Well-Done Hamburgers on a Charcoal or Gas Grill, including the optional cheese, adding the reserved bacon fat to the beef mixture in step 3, and topping each finished burger with 2 strips of bacon just before serving.

GETTING IT RIGHT:
Ensuring a Juicy Well-Done Burger

Our quest for a juicy well-done burger ended when we hit upon a surprisingly effective addition—a bread-and-milk paste (or panade). The panade prevented the burger at top from becoming dense and dried out, like the one at bottom.

Juicy Well-Done Burger
Add a bread-and-milk paste for a juicy, thick burger.

Dense and Dried Out Burger
Omit the panade, and you're left with a burger so dry it's literally hard to swallow.

Rating Presliced Cheddar Cheese

TWELVE AMERICA'S TEST KITCHEN STAFF MEMBERS EVALUATED NINE BRANDS OF PRESLICED CHEDDAR CHEESE, TASTING them plain, in grilled-cheese sandwiches, and on burgers. The cheeses are listed in order of preference and are available in supermarkets.

RECOMMENDED
Tillamook Sharp Cheddar
$4.99 for 12 ounces
Deemed the "cheddariest" by tasters, with a classic, slightly crumbly texture.

RECOMMENDED
Cabot All Natural Sharp Cheddar
$3.19 for 8 ounces
"Hearty," almost chewy texture was a nice foil for our burgers, as was the "great salty tang."

RECOMMENDED
Cracker Barrel Natural Sharp Cheddar
$3.99 for 8 ounces
Lacked the tang of the Tillamook and Cabot but was much creamier.

RECOMMENDED WITH RESERVATIONS
Sargento Deli Style Medium Cheddar
$3.39 for 8 ounces
Fullest flavor of the milder cheeses. One taster described this cheese as "kid-friendly cheddar."

RECOMMENDED WITH RESERVATIONS
Cabot All Natural Mild Cheddar
$3.19 for 8 ounces
A dead ringer for Monterey Jack cheese. Some found it "bland and rubbery."

RECOMMENDED WITH RESERVATIONS
Tillamook Medium Cheddar
$4.99 for 8 ounces
"Super-milky" but bland, with muted cheddar flavor.

RECOMMENDED WITH RESERVATIONS
Horizon Organic Cheddar
$3.49 for 8 ounces
"Bland-ola," said one taster. The mildest cheese in the lineup reminded tasters of many cheeses— but not cheddar.

RECOMMENDED WITH RESERVATIONS
Kraft Deli Deluxe Sharp Cheddar
$3.39 for 8 ounces
This processed cheese's waxy texture "sticks to your teeth," with an "oddly sweet" flavor.

RECOMMENDED WITH RESERVATIONS
Kraft 2% Milk Singles Sharp Cheddar
$3.99 for 12 ounces
As one taster summed up the taste of this processed cheese, "more Velveeta than cheddar."

TASTING LAB: Presliced Cheddar Cheese

TANGY, SALTY CHEDDAR IS THE TEST KITCHEN'S FAVORITE cheese for topping a hamburger. Beckoned by the ease and convenience of presliced cheese, we rounded up nine packages from the supermarket dairy case. Whether tasted straight up, in grilled-cheese sandwiches, or on burgers, the "sharp" cheddars carried the day over their "mild" and "medium" counterparts. Aged for at least nine months, sharp cheddar cheese has a strong, tangy flavor that tasters preferred in every application. Mild and medium cheddars—aged for days rather than months—tasted more like mild Monterey Jack. The biggest surprise came when tasters sampled two cheeses from Kraft that tasted nothing like the others. Prominently labeled "sharp cheddar," these two products were actually "pasteurized process cheese" loaded with added moisture and emulsifiers to make for smoother melting—a process identical to that used to make American cheese. The label simply refers to the intended flavor, but our tasters found nothing sharp about them, ranking them lowest in every round.

OVEN-FRIED ONION RINGS

WHAT WE WANTED: Tender rounds of sweet onion coated in a thick, rich batter so crunchy they rival deep-fried rings.

Oven-fried onion ring recipes promise to eliminate the mess associated with deep-frying, but they don't really work—at least none of the recipes we've tried. With the oven, we have gotten dehydrated onion rings, tough onion rings, and soggy onion rings but have never come close to the deep-fried crunch and flavor of the real thing.

Deep-fried onion rings start with sliced onions that are dunked in a thick batter, usually made with flour, egg, and liquid. When fried, the batter forms a crisp shell that helps the onions steam and become tender. When we tried it in the oven, however, the batter slid off the rings and stuck to the baking sheet instead. Dredging the onion rings in flour first helped—the batter now had something to

cling to. As for what went into the batter, we dismissed milk (too thin) and mayonnaise (too thick) before hitting on the right combination of buttermilk, egg, and flour.

This batter was pretty good, but we wanted more crunch and thought an additional crumb coating might help. Tossing the batter-dipped onion rings with bread crumbs was a step in the right direction, but tasters wanted even more crunch.

At the local supermarket, we bought anything that looked like it might make a good crumb coating, including cornmeal, corn flakes, Melba toast, Weetabix cereal, Ritz crackers, and saltines. Back in the test kitchen, only the saltines were met with even a lukewarm reception; their salty kick was well liked, but the crumbs were too powdery.

We headed back to the market and searched for less obvious options. If we wanted deep-fried flavor, then what about mixing the saltines with potato chips? This worked far better than we expected. It was almost impossible to tell that these super-crunchy onion rings had come out of the oven.

For four to six servings of rings made from two large onions, 6 tablespoons of vegetable oil was just right, giving the rings a good sear without making them too oily. We also learned that preheating the oil did wonders for encouraging a crisp crust. Admittedly, these onion rings, like many oven-fried recipes, are not low in fat, but that was not our goal. We wanted deep-fried flavor without the mess or the smell—and this recipe delivers on both counts.

WHAT WE LEARNED: Coat the onions in flour to encourage the batter (made from buttermilk, egg, and flour) to adhere. Fortify the batter with a crumb coating consisting of saltine crackers and potato chips. And to encourage a crisp crust, preheat the oil directly on the baking sheets, before adding the breaded onion rings and baking them.

OVEN-FRIED ONION RINGS

makes 24 rings, serving 4 to 6

Slice the onions into ½-inch-thick rounds, separate the rings, and discard any rings smaller than 2 inches in diameter.

½	cup unbleached all-purpose flour
1	large egg, at room temperature
½	cup buttermilk, at room temperature
¼	teaspoon cayenne pepper
½	teaspoon salt
¼	teaspoon ground black pepper
30	saltines
4	cups kettle-cooked potato chips
2	large yellow onions, cut into 24 large rings (see note)
6	tablespoons vegetable oil

1. Adjust the oven racks to the lower-middle and upper-middle positions and heat the oven to 450 degrees. Place ¼ cup of the flour in a shallow baking dish. Beat the egg and buttermilk in a medium bowl. Whisk the remaining flour, the cayenne, salt, and pepper into the buttermilk mixture. Pulse the saltines and chips together in a food processor until finely ground; place in a separate shallow baking dish.

2. Working one at a time, dredge each onion ring in the flour, shaking off the excess. Dip in the buttermilk mixture, allowing the excess to drip back into the bowl, then drop into the crumb coating, turning the ring over to coat evenly. Transfer to a large plate. (At this point, the onion rings can be refrigerated for up to 1 hour. Let them sit at room temperature for 30 minutes before baking.)

3. Pour 3 tablespoons oil onto each of two rimmed baking sheets. Place in the oven and heat until just smoking, about 8 minutes. Carefully tilt the heated sheets to coat evenly with the oil, then arrange the onion rings on the sheets. Bake, flipping the onion rings over and switching and rotating the position of the baking sheets halfway through baking, until golden brown on both sides, about 15 minutes. Briefly drain the onion rings on paper towels. Serve immediately.

GETTING IT RIGHT: Deep-Fried Coating Without Deep-Frying

Our oven-fried onion rings are so crisp and crunchy that you'd swear they came straight from the fryer. The secret is a coating made with kettle-cooked potato chips and saltines ground to fine crumbs.

Kettle Chips
When crumbled, these chips produce a golden brown crust that almost seems deep-fried.

Saltines
Crushed crackers add a nice salty kick and absorb excess grease from the potato chips.

Before topping our pan pizza, we precook the pepperoni slices in the microwave. This step releases excess grease, which can then be blotted away, so that the finished pizza bakes up meaty, not greasy.

PIZZA PARTY

CHAPTER 16

Pizza is a terrific option for many casual gatherings. And pan pizza (often called deep-dish pizza), with its crisp, almost buttery crust and chewy, soft interior, can make dinner all the more special. Most of us have enjoyed takeout pan pizza, but takeout often falls short (heavy, oily crusts and greasy toppings are a few of the problems we've run into). We set out to develop a better-than-takeout pizza where the crust shares equal billing with the toppings and each is full of flavor—not grease. And because this is casual fare, we wanted a recipe that came together in a reasonable amount of time.

Antipasto pasta salad is another good option when entertaining—and because it's so hearty (rich with Italian meats and cheese), this pasta salad is also a terrific choice for picnics or potluck get-togethers. But dull flavors, greasy meat, and bloated pasta are a few of the ways in which a good pasta salad can go bad. The test kitchen aimed to solve these problems and more for a full-flavored main-course salad that will please everyone.

PEPPERONI PAN PIZZA

WHAT WE WANTED: Pan pizza with a thick crust that's tender and chewy on the inside and crisp on the outside, topped with zesty tomato sauce, gooey cheese, and meaty (not greasy) pepperoni.

Great pan pizza—named for the pan in which the dough is risen and cooked—has an irresistible crust that's crispy on the bottom and soft and chewy in the middle. The generous amount of oil first poured into the pan creates the crisp bottom; the soft interior is harder to figure out.

Pan pizza isn't something you find in most cookbooks, so we turned to the Internet. After a few clicks, we found a Web site that claimed to reveal the secret Pizza Hut formula. We doubted the recipe was authentic, but decided to try it because it included a novel ingredient: powdered milk.

Classic pizza dough contains flour, yeast, water, and olive oil, but never milk. We knew, though, that many tender yeast breads are made with milk. Could powdered milk be the key to soft pizza dough?

This dough was tender, with just the right chew. Because most cooks don't have powdered milk on hand, we wondered if fresh milk would work. It did. In fact, the texture of the crust was even better. Whole milk was fine, but dough made with skim milk rose better and baked up especially soft and light.

All-purpose flour, which yields softer baked goods than bread flour, was the right choice, as was a healthy dose of olive oil (2 tablespoons). Although sugar is not traditional in pizza, tasters thought a little (just 2 teaspoons) made the dough taste better, and we knew that sugar gives yeast a nice jump start. To deliver our pan pizzas to the table in record time, we used a warm, turned-off oven to help the dough rise faster. Thirty minutes later, we had dough that was ready to shape.

After producing some less-than-stellar crusts, we discovered it was important not to overwork the dough. Beating the dough into submission with a rolling pin caused it to tear or snap back like a rubber band. In the end, we developed the following hybrid method: we used a rolling pin for the first (and easy) part of the process and then stretched the dough over the tops of our knuckles to finish the job—gently.

With the dough nice and tender, it was time to fine-tune the crispness factor. Three tablespoons of oil per pan delivered maximum crispness without greasiness. After trying various oven temperatures, we settled on 400 degrees as the best compromise between a crisp bottom and scorched toppings.

Everything was perfect—except for the grease on top of our pies. When just plopped onto the pizza and baked, the pepperoni floated in pools of orange grease. Our first thought was to fry it, just as we'd do with bacon. But this made the pepperoni too crisp and turned it an ugly shade of brown. A colleague suggested the microwave. Layered between paper towels, the pepperoni slices emerged pliable and brightly colored, while the paper towels were soaked with orange fat—the microwave had done its job.

From beginning to end, this pizza can be made in 90 minutes. Not as quick as delivery, but less greasy and with the same great crust.

WHAT WE LEARNED: Adding skim milk to the pizza dough gives the crust a light, tender texture; olive oil and sugar add flavor and richness. To speed the dough's rising, place it in a warmed turned-off oven. To prevent grease slicks on top of the pizza, microwave the pepperoni between sheets of paper towel, which will absorb the excess oil.

PEPPERONI PAN PIZZA

makes two 9-inch pizzas, serving 4 to 6

Packaged sliced pepperoni and preshredded mozzarella are great timesaving options here.

dough

½ cup olive oil

¾ cup plus 2 tablespoons skim milk, warmed to 110 degrees

2 teaspoons sugar

2⅓ cups unbleached all-purpose flour, plus extra for the work surface

1 package instant yeast

½ teaspoon salt

topping

1 (3.5-ounce) package sliced pepperoni

1⅓ cups Basic Pizza Sauce (recipe follows)

3 cups shredded part-skim mozzarella cheese

1. TO MAKE THE DOUGH: Adjust an oven rack to the lowest position and heat the oven to 200 degrees. When the oven reaches 200 degrees, turn it off. Lightly grease a large bowl with cooking spray. Coat each of two 9-inch cake pans with 3 tablespoons of the oil.

2. Mix the milk, sugar, and remaining 2 tablespoons oil in a measuring cup.

3. IF USING A STANDING MIXER: Mix the flour, yeast, and salt in a standing mixer fitted with a dough hook. Turn the machine to low and slowly add the milk mixture. After the dough comes together, increase the speed to medium-low and mix until the dough is shiny and smooth, about 5 minutes.

4. IF MIXING BY HAND: Mix the flour, yeast, and salt together in a large bowl. Make a well in the flour, then pour the milk mixture into the well. Using a wooden spoon, stir until the dough becomes shaggy and difficult to stir. Turn out onto a heavily floured work surface and knead, incorporating any shaggy scraps. Knead until the dough is smooth, about 10 minutes.

5. Turn the dough onto a lightly floured work surface, gently shape into a ball, and place in the greased bowl. Cover with plastic wrap and place in the warm oven until doubled in size, about 30 minutes.

6. TO SHAPE AND TOP THE DOUGH: Transfer the dough to a lightly floured work surface, divide in half, and lightly roll each half into a ball. Working with 1 dough ball at a time and following the photos on page 190, roll and shape the dough into a 9½-inch round and press into the oiled pan. Cover with plastic wrap and set in a warm spot (not in the oven) until puffy and slightly risen, about 20 minutes. Meanwhile, heat the oven to 400 degrees.

7. While the dough rises, put half of the pepperoni in a single layer on a microwave-safe plate lined with 2 paper towels. Cover with 2 more paper towels and microwave on high for 30 seconds. Discard the towels and set the pepperoni aside; repeat with new paper towels and the remaining pepperoni.

8. Remove the plastic wrap from the dough. Ladle ⅔ cup sauce on each round, leaving a ½-inch border around the edges. Sprinkle each with 1½ cups cheese and top with the pepperoni. Bake until the cheese is melted and the pepperoni is browned around the edges, about 20 minutes. Remove from the oven; let the pizzas rest in the pans for 1 minute. Using a spatula, transfer the pizzas to a cutting board and cut each into 8 wedges. Serve.

BASIC PIZZA SAUCE

makes 2⅔ cups

This recipe makes enough for four pan pizzas, so you will need only half when making the Pepperoni Pan Pizza on page 189. Freeze the remaining sauce for future pizza making.

- 1 tablespoon olive oil
- 2 medium garlic cloves, minced or pressed through a garlic press (about 2 teaspoons)
- 1 (28-ounce) can crushed tomatoes
  Salt and pepper

Cook the oil and garlic in a medium saucepan over low heat until fragrant, about 2 minutes. Add the tomatoes, increase the heat to medium, and cook until slightly thickened, 10 to 15 minutes. Season with salt and pepper to taste.

GETTING IT RIGHT:
Preventing Greasy Pepperoni

Microwaving pepperoni eliminates the possibility that it will turn your pizza into a grease trap. You can see how much fat is rendered in only 30 seconds by comparing the size of the slices before and after microwaving.

Before
Pepperoni slices straight out of the bag will bake into greasy pools on pizza.

After
Microwaving the pepperoni first, then baking, results in pizza with meaty, not greasy, pepperoni.

TECHNIQUE:
How to Make Pan Pizza

1. Roll
Place the dough on a lightly floured work surface and roll the dough outward from the center in all directions to form a 7-inch circle.

2. Stretch
With the dough draped over your knuckles, gently stretch it, using the weight of the dough to make a 9½-inch circle that is slightly thinner at the center.

3. Pat
Place the dough in the oiled cake pan and gently push it to the edge, taking care not to let too much oil spill over the top.

ANTIPASTO PASTA SALAD

WHAT WE WANTED: A hearty pasta salad chock-full of Italian meats, cheese, and vegetables in a zesty, not heavy, dressing.

An antipasto platter includes a variety of cured meats, cheeses, and pickled vegetables. As a whole, it's full-flavored and hearty—perfect attributes for a main-course pasta salad. But the recipes we tried for this type of salad were greasy and heavy, with lackluster dressing and not enough flavor in the pasta itself.

We started with the deli meats. We tried a variety of meats from our supermarket deli. We were surprised to find that prosciutto fared poorly. Its flavor was just too delicate for this salad. We did like pepperoni and sopresatta (a spicy, cured Italian sausage), and salami works well, too. From previous testing, we learned that microwaving the meat, wrapped in paper towels, helps remove excess grease. When ordering your meat at the deli counter, be sure to have it sliced thick—thin sliced meat gets lost in this salad.

Next we moved on to the cheese. Tasters dismissed mild-flavored cheeses like mozzarella and regular provolone, but aged provolone, with its sharp cheesy flavor, won everyone over. Tasters liked this strong cheese more when we grated it into the salad for even distribution.

For vegetables, we didn't want to stray too far from the items you'd find on an antipasto platter—olives, roasted red peppers, pepperoncini, marinated mushrooms, artichoke hearts, and sliced fennel were just some of the vegetables we chose for our tests. In the end, tasters preferred roasted red peppers for sweetness, pepperoncini for heat, and mushrooms for earthy flavor. (Kalamata olives and jarred artichoke hearts were close runners-up, so they're good options if you have them on hand.) While we used jarred roasted red peppers and pepperoncini, we felt we needed to go the homemade route with the marinated mushrooms—jarred versions we tried

were not worth the expense. After a little testing we found an easy way to infuse our mushrooms with flavor in just a few minutes—by sautéing them in a portion of the vinaigrette.

Pasta salads typically use a 2-to-1 ratio of oil to vinegar, but since the meats and cheese were so rich, we found that we had to nearly reverse this ratio. Some vinegary brine from the pepperoncini further sharpened the dressing. We felt that we were almost there, but the dressing seemed too thin. We needed some sort of thickening agent to emulsify it. First, we tried mustard, but its flavor overshadowed the dressing. On our next test, we added a few tablespoons of mayonnaise. This was perfect—it added body to help the dressing cling to the pasta, and its mild flavor didn't mute or detract from the dressing's other seasonings.

For the pasta, we liked short, curly pasta shapes best—their curves catch the dressing and cradle the meats, cheese, and vegetables far better than short straight pasta shapes like ziti or rigatoni. Most pasta salad recipes call for rinsing the cooked noodles, but this method left us with bloated pasta that didn't absorb any flavor from the dressing. Tossing the hot pasta with the dressing and extra vinegar made the pasta an equal partner in this bold Italian-style salad supper.

WHAT WE LEARNED: Short, curly pasta is the best choice, as its curves catch hold of the salad's other components, making for a more cohesive dish. Quickly rendering the meats in the microwave helps keep this salad from becoming greasy. Use an increased ratio of vinegar to oil in the dressing—the sharp, bright flavors cut the richness of the meats and cheese for a brighter-tasting salad. For well-seasoned pasta, toss the hot pasta with the dressing—hot dressing absorbs the dressing better than cold pasta. Use thickly sliced meats so their hearty flavor isn't lost among the pasta. And grate the cheese, rather than cutting it into chunks, so its sharp flavor is evenly distributed.

ANTIPASTO PASTA SALAD

serves 6 to 8

We also liked the addition of 1 cup chopped, pitted kalamata olives or 1 cup jarred artichokes, drained and quartered, to this salad.

8	ounces sliced pepperoni, cut into ¼-inch strips
8	ounces thick-sliced sopresatta or salami, halved and cut into ¼-inch strips
½	cup plus 2 tablespoons red wine vinegar
6	tablespoons extra-virgin olive oil
3	tablespoons mayonnaise
1	(12-ounce) jar pepperoncini, drained (2 tablespoons juice reserved), stemmed, and chopped coarse
4	garlic cloves, minced or pressed through a garlic press (about 4 teaspoons)
¼	teaspoon red pepper flakes Salt and ground black pepper
1	pound short, curly pasta, such as fusilli or campanelle
1	pound white mushrooms, wiped clean and quartered
4	ounces aged provolone cheese, grated (about 1 cup)
1	(12-ounce) jar roasted red peppers, drained, patted dry, and chopped coarse
1	cup minced fresh basil leaves

1. Bring 4 quarts water to a boil in a large pot for the pasta. Meanwhile, place the pepperoni on a large paper towel–lined plate. Cover with another paper towel and place the sopresatta on top. Cover with another paper towel and microwave on high for 1 minute. Discard the paper towels and set the pepperoni and sopresatta aside.

2. Whisk 5 tablespoons of the vinegar, the olive oil, mayonnaise, pepperoncini juice, garlic, pepper flakes, ½ teaspoon salt, and ½ teaspoon pepper together in a medium bowl.

3. Add 1 tablespoon salt and the pasta to the boiling water. Cook, stirring often, until the pasta is just past al dente. Drain the pasta and return it to the pot. Pour ½ cup of the dressing and the remaining vinegar over the pasta and toss to combine. Season with salt and pepper to taste. Spread the pasta on a rimmed baking sheet and cool to room temperature, about 30 minutes.

4. Meanwhile, bring the remaining dressing to a simmer in a large skillet over medium-high heat. Add the mushrooms and cook until lightly browned, about 8 minutes. Transfer to a large bowl and cool to room temperature.

5. Add the meat, provolone, roasted red peppers, basil, and cooled pasta to the mushrooms and toss to combine. Season with salt and pepper to taste before serving.

> ### TECHNIQUE: Mincing Basil
> Stack a few leaves of fresh basil, then roll the leaves tightly like a cigar and slice thinly.
>
>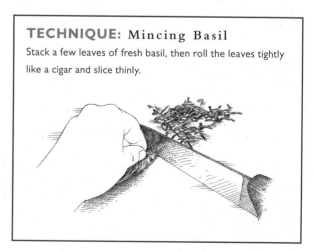

TASTING LAB: Frozen Pizza

IF WE DON'T MAKE OUR OWN PIZZA, WE'LL DIAL-UP A pie from our favorite pizza joint. But what about frozen pizza? Americans spent more than $2.6 billion on frozen pizza last year. To find out how good today's frozen pizzas are, we rounded up nine national brands and fired up the test kitchen ovens.

Wanting no distractions, we selected plain cheese pizzas with thin or "regular" crusts and no fancy ingredients. We prepared each pizza according to the instructions on the box and served hot slices to our tasters. Our tasting panel rated the crust, sauce, cheese, and overall quality of each sample.

So what did we find out? Frozen pizza is not going to fool anybody into thinking it's fresh. That said, our winning pizza, California Pizza Kitchen Margherita, tastes very good, and several tasters said they'd be happy to have it in their home freezers. In fact, our panel recommends the top four pizzas listed on page 194. As for the remaining pies, they ranged from imperfect (with muted flavors and soggy crusts) to inedible.

What separates the good from the bad? The top-scoring pizzas all tasted fresh (not freezer burnt) and lacked offensive or off flavors—in other words, they didn't taste mass-produced. Most of our winning pizzas had shorter, simpler ingredient lists (Tombstone lists 13 ingredients total), whereas the pies with lots of ingredients—including preservatives that are supposed to retain freshness—tasted old and tired (Celeste has 13 ingredients in its imitation cheese alone and another 13 in its crust).

Rating Frozen Pizzas

NINE FROZEN PIZZAS WERE SAMPLED BY 18 MEMBERS OF THE AMERICA'S TEST KITCHEN STAFF AND RATED ON FLAVOR, freshness, and overall quality. The pizzas are listed in order of preference and are available in supermarkets.

RECOMMENDED
California Pizza Kitchen Crispy Thin Crust Margherita
$5.99 for 12.8 ounces

This sauceless pizza had "nice" chunks of fresh tomato that tasters praised for their ability to make it "seem less like frozen pizza." Most tasters agreed that this pizza had a "nice overall combination of flavors."

RECOMMENDED
Freschetta Ultra Thin Golden Baked Crispy 5-Cheese Pizza
$6.29 for 12.8 ounces

This pizza scored especially well for its "thin and flaky," "crispy" crust and "complex" cheese flavor that "actually tastes like real cheese." With a better sauce (this one was "dusty and oregano-y"), this might have been the winner.

RECOMMENDED
Tombstone Extra Cheese Original
$5.19 for 20.5 ounces

Tasters found this pizza met expectations, noting that it "tastes like frozen pizza, in the best possible way." It scored well for its "very good" cheese and "nice and crunchy" crust.

RECOMMENDED
Amy's Cheese Pizza
$3.99 for 13 ounces

This organic product had a distinctive whole-grain crust that one taster said was "full of flavor, like real bread." The sauce was praised for being "tomatoey, with good herb flavor." The cheese was called "just okay."

RECOMMENDED WITH RESERVATIONS
Tony's Original Crust Cheese Pizza
$3.99 for 15.1 ounces

"Sweet sauce, which I like," said one taster, while another countered that it "takes me back to my high school cafeteria." The crust lost points for being "flabby."

RECOMMENDED WITH RESERVATIONS
Red Baron Thin Crust 5-Cheese Pizza
$6.49 for 19 ounces

Ingredients include vinegar, molasses, soy sauce solids, and smoke flavor. One taster called the sauce "too spicy, with strange flavors," while another called it "smoky and strangely sweet." "Plasticky" cheese.

RECOMMENDED WITH RESERVATIONS
DiGiorno Thin Crispy Crust Four Cheese Pizza
$6.29 for 23 ounces

"Like the frozen pizza from my childhood—sauce is too sweet, and the cheese tastes processed," said one taster. "Cheese is chewy, fake, and bland—what's it made of?" asked another. Another taster simply stated, "Decent."

NOT RECOMMENDED
Mr. P's Crispy Thin Crust Cheese Pizza
$1.00 for 6.5 ounces

"Pizza candy—way too sweet," said one taster. With a crust "like a wet cracker" and "chewy, rubbery" cheese, one taster asked, "Is it prison pizza?"

NOT RECOMMENDED
Celeste Original Pizza for One
$1.69 for 5.58 ounces

"Rancid" and "a sad specimen," said the panel. "You eat it and then ask yourself, 'Why did I just eat that?'"

EQUIPMENT CORNER: Toaster Ovens

IF YOU'RE LIKE A LOT OF PEOPLE, YOU GREW UP USING toaster ovens to make toast, melt cheese on sandwiches, or crisp up cold slices of pizza. But if you were to go shopping to replace that simple toaster oven, you'd be in for a surprise. Today, manufacturers are building toaster ovens bigger and fancier than they've ever been. Custom settings, convection capability, sleek design, digital displays, and their own cookware come along with higher prices—up to $200—for what used to be a pretty humble appliance in the $25 to $30 range.

Are these tricked-out toaster ovens really useful? Or have manufacturers gone too far and made something nobody needs? We bought eight models, all claiming to be big enough for six slices of toast or a 12-inch pizza and all with convection, the most widespread new feature. With their inflated size, they are sometimes called countertop ovens and are promoted as being able to do anything a full-size oven can do. We decided to find out if they really deliver.

This much was obvious: These bigger toaster ovens can't approach the capacity of a full-size oven. A standard 13 by 9-inch casserole dish could not fit inside any of the models in our lineup. If you want to bake cookies, you're restricted to the tiny baking sheet that comes with the appliance, which is capable of baking only six to eight cookies at a time. And only smaller whole chickens (less than 3½ pounds) fit without being too close to the heating elements.

Toaster ovens' smaller size means they preheat quickly, which is great if you're in a rush or don't want to heat up the kitchen. Even the slowest model in our lineup took half the time of a full-size oven, reaching 350 degrees in just over five minutes, compared with 11 to 12 minutes for a full-size oven. (The fastest took 1 minute, 47 seconds.) A toaster oven also uses roughly half the energy of a full-size oven. Still, if we are going to invest in a high-priced, souped-up toaster oven, we want oven-like consistency of cooking. We decided to test six foods that would each address a different aspect of the ovens' performance.

We were surprised to find that it is possible to roast a decent whole chicken in a toaster oven, though you get much better results using convection, in which a fan circulates the heat. If you don't use convection, the chicken browns only on top, where it faces the heating elements, leaving yellow skin on the sides and bottom. Without convection, we found that the side of the chicken near the back of the oven tended to cook faster, overcooking before the "door side" was done.

All the ovens claimed they could cook a frozen 12-inch pizza, but not one model produced a great-looking pie. All were patchy; some areas were overbrowned, while in other spots the cheese barely melted. The instruction booklet for the Krups model suggested rotating the pizza halfway through cooking, which helped. With less surface area, tuna melts fared better.

Switching to delicate baked goods, we prepared our own slice-and-bake lemon cookies on both convection and regular settings. Though convection proved a little better, most ovens baked up cookies with varying degrees of doneness, from too brown to slightly underdone. On the other hand, getting a baked potato cooked just right allowed all the ovens to shine.

Traditionally, toaster ovens have been known for making lousy toast, brown on top and white on the bottom. Since a recent appliance industry survey found that most people still buy toaster ovens primarily for making toast, we set toast as our gold standard. Although all of our models claimed they could fit six slices of bread, several of them couldn't. On the medium setting, after nearly five minutes, two of the toaster ovens produced a barely crisped slice of white bread. With most of the others, the top of the toast browned but the bottom remained predominantly white. On the dark setting, half of the ovens produced charcoal. In this critical test, only two, by Black & Decker and Krups, made good-looking stacks of toast in short order.

So why did these toaster ovens perform so inconsistently? While manufacturers have given them a sleek new look, few have actually improved on the traditional problem of toaster oven cooking: The heating elements tend to be nothing more than pairs of narrow, exposed bars across the top and the bottom of the oven. You get intense heat in proximity to the bars, which cycle on and off to regulate overall temperature. (The bars contain a nickel-chromium wire coil—the same wire that heats up inside a regular toaster—covered in ceramic and metal.) Their position also explains why toasting is so inefficient in a toaster oven.

Bread might be four or more inches from the elements. Ordinary toasters, however, have eight to 10 wires on each side of the toaster slot, less than an inch from the surface of the bread.

Manufacturers have made a few technical advances, most notably adding convection, which helps with heat distribution. Others simply cover the bars with pierced metal shields to help diffuse the heat or vary the number and placement of the bars. A few of the newest models sheath the bars with quartz instead of steel. "Quartz has less thermal mass [than metal], so the coil starts to radiate the heat out a lot quicker," said John Stein, president of Quartz Tubing Inc. of Bensalem, Pa. He explained that quartz also cools down more quickly, which makes the ovens less prone to overheating. With the most heating elements (six quartz bars), we found that the Krups cooked food more evenly than the other models.

Because of their fast cooking and tendency to scorch, you must be vigilant when cooking with toaster ovens. For multitasking cooks, toaster ovens with automatic shutoff and a digital countdown timer rather than a hard-to-interpret dial are valuable features. Krups was one of the few models we tested to offer these. After poring over instruction booklets with charts of rack positions and settings for every cooking task, we came to prefer toaster ovens in which the controls were self-evident. Again, the Krups oven stood out, with basic buttons that quickly became familiar.

Offering reliable cooking, user-friendly controls, solid construction, and even decent toast, the Krups emerged as the model that performed most like a full-size oven. If you want to invest in a higher-end toaster oven for small cooking projects, the $200 Krups might deserve a place in your kitchen. But you can do equally well (and save a lot of money) with an ordinary toaster and your full-size oven.

Rating Toaster Ovens

WE TESTED EIGHT TOASTER OVENS, ALL WITH CONVECTION CAPABILITY AND ALL CLAIMING TO HOLD A 12-INCH pizza or six slices of toast. We measured the accuracy of temperature controls and evaluated ease of operation and cleanup. Functionality of layout and user-friendliness received major emphasis. The ovens are listed in order of preference. See www.americastestkitchen.com for up-to-date prices and mail-order sources for top-rated products.

RECOMMENDED
Krups 6-Slice Digital Convection Toaster Oven FBC412
$199.99

Easiest to use of all the ovens, with clear instructions and digital controls. Display counts down cook time. Dark toast was "beautiful deep brown." Cooked quickly, cleaned up easily.

RECOMMENDED WITH RESERVATIONS
Oster Counterforms Digital Convection 6-Slice Toaster Oven 6292
$98.95

Easy digital controls. Interior light was a plus; lack of countdown timer a minus. Pans hard to clean; pieces of coating broke off. Toast incinerated on dark setting; burned underside of toast and cookies (on regular bake). Can't hold 6 slices of bread.

RECOMMENDED WITH RESERVATIONS
Cuisinart Toaster Oven Broiler TOB-175BC
$179

Easy-to-use touch-pad controls. Does not quite hold a 12-inch pizza or 6 slices of toast. Toast browned on top, stayed white on bottom on medium setting; burned on dark.

NOT RECOMMENDED
Hamilton Beach Toaster Oven 31180
$75.33

Took "forever" to bake, broil, or roast; temperature controls were too low by 50 degrees. Timer/toast knob must be dialed past 10 minutes before setting, and must be set to "stay on" if cook time is to exceed 30 minutes.

NOT RECOMMENDED
De'Longhi Convection Oven EO1258
$129.95

Cooks well, but the oven door snapped closed when inserting racks, resulting in burned forearms on 2 testers. Lacks timer or automatic shutoff (except for toasting). Runs more than 50 degrees hotter than setting.

NOT RECOMMENDED
Rival Counter Top Oven CO606
$69.95

Can't hold 6 slices of bread. Toast was blond underneath on medium setting, scorched on dark setting. Pizza overcooked along front and back, undercooked in center. Convection only.

NOT RECOMMENDED
Black & Decker Countertop Convection Oven CTO 100
$86

Timer knob is imprecise and hard to read. Oven too tall to brown foods. Piece of toast still was white after 5½ minutes. Cookies were pale on top, overbrowned underneath. Helpful dial shows when the oven is preheated. Runs hot; averaged 400 degrees when set to 350.

NOT RECOMMENDED
Toastmaster Convection Toaster Oven Broiler COV76OB
$49.99

Took almost twice as long as the winning oven to make toast. Imprecise, illegible controls are metal-painted plastic knobs with raised arrows. Browning was uneven; toast and cookies scorched.

Chris explains that while some chicken stews taste like they were made with a rubber bird, our Coq au Vin does not. In using a mix of chicken parts, we start the longer-cooking legs and thighs first, adding the breasts later, so that all the meat finishes cooking at the same time.

FRENCH classics

Coq au vin may have an old-fashioned name, but the appeal of this French classic is timeless. A chicken stew flavored with a hefty dose of red wine, bacon, and onions, it is eminently satisfying. We remember discovering this dish in the late 1960s when French food was taking hold in American kitchens. But if we've cooked this dish in the past 20 years, we don't remember; it simply isn't a dish we make at home. We wondered why. Perusing the recipe, it quickly came back to us—peeling all those baby onions takes time, the sauce relies on veal stock, another time-consuming chore, and then the dish is often finished with a flambé of cognac. Fussy, fussy, fussy. We set out to make this dish a little less overwhelming—but still just as delicious as we remembered.

Pot de crème is a French-style chocolate custard with an alluring satiny texture. Finding the right combination of chocolate, eggs, and cream can be perplexing—some pots de crème can taste heavy or dull instead of complex and rich. Preparing this French classic can also take some patience—the custards are cooked in individual ramekins in a water bath (the ramekins are set in a large pan of water), to ensure gentle cooking. The downside is that often the custards don't cook through at the same rate, which means removing some from the water bath before others—a messy endeavor. We wanted to simplify the process without compromising this decadent dessert's rich flavor or ethereal texture.

IN THIS CHAPTER

THE RECIPES

Coq au Vin

Chocolate Pots de Crème
Milk Chocolate Pots de Crème

EQUIPMENT CORNER

Inexpensive Dutch Ovens

SCIENCE DESK

Does Cooking Remove All the Alcohol?

Is Scalding Cream Necessary?

COQ AU VIN

WHAT WE WANTED: A streamlined version of this French-style chicken fricassee—juicy, tender chicken infused with the flavors of red wine, onions, mushrooms, and bacon—made in hours, not days.

This classic fricassee of cut-up chicken is cooked in a red wine sauce and finished with a garnish of bacon, tiny glazed pearl onions, and sautéed mushrooms. At its best, coq au vin is enormously flavorful, the acidity of the wine rounded out by rich, salty bacon and sweet caramelized onions and mushrooms. The chicken acts like a sponge, soaking up those same dark, compelling flavors. We set about creating a recipe that would satisfy our appetite for a really great coq au vin. The problem is that many versions contain some ingredients the home cook probably won't have on hand, like chicken livers, or want to spend the time preparing, such as veal stock. We wanted a more practical approach for today's cook.

We started out by cooking and tasting a number of recipes from French cookbooks. We noticed that the recipes fell into two categories: those that were simple and rustic in character, and ones that were a bit more complicated, but promised a more refined dish. The recipes in the first category were versions of a straightforward brown fricassee. Tasting these simpler versions, we recognized them as the serviceable renditions of recent memory: The sauces were good but not extraordinary; the chicken tasted mostly like chicken. OK, yes, but not what we were looking for.

We moved on to testing a handful of much more complicated recipes. One of them, also a brown fricassee, was a two-day affair with a much more elaborate sauce. The recipe began by combining red wine with the aforementioned veal stock and browned vegetables and reducing this mixture by about half. The chicken was then browned and the pan deglazed with the reduced wine mixture. Once the chicken was cooked, the sauce was strained, bound first with beurre manié (a paste of mashed butter and flour), and then with a bit of chicken liver pureed with heavy cream, and finished with flambéed cognac.

Although this particular recipe was built on the same basic model as the others, this dish was in a whole different league. It was what a good coq au vin ought to be—the sauce was beautifully textured, clean-flavored, and rich without being heavy or murky. The chicken was drenched in flavor, but the recipe unquestionably demanded more time, more last-minute fussing, and a lot more dishes.

In trying to simplify this recipe, two techniques stood out when we compared it with the others. First, our working recipe bound the sauce differently, using beurre manié and chicken liver rather than sprinkling the meat or vegetables with flour at the beginning. This recipe also used all chicken legs instead of both legs and breasts, which is traditional.

We first tested a coq au vin bound with beurre manié and compared it with one in which the vegetables were sprinkled with flour. We liked the streamlined method of sprinkling the flour over the vegetables to give the sauce some viscosity, but felt the richness of the butter in the beurre manié was missing in this leaner sauce. To solve that, we whisked cold butter into the finished sauce, which rounded out the flavors with the added benefit of thickening the sauce. And the veal stock? Chicken broth did just fine here. After all, we were also using an entire bottle of fruity red wine, which, in conjunction with bacon, provided lots of flavor. We then ran some final tests to find out if the addition of cognac, chicken liver, and tomato paste we found in several recipes improved the sauce enough to merit the extra trouble. Only tomato paste made the cut, as it's easy to whisk in and added extra flavor and body to the finished dish.

Traditionally coq au vin makes use of an entire bird, so when we tasted the version that used legs only, many tasters missed the white meat. Other tasters felt all dark meat made sense for gauging the cooking time since white and dark meats cook at a different rate. The bottom line: use the cuts you like. As long as the thighs get a head start cooking before the breasts are added to the pot, the end result is just as good either way.

WHAT WE LEARNED: Using chicken parts allows you to choose the parts you like best. If you choose a mix of dark and white meat, start the dark before the white, so that all the meat finishes cooking at the same time. Flour sprinkled over the vegetables after sautéing helps thicken the stewing liquid, and butter whisked in toward the end of cooking adds welcome richness. While it's not as rich, chicken broth stands in for veal stock, and bacon and an entire bottle of red wine provide a great base of flavor. Tomato paste is a fuss-free way to add extra depth and body to the sauce.

COQ AU VIN

serves 4

Regular bacon can be substituted for the thick-cut. Use any $10 bottle of fruity, medium-bodied red wine such a Pinot Noir, Côtes du Rhône, or Zinfandel. If using both chicken breasts and thighs/drumsticks, we recommend cutting the breast pieces in half so that each person can have some white meat and dark meat. The breasts and thighs/drumsticks do not cook at the same rate; if using both, note that the breast pieces are added partway through the cooking time. Serve with egg noodles.

6   ounces thick-cut bacon (about 5 slices), chopped medium
    Vegetable oil, as needed
4   pounds bone-in, skin-on chicken pieces (split breasts cut in half, drumsticks, and/or thighs)
    Salt and ground black pepper
5   ounces frozen pearl onions, thawed (about 2 cups)
10 ounces white mushrooms, wiped clean and quartered
2   medium garlic cloves, minced or pressed through a garlic press (about 2 teaspoons)
1   tablespoon tomato paste
3   tablespoons unbleached all-purpose flour
1   (750-ml) bottle medium-bodied red wine (about 3 cups, see note)
2½ cups low-sodium chicken broth
1   teaspoon minced fresh thyme leaves, or ¼ teaspoon dried
2   bay leaves
2   tablespoons unsalted butter, cut into 2 pieces, chilled
2   tablespoons minced fresh parsley leaves

1. Fry the bacon in a large Dutch oven over medium heat until crisp, 5 to 7 minutes. Transfer the bacon to a paper towel–lined plate, leaving the fat in the pot (you should have about 2 tablespoons fat; if necessary add some vegetable oil).

2. Pat the chicken dry with paper towels and season with salt and pepper. Return the pot with the bacon fat to medium-high heat until shimmering. Brown half of the chicken on both sides, 5 to 8 minutes per side, reducing the heat if the pan begins to scorch. Transfer the chicken to a plate, leaving the fat in the pot. Return the pot with fat to medium-high heat and repeat with the remaining chicken; transfer the chicken to the plate.

3. Pour off all but 1 tablespoon of the fat in the pot (or add vegetable oil if needed). Add the pearl onions and mushrooms and cook over medium heat, stirring occasionally, until lightly browned, about 10 minutes. Stir in the garlic and tomato paste and cook until fragrant, about 30 seconds. Stir in the flour and cook for 1 minute. Stir in the wine, broth, thyme, and bay leaves, scraping up any browned bits.

4. Nestle the chicken, along with any accumulated juices, into the pot and bring to a simmer. Cover, turn the heat to medium-low, and simmer until the chicken is fully cooked and tender, about 20 minutes for the breasts (160 degrees on an instant-read thermometer), or 1 hour for the thighs and drumsticks. (If using both types of chicken, simmer the thighs and drumsticks for 40 minutes before adding the breasts.)

5. Transfer the chicken to a serving dish, tent loosely with foil, and let rest while finishing the sauce. Skim as much fat as possible off the surface of the sauce and return to a simmer until the sauce is thickened and measures about 2 cups, about 20 minutes. Off the heat, remove the bay leaves, whisk in the butter, and season with salt and pepper to taste. Pour the sauce over the chicken, sprinkle with the reserved bacon and the parsley, and serve.

SCIENCE DESK:
Does Cooking Remove All the Alcohol?

IT IS A COMMONLY HEARD REFRAIN: "COOKING removes all the alcohol." But the truth is much more complex. To clarify things, we decided to look at two ways in which alcohol is used in cooking and if the alcohol really does "cook out" by the time the dish is finished.

To find out if alcohol cooks off in a long-cooking stew, we measured the alcohol content of the stew before it went into the oven. Every hour, we sampled the liquid to measure the alcohol concentration, and every time, it had dropped—but not as much as might be expected. After three hours of stewing (the recipe calls for two to three hours stewing), the alcohol concentration of the stew liquid had decreased by 60 percent. A major reason for the retention of alcohol in this dish is the use of a lid. If the surface of the liquid is not ventilated, alcohol vapor will accumulate, reducing further evaporation. Because most stews and braises are cooked in lidded pots, significant alcohol retention is the rule rather than the exception.

What about a faster way to cook alcohol out of a dish? One way is to ignite the vapors from the alcohol that lie above the pan, a technique known as flambéing. But the degree to which a flambé will remove alcohol depends partly on the heat applied to the liquid underneath. We found that brandy ignited over high heat retains 29 percent of its original alcohol concentration, while brandy flamed in a cold pan held 57 percent. In the case of a flambé, the addition of heat (not just the flame from a match) can make a significant difference in the strength of the finished sauce. Practically, what does this mean? Steak Diane, which is cooked on the stovetop, will lose more alcohol than Cherries Jubilee, in which flaming liquid is poured over ice cream.

Our conclusion? Though it is possible to remove the majority of alcohol in food through cooking, traces will almost always remain.

CHOCOLATE POTS DE CRÈME

WHAT WE WANTED: A user-friendly method for producing a lush and silky custard with deeply rich chocolate flavor.

Literally translated, *pots de crème* means pots of cream, but "cream" in this case refers to custard, a word the French simply don't have a translation for. Once we tasted our first pots de crème, we understood exactly why tiny Limoges china pots were commissioned especially for this exotic pudding-like dessert. The custard is so remarkably rich, so intensely flavored that just a small amount satisfies. When properly made, this rich custard boasts a satiny texture and intense chocolate flavor, but we've had versions that are no better than cafeteria pudding. We set out to develop a recipe for this dessert that was not only authentic, but foolproof as well.

We started with a handful of authentic recipes. Not surprisingly, the ingredients were more or less the same across the board: chocolate, eggs, sugar, and cream (or other such dairy). The difference lay in the ratio of ingredients and the way the custard was cooked. Most of the recipes employed the usual treatment for baked custard: a hot

water bath and a moderately low oven. But two out of the 20 or so recipes we found employed an unconventional method in which the custard is cooked on the stovetop in a saucepan, then poured into ramekins. Very interesting.

The downfall of the other recipes was that they required a roasting pan large enough to accommodate all the ramekins and a hot water bath that threatened to splash the custards every time the pan was moved. In addition, the individual custards didn't always cook at the same rate, which meant going in and out of the oven multiple times to gauge doneness and plucking hot ramekins from the water bath only to have them drip onto their neighbors. We wanted a simpler recipe that would be as user-friendly as possible.

Using the standard baked custard method for the time being, we went to work on ingredients. We started with the dairy. To serve eight, a chocolate pot de crème recipe requires about two cups of milk, half-and-half, or heavy cream. The richest recipes use heavy cream exclusively, but most call for a combination of cream and milk. We tested it all, in different ratios, and decided that 1½ cups of cream and ¾ cup of half-and-half had just the right amount of richness and body. Next up were eggs, which enrich and help thicken the custard. Most recipes use just the yolks. We experimented with as many as eight and as few as four. Five was the right number to make a luxurious custard. This is fewer than many recipes call for, but we wanted to use a lot of chocolate, which would also help the custard to set up.

Intensity of flavor was key, so we passed over milk chocolate (reserving it for a variation) and semisweet chocolate because we knew they'd be too mild. Cocoa powder and unsweetened chocolate were too gritty, so we focused our testing on bittersweet chocolate. With only 4 ounces of this dark chocolate, the pots de crème were too milky; with a whole pound, they were unpalatably rich. Our tastes tended toward a recipe made with 12 ounces—it was incredibly thick and chocolatey—but since most tasters couldn't abide the heavy texture, we went with 10 ounces. With only one exception, this was at least 50 percent more chocolate than in any other recipe that we encountered. In addition we bolstered the chocolate flavor with espresso, as is common in chocolate desserts.

It was now time to settle the matter of cooking method. Using the same ingredients, we made two versions of pots de crème. We baked one in a moderately low oven in a water bath, covered with foil to prevent the surface of the custards from drying out; the other we made on the stovetop in the style of a stirred custard, or crème anglaise in the culinary vernacular. It was unequivocal. The crème anglaise method was immensely easier than the traditional (and cumbersome) baking method—and the results were close to identical. (The baked custards were ever so slightly firmer and more set than the stirred ones, but tasters weren't the least bit concerned.) What wasn't identical was the hassle factor: The crème anglaise method was easy and reliable. The eggs, sugar, and dairy are cooked on the stovetop, the resulting custard is poured over the chocolate, and then the mixture is gently whisked until combined. The only equipment required is a saucepan and a heatproof spatula; no roasting pan and no water bath. Even better, when cooked on the stovetop the pots de crème were finished in a fraction of the time they took to bake. To our delight, we had not only made this refined French classic foolproof, we'd simplified it as well.

WHAT WE LEARNED: Cooking the custard on the stovetop, then pouring it into ramekins, is a more foolproof method than the traditional route of baking them in a water bath—and it is faster too. For richness and body use a mix of heavy cream and half-and-half along with five egg yolks. For intense chocolate flavor, bittersweet chocolate (reinforced with a little espresso) is best, and using 50 percent more than traditional recipes call for gives our recipe a depth and richness missing from others.

CHOCOLATE POTS DE CRÈME
serves 8

We prefer pots de crème made with 60 percent cocoa bittersweet chocolate (our favorite brands are Ghirardelli, Callebaut, Valrhona, and El Rey), but 70 percent bittersweet chocolate can also be used. If using a 70 percent bittersweet chocolate (we like Lindt, El Rey, and Valrhona), reduce the amount of chocolate to 8 ounces. A tablespoon of strong brewed coffee may be substituted for the instant espresso and water. Covered tightly with plastic wrap, the pots de crème will keep for up to 3 days in the refrigerator, but the whipped cream must be made just before serving.

pots de crème

10	ounces bittersweet chocolate (see note), chopped fine
5	large egg yolks
5	tablespoons (1¼ ounces) sugar
¼	teaspoon salt
1½	cups heavy cream
¾	cup half-and-half
1	tablespoon vanilla extract
½	teaspoon instant espresso mixed with 1 tablespoon water (see note)

whipped cream and garnish

½	cup heavy cream, cold
2	teaspoons sugar
½	teaspoon vanilla extract
	Cocoa for dusting (optional)
	Chocolate shavings for sprinkling (optional)

1. FOR THE POTS DE CRÈME: Place the chocolate in a medium heatproof bowl; set a fine-mesh strainer over the bowl and set aside.

2. Whisk the yolks, sugar, and salt together in a medium bowl until combined, then whisk in the heavy cream and half-and-half. Transfer the mixture to a medium saucepan. Cook the mixture over medium-low heat, stirring constantly and scraping the bottom of the pot with a wooden spoon, until it is thickened and silky and registers 175 to 180 degrees on an instant-read thermometer, 8 to 12 minutes. (Do not let the custard overcook or simmer.)

3. Immediately pour the custard through the strainer over the chocolate. Let the mixture stand to melt the chocolate, about 5 minutes. Whisk gently until smooth, then whisk in the vanilla and dissolved espresso. Divide the mixture evenly among eight 5-ounce ramekins. Gently tap the ramekins against the counter to remove any air bubbles.

4. Cool the pots de crème to room temperature, then cover with plastic wrap and refrigerate until chilled, at least 4 hours or up to 72 hours. Before serving, let the pots de crème stand at room temperature for 20 to 30 minutes.

5. FOR THE WHIPPED CREAM AND GARNISH: Using an electric mixer, whip the cream, sugar, and vanilla on medium-low speed until small bubbles form, about 30 seconds. Increase the speed to medium-high and continue to whip the mixture until it thickens and forms stiff peaks, about 1 minute; set aside. Dollop each pot de crème with about 2 tablespoons of whipped cream and garnish with cocoa or chocolate shavings, if desired.

VARIATION

MILK CHOCOLATE POTS DE CRÈME

Milk chocolate behaves differently in this recipe than bittersweet chocolate and more of it must be used to ensure that the custard sets. And because of the increased amount of chocolate, it's necessary to cut back on the amount of sugar so that the custard is not overly sweet.

Follow the recipe for Chocolate Pots de Crème, substituting 12 ounces milk chocolate for the 10 ounces of bittersweet chocolate. Reduce the sugar to 2 tablespoons and proceed as directed.

TECHNIQUE: When Is the Crème Anglaise Ready?

An instant-read thermometer is the most reliable way to judge when crème anglaise has reached the proper temperature of 175 to 180 degrees. But you can also judge the progress of a custard sauce by its thickness. Dip a wooden spoon into the custard and run your finger across the back. (Yes, this old-fashioned method really does work.)

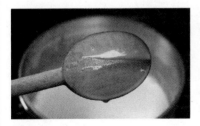  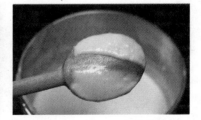

Not Yet

When its temperature is between 165 and 170 degrees, the custard will still be thin, and a line drawn on the back of the spoon will not hold.

Ready

When its temperature is between 175 and 180 degrees, the custard will coat the spoon, and the line will maintain neat edges.

Too Far

When its temperature goes above 180 degrees, small chunks will become visible in the curdled custard.

SCIENCE DESK:
Is Scalding Cream Necessary?

CRÈME ANGLAISE IS A CLASSIC FRENCH PREPARATION for a pourable custard that's used as a dessert sauce or as a base for ice creams and Bavarians. It's also the base for our chocolate pots de crème. The procedure for making crème anglaise that's taught in cooking schools everywhere goes like this: The cream (or half-and-half or milk) is scalded (that is, brought to a boil); the yolks and sugar are ribboned (that is, whisked together until light in color and the sugar dissolves); the yolk/sugar mixture is tempered (that is, some of the hot scalded cream is slowly whisked in to prevent the yolks from scrambling); the tempered mixture is returned to the saucepan; and the custard is cooked gently with constant stirring.

Fans of shortcuts, we tried making the crème anglaise base for our chocolate pots de crème without scalding the cream and tempering the eggs. Basically, we took cold or room-temperature ingredients, whisked them together, then cooked the mixture as usual. The result? A perfectly good crème anglaise. Why would this lazy-man's method work just as well as a classic and more complicated method?

It turns out the scald-and-temper method is scientifically out of date. This technique was developed to ensure smooth, uncurdled crème anglaise at a time when the quality of cream and milk was inconsistent. The unpasteurized and unhomogenized dairy products of yesteryear were more susceptible to curdling when they met heat. Today, dairy simply does not need to be scalded to check quality, and, consequently, there's no need to temper the egg yolks since they can be combined with the cold cream.

EQUIPMENT CORNER:
Inexpensive Dutch Ovens

WHEN WE TESTED DUTCH OVENS IN 1998, THE TOP performers were pots made by All-Clad and Le Creuset. Nearly a decade later, the only flaw we might find in these workhorses is their hefty price—roughly $250. These top-of-the-line pots now have plenty of imitators. Could any of them challenge our pricey favorites? Frankly, we were skeptical. But given that some of the cheaper options cost $200 less than our previous winners, it seemed worth a shot.

A good Dutch oven (variously called a stockpot, round oven, French oven, or casserole) is a kitchen essential.

Heavier and thicker than typical stockpots, allowing them to retain and conduct heat more effectively, and deeper than a skillet, so they can handle large cuts of meat and cooking liquid, Dutch ovens are the best choice for braises, pot roasts, and stews, as they can go on the stovetop to sear foods and then into the oven to finish cooking. Their tall sides make them useful for deep-frying, and many cooks press Dutch ovens into service for jobs like boiling pasta.

For our first test, we prepared a beef stew that starts on the stovetop and then moves to the oven. In each pan, we browned cubes of beef in batches, and as the meat seared, we observed whether the pan heated evenly and consistently without burning the drippings. After the long, slow cooking in the oven, we tasted the stew to see if the meat had become fork-tender and the broth had reduced to intense flavor. Of all the tests we did, this was the most important, because it focused on the unique abilities of Dutch ovens. As expected, the Le Creuset and All-Clad pots sailed through with flying colors. Surprisingly, so did a few of the others.

We noticed a few trends. Our favorite pots from All-Clad and Le Creuset measure 9¾ inches across, enabling them to brown 3½ pounds of beef in three batches, something narrower pots couldn't do. The Innova, which measures just 7⅝ inches across, required five batches—a big flaw. The Emerilware and Chefmate pans were slightly bigger (8 inches and 8¼ inches, respectively) and handled the beef in four batches—a minor flaw. The stew made in the Chefmate pot was great; the Emerilware pot browned the beef unevenly—an imperfection we also noticed in the too-light pot from Tramontina.

For the next test, we put two quarts of canola oil in each pan, clipped on a deep-fry thermometer, and cooked a pound of frozen french fries to test heat transfer and retention. Here again, our costly favorites met our high expectations but were well matched by a few contenders. The best pans retain heat well enough to prevent the temperature of the oil from dropping too precipitously when food is added. If the temperature drops too far, the fries will be soggy and

greasy. The Tramontina pot won this test—the temperature of the oil dropped just 45 degrees when the fries were added, and the recovery time for the oil, at 5 minutes and 45 seconds, was also the best. In contrast, oil in the Calphalon pot (the lowest-rated entry in this test) dropped 76 degrees and took more than 10 minutes to recover. As a result, the fries cooked in the Calphalon pot weren't crisp enough. The Innova pot suffered from similar problems.

An unexpected issue emerged during this test. Fries cooked in the Emerilware cast iron pan tasted rusty; evidently, the preseasoned surface had failed. Cast iron is a great choice for a Dutch oven, because it holds on to heat so well. But cast iron will also react with many foods. Some manufacturers (Le Creuset, Chefmate, Mario Batali, and Innova) coat their cast iron with a layer of brightly colored enamel. Other manufacturers preseason their pots—basically spraying them with oil and baking on the seasoning. But, as we discovered, it's possible to wash away the preseasoning. We boiled water in all the pots and noticed that the water turned yellow in both of the preseasoned cast iron pots, made by Emerilware and Lodge. As a result, neither pot can be used to boil water for pasta, and we worry that the cast iron may react with acidic cooking liquids, such as wine or tomatoes. Yes, you could reseason the pots yourself, but that seems like a hassle. An enamel coating on the cast iron surface will last a lifetime and makes a Dutch oven much more versatile.

For our last test, we steamed a triple batch of white rice in each Dutch oven to see how they simmered on very low heat. All but one pot made fluffy rice with intact grains. The Innova pot, which had trouble with heat retention in the french-fry test, overcooked the rice.

When all the smoke and sizzling fry oil cleared, our favorite pots (the ones we've used almost daily in the test kitchen for nearly 10 years) came out on top. Other than price, it's hard to quibble with the pots made by All-Clad and Le Creuset.

Although we weren't surprised by our winners, we were shocked at their narrow margin of victory. How could a $40 Dutch oven hold its own against pans costing six times as much? The Target Chefmate Casserole looks like a slightly smaller Le Creuset, down to the shape of the handles and the knob on the top. In fact, it kept up with the winners in every test. Because the Chefmate casserole is smaller than our top choices, you will need to brown meat for stew in more batches, and the biggest pot roasts will be a tight fit. While our test cooks are not ready to trade in their favorite Dutch ovens, the Chefmate is a real find for budget-minded cooks.

If you're willing to spend $100 on a Dutch oven, and you have the biceps to handle it, the 15-pound Mario Batali pot is comparable in size to the Le Creuset and All-Clad pots and performs nearly as well. Yes, the browning wasn't perfect, but that seems like a minor quibble most cooks would never notice. Two good choices, and both reasonably priced.

Rating Inexpensive Dutch Ovens

WE RATED SEVEN INEXPENSIVE DUTCH OVENS (PRICED UNDER $100) ALONG WITH PREVIOUS TEST KITCHEN winners made by All-Clad and Le Creuset (both priced in excess of $200). Ratings of good, fair, or poor for three kitchen tests (beef stew, french fries, and steamed white rice) were given to each pot. The Dutch ovens are listed in order of preference. See www.americastestkitchen.com for up-to-date prices and mail-order sources for top-rated products.

RECOMMENDED
All-Clad Stainless 8-quart Stockpot
$257.95; Stainless steel with aluminum core; 8 quart capacity; 6 pounds
This pot produced "golden and gorgeous" fond. Starred in the french-fry test, with rapid recovery of cooking temperature after fries were added. The best choice for cooks who prefer a lighter pot.

RECOMMENDED
Le Creuset 7¼-quart Round French Oven
$229.95; Enameled cast iron with phenolic lid knob; 7¼-quart capacity; 13.7 pounds
The "gold standard" of Dutch ovens put a "gorgeous, golden crust" on meat and created great fond. A kitchen workhorse that's heavy but not excessively so.

RECOMMENDED
Chefmate Round Enameled Cast Iron Casserole for Target
$39.99; Enameled cast iron with phenolic lid knob; 5-quart capacity; 11.6 pounds
Similar to Le Creuset, only smaller and a lot cheaper. Less cooking surface meant that stew meat was browned in four batches rather than three. Lid has a tight fit, and stew barely reduced in oven, although meat was tender and sauce flavorful.

RECOMMENDED
Mario Batali Italian Essentials Pot by Copco
$99.99; Enameled cast iron with cast stainless lid knob; 6-quart capacity; 15.2 pounds
This very heavy pan was slow to heat up but demonstrated quick recovery after fries were added to the oil. The "self basting" spikes inside the lid work— we never had to shake condensation off this lid after opening it.

RECOMMENDED WITH RESERVATIONS
Lodge Pro-Logic Pre-Seasoned Dutch Oven
$39.99; Preseasoned cast iron; 7-quart capacity; 17.2 pounds
Although it was hard at first to see the fond developing in this black pot, the meat had "excellent, deep browning." Large looping handles make it easy to manipulate this heavy-weight pot.

RECOMMENDED WITH RESERVATIONS
Calphalon One Infused Anodized Dutch Oven
$99.99; Heavy-gauge aluminum infused with polymer; stainless steel lid; 8½-quart capacity; 6.8 pounds
In the fries test, the temperature of oil dropped the farthest when potatoes were added, then fluctuated more than the other pans.

RECOMMENDED WITH RESERVATIONS
Tramontina Sterling ii 18/10 Stainless Steel Covered Dutch Oven
$69.95; Stainless steel with aluminum core bottom; 7-quart capacity; 6.4 pounds
Pan is big, light, and easy to handle, and it did a nice job browning meat. However, the stew liquid did not reduce at all in the oven and tasted soupy.

RECOMMENDED WITH RESERVATIONS
Emerilware from All-Clad Cast Iron Dutch Oven
$34.95; Preseasoned cast iron; 6-quart capacity; 15.9 pounds
Deep, narrow pan was slow to heat up but developed a nice fond for stew once it did. Meat had to be browned in four batches rather than three. Boiled water appeared yellow, and fries had a distinctly rusty taste.

RECOMMENDED WITH RESERVATIONS
Innova Color Cast Porcelain Enameled Cast Iron 5-quart Round Dutch Oven
$49.99; Enameled cast iron; 5-quart capacity; 11.3 pounds
We had to brown the meat for the stew in five batches rather than three. The pan also runs slightly hot.

IDAHO
Potatoes

Fresh

NET WT 5 LBS (2.27kg)

PRODUCE OF U.S.A.

GROWN IN IDAHO

We tested a variety of potatoes for our Garlic and Olive Oil Mashed Potatoes. What came out on top? Russets, which were prized for their earthy potato flavor and light, fluffy texture.

BISTRO STEAK
dinner

CHAPTER 18

A nicely charred thick-cut steak certainly looks appealing. But cutting into the steak to find that the rosy meat is confined to a measly spot in the center—with the rest a thick band of overcooked gray—is a great disappointment. This is the problem with thick-cut steaks—traditional methods pan-sear the meat over high heat (to ensure that flavorful crust), but even using lower heat to cook the rest of the steak through is still not gentle enough to prevent overcooking all but the very center. We needed to find a sure-fire method for pan-searing thick-cut steaks that could deliver both a flavorful crust and juicy, rosy meat throughout.

While we've enjoyed creamy, buttery mashed potatoes with steak, roast chicken, and more, we've often wondered if there is an alternative to dairy-rich potatoes. We suspected that we might have found our answer with Mediterranean-style mashed potatoes, which rely on olive oil (and often garlic) in lieu of butter and cream. But it's not as simple as swapping in olive oil and garlic for the dairy. These bold flavors have a tendency to overwhelm and we found the texture compromised as well—instead of lithe, smooth potatoes, the mash can turn pasty. With a little testing and a lot of tasting, we were determined to find a way to make these Mediterranean mashed potatoes work.

IN THIS CHAPTER

THE RECIPES
Pan-Seared Thick-Cut Steaks
Red Wine–Mushroom Pan Sauce
Tequila-Poblano Pan Sauce
Sun-Dried Tomato Relish
Thai Chili Butter

Garlic and Olive Oil Mashed
    Potatoes

EQUIPMENT CORNER
Slotted Spoons

SCIENCE DESK
What Makes Steaks Tender?

PAN-SEARED THICK-CUT STEAKS

WHAT WE WANTED: Thick-cut steak with a browned, flavorful crust and rosy, juicy meat throughout, not just in the center.

Cooking a standard supermarket steak is easy; we've been doing it for years—just get an oiled pan smoking hot and slap in your steak. A flip and a quick rest before serving, and you have dinner. But try this method with a thick-cut strip steak (we're talking almost as thick as it is wide) and you run into some problems. By the time a good crust has developed and the very center of the steak has reached medium-rare (130 degrees), the bulk of the meat is dry and gray. We were

convinced that there was a better way to cook thick steaks, a new method that would give them the tender treatment they deserve.

To begin, we had to figure out what was causing our meat to turn gray. When beef reaches temperatures above 140 degrees, it undergoes structural and chemical changes that cause it to dry out and toughen, as well as lose its red color. We wanted to keep as much of the meat below this critical temperature as possible. However, the Maillard reaction (which is responsible for the deep color and rich meaty flavor of a well-browned crust) occurs at temperatures closer to 300 degrees. The ideal technique would entail quickly searing the exterior to develop a crust while slowly cooking

the interior to allow for more even heat distribution. Our job was to reconcile these two conflicting goals.

Our first attempt was using a technique proposed by food scientist and writer Harold McGee: We flipped the meat as often as once every 15 seconds, so the heat would diffuse gradually through it, resulting in a more evenly cooked steak. This method did provide a uniform crust and a fairly evenly cooked interior, but to cook four steaks at a time, we had to flip one about every four seconds. With 176 flips required over the course of the 11-minute cooking time, we'd flipped the equivalent of 88 pounds of meat—maybe doable for a short-order cook on steroids, but not for your average home cook.

Next we tried pan-roasting, which involves searing the steaks in a hot pan, then transferring them—pan and all—to a blazing 450-degree oven to quickly finish cooking. This resulted in the familiar gray band and chewy meat. We wanted our steaks to finish cooking more gently, so the next time around we transferred them out of the hot pan and onto a rack and lowered the oven temperature to a mild 275 degrees. Thirty-two minutes later, the steaks were noticeably more tender in the center—due to increased enzymatic action (see "What Makes Steaks Tender?" on page 216)—but still had ¼-inch-thick gray zones around their perimeters.

Comparing cross-sections of a steak at different cooking stages revealed that this gray band was created during the initial browning. It seemed that a low oven was the path to tender meat, but we needed to speed up the searing process so that the meat just underneath the surface would not have time to overcook.

Basic thermodynamics: When a 40-degree steak is placed in a 400-degree pan, the temperature of the pan drops significantly. Until it reheats to 300 degrees, no browning can take place. A cold, thick steak added to a hot pan can take upward of four minutes per side to form a good crust—during which time the meat beneath the surface is overcooking. Preheating the pan longer and with more oil only sent our hopes up in flames. But what if we upped the starting temperature of the meat? We put the steaks in a zipper-lock bag and submerged them in 120-degree tap water; 30 minutes later, they had reached 100 degrees. Convinced that this was the solution, we transferred the warmed steaks to a preheated pan—where, alas, it still took more than six minutes to brown both sides properly.

While racking our gray matter, we recalled a grade school science experiment. A paper cup full of water was placed directly over the flame of a candle, yet the paper did not burn. The cup was left over the flame until all the water had boiled away, at which point the cup finally ignited. Turned out that as long as there was still water in the cup, all the heat from the candle was being used to boil and vaporize the water, preventing the cup from ever going above 212 degrees (the boiling point of water). Our point? Just as a paper cup can't burn if there is any water in it, a steak can't brown until all of its surface moisture has evaporated.

That explained our failed zipper-lock bag test. The moisture that was sweating out of the warming steaks was coming into direct contact with the pan, thereby reducing the rate at which it could heat up. It struck us: To get well-browned, juicy steaks, start with warm, dry meat. We seasoned some steaks as usual, this time moving them straight from the fridge into a 275-degree oven. After 25 minutes, they had warmed to 95 degrees and the surfaces looked like desiccated lunar landscapes. We began to doubt our theory, but then we seared them; they developed beautiful brown crusts in less than four minutes. We held our breath while they rested. As the knife cut through the crispy crust, it revealed pink, juicy, tender meat—the gray zone was all but gone.

WHAT WE LEARNED: For juicy, rosy meat throughout, start the steaks in the oven—place on a wire rack set over a baking sheet and cook at a gentle 275 degrees. To finish the steaks and develop a browned crust, transfer the parcooked steaks to a skillet and pan-sear. Let rest for 10 minutes so the juices have time to redistribute throughout the meat.

PAN-SEARED THICK-CUT STEAKS

serves 4

Rib-eye or filet mignon of similar thickness can be substituted for strip steaks. If using filet mignon, buying a 2-pound center-cut tenderloin roast and portioning it into four 8-ounce steaks yourself will produce more consistent results. If using filet mignon, increase the oven time by about 5 minutes. When cooking lean strip steaks (without an external fat cap) or filet mignon, add an extra tablespoon of oil to the pan. If desired, serve with one of the sauces, the relish, or butter that follow.

2   boneless strip steaks, 1½ to 1¾ inches thick
     (about 1 pound each) (see note)
     Kosher salt and ground black pepper
1   tablespoon vegetable oil

1. Adjust an oven rack to the middle position and heat the oven to 275 degrees. Pat the steaks dry with paper towels. Cut each steak in half vertically to create four 8-ounce steaks. Season the steaks liberally with salt and pepper; using your hands, gently shape into a uniform thickness. Place the steaks on a wire rack set in a rimmed baking sheet; transfer the baking sheet to the oven. Cook until an instant-read thermometer inserted horizontally into the center of the steaks registers 90 to 95 degrees for rare to medium-rare,

20 to 25 minutes, or 100 to 105 degrees for medium, 25 to 30 minutes.

2. Heat the oil in a 12-inch heavy-bottomed skillet over high heat until smoking. Place the steaks in the skillet and sear until well browned and crusty, 1½ to 2 minutes, lifting once halfway through to redistribute the fat underneath each steak. (Reduce the heat if the fond begins to burn.) Using tongs, turn the steaks and cook until well browned on the second side, 2 to 2½ minutes. Transfer the steaks to a clean rack and reduce the heat under the pan to medium. Use tongs to stand 2 steaks on their sides. Holding the steaks together, return to the skillet and sear on all edges until browned, about 1½ minutes (see the photo below left). Repeat with the remaining 2 steaks.

3. Return the steaks to the wire rack and let rest, loosely tented with foil, for about 10 minutes. If desired, cook the sauce in the now-empty skillet. Serve immediately.

TECHNIQUE:
Searing Two Steaks at Once

Use tongs to sear the sides of two steaks at the same time.

GETTING IT RIGHT:
Ensuring Rosy, Not Gray, Meat

Traditional Way
By the time thick steaks come up to temperature in the middle, a wide band of dry gray meat has developed below the crust.

Our Method
Our method starts the steaks in a low oven to gently raise their temperature. The rosy interior extends nearly to the crust.

RED WINE–MUSHROOM PAN SAUCE

makes about 1 cup, enough to sauce 4 steaks
Prepare all the ingredients for the pan sauce while the steaks are in the oven.

1 tablespoon vegetable oil
8 ounces white mushrooms, wiped clean, trimmed, and sliced thin (about 3 cups)
1 small shallot, minced (about 1½ tablespoons)
1 cup dry red wine
½ cup low-sodium chicken broth
1 tablespoon balsamic vinegar
1 teaspoon Dijon mustard
2 tablespoons cold unsalted butter, cut into 4 pieces
1 teaspoon minced fresh thyme leaves
Salt and ground black pepper

Pour off the fat from the skillet in which the steaks were cooked. Heat the oil over medium-high heat until just smoking. Add the mushrooms and cook, stirring occasionally, until beginning to brown and the liquid has evaporated, about 5 minutes. Add the shallot and cook, stirring frequently, until beginning to soften, about 1 minute. Increase the heat to high; add the red wine and broth, scraping the bottom of the skillet with a wooden spoon to loosen any browned bits. Simmer rapidly until the liquid and mushrooms are reduced

to 1 cup, about 6 minutes. Add the vinegar, mustard, and any juices from the resting steaks; cook until thickened, about 1 minute. Off the heat, whisk in the butter and thyme; season with salt and pepper to taste. Spoon the sauce over the steaks and serve immediately.

TEQUILA-POBLANO PAN SAUCE

makes ⅔ cup, enough to sauce 4 steaks
Prepare all the ingredients for the pan sauce while the steaks are in the oven.

1 small shallot, minced (about 1½ tablespoons)
1 poblano chile, seeded and diced (about ⅓ cup)
½ teaspoon ground cumin
½ cup tequila, white or gold
½ cup low-sodium chicken broth
1 tablespoon juice from 1 lime
3 tablespoons cold unsalted butter, cut into 6 pieces
1 tablespoon chopped fresh cilantro leaves
Salt and ground black pepper

Pour off all but 1 tablespoon fat from the skillet in which the steaks were cooked. Return the pan to high heat and add the shallot and poblano; sauté, stirring and flipping frequently, until lightly browned and fragrant, 1 to 2 minutes. Add the cumin and continue to cook 30 seconds. Transfer the pan contents to a bowl. Reserving 2 teaspoons of the tequila, add the remaining to the now-empty pan off the heat and then return the pan to high heat. Using a long match or kitchen lighter, ignite the tequila. Let the flames subside. Add the chicken broth and 2 teaspoons of the lime juice. Simmer rapidly until reduced to about ⅓ cup, about 6 minutes, scraping up any browned bits from the bottom of the pan with a wooden spoon. Add the remaining 2 teaspoons tequila, remaining teaspoon of lime juice, and any meat juices to the pan. Remove from the heat and whisk in the butter, cilantro, and reserved poblano and shallot; season to taste with salt and pepper. Spoon the sauce over the steaks and serve immediately.

SUN-DRIED TOMATO RELISH

makes ½ cup, enough for 4 steaks

If you desire more heat after tasting this highly flavorful relish, add another small pinch of red pepper flakes.

½ cup low-sodium chicken broth
  Pinch red pepper flakes (see note)
2 tablespoons oil-packed sun-dried tomatoes, drained and chopped
1 tablespoon capers, drained and chopped
1 teaspoon honey
1 tablespoon extra-virgin olive oil
2 teaspoons juice from 1 lemon
2 tablespoons chopped fresh parsley leaves
1 tablespoon minced fresh mint leaves
  Salt and ground black pepper

Pour off all the fat from the skillet and return to high heat. Add the chicken broth and scrape the browned bits from the bottom of the pan with a wooden spoon. Add the pepper flakes and boil until the liquid is reduced to 2 tablespoons, about 5 minutes. Add any meat juices to the pan. Add the tomatoes, capers, honey, olive oil, and lemon juice to the pan and swirl vigorously to emulsify. Remove the pan from the heat and add the parsley and mint. Season with salt and pepper to taste. Spoon over the steaks and serve immediately.

THAI CHILI BUTTER

makes about 6 tablespoons, enough for 4 steaks

If red curry paste isn't available, increase the chili-garlic sauce to 2½ teaspoons.

4 tablespoons (½ cup) unsalted butter, softened
1 scallion (green part only), sliced thin
1 tablespoon chopped fresh cilantro leaves
2 teaspoons Asian chili-garlic sauce (preferably Thai)
1 small garlic clove, minced or pressed through a garlic press (about ½ teaspoon)
½ teaspoon red curry paste (preferably Thai)
2 teaspoons juice from 1 lime
  Salt

Beat the butter vigorously with a spoon until soft and fluffy. Add the scallion, cilantro, chili-garlic sauce, garlic, and red curry paste; beat to incorporate. Add the lime juice a little at a time, beating vigorously between each addition until fully incorporated. Add salt to taste. Serve a dollop over each steak, giving it time to melt.

SCIENCE DESK:
What Makes Steaks Tender?

OUR STEAKS SPEND A LONG TIME IN A WARM OVEN, yet taste more tender than traditionally prepared steaks, which can be tough and chewy. The explanation? Meat contains active enzymes called cathepsins, which break down connective tissues over time, increasing tenderness (a fact that is demonstrated to great effect in dry-aged meat). As the temperature of the meat rises, these enzymes work faster and faster until they reach 122 degrees, where all action stops. While our steaks are slowly heating up, the cathepsins are working overtime, in effect "aging" and tenderizing our steaks within half an hour. When steaks are cooked by conventional methods, their final temperature is reached much more rapidly, denying the cathepsins the time they need to properly do their job.

GARLIC AND OLIVE OIL MASHED POTATOES

WHAT WE WANTED: Mediterranean-style mashed potatoes—light, smooth, and rich with olive oil and discernible, but not harsh, garlic flavor.

A heaping mound of rich yet fluffy traditional mashed potatoes is to many main dishes what a scoop of vanilla ice cream is to dessert: a great all-American side. But in the Mediterranean, another take on mashed potatoes exists that incorporates the distinct flavors of extra-virgin olive oil (used in lieu of dairy products like butter and cream) and garlic. For example, the Greeks have skordalia, a puree of cooked potatoes, extra-virgin olive oil, garlic, and lemon served meze-style as a spread or dip. We wanted to translate these same bold (but often overpowering) flavors into a light and creamy mashed potato side dish to partner with simple grilled meats or fish.

First, we needed the ideal potato base, so we began with the test kitchen's established methods. Rather than simmering peeled, cut potatoes, we opted for whole potatoes in their skins. This minimizes the opportunity for water to enter and bind with the potato's starch molecules, thus keeping the mashed potatoes from becoming thin, water-logged, and bland.

While Yukon Golds provided a nice golden color and a creamy, dense texture, russet potatoes yielded lighter, fluffier mashed potatoes that our tasters preferred. Putting the drained, peeled, still-hot potatoes through a ricer or food mill rather than using a potato masher ensured a smooth, fine texture.

We knew that replacing the full 1½ cups of fat (butter and half-and-half) in our traditional recipe with extra-virgin olive oil would be a disaster (more like potato-flavored olive oil). Reducing the oil to a little more than ½ cup made the mashed russets smooth and creamy without being watery, greasy, or pasty. Now the texture was right, but the flavor of the extra-virgin olive oil was still overwhelming, so we tried other options. Extra-light olive oil had all the flavor of vegetable oil, while regular olive oil was only slightly better. Stumped, we took a break from the olive oil problem to focus on the garlic.

We quickly learned that stirring raw minced garlic into the mashed potatoes made for a harsh flavor. Next, we tried smashing raw minced garlic with kosher salt into a smooth paste. This improved the texture by eliminating pockets of grainy garlic but did nothing for the harsh bite. Boiling whole peeled cloves reduced the flavor to almost nothing. Pan-toasting unpeeled cloves was a winner—the resulting flavor was sweet and roasted. Slowly cooking the garlic paste in oil over low heat, however, provided a similarly mild-sweet flavor with an added benefit: we had inadvertently made a mild garlic oil.

This was the solution we'd been looking for. The 10 tablespoons of raw extra-virgin olive oil we had been using was too potent, but using less than half that amount (4 tablespoons, or ¼ cup) to simmer the garlic tempered the oil's raw flavor (heat alters the oil's taste) and added a hint of garlic. Next, we added the cooked garlic oil to the potatoes along with the remaining 6 tablespoons of uncooked oil. The result? Very nice, but tame. The answer was to add just 1 teaspoon of freshly made garlic paste for a full—but not overwhelming—flavor.

To lighten and brighten these mashed potatoes without making them sour or overly citrusy, we added just a splash (2 teaspoons) of lemon juice. Smooth and creamy, with distinct but balanced flavors, our Mediterranean-style mashed potatoes were finally ready for side-dish duty.

WHAT WE LEARNED: Russets are preferred to other potatoes in this dish for their light, fluffy texture. For potatoes with full and balanced, not harsh, garlic flavor, use a blend of cooked and raw garlic. Use restraint with the olive oil—just a little over ¼ cup is enough to add flavor and richness. And a splash of lemon juice brightens the flavor of these Mediterranean—style spuds.

GARLIC AND OLIVE OIL MASHED POTATOES

serves 6

As this dish is denser and more intensely flavored than traditional mashed potatoes, our suggested serving size is smaller than you might expect. These potatoes make a fine accompaniment to simply seasoned grilled meats, fish, and poultry.

2   pounds russet potatoes, unpeeled and scrubbed
5   medium garlic cloves, peeled
2   teaspoons plus ⅛ teaspoon kosher salt
½   cup plus 2 tablespoons extra-virgin olive oil
½   teaspoon ground black pepper
2   teaspoons juice from 1 lemon

1. Place the potatoes in a large saucepan with water to cover by 1 inch. Bring to a boil over high heat; reduce the heat to medium-low and cook at bare simmer until just tender (the potatoes will offer very little resistance when poked with a paring knife), 40 to 45 minutes.

2. While the potatoes are simmering, mince 1 garlic clove (or press through a garlic press). Place the minced garlic on a cutting board and sprinkle with ⅛ teaspoon of the kosher salt. Using the flat side of a chef's knife, drag the garlic and salt back and forth across the cutting board in small circular motions until the garlic is ground into a smooth paste. Transfer to a medium bowl and set aside.

3. Mince the remaining 4 garlic cloves (or press through a garlic press). Place in a small saucepan with ¼ cup of the olive oil and cook over low heat, stirring constantly, until the garlic foams and is soft, fragrant, and golden, about 5 minutes. Transfer the oil and garlic to the bowl with the raw garlic paste.

4. Drain the cooked potatoes; set a food mill or ricer over the now-empty saucepan. Using a potholder (to hold the potatoes) and a paring knife, peel the skins from the

potatoes. Working in batches, cut the peeled potatoes into large chunks and process through a food mill or ricer into the saucepan.

5. Add the remaining 2 teaspoons salt, the pepper, lemon juice, and remaining 6 tablespoons olive oil to the bowl with the garlic and cooked oil and whisk to combine. Fold the mixture into the potatoes and serve.

EQUIPMENT CORNER: Slotted Spoons

A SLOTTED SPOON IS INDISPENSABLE FOR FISHING food out of boiling water. But after damaging delicate gnocchi and dropping dozens of green peas as we tested eight models, we learned that not just any combination of handles and holes would do. Our testers preferred lengthy handles, deep bowls, and enough small slits or punctures to quickly drain water without losing as much as one petite pea. A stainless steel spoon from Calphalon ($9.95) and nonstick nylon models from Messermeister ($2.95) and OXO ($5.95) all met our demands, though the slightly flimsy Messermeister was downgraded for its smaller capacity. With its lighter weight and slimmer price tag, OXO just edged out Calphalon for top honors.

Rating Slotted Spoons

WE TESTED EIGHT SLOTTED SPOONS. TESTS INCLUDED RETRIEVING DELICATE GNOCCHI AND PETITE PEAS FROM boiling water. The spoons are listed in order of preference. See www.americastestkitchen.com for up-to-date prices and mail-order sources for top-rated products.

HIGHLY RECOMMENDED
OXO Good Grips Nylon Slotted Spoon
$5.95
A deep bowl, plenty of holes, and lightweight design slotted this spoon at the top of the charts.

RECOMMENDED
Calphalon Stainless Steel Slotted Spoon
$9.95
This stainless steel spoon was a close second and might be a better option for those who prefer a sturdier tool.

RECOMMENDED
Messermeister Nylon Slotted Spoon
$2.95
This lightweight, bargain spoon felt slightly flimsy to some and held less food, but generally performed fine.

RECOMMENDED WITH RESERVATIONS
Cuisipro Tempo Slotted Spoon
$14.95
Heavy and bearing an overly offset handle, this stainless steel model lost most credit for sporting only three razor-thin slits and a pinhole, making it slow to drain.

RECOMMENDED WITH RESERVATIONS
Kuhn Rikon SoftEdge Cooks' Slotted Spoon
$17.95
More of a hindrance than a help, the silicone edge on this deep-bowled, oddly shaped model ended up nicking and sticking to the delicate gnocchi.

NOT RECOMMENDED
OXO Good Grips Large Wooden Slotted Spoon
$4.99
Awkwardly stiff and shallow, this wooden model also managed to lodge some peas in its wide slits.

NOT RECOMMENDED
All-Clad Stainless Steel Slotted Spoon
$19.95
Very solidly made and comfortable to hold, but this model's small cluster of holes in its shallow basin lost far too many peas to the drain.

NOT RECOMMENDED
KitchenAid Hollow Handle Slotted Serving Spoon
$9.99
Far too short, with holes that were far too big, this model held only three gnocchi and lost most of the peas to the sink.

With all the burners fired up and barely an inch of counter space free, the test kitchen readies dishes for an episode on Indian favorites.

INDIAN·FAVORITES,
CHAPTER 19
simplified

Put away your takeout menus. Now that many supermarkets boast expansive aisles containing a variety of ethnic ingredients, cooking "internationally" has become easier than ever. For this chapter, we chose to develop home-cook-friendly versions of two Indian favorites: vegetable curry and chicken tikka masala.

Finding the right vegetables to carry the rich, complex flavors of curry can be a challenge. A good curry can also be elusive, turning bland and greasy, rather than bold and complex. And it's no secret that preparing curry can often be quite labor intensive. We wanted a curry that we could turn out on a weeknight—relatively quick, but full of flavor.

Chicken tikka masala is said to have been created in a London restaurant by a cook looking to please a patron who was unsatisfied by his plate of chicken tikka (skewered grilled chicken). He added a lightly spiced tomato sauce enriched with cream and returned it to the waiting diner, who was, indeed, pleased by the flavorful combination. Unfortunately, not all cooks (or recipes) are so accommodating. We've eaten our fair share of substandard tikka masala—bone-dry chicken in a heavily spiced harsh sauce or one overly rich with cream. We aimed to develop a reliable, foolproof version of chicken masala—juicy chunks of chicken in a lightly spiced sauce just rich enough to cling to the meat and moisten the rice served alongside.

VEGETABLE CURRY

WHAT WE WANTED: A vegetable curry we could make on a weeknight in less than an hour—without sacrificing flavor or overloading the dish with spices.

The term "curry" is derived from the Tamil word *kari*, which simply means "sauce" or "gravy." There are thousands of ways to make curry. When flavorful beef or lamb is the main ingredient, even a mediocre recipe usually yields a decent outcome. But vegetable curry is a different story: It's all too easy to turn out a second-rate, if not awful, dish. Delicate vegetables are often watery carriers for the sauce, offering little personality of their own.

Vegetable curries can be complicated affairs, with lengthy ingredient lists and fussy techniques meant to compensate for the lack of meat. But we wanted something simpler—a curry we could make on a weeknight in less than an hour. Most streamlined recipes we tried, however, were uninspired. A few attempted to make up for the flavor deficit by overloading the dish with spices, and the results were harsh and overpowering. We had our work cut out for us.

While some curries are made with exotic whole and ground spices (fenugreek, asafetida, dried rose petals, and so on), we decided to limit ourselves to everyday ground spices such as cumin, cloves, cardamom, cinnamon, and coriander. Our testing dragged on for days, and it was hard to reach consensus in the test kitchen. Frankly, most of the homemade spice mixtures we tried were fine.

We had been reluctant to use store-bought curry powder, assuming its flavor would be inferior to a homemade blend, but it seemed worth a try. We were surprised when tasters liked the curry powder nearly as well as a homemade mixture made with seven spices. It turns out that store-bought curry powder contains some of the exotic spices we had dismissed at the outset. As long as we used enough, our recipe had decent flavor.

Looking for ways to improve the flavor of the curry powder, we tried toasting it in a skillet until the seductive aroma of the spices emerged. This simple step took just one minute and turned commercial curry powder into a flavor powerhouse. Why was toasting so beneficial? When added to a simmering sauce, spices can be heated to only 212 degrees. In a dry skillet, temperatures can exceed 500 degrees, causing flavors to explode.

With the spices settled, we turned to building the rest of our flavor base. Many classic recipes begin with a generous amount of sautéed onion, which adds depth and body to the sauce, and we followed suit. Ghee (clarified butter) is traditionally used to sauté the onions. It adds terrific richness, though we found that vegetable oil was a fine substitute. Almost all curry recipes—meat and vegetable alike— add equal amounts of garlic and ginger to the onions, and we found no reason to stray from this well-balanced tradition. Wanting to take our meatless sauce to the next level, we stirred in a minced fresh chile for heat and a spoonful of tomato paste for sweetness. The latter ingredient was decidedly inauthentic, but we found it really helped. As the onions caramelized with the other ingredients, fond (flavorful dark bits) developed in the bottom of the pan, mimicking the phenomenon that occurs when browning meat. We then added the toasted curry powder to the pan and let it dissolve. Creating a supercharged base for our curry took just 15 minutes.

We decided to include chickpeas and potatoes for heartiness, along with one firm and one soft vegetable. Eventually, we settled on a classic pairing of cauliflower and peas. Although the combination of textures and colors was good, the vegetables were a bit bland. For meat curries, the beef or lamb is often added to the sauce without any prior flavor development, but we figured our vegetables should bring something to the dish. Oven roasting the potatoes definitely helped but took too much time. Instead, we tried browning them along with the onions. This unconventional

move was an unqualified success, substantially boosting the flavor of the potatoes.

Could we bring up the flavor of the other vegetables, too? An Indian cooking method called *bhuna* involves sautéing the spices and main ingredients together to enhance and meld flavors. We tried this technique with cauliflower, as well as eggplant and green beans (used in a recipe variation), and they all developed a richer, more complex flavor. Next, we determined that a combination of water and pureed canned tomatoes, along with a splash of cream or coconut milk, allowed the delicate vegetables and fragrant spices to shine.

Lastly, we experimented with garam masala, a spice blend often sprinkled on Indian dishes before serving. Like curry powder, garam masala varies among cooks but usually includes warm spices such as black pepper, cinnamon, coriander, and cardamom (its name means "hot spice" in Hindi). Following our success with the curry powder, we decided to buy a jar of commercial garam masala. But when we added a few pinches to the curry post-cooking, the result was raw and harsh-tasting. What if we toasted the garam masala in a skillet along with the curry powder? Lightning did strike twice, as the garam masala mellowed into a second wave of flavor that helped the curry reach an even more layered complexity. Here was a robust, satisfying vegetable curry that relied on supermarket staples.

WHAT WE LEARNED: Toasting the curry powder in a skillet turns it into a flavor powerhouse. Adding a few pinches of garam masala adds even more spice flavor. To build the rest of the flavor base start with a generous amount of sautéed onion, vegetable oil, garlic, ginger, fresh chile, and tomato paste for sweetness. Sauté the spices and main ingredients (chickpeas and potatoes for heartiness, and cauliflower and peas for texture and color) together to enhance and meld the flavors. A combination of water, pureed canned tomatoes, and a splash of cream or coconut milk rounds out the flavors in the sauce.

INDIAN-STYLE CURRY WITH POTATOES, CAULIFLOWER, PEAS, AND CHICKPEAS

serves 4 to 6 as a main course

This curry is moderately spicy when made with one chile. For more heat, use an additional half chile. For a mild curry, remove the chile's ribs and seeds before mincing. Onions can be pulsed in a food processor. You can substitute 2 teaspoons ground coriander, ½ teaspoon ground black pepper, ¼ teaspoon ground cardamom, and ¼ teaspoon ground cinnamon for the garam masala.

2	tablespoons sweet or mild curry powder (see page 225)
1½	teaspoons garam masala (see page 225)
¼	cup vegetable oil
2	medium onions, chopped fine (about 2 cups)
12	ounces Red Bliss potatoes, scrubbed and cut into ½-inch pieces (about 2 cups)
3	medium garlic cloves, minced or pressed through a garlic press (about 1 tablespoon)
1	tablespoon finely grated fresh ginger
1–1½	serrano chiles, ribs, seeds, and flesh minced (see note)
1	tablespoon tomato paste
½	medium head cauliflower, trimmed, cored, and cut into 1-inch florets (about 4 cups)
1	(14.5-ounce) can diced tomatoes, pulsed in a food processor until nearly smooth with ¼-inch pieces visible
1¼	cups water
1	(15-ounce) can chickpeas, drained and rinsed Salt
8	ounces frozen peas (about 1½ cups)
¼	cup heavy cream or coconut milk

condiments

Plain whole milk yogurt
Onion Relish (recipe follows)
Cilantro-Mint Chutney (recipe follows)
Mango chutney

1. Toast the curry powder and garam masala in a small skillet over medium-high heat, stirring constantly, until the spices darken slightly and become fragrant, about 1 minute. Remove the spices from the skillet and set aside.

2. Heat 3 tablespoons of the oil in a large Dutch oven over medium-high heat until shimmering. Add the onions and potatoes and cook, stirring occasionally, until the onions are caramelized and the potatoes are golden brown on the edges, about 10 minutes. (Reduce the heat to medium if the onions darken too quickly.)

3. Reduce the heat to medium. Clear the center of the pan and add the remaining tablespoon oil, the garlic, ginger, chile, and tomato paste; cook, stirring constantly, until fragrant, about 30 seconds. Add the toasted spices and cook, stirring constantly, about 1 minute longer. Add the cauliflower and cook, stirring constantly, until the spices coat the florets, about 2 minutes longer.

4. Add the tomatoes, water, chickpeas, and 1 teaspoon salt; increase the heat to medium-high and bring the mixture to a boil, scraping the bottom of the pan with a wooden spoon to loosen any browned bits. Cover and reduce the heat to medium. Simmer briskly, stirring occasionally, until the vegetables are tender, 10 to 15 minutes. Stir in the peas and cream; continue to cook until heated through, about 2 minutes longer. Season with salt to taste and serve immediately, passing the condiments separately.

CILANTRO-MINT CHUTNEY

makes about 1 cup

The chutney can be refrigerated in a covered container for 1 day.

2	cups packed fresh cilantro leaves
1	cup packed fresh mint leaves
⅓	cup plain yogurt
¼	cup minced onion
1	tablespoon juice from 1 lime
1½	teaspoons sugar
½	teaspoon ground cumin
¼	teaspoon salt

Process all the ingredients in a food processor until smooth, about 20 seconds, scraping down the sides of the bowl with a rubber spatula after 10 seconds.

VARIATION

INDIAN-STYLE CURRY WITH SWEET POTATOES, EGGPLANT, GREEN BEANS, AND CHICKPEAS

Follow the recipe for Indian-Style Curry with Potatoes, Cauliflower, Peas, and Chickpeas, substituting peeled sweet potatoes, cut into ½-inch dice, for the Red Bliss potatoes. Substitute 1½ cups green beans, trimmed and cut into 1-inch pieces, and 1 medium eggplant, cut into ½-inch pieces (about 3 cups), for the cauliflower. Omit the peas.

ONION RELISH

makes about 1 cup

If using a regular yellow onion, increase the sugar to 1 teaspoon. The relish can be refrigerated in an airtight container for 1 day.

1	medium Vidalia onion, finely diced (about 1 cup) (see note)
1	tablespoon juice from 1 lime
½	teaspoon sweet paprika
½	teaspoon sugar
⅛	teaspoon salt
	Pinch cayenne pepper

Mix all the ingredients in a medium bowl.

SHOPPING NOTES: Curry in a Hurry

Hoping we could skip the step of grinding our own spices for curry, we substituted store-bought curry powder and garam masala. Tasters found this shortcut to be long on flavor, provided we chose the right brands and toasted the spice blends in a dry skillet.

THE BEST
CURRY POWDER

Penzeys Curry Powder

THE BEST
GARAM MASALA

McCormick Garam Masala

TASTING LAB: Mango Chutney

MANGO CHUTNEY (SOMETIMES CALLED MAJOR GREY'S chutney) is a welcome accompaniment to many curries and roasted meats. The name "Major Grey" is based on a fictional British soldier who supposedly enjoyed the sweet-and-sour punch of chutneys so much that he bottled his own. The name is not copyrighted and any bottled chutney can carry it.

Classic preparations cook unripe green mangos with sugar, vinegar, and aromatic spices. But high levels of fructose corn syrup and caramel color cloud many store-bought varieties, and any natural mango flavors are often overshadowed.

Many of the supermarket brands we tested were sickeningly sweet, with insipid, weak flavor. Tasters disliked the unnatural mango flavor in Crosse and Blackwell Major Grey's Chutney. A substantial dollop of ginger oil spiced Patak's Sweet Mango Chutney so heavily that tasters were torn; some appreciated the pungent, perfumed zing, while others complained about the ginger overload. Tasters liked the balanced sweetness and acidity of both Sharwood's Major Grey Mango Chutney and The Silver Palate Mango Chutney. In the end, the addition of lemon juice and peel gave The Silver Palate Mango Chutney a tangy boost that made it our favorite.

THE BEST MANGO CHUTNEY
A good mango chutney, like this one from The Silver Palate, offers a tangy, sweet, fruity complement to spicy curries.

BASMATI RICE, PILAF-STYLE
serves 4 as a side dish

1 tablespoon canola oil, vegetable oil, or corn oil
1 (3-inch) piece cinnamon stick, halved
2 green cardamom pods
2 whole cloves
¼ cup thinly sliced onion
1 cup basmati rice
1½ cups water
1 teaspoon salt

1. Heat the oil in a medium saucepan over high heat until almost smoking. Add the whole spices and cook, stirring until they pop. Add the onion and cook, stirring until translucent, about 2 minutes. Stir in the rice and cook, stirring, until fragrant, about 1 minute.

2. Add the water and salt; bring to a boil. Reduce the heat, cover tightly, and simmer until all the water has been absorbed, about 17 minutes. Let stand, covered, at least 10 minutes, fluff with a fork, and serve.

CHICKEN TIKKA MASALA

WHAT WE WANTED: An approachable method for producing moist, tender chunks of chicken in a rich, lightly spiced tomato sauce.

It is said that in the 1970s, a plateful of overcooked chicken tikka—boneless, skinless chicken chunks, skewered and cooked in a tandoor oven—was sent back to the kitchen of a London curry house by a disappointed patron. The Bangladeshi chef in charge acted quickly, heating canned tomato soup with cream, sprinkling in Indian spices, and pouring it over the chicken before sending it back out to the dining room. His inventive creation of chicken tikka masala satisfied the demanding customer, and as the recipe was perfected, diners worldwide (including those in India) fell in love with the tender, moist pieces of chicken napped with a lightly spiced tomato cream sauce. In fact, chicken tikka masala is so adored that it went on to overtake the likes of Yorkshire pudding and fish and chips as the "true national dish" of Great Britain, according to former British Foreign Secretary Robin Cook.

Despite its popularity in restaurants, recipes for chicken tikka masala were absent from some of our favorite Indian cookbooks, a testament to its lack of authenticity as an Indian dish. The recipes we did find had much in common. They all called for marinating chicken breast chunks in yogurt, often for 24 hours, then skewering them, kebab-style, for cooking. The tandoor oven was replaced with a broiler or grill. The masala ingredients varied, but the sauces were all as easy to prepare as a quick Italian tomato sauce.

But the similarities didn't end there: In all of the recipes, the chicken was either mushy or dry and the sauces were unbearably rich and overspiced. The good news is that these problems did not seem impossible to overcome, and the promise of a new way to cook chicken with exotic flavors held plenty of appeal. We just needed a decent recipe.

We wanted a four-season dish, so we chose the broiler (not the grill) as our cooking medium and began to analyze the yogurt marinade for the chicken. The marinade is meant to tenderize the meat and infuse it with the essence of spices and aromatics. While overnight marinades did adequately flavor the chicken, they also made its texture too tender, bordering on mushy. Given enough time, the lactic acid in yogurt breaks down the protein strands in meat.

Using shorter marinating times, we embarked on a series of tests intended to improve the texture of the chicken, including marinating in heavily salted yogurt, lightly salted yogurt, watered-down yogurt, and in yogurt flavored with spices. Most of the chicken we produced still missed the mark. Two or three hours of marinating desiccated the outer layer of the chicken, while really short marinades didn't do much at all.

Cooking the boneless breasts whole and cutting them into pieces only after they were broiled was a step in the right direction. The larger pieces of chicken didn't dry out as quickly under the searing heat of the broiler. It also got rid of the fussy step of skewering raw, slippery chicken pieces. But the chicken still wasn't juicy enough.

We weren't having much luck with the yogurt marinade and were tempted to abandon it altogether. But yogurt is so fundamental to this recipe that excluding it felt like a mistake. Could we find a different way to use it? We considered salting, a technique we have used for steaks, roasts, chicken parts, and whole turkeys. Salt initially draws moisture out of protein; then, the reverse happens and the salt and moisture flow back in. What if we salted the chicken first, then dipped it in yogurt right before cooking?

We rubbed the chicken with a simple mixture of salt and everyday spices common in Indian cookery: coriander, cumin, and cayenne. We set it aside for 30 minutes, which gave us time to prepare the masala sauce, then dunked the chicken in yogurt and broiled it. The result was the best tikka yet—nicely seasoned with spices and tender but not soft. In just half an hour's time, the salt rub had done its job of flavoring the chicken and keeping it moist, and the yogurt

spices such as cardamom, black pepper, cinnamon, and coriander in one jar. To bloom the flavor of the garam masala, we sautéed it in oil along with the aromatics instead of adding it to the simmering sauce, as some recipes suggest. There was just one problem: Many commercially prepared masala sauces contain tartrazine, an artificial coloring. Without it, the spices lent our sauce an unappealing gray cast. A tablespoon of tomato paste easily restored a pleasant shade of red.

Most versions of chicken tikka masala call for a cup or more of cream, but tasters wanted less. After experimenting with heavy cream, half-and-half, and even yogurt, we decided on ⅔ cup heavy cream, which was luxurious but not so rich that it was impossible to finish a whole serving.

At this point, our recipe was getting rave reviews, but we had the nagging feeling that something was missing. We scanned through our flavor checklist: Salt? No. Acidity? No. Heat? No. Sweetness? That was it. We stirred a teaspoon of sugar into the pot, then another. Our work was done, the sugar having successfully rounded out the flavors of the sauce. When we spooned the chicken over basmati rice and sprinkled it with fresh cilantro, we knew we had a dish worth staying home for.

mixture acted as a protective barrier, shielding the lean meat from the powerful heat of the broiler.

But we didn't stop there. To encourage gentle charring on the chicken, we fattened up the yogurt by adding two tablespoons of oil. We also took advantage of the yogurt's thick texture, mixing it with minced garlic and freshly grated ginger. The aromatics clung to the chicken as it cooked, producing tikka that was good enough to eat on its own.

Having perfected the chicken, we shifted our focus to the sauce. Masala means spice mixture, and the ingredients in a masala sauce depend largely on the whims of the cook. When the masala is to be served as part of chicken tikka masala, however, tomatoes and cream always form the base. Working with a mixture of sautéed aromatics (onions, ginger, garlic, and chiles) simmered with tomatoes (crushed tomatoes were favored over diced canned or fresh because of their smooth consistency) and cream, we tested combination after combination of spices. With plenty of winners and no real losers, we eventually settled on the simplest choice of all: commercial garam masala. Garam masala blends warm

WHAT WE LEARNED: Broiling the chicken (instead of grilling) allows you to make this dish year-round. Sprinkling the chicken with a salt and spice mixture seasons the meat and helps keep it moist under the broiler. To further ensure juicy chicken, dunk the chicken in yogurt (seasoned with ginger and garlic) just before broiling—the yogurt acts as a protective barrier over the chicken and adds tangy flavor to the meat. For the masala sauce, canned crushed tomatoes work better than diced canned or fresh because of their smooth consistency and year-round availability. Garam masala (a blend of warm Indian spices) adds complex flavor and depth to the sauce, and a modest amount of heavy cream (just ⅔ cup) adds a velvety richness without turning the sauce heavy.

CHICKEN TIKKA MASALA

serves 4 to 6

This dish is best when prepared with whole milk yogurt, but low-fat yogurt can be substituted. If you don't own a ceramic ginger grater, use a Microplane or the small holes on a box grater. For a spicier dish, do not remove the ribs and seeds from the chile. If you prefer, substitute 2 teaspoons ground coriander, ¼ teaspoon ground cardamom, ¼ teaspoon ground cinnamon, and ½ teaspoon ground black pepper for the garam masala. Ghee, a clarified butter that is often used in Indian cooking, can be used in place of the vegetable oil in the sauce. The sauce can be made ahead, refrigerated for up to 4 days in an airtight container, and gently reheated before adding the hot chicken. Serve with basmati rice—see out tasting on page 177.

chicken tikka

- 1 teaspoon salt
- ½ teaspoon ground cumin
- ½ teaspoon ground coriander
- ¼ teaspoon cayenne pepper
- 2 pounds boneless, skinless chicken breasts, trimmed of fat
- 1 cup plain whole milk yogurt (see note)
- 2 tablespoons vegetable oil
- 2 medium garlic cloves, minced or pressed through a garlic press (about 2 teaspoons)
- 1 tablespoon grated fresh ginger

masala sauce

- 3 tablespoons vegetable oil
- 1 medium onion, diced fine (about 1¼ cups)
- 1 tablespoon garam masala (see page 225)
- 1 tablespoon tomato paste
- 2 medium garlic cloves, minced or pressed through a garlic press (about 2 teaspoons)
- 2 teaspoons grated fresh ginger
- 1 serrano chile, ribs and seeds removed, flesh minced
- 1 (28-ounce) can crushed tomatoes

- 2 teaspoons sugar
- ½ teaspoon salt
- ⅔ cup heavy cream
- ¼ cup chopped fresh cilantro leaves

1. FOR THE CHICKEN: Combine the salt, cumin, coriander, and cayenne in a small bowl. Sprinkle both sides of the chicken with the spice mixture, pressing gently so the mixture adheres. Place the chicken on a plate, cover with plastic wrap, and refrigerate for 30 to 60 minutes. In a large bowl, whisk together the yogurt, oil, garlic, and ginger; set aside.

2. FOR THE SAUCE: Heat the oil in a large Dutch oven over medium heat until shimmering. Add the onion and cook, stirring frequently, until softened and light golden, 8 to 10 minutes. Add the garam masala, tomato paste, garlic, ginger, and chile; cook, stirring frequently, until fragrant, about 3 minutes. Add the crushed tomatoes, sugar, and salt; bring to a boil. Reduce the heat to medium-low, cover, and simmer for 15 minutes, stirring occasionally. Stir in the cream and return to a simmer. Remove the pan from the heat and cover to keep warm.

3. While the sauce simmers, adjust an oven rack to the upper-middle position (about 6 inches from the heating element) and heat the broiler. Line a rimmed baking sheet or broiler pan with foil and set a wire rack on it. Using tongs, dip the chicken into the yogurt mixture (the chicken should be coated with a thick layer of yogurt) and arrange on the wire rack. Discard the excess yogurt mixture. Broil the chicken until the thickest parts register 160 degrees on an instant-read thermometer and the exterior is lightly charred in spots, 10 to 18 minutes, flipping the chicken halfway through cooking.

4. Let the chicken rest 5 minutes, then cut into 1-inch chunks and stir into the warm sauce (do not simmer the chicken in the sauce). Stir in the cilantro, season with salt to taste, and serve.

GETTING IT RIGHT: Key Ingredients in Chicken Tikka Masala

All of the ingredients for Chicken Tikka Masala are available at the supermarket. Here are notes on what to buy.

Chicken Breasts

Lean boneless, skinless chicken breasts (preferably a natural brand like Bell and Evans) pair well with the rich tomato-cream masala sauce.

Garlic and Ginger

Garlic and ginger flavor both the chicken and the sauce.

Plain Yogurt

A coating in whole milk yogurt helps aromatics cling to the chicken and seals in moisture. Brown Cow Cream Top is the test kitchen's favorite brand.

Crushed Tomatoes

Smooth crushed tomatoes form the base of the masala sauce. Tuttorosso and Muir Glen are our preferred brands.

Garam Masala

This combination of warm spices seasons the tomato-cream sauce. McCormick won a recent test kitchen tasting.

TECHNIQUE: Five Key Steps to Chicken Tikka Masala

1. Rub: Coat the chicken in a mixture of salt and spices and refrigerate.

2. Make Sauce: Prepare the creamy tomato-masala sauce.

3. Dip: Dunk the chicken in a protective coating of yogurt and oil.

4. Broil: Broil the chicken, then allow to rest.

5. Combine: Cut the chicken into chunks and add to the sauce.

TASTING LAB:
Canned Crushed Tomatoes

IN THE TEST KITCHEN, WE'VE OFTEN AVOIDED USING crushed tomatoes because the differences among leading brands are so dramatic. The textures vary from watery and thin to so thick you could stand a spoon in it. You might get peels or no peels; plentiful seeds or none; big, rough-cut chunks of tomato or a smooth, sauce-like consistency with no chunks at all.

Why is it that manufacturers can't seem to agree on what crushed tomatoes are? Simple. The United States government regulates the appearance and consistency of other types of canned tomatoes, but not crushed tomatoes. As a result, each brand offers its own definition of "crushed."

Our solution to this problem has been to crush our own tomatoes by pulsing whole or diced canned tomatoes in the food processor. Given the extra work (and mess) this entails, it seemed time to tackle the issue head-on.

In our quest to find the perfect canned crushed tomatoes, we bought 10 varieties to test alongside our preferred brands of whole and diced tomatoes (which we pulsed in the food processor). We started by tasting them all uncooked. Then we reduced them on the stove to a thick, spoonable consistency, adding olive oil and garlic, per our recipe for our quick tomato sauce for pizza. A panel of 20 tasters rated the tomatoes, both cooked and raw, on their freshness of flavor, sweetness, acidity, and overall appeal.

The good news is that we can put away the food processor. Our tasters liked some brands of crushed tomatoes more than the diced or whole tomatoes pulsed in the machine, which fell into the middle of the rankings.

So what makes a great can of crushed tomatoes? We knew texture would be very important. To get to the bottom of this, we investigated how much solid tomato—as opposed to liquid—you get in each can. We poured them into sieves suspended over glass measuring cups, wrapped them in plastic to prevent evaporation, and let the liquids drain for

24 hours. When we weighed the solids that remained, the results were dramatic: Tomato solids in the different brands ranged from a high of 71 percent to a low of 50 percent. But did more tomatoes equal better crushed tomatoes? Surprisingly, no. The thickest samples were criticized for having a "tomato paste" consistency, while the top two brands were 51 percent and 57 percent tomatoes, respectively. Looking over tasters' comments, it was clear that we preferred our crushed tomatoes chunky, not thick like tomato paste or smooth like tomato sauce. The ideal can of crushed tomatoes contains actual tomato pieces and a fair amount of liquid.

Fresh tomato taste is another essential. Canned tomatoes can actually have a fresher taste than supermarket tomatoes, as those tomatoes in the produce section are picked green and hard in order to survive shipping, then sprayed with ethylene gas—which, though it turns them red, can't do much about their undeveloped flavor. By contrast, tomatoes destined for the can are picked ripe and processed quickly. But which of these brands did the best job of preserving that vine-ripened flavor?

How they're processed makes a big difference, experts say. Generally, the fruit that will become canned crushed tomatoes is harvested by machine, explained Rich Rostomily, formerly of Morning Star Packing Company in Williams, Calif., one of the largest tomato-packing companies in the world.

If they are to be peeled, this is done either by steam or with a lye bath. Next, he said, the tomatoes are sorted to remove those with "yellow shoulders" (parts that are not red), blemishes, and, if the product is to be peel-free, any peel still attached. The tomatoes are crushed by a machine called a disintegrator, described by Gerald Harter, who works in Morning Star's Santa Nella, Calif., canning facility, as "looking like a big cheese grater." Then they're heated to remove microorganisms, either at a lower temperature (between 160 and 185 degrees) for a longer time or a higher temperature (over 200 degrees) for a shorter time.

Here is where the flavor is most affected. "Typically,

Seeing Red   **Gold Standard**

you'll have a better-tasting tomato if it's processed at a lower temperature," Rostomily said. Lower temperatures preserve an enzyme called lipoxygenase, which is vital to the formulation of the volatiles that contain tomato flavor. So why the high temperatures? For texture, he said. Heating tomatoes over 185 degrees, a process called "hot break," deactivates enzymes that would break down the pectin binding the cells together in the tomatoes. Though heat will give you a thicker product that won't separate, you'll lose tomato taste.

When we separated liquids from solids in the sieve, we were surprised to see that after 24 hours, our top-ranking tomatoes had exuded a golden-colored liquid, while the lower-ranked ones had produced bright red juice. Rostomily said the golden juice is a product of cooler-temperature processing, where the enzymes were left to break down the pectin, leading to what he called serum separation. Our tasters confirmed Rostomily's claim: Better-tasting crushed tomatoes are processed at a lower temperature.

In the next step of processing, the cans are topped with tomato puree or juice, according to manufacturer preference. Puree must be cooked for a long time to break down the tomatoes, and therefore imparts a more cooked—rather than fresh—taste to the final product, Rostomily said. Indeed, the lower-ranking crushed tomatoes in our lineup generally featured tomato puree as the first ingredient on the label, while the top four all started their ingredient lists with tomatoes. What's more, Rostomily noted, manufacturers often disguise less-than-perfect tomatoes with puree, which imparts a deeper red color to the contents of the can. The lesson? A fresh-tasting can of crushed tomatoes won't list puree first on the ingredient list.

While sugar levels differ from brand to brand, no sugar is added. Manufacturers do add salt to boost the flavor and help preserve the contents. Some added salt is a good thing, Harter said, as it makes the tomatoes taste sweeter: "Too much and the tomatoes will taste salty; too little and they're bland." Indeed, our lowest-ranking tomato had no added salt.

Manufacturers may also add calcium chloride to maintain a firm texture. Amounts matter, said Harter: "If you get too high, you'll have a metallic taste." Rostomily added that too much can also give a "rubbery" texture to the tomato pieces. In our lineup, three of the four lowest-ranking tomatoes contained calcium chloride, while none of the top-ranked ones did.

Finally, citric acid appeared in every brand except our lowest-ranked. It's there to correct the acid level of the tomatoes, Harter said. "You want to balance the sugar-to-acid ratio," he explained. "An overripe tomato will have more sugar than acid, and you want a certain pH, usually 4.2 or lower, in a canned tomato." Our lowest-ranked brand came in at 4.3, meaning it was the least acidic of the bunch, leading to less-than-bright flavor. A lower pH also means more acid to preserve the tomatoes, so they will require less cooking, Harter said, and you'll get fresher taste.

Our two top-ranked crushed tomatoes, Tuttorosso and Muir Glen, brought all these desirable attributes together. Tuttorosso is available only in New York, New England, and Florida, but Muir Glen tomatoes are distributed nationally. Both are recommended. Tuttorosso crushed tomatoes also come in "New World Style," in a green can; this is not the same product and was disliked by many of our tasters.

Rating Crushed Tomatoes

TWENTY AMERICA'S TEST KITCHEN STAFF MEMBERS TASTED 10 BRANDS OF CRUSHED TOMATOES. THE TOMATOES WERE tasted poured from the can and reduced with olive oil and garlic to a spoonable consistency. We rated the crushed tomatoes on their freshness of flavor, sweetness, acidity, and overall appeal. The tomatoes are listed in order of preference and are available in supermarkets.

RECOMMENDED
Tuttorosso Crushed Tomatoes in Thick Puree with Basil

$1.69 for 28-ounce can; Tomato solids: 51 percent; Sugar: 4 g; Sodium: 240 mg
Tasters declared Tuttorosso "chunky, with dimensional flavor and bright tomato taste." In the sauce, we liked its "deep roasted tomato flavor."

RECOMMENDED
Muir Glen Organic Crushed Tomatoes with Basil

$2.69 for 28-ounce can; Tomato solids: 57 percent; Sugar: 6 g; Sodium: 380 mg
"Very fresh, spicy, like pizza topping," with "good-sized chunks of tomato." In the sauce, tasters said it "tastes like a well-cooked marinara," with a "balanced," "bright tomato flavor."

RECOMMENDED
Hunt's Organic Crushed Tomatoes

$2.50 for 28-ounce can; Tomato solids: 64 percent; Sugar: 6 g; Sodium: 220 mg
Right out of the can, this brand came across as "fresh and peppery" and "thick, rich, and tomatoey." In the sauce, it was "ultrathick, with great flavor, not overly sweet or acidic."

RECOMMENDED
RedPack Crushed Tomatoes in Thick Puree

$1.99 for 28-ounce can; Tomato solids: 55 percent; Sugar: 4 g; Sodium: 240 mg
Uncooked, this brand "actually tastes like real tomatoes!" But in the sauce, several tasters complained that it was "bland."

RECOMMENDED
Progresso Crushed Tomatoes with Added Puree

$1.79 for 28-ounce can; Tomato solids: 55 percent; Sugar: 4 g; Sodium: 190 mg
Tasters praised the "large, diced chunks," though they disliked the "thin, watery" consistency. It had a well-liked "sweet, roasted tomato" taste in the sauce.

RECOMMENDED WITH RESERVATIONS
Pastene Kitchen Ready Ground Peeled Tomatoes

$1.50 for 28-ounce can; Tomato solids: 71 percent; Sugar: 8 g; Sodium: 170 mg
"Too sweet" and "ketchupy" to many, with a "mushy" texture.

RECOMMENDED WITH RESERVATIONS
Hunt's Crushed Tomatoes

$2.50 for 28-ounce can; Tomato solids: 59 percent; Sugar: 5 g; Sodium: 340 mg
Raw, these tomatoes were "candy-like but bold." In the sauce, they were drubbed for having a "pureed" texture and "lots of skins."

RECOMMENDED WITH RESERVATIONS
Del Monte Organic Crushed Tomatoes

$2.50 for 28-ounce can; Tomato solids: 50 percent; Sugar: 4 g; Sodium: 300 mg
"Thin" and "watery" came up again and again. In the sauce, some tasters found it had a "nice balance of sweet and acidic"; to others it was "uninspired."

RECOMMENDED WITH RESERVATIONS
Contadina Crushed Roma Style Tomatoes

$1.89 for 28-ounce can; Tomato solids: 52 percent; Sugar: 4 g; Sodium: 300 mg
"Watery, awful texture," with "lots of skin and seeds." Cooked, these tomatoes took on an "Olive Garden-esque" marinara flavor.

NOT RECOMMENDED
Cento All-Purpose Crushed Tomatoes

$1.39 for 28-ounce can; Tomato solids: 68 percent; Sugar: 8 g; Sodium: 40 mg
"Flat," with a "canned puree flavor" that's "megathick" and "sweet." "This isn't crushed, it's puree." Cooked, this brand made a "pasty," "bland" sauce.

Most vegetable stir-fries simply aren't hearty or flavorful enough—even for a dummy. The test kitchen discovered that meaty portobello mushrooms, supported by lots of other vegetables and a brightly flavored sauce, are so satisfying, no one will miss the meat.

ASIAN TAKEOUT
CHAPTER 20
at home

A good bowl of chicken soup is always satisfying.
But exciting? Not really. Thai-style chicken soup, however, delivers on
both fronts. This creamy chicken soup is fragrant with coconut and
lemon grass and derives its complex flavors from more than a dozen
ingredients, including kaffir lime leaves, bird's eye chiles, galangal, and
oyster mushrooms. Shopping for such exotic ingredients, not typically
found in a supermarket, can give the home cook pause. We wanted to
develop a reasonable interpretation of this Thai favorite (using supermarket ingredients) without sacrificing its enticing flavors.

Order a takeout vegetarian stir-fry and chances are you'll be disappointed. Too often these stir-fries are skimpy on the vegetables. And
the vegetables these stir-fries do include are typically green vegetables
like broccoli and bok choy, which are simply not hefty enough to take
center stage as a main course. Our goal was to develop a vegetarian stir-
fry so hearty even carnivores would be satisfied and no one would be
driven to raid the refrigerator an hour after dinner.

THAI-STYLE CHICKEN SOUP

WHAT WE WANTED: A rich, complex, and balanced Thai chicken soup made with supermarket ingredients.

One of our favorite ways to begin a meal at a Thai restaurant is with a bowl of *tom kha gai,* or the easier-to-pronounce translation: Thai chicken soup. It doesn't look like much—a creamy, pale broth laced with chicken slices, mushrooms, and cilantro—but what it lacks in looks it makes up for in flavor. Sweet and sour components balance the richness of lemon grass–and-lime-infused coconut milk, which, in turn, tempers a slow-building chili burn.

This classic Thai soup is relatively easy to make if you can find all of the proper ingredients, which not all of us can. Its complex flavor is largely derived from such exotica as galangal, kaffir lime leaves, and lemon grass. We'd be hard-pressed to find most of these ingredients at our local market. Instead we aimed to make the most authentic version possible with widely available ingredients. We found a handful of "simplified" or "Americanized" Thai chicken soup recipes that, while largely informative regarding substitutions, mostly missed the mark. Each lacked the taut balancing of hot, sour, salty, and sweet components that makes Thai cooking so compelling. (Appropriately enough, that balance, in Thai, is called *yum.*) So, for the time being at least, we stuck with the classic recipes. We'd address substitutions once we knew how best to prepare the soup.

Variation in Thai chicken soup recipes tends to center on two basic components: broth and garnishes. Traditional recipes typically prepare the broth using one of two methods. The first involves poaching a whole chicken in water with aromatics, after which the broth is blended with coconut milk and further seasoned. The chicken is then shredded and stirred in with the mushrooms. In the second approach, chicken broth and coconut milk are simmered with the aromatics, after which thin-sliced raw chicken and the remaining ingredients and seasonings are added. Both methods

have their merits, but we much preferred the latter, which took half the effort and time without any apparent injury to flavor. The richness of the coconut milk and assertive seasonings added big flavor fast.

How long did the broth and aromatics need to simmer for the best results? We used broth ingredients from the best recipes we had tried—a blend of chicken broth, coconut milk, lemon grass, shallots, galangal, and cilantro. After sautéing the aromatics for a few minutes to bring out and deepen their flavors, we added the broth and noted that a scant 10 minutes of simmering proved perfect. Much longer and the broth tasted bitter and vegetal.

After preparing a few more batches with varying ratios of chicken broth to coconut milk, we settled on equal parts of each. Rich tasting without being cloying, and definitely chicken flavored, the blend was perfectly balanced. We also tried a technique we had come across in a couple of recipes. We added the coconut milk in two parts: half at the beginning and the remainder just before serving. What seemed fussy made a big difference, allowing the coconut flavor to come through clearly.

Now came the hard part: making substitutions. Most of the "simplified" recipes we tried or reviewed replaced the lemon grass with lemon zest, but we found the swap objectionable. Lemon zest—in conjunction with the sweet coconut milk—made for a broth with an odd, candy-like flavor. Dried lemon grass also failed to impress, as it lacked any of the depth of the fresh stuff. Luckily, we discovered lemon grass to be more readily available than we had assumed.

Galangal is a knotty, peppery-flavored rhizome distantly related to ginger, which most food writers suggest is the perfect substitute. While it wasn't perfect to us—ginger lacks the depth of flavor and piney finish of galangal—we decided it would do.

Kaffir lime leaves, the fresh or dried leaves from a potent variety of tropical lime, lend the broth a particularly floral, deep flavor and alluring aroma. Lime zest is the usual substitute, but one we felt lacked the intensity of the leaves. Once again, the substitute felt like a distant second.

This was a bad trend. Replacing the authentic ingredients was not working as well as we hoped, and the soup didn't taste nearly as good as we expected. Perhaps authentic flavor really wasn't possible without the proper ingredients.

Then we found our magic bullet. After one taste test, a colleague suggested red curry paste, an ingredient we hadn't considered to that point. While it is never added to traditional Thai chicken soup, the curry paste did include all the exotic ingredients for which we were trying so hard to find acceptable substitutions. We whisked a small spoonful

of the paste into the soup in front of us and were struck by the surprising transformation from boring to—dare we say?—authentic.

Curry paste is usually added early on in cooking to mellow its potent flavor, but we found this flattened the flavors too much. Adding a dollop at the very end of cooking—whisked together with pungent fish sauce and tart lime juice—allowed the sharpness of the galangal, the fragrance of the kaffir lime leaves, and the bright heat of the chiles to come through loud and clear. Out went the mediocre ginger and lime zest and in went 2 teaspoons of easy-to-find red curry paste.

With the broth tasting great, we could finally tackle the chicken and mushrooms. We initially thought that rich-tasting thigh meat would be the best choice to stand up to the full-flavored broth, but it was too fatty; boneless, skinless breast meat was better.

As for the mushrooms, oyster mushrooms are traditional but hard to find and expensive. Supermarket options like cremini, shiitake, and white mushrooms each had their merits, but the latter proved to be the closest match to the mild flavor and chewy texture of oyster mushrooms. Sliced thin and submerged in the broth, they quickly softened and absorbed the soup's flavors like a sponge.

A sprinkle of cilantro usually suffices as a finishing touch, but tasters wanted more. The clean, bright heat of thin-sliced Thai chiles and sharp bite of scallions did the trick. With twenty-odd minutes of cooking and a minimum of hands-on effort, we had Thai chicken soup that tasted every bit as good as that served at our local Thai restaurant.

WHAT WE LEARNED: Equal parts chicken broth and coconut milk (adding the coconut milk in two stages: at the beginning and just before serving) yield a rich base for the soup. Jarred red curry paste, found in many supermarkets, includes all the exotic ingredients necessary for the dish. Just adding a dollop at the very end of cooking and whisking it with pungent fish sauce and tart lime juice allow all the classic flavors to come through loud and clear.

THAI-STYLE CHICKEN SOUP

serves 6 to 8 as an appetizer or 4 as a main course

Although we prefer the richer, more complex flavor of regular coconut milk, light coconut milk can be substituted for one or both cans. Don't be tempted to use jarred or dried lemon grass—their flavor is characterless. For a spicier soup, add additional red curry paste to taste.

1	teaspoon vegetable oil
3	stalks lemon grass, bottom 5 inches only, trimmed and sliced thin
3	large shallots, chopped coarse (about ¾ cup)
8	sprigs fresh cilantro, chopped coarse
3	tablespoons fish sauce
4	cups low-sodium chicken broth
2	(14-ounce) cans coconut milk
1	tablespoon sugar
½	pound white mushrooms, wiped clean, trimmed, and sliced ¼ inch thick
1	pound boneless, skinless chicken breasts (about 2 large breasts), halved lengthwise and sliced on the bias into ⅛-inch-thick pieces
3	tablespoons juice from 2 limes
2	teaspoons Thai red curry paste

garnish

½	cup loosely packed fresh cilantro leaves
2	fresh Thai, serrano, or jalapeño chiles, seeds and ribs removed, chiles sliced thin
2	scallions, sliced thin on the bias
1	lime, cut into wedges (for serving)

1. Heat the oil in a large saucepan over medium heat until just shimmering. Add the lemon grass, shallots, cilantro sprigs, and 1 tablespoon of the fish sauce, and cook, stirring frequently, until just softened but not browned, 2 to 5 minutes.

2. Stir in the chicken broth and 1 can of the coconut milk, and bring to a simmer over high heat. Cover, reduce the heat to low, and simmer until the flavors have blended, about 10 minutes. Pour the broth through a fine-mesh strainer, discarding the solids in the strainer. (At this point, the soup can be refrigerated in an airtight container for up to 1 day.)

3. Return the strained soup to a clean saucepan and bring to a simmer over medium-high heat. Stir in the remaining can of coconut milk and the sugar and return to a simmer. Reduce the heat to medium, add the mushrooms, and cook until just tender, 2 to 3 minutes. Add the chicken and cook, stirring constantly, until no longer pink, 1 to 3 minutes. Remove the soup from the heat.

4. Whisk the lime juice, curry paste, and remaining 2 tablespoons fish sauce together, then stir into the soup. Ladle the soup into individual bowls and garnish with the cilantro, chiles, and scallions. Serve with the lime wedges.

SHOPPING NOTES:
Thai Red Curry Paste

Why run all over town looking for authentic Thai ingredients like galangal, bird's eye chiles, and kaffir lime leaves when a jar of supermarket Thai red curry paste delivers all those flavors in super-concentrated form?

VEGETABLE STIR-FRIES

WHAT WE WANTED: A vegetable stir-fry that is hearty and satisfying enough to serve as a main course.

For a fast and easy weeknight dinner, it's hard to beat a stir-fry: Sliced meat and chopped vegetables are cooked quickly over high heat, then tossed with a bold-flavored sauce and served. Take out the meat, however, and this one-dish meal devolves into a side dish. The all-vegetable stir-fry has plenty of pleasing contrasts of flavor and texture but nothing substantial enough to anchor the dish firmly in entrée territory.

Unlike many of our colleagues, we were convinced there was a way to make a satisfying meal out of nothing but stir-fried vegetables. It wasn't the meat they were missing from these all-veggie stir-fries, we reasoned, but the meatiness. And with a few strategically chosen vegetables, we thought we could change the mind of even the most unapologetic carnivore in the test kitchen.

After we scanned the produce aisle of our supermarket, it wasn't hard to figure out where to start. If it was meaty heft and texture we were after, mushrooms were the obvious choice—specifically, hearty portobellos. To capitalize on their bulk and meatiness, we cut them into wedges large enough to stand out from the other vegetables.

The only problem now was the gills, which often broke off and muddied the sauce. We tried cooking the mushrooms on the tops only (to keep the gills intact), but this technique left the mushrooms leathery and raw-tasting. Scraping the gills off with a spoon before cooking solved the problem (see the illustration on page 242).

Now that we had settled on a cooking technique for our starring vegetable, it was time to move on to the supporting cast—and to more familiar territory. Using the kitchen's tried-and-true procedure for stir-fries, we simply plugged in the meaty portobellos where the sliced beef or chicken usually went. We cooked the portobellos in batches and set them aside; steam-sautéed the longer-cooking vegetables (such as carrots and broccoli; see the chart on page 241) and set them aside; stir-fried the softer vegetables (such as celery and bell pepper), greens (napa cabbage or bok choy), and aromatics (garlic and ginger); then added all of the vegetables back to the pan along with a flavorful sauce.

The technique worked without a hitch, but we thought the portobellos could still be more distinct from the other vegetables. Taking another cue from meat stir-fries, we experimented with marinades and coatings, but to no avail. Soaking the mushrooms in a soy-based marinade left them soggy, slimy, and difficult to sear. Dipping them in different combinations of egg and cornstarch created a distinct

crust initially, but the mushrooms' high moisture content eventually made the crust unappetizingly chewy and wet. Searing proved best after all, but we wondered if a simple glaze (made from our existing sauce ingredients) might help. Adding soy sauce, chicken broth, and sugar as the mushrooms finished cooking yielded a shiny, flavorful glaze that provided just the boost they had been lacking.

Surely portobellos were not the only vegetable that could anchor the dish. Summer squash was quickly ruled out: too watery and no substance. Sweet potatoes added bulk, but they remained starchy when stir-fried and fell apart when cooked through. Eggplant disintegrated into a mushy mess, but its meatiness was appealing enough for us to continue testing it. Dipping the eggplant first in beaten eggs and then in cornstarch provided just enough textural contrast to lift the eggplant out of vegetable obscurity.

While not exactly a vegetable, firm tofu (soybean curd) seemed promising as an easy stand-in for the eggplant. In practice, however, the egg/cornstarch coating created a crust that was too thick and chewy; tasters wanted something thinner. Because it's packaged in water, tofu already has a significant amount of moisture, so what if we skipped the egg and simply dredged the tofu in the cornstarch? Not only was this method simple (no pressing or freezing, as so many other recipes required), but the results pleased even the skeptics who claimed they didn't like tofu.

Now when we head to the supermarket, we don't have to look beyond the produce aisle to assemble a quick meal that will satisfy our craving for a substantial main course.

WHAT WE LEARNED: Replace the typical chicken or beef with hefty, meaty portobello mushrooms. Remove the gills to keep the mushrooms from tasting leathery and raw. Cook the mushrooms in batches, add a glaze to boost the flavor, and set them aside. Steam-sauté the longer-cooking vegetables (such as carrots and broccoli) next, then set them aside while the softer vegetables (such as celery, bell pepper, greens, and aromatics) are stir-fried. Finally, add everything back to the pan along with a flavorful sauce.

STIR-FRIED PORTOBELLOS WITH GINGER-OYSTER SAUCE

serves 3 to 4
Serve with steamed white rice.

glaze
¼ cup low-sodium chicken or vegetable broth
2   tablespoons soy sauce
2   tablespoons sugar

sauce
1   cup low-sodium chicken or vegetable broth
3   tablespoons oyster-flavored sauce
1   tablespoon soy sauce
1   tablespoon cornstarch
2   teaspoons toasted sesame oil

vegetables
2   medium garlic cloves, minced or pressed through a garlic press (about 2 teaspoons)
4   teaspoons minced fresh ginger
4   tablespoons vegetable oil
6–8 portobello mushrooms (each 4 to 6 inches), stems discarded, gills removed (see the illustration on page 242), and cut into 2-inch wedges (about 7 cups)
2   cups sliced carrots or other longer-cooking vegetable from the chart on page 241
½   cup low-sodium chicken or vegetable broth
1   cup snow peas or other quicker-cooking vegetable from the chart on page 241
1   pound leafy greens from the chart on page 241
1   tablespoon sesame seeds, toasted (optional)

1. Whisk the glaze ingredients in a small bowl; whisk the sauce ingredients in a separate small bowl. In a third small bowl, mix the garlic and ginger with 1 teaspoon of the vegetable oil. Set the bowls aside.

TECHNIQUE: Choosing and Preparing Vegetables for a Stir-Fry

Portobello mushrooms are the mainstay in our stir-fries. As for the other vegetables, use those called for in the recipe or swap them with another vegetable from the same category below. We recommend using one longer-cooking vegetable paired with one quicker-cooking vegetable and a leafy green (either napa cabbage or bok choy).

LONGER-COOKING VEGETABLES (to yield 2 cups)	AMOUNT	PREPARATION
Carrots	4 small	peeled, sliced on bias ¼ inch thick
Broccoli	½ pound	stalks discarded, florets cut into 1¼-inch pieces
Cauliflower	½ pound	core removed, florets cut into 1¼-inch pieces
Asparagus	1 pound medium	bottoms trimmed, cut on bias into 1½-inch lengths
Green Beans	½ pound	ends trimmed, cut on bias into 1½-inch lengths
QUICKER-COOKING VEGETABLES (to yield 1 cup)		
Bell Pepper	1 medium	stemmed, seeded, and cut into ½-inch dice
Snow Peas	3 ounces	strings and tough ends trimmed
Celery	3 medium ribs	ends trimmed, cut on bias ½ inch thick
Zucchini or Summer Squash	1 small	seeded, quartered lengthwise, and cut on bias ¼ inch thick
LEAFY GREENS (to yield 2 cups stems and 4 cups greens)		
Bok Choy or Napa Cabbage	1 small (about 1 pound)	stems/cores and greens separated, stems/cores cut into ¼-inch strips, greens into ¾-inch strips

2. Heat 3 tablespoons of the vegetable oil in a 12-inch non-stick skillet over medium-high heat until shimmering. Add the mushrooms and cook, without stirring, until browned on one side, 2 to 3 minutes. Using tongs, turn the mushrooms and reduce the heat to medium; cook until the second sides are browned and the mushrooms are tender, about 5 minutes. Increase the heat to medium-high; add the glaze mixture and cook, stirring, until the glaze is thick and the mushrooms are coated, 1 to 2 minutes. Transfer the mushrooms to a plate; rinse the skillet clean and dry with paper towels.

3. Heat 1 more teaspoon of the vegetable oil in the now-empty skillet over medium-high heat until just smoking. Add the carrots and cook, stirring occasionally, until beginning to brown, 1 to 2 minutes. Add the broth and cover the skillet; cook until the carrots are just tender, 2 to 3 minutes. Uncover and cook until the liquid evaporates, about 30 seconds. Transfer the carrots to the plate with the mushrooms.

4. Heat the remaining teaspoon vegetable oil in the now-empty skillet over medium-high heat until just smoking. Add the snow peas and bok choy stems or napa cabbage cores and cook, stirring occasionally, until beginning to brown and soften, 1 to 2 minutes. Add the leafy greens and cook, stirring frequently, until wilted, about 1 minute. Push the vegetables to the sides of the skillet to clear the center; add the garlic-ginger mixture to the clearing and cook, mashing the mixture with a spoon or spatula, until fragrant, 15 to 20 seconds, then stir the mixture into the greens.

5. Return all the vegetables to the skillet along with the sauce. Toss to combine and cook, stirring, until the sauce is thickened and the vegetables are coated, 2 to 3 minutes. Transfer to a serving platter, top with the sesame seeds, if using, and serve immediately.

STIR-FRIED PORTOBELLOS WITH SWEET CHILI-GARLIC SAUCE

Follow the recipe for Stir-Fried Portobellos with Ginger-Oyster Sauce, replacing the sugar in the glaze with 2 tablespoons honey. For the sauce, increase the soy sauce to 3 tablespoons, reduce the broth to ¾ cup, and replace the oyster-flavored sauce and sesame oil with 2 tablespoons honey, 1 tablespoon rice wine vinegar, and 1 teaspoon Asian chili sauce. Increase the garlic to 4 teaspoons.

STIR-FRIED TOFU WITH GINGER-OYSTER SAUCE

When coated with cornstarch and stir-fried, tofu develops a crisp exterior and a creamy interior. Most tofu is sold in 12-, 14-, or 16-ounce blocks. To cut tofu for a stir-fry, hold a chef's knife parallel to the cutting board and cut the block in half horizontally to form two rectangular planks. Cut each plank into six squares, then cut each square diagonally into two triangles.

Follow the recipe for Stir-Fried Portobellos with Ginger-Oyster Sauce through step 1. Cut 1 container extra-firm tofu into 24 triangles (see note above). Heat 3 tablespoons vegetable oil in a 12-inch nonstick skillet over medium-high until shimmering. While the oil is heating, sprinkle ⅓ cup cornstarch evenly into a baking dish. Place the tofu on top of the cornstarch and turn with your fingers until evenly coated. When the skillet is hot, add the tofu in a single layer and cook until golden brown, 4 to 6 minutes. Turn the tofu with tongs and cook until the second side is browned, 4 to 6 minutes more. Add the glaze ingredients and cook, stirring, until the glaze is thick and the tofu is coated, 1 to 2 minutes. Transfer the tofu to a plate; rinse the skillet clean and dry with paper towels. Proceed with the recipe from step 3.

TECHNIQUE:
Preparing Portobellos for Stir-Frying

After removing the stem, gently scrape the underside of the mushroom with a dinner spoon to remove the feathery gills, which can impart a muddy taste to the stir-fry.

Rating Ladles

WE TESTED EIGHT STAINLESS STEEL LADLES PRICED BETWEEN $4.49 AND $23.95. TESTS INCLUDED LADLING OUT PORTIONS of chicken noodle soup and beef stew. The ladles are listed in order of preference. See www.americastestkitchen.com for up-to-date prices and mail-order sources for top-rated products.

HIGHLY RECOMMENDED
Rösle Ladle with Pouring Rim and Hook Handle
$23.95
The all-around ladle of choice for its ergonomically designed handle, dripless pouring rim, and helpful hanging hook.

RECOMMENDED
Calphalon Stainless Steel Ladle
$9.95
A good all-purpose ladle, despite the lack of a hanging mechanism.

RECOMMENDED WITH RESERVATIONS
Next Day Gourmet 6-Ounce 1-Piece Stainless Steel Ladle
$17.70
Heavy, with a lengthy handle, but sturdy and helpful for deep stockpots.

RECOMMENDED WITH RESERVATIONS
Fantes 6-Ounce Stainless Steel Ladle
$4.49
The bargain of the bunch, this ladle could eventually break due to its two-piece construction.

RECOMMENDED WITH RESERVATIONS
OXO Steel Serving Ladle
$7.95
On the small side, but slightly offset and complete with OXO's traditionally comfortable grip.

RECOMMENDED WITH RESERVATIONS
Cuisipro Tempo 6-Ounce Serving Ladle
$14.95
This heavy ladle's bowl was plenty big, but the handle was bent so dramatically that it made it awkward to use.

NOT RECOMMENDED
Amco Stainless Steel Stand-Up 8-Ounce Ladle
$12.99
A ladle that stands up is a nice idea, but without an offset handle, pouring out soup cleanly is nearly impossible.

NOT RECOMMENDED
KitchenAid Hollow Handle Serving Ladle
$14.99
This ladle's small size and spouts are more suited for sauces than soups.

EQUIPMENT CORNER: Ladles

YOU MIGHT THINK ONE LADLE IS PRETTY MUCH THE same as the next. But after we had dunked eight stainless steel models (plastic stains and can melt on the stovetop) into pots of chicken noodle soup and hearty beef stew, scattered puddles on the test kitchen countertop made it clear that not all ladles are ergonomically equal.

Ladles with handles shorter than 9 inches, such as the KitchenAid Hollow Handle Serving Ladle ($14.99) and OXO Steel Serving Ladle ($7.95), simply sank in deeper pots; what's more, their small bowls were better suited to sauces than soups. However, more than 10 inches of grip on the Next Day Gourmet Stainless Steel Ladle ($17.70) and Fantes Stainless Steel Ladle ($4.49) proved cumbersome to maneuver, as did their lack of offset handles—a flaw shared by the Amco Stainless Steel Stand-Up Ladle ($12.99). Without some slight bend in the handle, cleanly transferring the ladle's contents into a bowl is nearly impossible.

A handle that bends too dramatically, however—the defect of the Cuisipro Tempo Serving Ladle ($14.95)—makes it difficult to dip the ladle into a tall, narrow stockpot. That left the Rösle Ladle with Pouring Rim and Hook Handle ($23.95), which worked very well. A hook handle and a drip-prevention pouring rim, which kept even wiggly noodles intact all the way to the bowl, earned the Rösle ladle our top rating.

TASTING LAB: Soy Sauce

MOST OF US HAVE RARELY GIVEN SOY SAUCE A SECOND thought, using it as a kind of liquid salt. But this 2,500-year-old ingredient, brewed first in China and since the seventh century in Japan, can offer nearly as much variety, complexity, and flavor as wine or olive oil, and it deserves serious consideration. In most supermarkets today, you will find a shelf of imported soy sauces, as well as American-brewed versions. How do they differ? Which tastes best as a dipping sauce for delicate sushi and savory dumplings? Cooked in stir-fries and glazes for meat and fish? And while we're at it, what is tamari?

We decided to sample nationally available brands, choosing a lineup of 12 soy sauces, including both tamari and regular soy sauce, from Japan, China, and the United States. We tasted them three times: first plain, then with warm rice, and finally cooked in a teriyaki sauce with ginger, garlic, and mirin and brushed over broiled chicken thighs. As we tasted them, we noticed a wide range of colors and flavors, from reddish-brown, delicate, and floral to dark brown, pungent, and assertive. We wondered where these differences came from and how well they played off the other flavors in a dish.

At its most basic, soy sauce is a fermented liquid made from soybeans and wheat. Soybeans contribute a strong, pungent taste, while wheat lends sweetness. Tamari is a type of soy sauce traditionally made with all soybeans and no wheat—though, confusingly, many tamaris do contain a little wheat. As a result, tamari has a more pungent flavor than soy sauce. Similarly, stronger, earthier Chinese soy sauce tends to be made with a lower proportion of wheat than the sweeter, lighter Japanese soy sauce.

Like many products with a long history, soy sauce is now made both artisanally using traditional methods and industrially using modern technology. All soy sauce begins with whole soybeans or defatted soy meal cooked and mixed with roasted grain, usually wheat (but sometimes barley or rice). This bean-grain mixture is inoculated with a mold called koji (technically, *Aspergillus oryzae* or *Aspergillus sojae*) and left for a few days to allow the mold to grow and spread. Then salt water and yeast are added to form a mash called moromi. And here comes the biggest factor in the difference in quality levels of soy sauce: The mash is fermented for anywhere from two days to four years. The brown liquid that is extruded from the mash is soy sauce, which is usually filtered, pasteurized, and bottled.

Experts claim that each soy sauce gets its particular flavor from the proportion and quality of the ingredients, including the local water where it's brewed, the koji "starter" mold (some companies brag of their proprietary koji, kept alive for centuries), the climate (a certain level of humidity is essential to make the mold grow), and the length of fermentation. Some industrially produced soy sauce starts with hydrolyzed vegetable protein (not necessarily soy) and may be sweetened with corn syrup and colored with caramel to mimic the flavor and color of fermented soy sauce.

Soy sauce is not all the same—there are five types in Japan alone. In the United States, however, we tend to use one kind of soy sauce for all purposes, and, since we prefer simplicity in the test kitchen, we were hoping one clear winner would emerge from our tasting. No such luck. Our tasters liked one type of soy sauce for plain, uncooked applications and an entirely different one for cooked dishes. How about being able to say the best soy sauce is made in one particular country? Sorry: The tasters chose two different nations' products, depending on how it was used. Method of brewing? Again, they split between an artisanal soy and a mass-produced one (albeit one aged for months, not days). Would saltiness be the favored attribute? No, one had the least salt of the 12 in our lineup, the other had the most. Clearly, these results underscored the fact that there's no "one-size-fits-all" soy sauce.

In the plain tasting, Ohsawa Nama Shoyu (a traditionally brewed import from Japan) came out on top. With 720 milligrams per tablespoon, it has the lowest sodium level of the 12 brands we tasted. When the sauces were drizzled

over warm rice and cooked into a teriyaki glaze, our tasters preferred a mass-produced Chinese brand, Lee Kum Kee Tabletop Soy Sauce, which has the highest sodium level of the lineup, at 1,200 milligrams per tablespoon. Ohsawa Nama Shoyu was described as having a "sweet," "delicate," even "floral" taste, while tasters dubbed Lee Kum Kee "salty," "malty," and "delicious." What could explain this flavor divide?

An important clue came when we tested lower-sodium (also called "light") soy sauces. (Lower-sodium soy sauces start as regular soy sauce, then some sodium is removed by filtering or ion exchange.) The lower-sodium soy sauces actually beat the regular soy sauces in a plain taste test but lost out in cooked applications. Why? Cutting down on the salt let some of the other flavors take the stage, leaving a delicate, complex soy taste in the foreground. But once cooked, the delicate flavors dissipated.

These delicate, nuanced flavors develop during the fermentation process, according to Dr. Joseph Frank, professor of food microbiology at the University of Georgia at Athens, who teaches courses in food fermentation and is an expert on soy sauce. "The koji mold produces a variety of enzymes that, when they get put in a salt solution with the soy and toasted wheat, convert proteins to amino acids and starches to sugars. The acids and alcohol that result combine to form esters—flavor compounds that give you fruitiness. This all takes time," he said. "Generally, the longer the soy sauce ages, the more flavor it will develop—like wine."

These flavorful esters are volatile, however, Frank said, and cook off when heated. "If you cook soy sauce for any length of time you'll drive off the aroma—it's sort of like using vanilla. You might want to add more [soy sauce] back at the end of cooking."

In the case of the Lee Kum Kee soy sauce, whose more robust flavor held up during the boiling and reduction of the teriyaki sauce, Frank said, "I think this soy sauce,

in its brewing process, is higher in the nonvolatile flavor components, what we call the Maillard components." In the Maillard reaction, sugars and amino acids react to heat, causing browning and bringing about a richer, more savory flavor—like searing meat before making pot roast. "That's what contributes to the depth of flavor in the [teriyaki] glaze," Frank said. And in fact, Lee Kum Kee was the only soy sauce we tasted that had significant sugar content: 2 grams per tablespoon. Combine that sugar with a high salt content and the overall flavor profile of the dish is improved, Frank noted. "It may not even taste salty [or sweet], per se, but it will change your perception of the flavor."

Our two winners represent two very different manufacturing styles. Lee Kum Kee is brewed and bottled in a 10-million-square-foot factory in Xinhui, China. It is fermented for three to six months in 20-foot-tall fiberglass holding tanks.

In contrast, Ohsawa Nama Shoyu (shoyu is the Japanese word for soy sauce; nama shoyu means it's unpasteurized) is made in the Japanese mountain village of Kamiizumi-mura, using the spring water from the mountain. The soy sauce is hand-stirred and fermented in sixty 150-year-old cedar kegs, in a wooden-post-and-beam factory surrounded by organic gardens. The flavor of Ohsawa Nama Shoyu develops over an unusually long period of time because it is double-fermented, according to Jean Richardson, president of its importer, San Diego–based Goldmine Natural Foods. After fermenting the sauce in the cedar vats for at least two summers, the makers add more soybeans and wheat and age it another two summers. "This makes a complex bouquet of aroma and flavor," Richardson said. "You don't really get that bite of salt. The aging makes it mellower."

Long-aging and importing costs explain why Ohsawa is the most expensive brand we tasted—$6.49 for 10 ounces. But spending a few extra dollars for a traditional, slow-brewed soy sauce is worth the investment, especially for use as a dipping sauce. However, the more robust Lee Kum Kee is our top choice for cooking.

Rating Soy Sauces

NINETEEN MEMBERS OF THE AMERICA'S TEST KITCHEN STAFF TASTED 12 SOY SAUCES, INCLUDING BOTH TAMARI and regular soy sauce samples. The sauces were rated on their saltiness, complexity, and overall flavor in three applications: plain, drizzled over warm rice, and cooked in a simple teriyaki glaze over chicken thighs. The soy sauces are listed in order of preference and are available in supermarkets.

RECOMMENDED
Lee Kum Kee Tabletop Soy Sauce
$1.99 for 5.1 ounces; Sodium: 1,200 milligrams per tablespoon
This Chinese brand won the rice and teriyaki tastings. Its flavor was described as "salty, sweet, roasted, pleasant." Contains more sodium than other brands tested.

RECOMMENDED
Ohsawa Nama Shoyu Organic Unpasteurized Soy Sauce
$6.49 for 10 ounces; Sodium: 720 milligrams per tablespoon
This Japanese brand won the plain tasting, with its flavor described as "clean," "caramel," and "rich and nuanced." Contains less sodium than other brands tested.

RECOMMENDED WITH RESERVATIONS
San-J Organic Shoyu Naturally Brewed Soy Sauce
$3.69 for 20 ounces; Sodium: 960 milligrams per tablespoon
Tasters described this Japanese-style soy sauce made in Virginia as "thin" and "light." With rice, it came across as slightly "earthy."

RECOMMENDED WITH RESERVATIONS
Kikkoman All-Purpose Soy Sauce
$1.79 for 10 ounces; Sodium: 920 milligrams per tablespoon
Many tasters identified this Japanese-style version made in Wisconsin as basic soy sauce: "Tastes like what you get in Asian restaurants."

RECOMMENDED WITH RESERVATIONS
Pearl River Bridge Superior Light Soy Sauce
$1.99 for 16.9 ounces; Sodium: 870 milligrams per tablespoon
Tasters noted a "beefy," "salty," even "smoky" flavor in this Chinese brand, though some described it as "lacking depth."

RECOMMENDED WITH RESERVATIONS
Eden Organic Naturally Brewed Tamari Soy Sauce
$3.99 for 10 ounces; Sodium: 860 milligrams per tablespoon
The "malty," "caramel" notes of this Japanese-style tamari made in Michigan appealed to some tasters, but many complained of "fishy," "pungent" flavors.

RECOMMENDED WITH RESERVATIONS
Eden Organic Traditionally Brewed Tamari Soy Sauce
$5.99 for 10 ounces; Sodium: 990 milligrams per tablespoon
Served with rice, there were some complaints about the saltiness of this Japanese tamari, and in teriyaki it was called "really pungent and strong."

RECOMMENDED WITH RESERVATIONS
Eden Organic Shoyu Soy Sauce
$3.99 for 10 ounces; Sodium: 1,040 milligrams per tablespoon
This Japanese import appealed to some tasters as "nice," with a "light caramel taste." However, salt and alcohol dominated other tasters' perceptions.

RECOMMENDED WITH RESERVATIONS
Kikkoman Naturally Brewed Organic Soy Sauce
$3.99 for 10 ounces; Sodium: 1,000 milligrams per tablespoon
"Pure salt; use sparingly," warned one taster; others agreed but enjoyed this Japanese brand's "nice flavor once the saltiness dissipates."

RECOMMENDED WITH RESERVATIONS
Kikkoman Naturally Brewed Tamari Soy Sauce
$3.29 for 10 ounces; Sodium: 980 milligrams per tablespoon
"Dark, rich, and malty," with "caramel" and "wheat" notes, this Japanese brand lost points for a "weird fishy aftertaste."

RECOMMENDED WITH RESERVATIONS
SAN-J Naturally Brewed Tamari Premium Soy Sauce
$2.99 for 10 ounces; Sodium: 960 milligrams per tablespoon
Some found this Virginia-made tamari "thick, sweet, and tasty," but many others called it "fishy" and "tinny."

NOT RECOMMENDED
La Choy Soy Sauce
$1.79 for 10 ounces; Sodium: 1,160 milligrams per tablespoon
The complaints about this American brand with hydrolyzed soy protein, corn syrup, and caramel color were many: "grainy, chemical taste," "artificial," "burnt," "stinky," and "acidic."

Bryan portions out brown sugar cookie dough onto parchment-lined baking sheets to prevent sticking. He also rolls the balls of dough in a mixture of granulated and brown sugar for some extra crunch and caramel flavor.

COOKIE JAR *favorites*

CHAPTER 21

Bakers tend to think of themselves as an elite lot, but cookie-making seems to level the playing field a bit. After all, who hasn't assisted a parent or grandparent with baking a batch? We turned our attention to developing two favorite cookies—the humble brown sugar cookie, a moist, chewy cookie packed with butterscotch flavor, and a triple chocolate cookie that is so chocolaty it's almost a brownie.

Brown sugar cookies are among the simplest cookies you can make. A combination of basic pantry ingredients, these cookies derive their flavor from the warm molasses notes of brown sugar. But some brown sugar cookies taste flat and bland. Could we find a way to inject our cookie with more flavor? We were ready to find out.

As for making a triple chocolate cookie, trying to pack a lot of chocolate into a cookie isn't without its hazards. The cookie can bake up overly gooey or candy-like. We wanted to strike the right balance, turning out a chocolate cookie that is undeniably rich, but not overly so.

BROWN SUGAR COOKIES

WHAT WE WANTED: A homey cookie—crisp and chewy, with warm brown sugar flavor.

There's nothing like a simple cookie done well. Take sugar cookies, for example: Made of nothing more than butter, sugar, flour, eggs, and leavener, they're rich and buttery with a crisp, sugary exterior. But a sugar cookie can seem too simple—even dull—at times. We love the butterscotch, vanilla, and caramel flavors that brown sugar gives coffee cakes and other baked goods. Could we replace the granulated sugar in a sugar cookie with brown sugar and create a simple cookie that was actually exciting? We had a clear vision of this cookie. It would be oversized, with a crackling crisp exterior and a chewy interior. And, like Mick Jagger, this cookie would scream "brown sugar."

We found a half-dozen recipes and got to work. Although they looked similar on paper, the baked cookies ranged in style from bite-sized puffs with a soft, cakey texture to thin disks with a short crumb. This first round of testing reminded us that cookies are deceptively difficult. Yes, most recipes can be executed by a young child, but even the tiniest alteration will make a significant difference in flavor and, especially, texture. To construct our ideal brown sugar cookie, we would need to brush up on the science of cookie making.

Most sugar cookie recipes start by creaming softened butter with sugar until fluffy, beating in an egg or two, and then adding the dry ingredients (flour, baking powder, and salt). Vanilla is often incorporated along the way.

Butter was the obvious choice for optimal flavor, but creaming the fat and sugar beat tiny air bubbles into the dough and the resulting cookies were cakey and tender—not what we had in mind. We tried cutting the butter into the flour (like you do when making pie dough), but this method produced crumbly cookies with a texture akin to shortbread. When we melted the butter, the cookies finally had the chewy texture we wanted.

So why does melted butter make chewy cookies? Butter is actually 20 percent water and 80 percent fat. When melted, the water and fat separate and the proteins in the flour absorb some of the water and begin to form gluten, the protein that gives baked goods, including breads, their structure and chew.

Cookies made with melted butter and an entire 1-pound box of brown sugar had plenty of flavor, but these taffy-textured confections threatened to pull out any expensive dental work. Using dark brown sugar rather than light brown sugar allowed us to get more flavor from less sugar. Cookies made with 1¾ cups dark brown sugar had the best texture and decent flavor. We decided to nail down the rest of our recipe before circling back to flavor issues.

Eggs add richness and structure to cookies. A single egg didn't provide enough of the latter— the cookies were too candy-like. Thinking that two eggs would solve the problem, we were surprised when a test batch turned out dry and cakey. Splitting the difference, we added one whole egg plus a yolk and were pleased with the results.

Too much flour gave the cookies a homogenous texture; too little and that candy-like chew reemerged. Two cups flour, plus a couple extra tablespoons, was the perfect match for the amounts of butter, sugar, and egg we'd chosen.

The choice of leavener is probably the most confusing part of any cookie recipe. Sugar cookies typically contain baking powder—a mixture of baking soda and a weak acid (calcium acid phosphate) that is activated by moisture and heat. The soda and acid create gas bubbles, which expand cookies and other baked goods. However, many baked goods with brown sugar call for baking soda. While granulated sugar is neutral, dark brown sugar can be slightly acidic. When we used baking soda by itself, the cookies had an open, coarse crumb and craggy top. Tasters loved the craggy top but not the coarse crumb. When we used baking

(½ teaspoon) balanced the sweetness and helped accentuate the more interesting flavor components in brown sugar. But our biggest success came from an unlikely refinement.

Browned butter sauces add nutty flavor to delicate fish and pasta dishes. We wondered if browning the melted butter would add the same nutty flavor to our cookies. We were hoping for a modest improvement, but our tasters thought the complex nuttiness added by the browned butter made a substantial difference.

We noticed that cookies made with browned butter were slightly drier than cookies made with melted butter; some of the water in the butter was evaporating when we browned it. Adding an extra 2 tablespoons of butter and browning most (but not all) of the butter restored the chewy texture to our cookies.

We tried a range of baking temperatures between 300 and 400 degrees and found that right down the middle (350 degrees) gave us the most consistent results. We had hoped to bake two sheets at the same time, but even with rotating and changing tray positions at different times during baking, we could not get two-tray baking to work. Some of the cookies had the right texture, but others were inexplicably dry. Baking one tray at a time allows for even heat distribution and ensures that every cookie has the same texture.

Our final recipe relies on pantry staples and delivers big brown sugar flavor. And although our technique isn't difficult (the cookies can be in the oven after just 15 minutes of work), it did require us to learn some chemistry and physics. After baking 1,200 brown sugar cookies, we think we've earned advanced degrees in both subjects.

WHAT WE LEARNED: Melting the butter before mixing it into the dough makes for perfectly chewy cookies, and browning the melted butter adds a complex nuttiness to the cookies' flavor. Dark brown sugar is preferred to light brown sugar for its concentrated flavor. To highlight the brown sugar flavor, add a healthy amount of vanilla and salt, and for increased flavor roll the dough balls in a combination of brown and granulated sugar.

powder by itself, the cookies had a finer, tighter crumb but the craggy top disappeared. After a dozen rounds of testing, we found that ¼ teaspoon of baking powder mixed with ½ teaspoon of baking soda moderated the coarseness of the crumb without compromising the craggy tops.

We had now developed a good cookie, but could we eke out even more brown sugar flavor? Riffing off a classic sugar cookie technique, we tried rolling the dough balls in brown sugar before baking them. The brown sugar clumped in some spots, but overall the crackling sugar exterior added good crunch and flavor. Cutting the brown sugar with granulated sugar solved the clumping problem.

To further ramp up the brown sugar flavor, we tested maple syrup, molasses, and vanilla extract. The maple and molasses were overpowering and masked the cookies' butterscotch flavor, but 1 tablespoon of vanilla extract properly reinforced the brown sugar flavor. A healthy dose of salt

BROWN SUGAR COOKIES

makes 2 dozen cookies

The most efficient way to bake these cookies is to portion and bake half of the dough. While the first batch is in the oven, the remaining dough can be prepared for baking. Avoid using a nonstick skillet to brown the butter. The dark color of the nonstick coating makes it difficult to gauge when the butter is sufficiently browned. Use fresh brown sugar, as older (read: harder and drier) brown sugar will make the cookies too dry.

14	tablespoons (1¾ sticks) unsalted butter
¼	cup (about 1¾ ounces) granulated sugar
2	cups (14 ounces) packed dark brown sugar
2	cups plus 2 tablespoons (about 10½ ounces) unbleached all-purpose flour
½	teaspoon baking soda
¼	teaspoon baking powder
½	teaspoon salt
1	large egg
1	large egg yolk
1	tablespoon vanilla extract

1. Heat 10 tablespoons of the butter in a 10-inch skillet over medium-high heat until melted, about 2 minutes. Continue to cook, swirling the pan constantly until the butter is dark golden brown and has a nutty aroma, 1 to 3 minutes. Remove the skillet from the heat and transfer the browned butter to a large heatproof bowl. Stir the remaining 4 tablespoons butter into the hot butter to melt; set aside for 15 minutes.

2. Meanwhile, adjust an oven rack to the middle position and heat the oven to 350 degrees. Line 2 large (18 by 12-inch) baking sheets with parchment paper. In a shallow baking dish or pie plate, mix the granulated sugar and ¼ cup of the packed brown sugar, rubbing between your fingers, until well combined; set aside. Whisk the flour, baking soda, and baking powder together in a medium bowl; set aside.

GETTING IT RIGHT: The Cookies You Want

By adjusting key ingredients, you can change the texture of any cookie recipe.

IF YOU WANT . . .	ADD . . .	EXPLANATION
Chewy cookies	Melted butter	Butter is 20 percent water. Melting helps water in butter mix with flour to form gluten.
Thin, candy-like cookies	More sugar	Sugar becomes fluid in the oven and helps cookies spread.
Cakey cookies	More eggs	Yolks make cookies rich, and whites cause cookies to puff and dry out.
An open, coarse crumb and craggy top	Baking soda	Baking soda reacts quickly with acidic ingredients (such as brown sugar) to create lots of gas bubbles.
A fine, tight crumb and smooth top	Baking powder	Baking powder works slowly and allows for an even rise.

---

3. Add the remaining 1¾ cups brown sugar and salt to the bowl with the cooled butter; mix until no sugar lumps remain, about 30 seconds. Scrape down the sides of the bowl with a rubber spatula; add the egg, yolk, and vanilla and mix until fully incorporated, about 30 seconds. Scrape down the bowl. Add the flour mixture and mix until just combined, about 1 minute. Give the dough a final stir with the rubber spatula to ensure that no flour pockets remain and the ingredients are evenly distributed.

4. Divide the dough into 24 portions, each about 2 tablespoons, rolling them between your hands into balls about 1½ inches in diameter. Working in batches, toss the balls in the reserved sugar mixture to coat and set on the prepared baking sheet, spacing them about 2 inches apart, 12 dough balls per sheet. (Smaller baking sheets can be used, but it will take 3 batches.)

5. Bake one sheet at a time until the cookies are browned and still puffy and the edges have begun to set but the centers are still soft (the cookies will look raw between the cracks and seem underdone; see the photo at right), 12 to 14 minutes, rotating the baking sheet halfway through baking. Do not overbake.

6. Cool the cookies on the baking sheet for 5 minutes; using a wide metal spatula, transfer the cookies to a wire rack and cool to room temperature.

TECHNIQUE: Checking Doneness

Achieving the proper texture—crisp at the edges and chewy in the middle—is critical to this recipe. Because the cookies are so dark, it's hard to judge doneness by color. Instead, gently press halfway between the edge and center of the cookie. When it's done, it will form an indentation with slight resistance. Check early and err on the side of underdone.

GETTING IT RIGHT:
Building Big Brown Sugar Flavor

Dark brown sugar was an obvious place to begin our efforts to create a cookie with a bold, nutty, butterscotch flavor. A whole tablespoon of vanilla helped, but everyone in the test kitchen was surprised how much impact browning the butter had on the flavor of these cookies.

Dark Brown Sugar   Lots of Vanilla   Browned Butter

TRIPLE CHOCOLATE COOKIES

WHAT WE WANTED: A soft and chewy cookie packed with serious, but balanced, chocolate flavor.

The most common trio of chocolates used to make triple-chocolate cookies consists of unsweetened, bittersweet, and semisweet. The unsweetened chocolate adds intense, earthy chocolate flavor (think brownies); the bittersweet chocolate adds a sophisticated, rich chocolate flavor; and the semisweet balances the two more bitter chocolates.

At least that's the theory behind this recipe. In reality, many recipe writers seem to believe this cookie is an excuse for excess. A triple-chocolate cookie shouldn't be a case of death by chocolate. All the same, this cookie ought to be rich and intense. But how do you build in so much chocolate and not end up with a piece of fudge?

Most cookies are made by creaming butter and sugar, then adding eggs and the dry ingredients. This method simply won't work with triple-chocolate cookies—there's no place to add all of that melted chocolate. The brownie method—melt chocolate and butter, add sugar, then eggs, then flour—was the most common choice in the recipes we found, but we had trouble getting the cookies to hold their shape.

We had better luck beating the eggs and sugar together until fluffy, then adding the melted chocolate along with the melted butter, and adding the dry ingredients last. Beating the eggs and sugar for four minutes gave the batter more structure. When baked, the cookies had a crisp shell, kind of like a meringue cookie, that tasters really liked.

Tasters liked a relatively small amount of unsweetened chocolate (too much was overpowering) balanced by equal amounts of bittersweet and semisweet. We found that premium bittersweet bar chocolates were actually too rich (and too greasy) for this recipe. We had better luck with bittersweet chocolate chips, which contain less fat than bittersweet chocolate bars. The melted chips improved the batter by making it less fluid, yet they also added the same grown-up, not-too-sweet flavor as the bittersweet bar chocolate. We also added coffee powder and vanilla to bolster the chocolate flavor.

The semisweet chocolate is the buffer that rounds out the harsh edges of the bittersweet and unsweetened chocolates. But when we added even a small amount of melted semisweet chocolate, the cookies became gooey and cloying. After much trial and error, we hit upon a novel idea. We added the semisweet chocolate in chip form once the batter was assembled. Because the chips softened but did not melt in the oven, they added chocolate flavor without increasing the fluidity of the batter or harming the texture of the cookies. We also found that the cookies retained their fudgy texture if they cooled directly on the baking sheet, rather than on a baking rack.

Our final recipe contains 1⅓ pounds of chocolate. Although most kids will like these cookies with a glass of milk, the grownups in the test kitchen enjoyed them straight up. Talk about chocolate decadence!

WHAT WE LEARNED: For a chewy, fudgy texture, beat the eggs and sugar together until fluffy, then add melted butter and melted chocolate. To prevent the cookies from becoming too gooey, melt only the unsweetened and bittersweet chocolate—add the semisweet chips whole. Coffee powder and a generous amount of vanilla deepen the chocolate flavor. Cool the cookies directly on the baking sheet, which contributes to their fudgy texture.

TRIPLE CHOCOLATE COOKIES

makes 26 cookies

Avoid using bittersweet bar chocolate—the cookies will be too rich and won't hold their shape. The key to the fudgy texture of these cookies is letting them cool directly on the baking sheets.

    3   ounces unsweetened chocolate, chopped
    1½ cups bittersweet chocolate chips
    7   tablespoons unsalted butter, cut into pieces
    2   teaspoons instant coffee
    2   teaspoons vanilla extract
    3   large eggs, at room temperature
    1   cup (7 ounces) sugar
    ½   cup (2½ ounces) unbleached all-purpose flour
    ½   teaspoon baking powder
    ½   teaspoon salt
    1½ cups semisweet chocolate chips

1. Melt the unsweetened chocolate, bittersweet chips, and butter in a heatproof bowl set over a saucepan of simmering water, stirring frequently, until completely smooth and glossy. Remove the bowl from the pan and set aside to cool slightly.

2. Stir the instant coffee and vanilla extract together in a small bowl until dissolved. Beat the eggs and sugar in a large bowl with an electric mixer at medium-high speed until very thick and pale, about 4 minutes. Add the vanilla-coffee mixture and beat until incorporated, 20 seconds. Reduce the speed to low, add the chocolate mixture, and mix until thoroughly combined, about 30 seconds.

3. Whisk the flour, baking powder, and salt together in a medium bowl. Using a large rubber spatula, fold the flour mixture and semisweet chips into the batter. Cover the bowl with plastic wrap and let stand at room temperature for 20 to 30 minutes until the batter firms up (it will more closely resemble thick brownie batter than cookie dough).

4. Meanwhile, adjust 2 oven racks to the upper- and lower-middle positions and heat the oven to 350 degrees. Line 2 large baking sheets with parchment paper. Using 1 heaping tablespoon of batter per cookie, place the cookies 2 inches apart on the prepared baking sheets. Bake until the cookies are shiny and cracked on top, 11 to 14 minutes, rotating the baking sheets top to bottom and front to back halfway through the baking time. Transfer the baking sheets to cooling racks and cool the cookies completely, on the baking sheets, before serving.

TECHNIQUE: How to Arrange Cookies

By staggering the rows of cookie batter, it's easy to fit 13 cookies on a single large baking sheet.

TECHNIQUE: Cookie Quick Tips

We can think of few baking tasks as approachable and fun as cookie making. To make most cookies, you need no more than a good-sized mixing bowl and a sturdy wooden spoon. And because cookies take far less time to bake (and cool) than most other baked goods, enjoying them is just minutes away. Here are a few tips we've gleaned over the years from making cookies in the test kitchen.

Freezing Cookie Dough

Keeping frozen dough on hand means you can bake just as many, or as few, cookies as you like. Most cookie doughs can withstand a month or so in the freezer.

Form the dough into balls and arrange them on a baking sheet lined with parchment or waxed paper. Place the baking sheet in the freezer. When the balls of dough are frozen, place them in a zipper-lock bag or small airtight container. When you want to make cookies, remove as many as you like and bake as directed, increasing the baking time by a minute or two.

Rotating Baking Sheets for Evenly Baked Cookies

Often when you have two sheets of cookies in the oven at once, the recipe will direct you to reverse them from front to back and top to bottom. In the bustle of a busy kitchen, however, it can be a challenge to keep track of the direction of the pans.

Line the baking sheets with parchment paper and mark the front edge of the paper, indicating which pan starts on the top and the bottom. This marking will help you keep track of which edge goes where when you reverse the pans' positions.

Handling Baking Pans

Pulling a hot pan of cookies from the oven while wearing oven mitts can be tricky, sometimes resulting in cookies with finger indents. Try this method instead.

We found that a common tool—pliers—gives you a secure grip on the hot pan without marring the cookies.

Keeping Cookies Fresh

Decorative cookie jars, like those made from ceramic, are convenient and attractive but not airtight, allowing fresh-baked cookies to go stale quickly. This method preserves the cookies' freshness and allows you to keep the pretty jar.

Line the inside of the jar with a large zipper-lock bag, place the cookies in the bag, and seal tightly.

EQUIPMENT CORNER:
Drip Coffee Makers

SINCE MR. COFFEE INTRODUCED THE FIRST AFFORDABLE automatic drip coffee maker in 1972, they have become staple appliances in American kitchens—24 million of them are sold each year. Although you can spend a few hundred dollars on high-end models, we were more interested in the under-$50 machines. Do they brew coffee reliably well? Are they easy to use? To find out, we rounded up eight popular models and headed to the test kitchen.

What did we find? Each of the machines made good (but not great) coffee that suffered somewhat because of low brewing temperature and slow brewing speed. To coax optimum flavor out of ground coffee, it should be brewed with water that is 195 to 200 degrees, and the brewing process for a full pot should take no longer than six minutes (lest overextraction—and the more bitter coffee it produces—occur). These inexpensive machines don't have the heating power to bring water to such high temperatures (only two machines, the Braun and Mr. Coffee, produced water hotter than 180 degrees), and they aren't designed to brew a full pot so quickly (the brew times ranged from 9:40 to 11:55).

Once coffee was brewed, we tasted it every 15 minutes for an hour, and the results were disappointing: The coffee was noticeably worse after only 15 minutes and progressively worse at each increment. Since coffee suffers with continued heating, we recommend immediately pouring the brewed coffee into a thermal carafe to retain freshness.

Since we didn't find much difference in coffee flavor, user-friendliness proved to be the most important factor. Testers were annoyed by machines with a small filling area, like the Proctor Silex model, which makes you pour the water into an opening just 1½ inches wide (by comparison, the Black & Decker well is 4½ inches wide at the pouring point). The accessibility and perceived solidity of the filter basket mechanism were also important, and the ratings for the Kenmore (flimsy feel) and Mr. Coffee (you have to manually push the hinged waterspout arm out of the way) machines suffered as a result. Testers also preferred coffee makers (Black & Decker, Braun, and DeLonghi) that offered easy one-handed access to the spent grounds.

We also examined the design of the carafe. The Kenmore carafe did not easily nestle back into the machine after being removed for pouring. The Braun, by contrast, felt solid and ergonomic, and clicked back into its nest on the first try.

So where did we end up? Making coffee should be easy. The Black & Decker and Braun machines felt solid and were very user-friendly. They earned top marks from our testers.

Rating Drip Coffee Makers

WE TESTED EIGHT DRIP COFFEE MAKERS PRICED BETWEEN $22.99 AND $49.99. THE COFFEE MAKERS WERE RATED ON flavor, freshness (the staying power of the coffee once brewed), and ease of use. The coffee makers are listed in order of preference. See www.americastestkitchen.com for up-to-date prices and mail-order sources for top-rated products.

RECOMMENDED
Black & Decker SmartBrew 12-Cup Coffeemaker, #DCM2000
$34.95; carafe capacity: 64 ounces; brew time: 11:21

Testers loved how easy it was to pour water into the wide tank of this model. All controls were intuitive and "dummy-proof." Very easy to clean and very accurate pouring.

RECOMMENDED WITH RESERVATIONS
Delonghi Caffe Elite, #DC76T
$49.99; carafe capacity: 60 ounces; brew time: 10:36

Testers liked the easy-to-read exterior water gauge and "good" feel of the carafe. Negatives include a narrow filling area and a filter-basket release button that swings the hot grounds open a little too fast for comfort.

RECOMMENDED
Braun AromaDeluxe, #KF 510
$49.95; carafe capacity: 48 ounces; brew time: 10:26

Felt very solid and well made, and testers praised the carafe's grip and handling. Accessing the grounds was easy. While some testers downgraded this machine for its lack of a program mode, most admitted they'd never use it.

RECOMMENDED WITH RESERVATIONS
Proctor Silex 12-Cup Programmable, #48574
$22.99; carafe capacity: 54 ounces; brew time: 11:14

Testers didn't like the narrow filling area for water, but they did appreciate that the pot resettled back into the machine effortlessly. Coffee strength dial deemed superfluous. Functional but unremarkable.

RECOMMENDED
Mr. Coffee 12-Cup Programmable, #VBX23
$29.99; carafe capacity: 60 ounces; brew time: 11:30

"Everything is easy and straightforward," said one tester. The only complaint was a swinging arm inside the machine, which a few testers thought was "just another thing that could break." "A very big carafe."

NOT RECOMMENDED
Hamilton Beach BrewStation Plus, #47665
$49.95; carafe capacity: 66 ounces; brew time: 9:40

No carafe—the coffee is brewed into an internal insulated chamber. The "landing pad" below the dispenser is too small to rest a mug on, meaning that your mug must hover while being filled. Definitely not intuitive.

RECOMMENDED WITH RESERVATIONS
Cuisinart Programmable Filter Brew 12-Cup Coffeemaker, #DCC-1000
$49.95; carafe capacity: 52 ounces; brew time: 9:43

Some odd design quirks (no hinged carafe lid, no markings under 6 cups on the carafe, and excessive height), but overall a solid machine with ergonomic pouring and a good system for accessing the grounds.

NOT RECOMMENDED
Kenmore 12-Cup Programmable Coffee Maker, #69327
$34.99; carafe capacity: 56 ounces; brew time: 11:55

Testers noted that the different components of the coffee maker didn't fit well together. Accessing the grounds was awkward, and the carafe felt dangerously unstable when full.

Brown Sugar Cookies **page 252**

Rice Salad with Oranges, Olives, and Almonds **page 175**

Pan-Roasted Chicken Breasts with Potatoes **page 20**

Pan-Seared Thick-Cut Steaks **page 214**

Pasta Caprese **page 50**

Skillet-Barbecued Pork Chops **page 36**

264

Shrimp Salad **page 27**

Pepperoni Pan Pizza **page** 189

266

Antipasto Pasta Salad **page 192**

Indian-Style Curry with Potatoes, Cauliflower, Peas, and Chickpeas **page 224**

Stir-Fried Portobellos with Ginger-Oyster Sauce **page 240**

Coq au Vin **page 201**

Apple Galette **page 318**

Lemon Layer Cake **page 310**

272

New York–Style Crumb Cake **page 285**

Low-Fat Chocolate Mousse **page 277**

274

LIGHTENING UP
chocolate
desserts

CHAPTER 22

Skipping dessert or eating a piece of fruit is an obvious
way to cut calories, but where's the fun in that? We set our sights on
revamping the fat and calories in two favorite chocolate desserts—
chocolate mousse and chocolate brownies.

What makes chocolate mousse so appealing? Sure, its intense
chocolate flavor is a draw, but its lush, creamy texture ensures the
popularity of this decadent dessert. And just what gives mousse such an
ethereal texture? Heavy cream, and lots of it. When you're cutting fat
and calories, cream is obviously not an option. We'd need to look for
other ways to mimic the almost fluffy texture of whipped cream. And
as for the chocolate, we'd have to weigh our options carefully so as not
to compromise the flavor in our low-fat mousse.

Brownies are not unknown to the low-fat canon, but so often
they're dry or gummy—or short on chocolate flavor (prune-flavored
brownies, anyone?). We wanted to inject our low-fat brownies with rich
chocolate flavor without relying on silly fat substitutes. And we aimed
to develop a low-fat brownie with an irresistible, fudgy texture similar
to traditional versions.

IN THIS CHAPTER

THE RECIPES
Low-Fat Chocolate Mousse
Fudgy Low-Fat Brownies

TASTING LAB
Light Vanilla Ice Cream

LIGHTENING UP CHOCOLATE DESSERTS **275**

LOW-FAT CHOCOLATE MOUSSE

WHAT WE WANTED: A low-fat chocolate mousse with a rich flavor and creamy, ethereal texture similar to traditional versions.

When presented with the challenge of developing a low-fat chocolate mousse recipe, we admit we were daunted. After all, traditional chocolate mousse—essentially melted chocolate, cocoa, beaten egg whites, and whipped cream—is mostly fat. Besides preserving the rich chocolate flavor, we wanted to keep that irresistible silky, fluffy texture. How were we going to pull this off? Since this dish is as much about texture as flavor, we were hoping to find an alternative to the whipped cream.

It didn't take us long to find a stack of "healthy" mousse recipes that relied on various low-fat dairy products. Even when we pureed them first, part-skim ricotta cheese and extra-firm tofu made mousses with unpleasant granular textures; mousse made with low-fat yogurt was runny and sour; and light cream cheese yielded a dense and gummy texture.

Leaving low-fat dairy behind, we tested unflavored gelatin, but tasters rejected its bouncy, "set" quality. Marshmallow crème (Fluff) gave mousse a light, lofty texture without any fat, but the Fluff lent a distinct marshmallow flavor that wasn't right for chocolate mousse. The Fluff did, however, remind us of seven-minute frosting, an old-fashioned icing made by beating egg whites with sugar over heat for seven minutes. We tried this and finally had some hope; there was no marshmallow flavor, but the airy frosting made the mousse too light.

Staying with cooked egg whites, we made an Italian meringue by beating egg whites in a mixer until fluffy, then "cooking" them by adding a hot sugar syrup. This fat-free mixture (which is denser than the seven-minute frosting) became suitably voluminous and gave the mousse the creamy texture we were looking for—without a drop of heavy cream. Using this Italian meringue as our base, we folded in melted chocolate (for richness) and cocoa powder (for intensity) and chilled our mousse. The texture was perfectly creamy and light. Now our tasters' only complaint was about the flavor—it was harsh, one-dimensional, and actually too chocolaty.

We tried scaling back the amount of chocolate, but we were just reducing the chocolate flavor, not the harshness. We played around with every amount and combination of semisweet, bittersweet, milk, and unsweetened chocolate, all to no avail. And then it hit us that there was one chocolate we hadn't tried: white chocolate. In the end, just ⅓ cup of white chocolate chips took the edge off the other chocolate and cocoa—and tacked on only 10 extra calories per serving.

Why did it work? White chocolate isn't actually chocolate—it's mostly fat and sugar. It turns out that chocolate and cocoa need fat to temper their harshness and bring out their full, well-balanced flavor. Without any cream in our mousse, the chocolate and cocoa were too harsh. A little white chocolate added just enough fat to keep them in check. And where did we end up in terms of fat and calories? A single 6-ounce serving of traditional chocolate mousse contains 380 calories and 32 grams of fat. The same serving size of our low-fat version contains 230 calories and only 10 grams of fat (5 grams saturated fat). Not bad at all!

WHAT WE LEARNED: An Italian meringue (egg whites beaten until fluffy, and then cooked in hot sugar syrup) makes a fat-free base that mimics the volume and texture of traditional mousse made with heavy cream. Semisweet chocolate and Dutch-processed cocoa add rich chocolate flavor, and a surprise ingredient—melted white chocolate chips—mellows and rounds out the flavors of each.

LOW-FAT CHOCOLATE MOUSSE

serves 6

The meringue and chocolate mixture are combined in two stages so the meringue doesn't collapse. For the best texture, chill the mousse overnight.

4   ounces semisweet chocolate, broken into pieces
⅓   cup white chocolate chips
2   tablespoons Dutch-processed cocoa powder
6   tablespoons plus ½ cup water
1   teaspoon vanilla extract
½   cup (3½ ounces) sugar
3   large egg whites
¼   teaspoon cream of tartar

1. Melt the semisweet chocolate, white chocolate, cocoa powder, 6 tablespoons of the water, and the vanilla in a medium bowl set over a pot of barely simmering water, stirring until smooth. Set aside to cool slightly.

2. Bring the remaining ½ cup water and the sugar to a vigorous boil in a small saucepan over high heat. Boil until slightly thickened and large bubbles rise to the top, about 4 minutes. Remove from the heat.

3. With an electric mixer on medium-low speed, beat the egg whites in a large bowl until frothy, about 1 minute. Add the cream of tartar and beat, gradually increasing the speed to medium-high, until the whites hold soft peaks, about 2 minutes. With the mixer running, slowly pour the hot syrup into the whites (avoid pouring the syrup onto the beaters or it will splash). Increase the speed to high and beat until the meringue has cooled to just warm and becomes very thick and shiny, 2 to 3 minutes.

4. Whisk one-third of the meringue into the chocolate mixture until combined, then whisk in the remaining meringue. Spoon the mousse into six 6-ounce ramekins or pudding cups. Cover tightly with plastic wrap. Chill overnight. (The mousse can be refrigerated for up to 4 days.)

GETTING IT RIGHT:
Three Chocolates Are Better Than One

Semisweet Chocolate
Adds rich chocolate flavor and creaminess.

Dutch-Processed Cocoa
Adds intense chocolate flavor.

White Chocolate Chips
Tempers the harshness of the chocolate and cocoa.

FUDGY LOW-FAT BROWNIES

WHAT WE WANTED: A moist and fudgy chocolate brownie with fewer calories and less fat than traditional versions.

We have tried many recipes for "healthy" brownies, but it usually takes just one bite to regret the effort. Either the texture is incredibly dry or the chocolate flavor is anemic. The best of the lot are usually cakey and spongy, which is OK if what you want is a flat piece of chocolate cake but not if you want a real brownie, which should be moist, fudgy, and packed with chocolate flavor. Fudgy brownies tend to rely on a generous amount of butter (usually an entire stick for an 8-inch pan) and unsweetened chocolate (at least 2 ounces, often more).

Many low-fat brownie recipes call for "alternative" ingredients such as applesauce, prune puree, or even yogurt, but the test kitchen's opinion of these stand-ins was unanimously negative. Applesauce masked the chocolate flavor and gave the brownies a texture that reminded tasters of an oily sponge. Prune puree yielded flavorless hockey pucks. Although yogurt produced a pleasing texture, tasters turned up their noses at the tart flavor.

We decided to stick with the test kitchen's favorite recipe for fudgy brownies and see where we might trim calories and fat. Cocoa powder, which is unsweetened chocolate with most of the fat removed, is a common ingredient in many low-fat chocolate recipes. Replacing all of the chocolate with cocoa powder is a mistake—the result was a very dry texture. Replacing all but 2 ounces was a vastly better approach. We also found that Dutch-processed brands contributed more flavor than "natural" cocoas. The last trick was to use bittersweet chocolate, which has less fat per ounce (by about 5 grams) than unsweetened chocolate.

Now it was time to confront the real problem with low-fat brownies: the butter. Leave it out and you might as well throw the brownies in the trash. But to make a significant dent in the calorie and fat count, we couldn't add more than 2 tablespoons—far less than the usual stick—and that meant dry, cakey brownies. We would have to find another source of moisture to make our brownies gooier. A squirt of chocolate syrup (such as Hershey's), which contains no fat and plenty of chocolate flavor, helped things along, but it wasn't enough.

In our research, we ran across several low-fat chocolate cake recipes that called for nonfat sour cream. Could it help our brownies? After our first test, we would have thought not. The brownies were still too dry. Then, in place of the nonfat sour cream, we tried low fat, which has only about one-third the fat of the regular stuff. These brownies were much better, not just moist and fudgy but also more tender. That's because the acidity in sour cream has a tenderizing effect on baked goods. We had trimmed more than half the calories and two-thirds of the fat from our favorite fudgy brownie recipe (110 calories per brownie, down from 220, and 4.5 grams of fat, down from 12 grams). And our low-fat brownies were good enough to merit a second, even a third bite—with no regrets.

WHAT WE LEARNED: Replacing some of the butter with low-fat sour cream yields moist, fudgy brownies, with less fat. A blend of cocoa powder and bittersweet chocolate (which has less fat per ounce than unsweetened chocolate) adds deep chocolate flavor. And to boost both the brownies' chocolate flavor and moisture without adding any fat, add chocolate syrup.

FUDGY LOW-FAT BROWNIES

makes 16 brownies

Melt the chocolate and butter together in a bowl set over a pan of simmering water or in a microwave set to medium power. For a truly fudgy consistency, don't overbake the brownies; as soon as a toothpick inserted into the center comes out with sticky crumbs attached, the brownies are done. If the toothpick emerges with no crumbs, the brownies will be cakey.

¾	cup unbleached all-purpose flour
⅓	cup Dutch-processed cocoa powder
½	teaspoon baking powder
¼	teaspoon salt
2	ounces bittersweet chocolate, chopped
2	tablespoons unsalted butter
2	tablespoons low-fat sour cream
1	tablespoon chocolate syrup
2	teaspoons vanilla extract
1	large egg plus 1 large egg white
1	cup (7 ounces) sugar

GETTING IT RIGHT:
Sour Cream in Brownies

We found that an unlikely ingredient—low-fat sour cream—helped keep our brownies fudgy even though they contain very little butter.

**Low-Fat Sour Cream =
Low-Fat Fudgy Brownies**

1. Adjust an oven rack to the middle position and heat the oven to 350 degrees. Fold two 12-inch pieces of foil or parchment paper lengthwise so each measures 7 inches wide. Fit 1 sheet into an 8-inch-square baking pan, pushing the foil into the corners and up the sides of the pan (the overhang will help in removal of brownies). Repeat with the second sheet, placing it in the pan perpendicular to the first sheet. Spray the foil with cooking spray.

2. Whisk the flour, cocoa, baking powder, and salt together in a medium bowl. Melt the bittersweet chocolate and butter in a large bowl until smooth (see note). Cool 2 to 3 minutes, then whisk in the sour cream, chocolate syrup, vanilla, egg, egg white, and sugar. Using a rubber spatula, fold the dry ingredients into the chocolate mixture until combined.

3. Pour the batter into the pan, spread into the corners, and level the surface with the spatula. Bake until slightly puffed and a toothpick inserted in the center comes out with a few sticky crumbs attached, 20 to 25 minutes. Cool the brownies completely in the pan on a wire rack, at least 1 hour. Remove the brownies from the pan using the foil handles. Cut into 2-inch squares and serve. To keep the brownies moist, do not cut until ready to serve. (The brownies can be wrapped in plastic and refrigerated for 3 days.)

TECHNIQUE: Easy Brownie and Bar Cookie Removal

1. Place two sheets of parchment paper or foil perpendicular to each other in the pan. Scrape the batter into the pan, pushing it into the corners.

2. After the brownies or bars have baked and cooled, use the paper or foil to transfer them to a cutting board, then slice into individual portions.

TASTING LAB: Light Vanilla Ice Cream

A NEW GENERATION OF LIGHT ICE CREAMS—APPEALINGLY described as "slow-churned," "double-churned," and the like—is filling supermarket freezer cases. How do they taste? To find out, we rounded up four samples.

Low-fat ice creams and ice milks used to be grainy and icy, because they didn't contain enough fat to counterbalance the ice crystals that inevitably form when ice cream is churned. For the past year or two, manufacturers have been using a process called low-temperature extrusion, which freezes light ice cream at an extremely low temperature. The idea is to freeze the ice cream so quickly that the air-fat-water emulsion does not break and grainy ice crystals never have a chance to form.

Overall, our tasters weren't terribly impressed. They gave low marks to Turkey Hill—the leanest sample in the group, with just 2.5 grams of fat per half-cup serving. Breyers and Edy's (which is sold under the Dreyer's label on the West Coast) scored slightly higher but didn't elicit much enthusiasm. Tasters genuinely liked Häagen-Dazs, the only brand in the lineup made without stabilizers or emulsifiers. But with 7 grams per half-cup serving, Häagen-Dazs Light has as much fat as many brands of regular ice cream.

How can something with so much fat be considered "light"? Federal labeling allows manufacturers to use the term "light" on ice cream with no more than half the fat and two-thirds the calories of the company's regular ice cream. Regular Häagen-Dazs has much more fat than the competition, so its light offering does, too.

Rating Light Vanilla Ice Cream

ELEVEN TASTERS TASTED FOUR LIGHT VANILLA ICE CREAMS rating them on flavor and texture. The brands are listed in order of preference and are available in supermarkets.

RECOMMENDED
Häagen-Dazs Light Vanilla Bean Ice Cream
$3.49 for 1 pint
Tasters liked the "clean" vanilla flavor in this brand made without stabilizers or emulsifiers.

RECOMMENDED WITH RESERVATIONS
Edy's/Dreyer's Slow-Churned Light Vanilla Bean Ice Cream
$4.19 for 1.75 quarts
Most tasters found this sample "creamy" and "rich," but complained "not much flavor."

RECOMMENDED WITH RESERVATIONS
Breyers Double-Churned Light Vanilla Bean Ice Cream
$5.39 for 1.75 quarts
This brand was deemed "creamy" and "rich," but "really, really sweet."

NOT RECOMMENDED
Turkey Hill Light Recipe Vanilla Bean Ice Cream
$5.69 for 1.75 quarts
"Gummy" was the common complaint here, with a few tasters noting a "chewy" texture.

TECHNIQUE:
Keeping Ice Cream Fresh
Once opened, ice cream is apt to lose its fresh flavor and form ice crystals on its surface. We found that an extra layer of insulation helps prevent these problems. Before returning the ice cream to the freezer, cover the portion remaining in the carton with heavy-duty plastic wrap, pressing the wrap flush against the surface of the ice cream. Replace the carton cover and return it to the freezer.

Lots of blueberries and a sprinkle of cinnamon sugar infuse our coffee cake, Blueberry Boy Bait, with a light sweetness.

OLD-FASHIONED
CHAPTER 23 breakfast cakes

A slice of a warm, cinnamon-y breakfast cake is a very pleasant way to ease into the day. And crumb cake is as good with a cup of coffee in the afternoon as it is at breakfast. But bakery versions of this cake often fall short—the crumb topping can be too skimpy or dry and brittle, rather than tender. And the cake can suffer too, baking up too dry or not sturdy enough, so that the crumb topping simply sinks into the cake. We wanted to tackle these issues to develop the ultimate crumb cake—a buttery vanilla-scented cake topped with the perfect amount of soft, sweet crumb topping.

Have you heard of blueberry boy bait? Perhaps not. Developed by a Pillsbury bake-off contest winner in the Midwest, this blueberry coffee cake is simply addictive. We gathered together versions of this buttery cake studded with blueberries and topped with cinnamon sugar, ready to test and tweak, because everyone should know how to make this charming, delicious cake.

CRUMB CAKE

WHAT WE WANTED: A buttery yellow cake with a tender crumb, sturdy enough to support a thick, lightly spiced crumb topping.

Crumb cake has been around for a long time, but surprisingly few people can distinguish it from a regular streusel-topped coffee cake. This is because this quirky yet elegant cake has its origins deeply rooted in just one part of the United States, New York, where it arrived with the influx of German immigrants who came to the area in the late 1800s, their recipes for krummelkuchen in hand. The New York bakeries that originally made this especially rich yeasted Danish dough topped with thick chunks of lightly spiced crumb topping are all but extinct. Our research uncovered only one still operating, the family-run Holtermann's Bakery on Staten Island.

Many people associate crumb cake with Entenmann's, a Brooklyn bakery that has expanded into a national supermarket brand. Laden with shelf-stabilizing preservatives, this popular version of crumb cake doesn't do justice to the bakery-fresh original. Because we think everyone deserves a proper taste of this classic confection, our goal was to come up with a recipe to make at home—one that would stand up to the legacy of authentic crumb cake.

A sampling of recipes showed that many modern versions are made with butter cake (even Entenmann's now offers this style). This was good news for us and made a lot of sense, as we didn't want to spend all day watching dough rise in order to make this cake. These recipes served as a primer on the potential problems with crumb cake. If the cake was too tender and delicate, the crumbs had a tendency to sink in the center. Drier, sturdier cakes provided little contrast between cake and crumb. Skimping on crumb topping—which is how some recipe writers avoid sinking crumbs—was not an option.

We decided to try one promising approach. Some recipes call for combining all of the flour, sugar, and butter and then reserving a portion for the topping and adding the remaining ingredients—such as eggs, milk, and baking powder—to the rest to make the cake batter. While this method was efficient, tasters found the results to be lackluster. The crumb needed more butter and sugar than flour, and the cake cried out for just the opposite. Clearly a wrong turn: For the ultimate crumb cake, each component would need its own recipe.

Starting with the test kitchen's favorite yellow cake recipe, we divided it in half to make room for the crumb layer. Part of this cake's appeal is its rich butteriness; once topped with redundantly buttery crumbs, it crossed over the line to greasiness. Reducing the butter lightened the cake but also made it dry and lean. Increasing the milk moistened the cake but made it less sturdy; while in the oven, the crumbs promptly sank through the wet batter. We tried thicker dairy ingredients: buttermilk, sour cream, and yogurt. Buttermilk was the clear winner, although it required a switch from baking powder to baking soda to neutralize some of its acidity.

The cake was still a little too rubbery, which we suspected was due to its being egg-heavy. We tried removing an egg, but again the careful structure of the cake was compromised. We added back a yolk, and our cake problems were finally solved.

The pièce de résistance of all crumb cakes is, of course, the crumb topping. And this is where many recipes go wrong, veering more toward a streusel topping than a crumb topping. While these both begin with the same ingredients—flour, sugar, butter, and a pinch of salt—a subtle shift in the ratios gives very different results. Streusel is fine and crunchy and may include other textural additions such as nuts or oatmeal. It's more of a sugary topping, while a crumb topping is less sweet and more substantial, sharing equal billing with the cake. Streusel also has less butter, giving it a sandy quality. Crumb topping is softer, more cookie-like, and contains only cinnamon as a flavoring.

Once we had acknowledged these distinctions, we adjusted our recipe. Less sugar, however, gave the crumbs the texture of powdery snow. To make them more cohesive, we tried using brown sugar instead of granulated. These crumbs were too chewy but had a welcome butterscotch flavor; half of each sugar was the winning compromise. Getting the butter right proved to be even more challenging. Too much and the crumbs melted into a solid mass when baked; too little and they reverted back to streusel. Switching from softened butter to melted butter gave the raw topping a unified, dough-like consistency—one we broke apart with our fingers before sprinkling over the cake batter. As we had hoped, these cohesive little nuggets held together when baked, giving us the quintessential crumb cake crumbs: sturdy on the outside, moist and tender on the inside.

Just the right amount of cinnamon (¾ teaspoon) finished the crumbs off with some warm spice flavor. Reducing the oven temperature, lengthening the baking time, and raising the oven rack to the upper-middle position gave the crumbs their irresistible golden edges. We had finally captured the essence of what made this cake a classic. Plus we could enjoy it at home whenever we wanted, still warm from the oven—something you can't get out of any cake box.

WHAT WE LEARNED: A less rich classic yellow cake compensates for the richness of the buttery crumb topping. Buttermilk provides moisture and removing one egg white keeps the cake from being too rubbery. For a soft, more cookie-like topping, use a blend of brown and granulated sugars and melt the butter to give the raw topping a unified, dough-like consistency. Using just one spice, cinnamon, provides enough flavor and warmth. For the right texture, the topping is broken into little nuggets and sprinkled over the cake batter. The nuggets hold together when baked, creating sturdy crumbs that remain moist and tender on the inside.

NEW YORK–STYLE CRUMB CAKE

serves 8 to 10

Don't be tempted to substitute all-purpose flour for the cake flour, as doing so will make a dry, tough cake. If you can't find buttermilk, you can substitute an equal amount of plain, low-fat yogurt, but do not substitute powdered buttermilk because it will make a sunken cake. When topping the cake, take care to not push the crumbs into the batter. This recipe can be easily doubled and baked in a 13 by 9-inch baking dish. If doubling, increase the baking time to about 45 minutes.

crumb topping

⅓ cup (2⅔ ounces) granulated sugar
⅓ cup (2⅔ ounces) dark brown sugar
¾ teaspoon ground cinnamon
⅛ teaspoon salt
8 tablespoons (1 stick) unsalted butter, melted and still warm
1¾ cups (7 ounces) cake flour

cake

1¼ cups (5 ounces) cake flour
½ cup (3½ ounces) granulated sugar
¼ teaspoon baking soda
¼ teaspoon salt
6 tablespoons (¾ stick) unsalted butter, cut into 6 pieces, softened but still cool
1 large egg plus 1 large egg yolk
1 teaspoon vanilla extract
⅓ cup buttermilk
Confectioners' sugar for dusting

1. FOR THE TOPPING: Whisk the sugars, cinnamon, salt, and butter in a medium bowl to combine. Add the flour and stir with a rubber spatula or wooden spoon until the mixture resembles a thick, cohesive dough; set aside to cool to room temperature, 10 to 15 minutes.

2. FOR THE CAKE: Adjust an oven rack to the upper-middle position and heat the oven to 325 degrees. Cut a 16-inch length of parchment paper or aluminum foil and fold lengthwise to a 7-inch width. Spray an 8-inch square baking dish with nonstick cooking spray and fit the parchment into the dish, pushing it into the corners and up the sides; allow the excess to overhang the edges of the dish.

3. In the bowl of a standing mixer fitted with the paddle attachment, mix the flour, sugar, baking soda, and salt on low speed to combine. With the mixer running at low speed, add the butter one piece at a time; continue beating until the mixture resembles moist crumbs, with no visible butter chunks remaining, 1 to 2 minutes. Add the egg, egg yolk, vanilla, and buttermilk; beat on medium-high speed until light and fluffy, about 1 minute, scraping once if necessary.

4. Transfer the batter to the baking pan; using a rubber spatula, spread the batter into an even layer. Following the photos, break apart the crumb topping into large pea-sized pieces and spread in an even layer over the batter, beginning with the edges and then working toward the center. Bake until the crumbs are golden and a wooden skewer inserted into the center of the cake comes out clean, 35 to 40 minutes. Cool on a wire rack for at least 30 minutes. Remove the cake from the pan by lifting the parchment overhang. Dust with confectioners' sugar just before serving.

TECHNIQUE:
Secrets to Bigger Crumbs

Using both hands, break apart the crumb dough, rolling the broken dough between your thumb and forefinger to form crumbs about the size of large peas. Continue until all the dough has been broken down into crumbs. Sprinkle the crumbs evenly over the cake batter, breaking apart any larger chunks. Spread the crumbs from the outside of the cake toward the center so as to not make the center too heavy.

Breaking the Dough   **Perfect-Sized Crumbs**

EQUIPMENT CORNER: Square Cake Pans

A SQUARE CAKE PAN IS A KITCHEN ESSENTIAL, BUT should you buy a glass, nonstick, or traditional metal model? We tested crumb cakes and cornbread in seven 8-inch pans to see how the various options performed. Pallid crusts plagued items baked in shiny metal pans made by Kaiser Tinplate ($6), Magic Line ($17.50), and Kitchen Supply ($14.98). The Pyrex square glass pan ($9) turned out respectable color on our cornbread and crumb cake, though it was outshone by the deep, evenly golden sides and bottoms on baked goods prepared in the three nonstick options—Chicago Metallic Gourmetware ($6.00), Calphalon Classic nonstick ($18.95), and Williams-Sonoma Goldtouch nonstick square pan ($21). The Williams-Sonoma pan yielded baked goods that stood a full 2 inches tall and sported straight (rather than flared) sides, making it easier to cut symmetrical pieces and split cakes into two even layers.

Rating Square Cake Pans

WE TESTED SEVEN 8-INCH SQUARE CAKE PANS BETWEEN $6 AND $21. TESTS INCLUDED BAKING CORNBREAD and crumb cake. The pans are listed in order of preference. See www.americastestkitchen.com for up-to-date prices and mail-order sources for top-rated products.

HIGHLY RECOMMENDED

Williams-Sonoma Goldtouch Nonstick Square Cake Pan

$21

Perfectly even gold color on our crumb cake and cornbread crowned this pan the winner.

RECOMMENDED

Calphalon Classic Nonstick Bakeware 8-Inch Square Cake Pan

$18.95

Nearly identical to the winning pan, but with a dark, charcoal-gray surface.

RECOMMENDED WITH RESERVATIONS

Chicago Metallic Gourmetware 8-Inch Square Cake Pan

$6

Performed as well as the Calphalon (and equipped with handles), but lacking the clean, sharp edges and full 2-inch depth we prefer.

RECOMMENDED WITH RESERVATIONS

Pyrex 8-Inch Square Glass Baking Dish

$9.00

Classic, durable, and respectable, but slightly uneven browning; with sloped sides.

NOT RECOMMENDED

Magic Line Pan 8-Inch Square

$17.50

The best of the pale metals for its straight sides and sturdy, heavy-gauge aluminum material, but still a poor choice for browning.

NOT RECOMMENDED

Kaiser Tinplate 8-Inch by 8-Inch by 2-Inch Square Cake Pan

$6

Not surprisingly, tin feels flimsy and its bright silver color produced uniformly pale bottom crusts on our baked goods.

NOT RECOMMENDED

Kitchen Supply Stainless Steel 8-Inch Square Cake/Brownie Pan

$14.98

A baking disaster from every angle—except its handles. Stainless steel is a poor heat conductor and made for a downright soupy loaf of cornbread.

BLUEBERRY BOY BAIT

WHAT WE WANTED: A moist coffee cake studded with blueberries and topped with a light streusel.

Recently, a friend brought a cake to the test kitchen: a blueberry-studded coffee cake she called "blueberry boy bait." Much more than a yellow sheet cake topped with a layer of blueberries and crisp cinnamon sugar, it was possibly the best coffee cake we'd ever eaten—despite its funny name. The cake was developed by a 15-year-old girl who entered the recipe in the 1954 Pillsbury Grand National Baking Contest—she won second place. She named the cake (a family recipe) for the effect it had on teenage boys—one bite and they were

hooked. The only problem was that the friend who shared her cake with us refused to share her recipe. No problem, we'd track down the contest winner ourselves.

We were happy to find the recipe, but it was tricky; time and again our streusel came out dry and then there was a problem with the blueberries. There didn't seem to be enough berry flavor throughout the cake, and when we added more, the cake turned soggy. We found a simpler version of the recipe in the 1969 Pillsbury's Bake Off Dessert Cookbook. This cake was moist and tender, and we especially liked that blueberries were stirred into the cake batter as well as added on top, making every bite berry-packed without it turning soggy. But the best part was the topping. No more dry, crumbly streusel—just a sprinkling of sugar and cinnamon, which baked up into sweet, crispy flakes, just like our friend's cake. Still, we saw room for improvement.

Our adjustments were minor. For deeper flavor, we exchanged butter for the shortening called for in the Pillsbury recipe, and brown sugar for half of the granulated sugar. For more structure, we added an extra egg. And since this cake has "blueberry" in its name, we increased the amount—with our sturdier cake, the cake didn't turn mushy from the extra berries. We invited our friend to the test kitchen for a piece of cake. After a few bites, she sheepishly asked for the recipe.

WHAT WE LEARNED: For richer, deeper flavor, exchange butter for the shortening and brown sugar for half of the granulated sugar. For more fruit impact, double the amount of blueberries, putting half into the cake batter and half on top. A simple sprinkling of cinnamon sugar makes a light, crisp topping—better than heavy streusel.

BLUEBERRY BOY BAIT

serves 12

If using frozen blueberries, do not let them thaw, as they will turn the batter a blue-green color.

cake

 2 cups (10 ounces) plus 1 teaspoon unbleached all-purpose flour
 1 tablespoon baking powder
 1 teaspoon salt
 16 tablespoons (2 sticks) unsalted butter, softened
 ¾ cup (5¼ ounces) packed light brown sugar
 ½ cup (3½ ounces) granulated sugar
 3 large eggs
 1 cup whole milk
 ½ cup blueberries, fresh or frozen (see note)

topping

 ½ cup blueberries, fresh or frozen (see note)
 ¼ cup (1¾ ounces) granulated sugar
 ½ teaspoon ground cinnamon

1. FOR THE CAKE: Adjust an oven rack to the middle position and heat the oven to 350 degrees. Grease and flour a 13 by 9-inch baking pan.

2. Whisk 2 cups of the flour, the baking powder, and salt together in a medium bowl. With an electric mixer, beat the butter and sugars on medium-high speed until fluffy, about 2 minutes. Add the eggs, one at a time, beating until just incorporated. Reduce the speed to medium and beat in one-third of the flour mixture until incorporated; beat in ½ cup of the milk. Beat in half of the remaining flour mixture, then the remaining ½ cup milk, and finally the remaining flour mixture. Toss the blueberries with the remaining 1 teaspoon flour. Using a rubber spatula, gently fold in the blueberries. Spread the batter into the prepared pan.

3. FOR THE TOPPING: Scatter the blueberries over the top of the batter. Stir the sugar and cinnamon together in a small bowl and sprinkle over the batter. Bake until a toothpick inserted in the center of the cake comes out clean, 45 to 50 minutes. Cool in the pan for 20 minutes, then turn out and place on a serving platter (topping side up). Serve warm or at room temperature. (The cake can be stored in an airtight container at room temperature up to 3 days.)

TASTING LAB: Hot Cocoa Mixes

A STEAMING MUG OF HOT COCOA IS THE ULTIMATE comfort drink, and there's no shortage of instant hot cocoa mixes to choose from when you need a fix. To determine the best hot cocoa, we gathered eight mixes from the supermarket and well-known chocolate companies. Most of the supermarket brands were made with water, as instructed, while Godiva, Lindt, Lake Champlain, and Ghirardelli required a cup of whole milk per serving.

The result: Tasters like their hot cocoa both sweet (but not too sweet) and creamy. Surprisingly, tasters found that the water-based cocoas tasted creamier than those made with whole milk. To make sense of our results, we took a look at each cocoa's label.

A dollop of whipped cream is the old-fashioned way to give a rich, creamy texture to hot cocoa, but additives can be used to achieve similar results. For example, mono- and diglycerides are emulsifiers that keep fats in foods bonded. When fats are emulsified, they lend a thick, silky texture to foods. Other additives that can be used to improve the texture or mouthfeel of foods include cellulose gum, carrageenan, and guar gum, which stabilize food and improve viscosity. Once we examined our hot cocoa labels, the results of our taste test made more sense.

Land O' Lakes Supreme Chocolate Hot Cocoa Mix was our tasters' first choice—they praised its buttery milk

only premium hot cocoa in our lineup to satisfy a majority of tasters with a well-balanced chocolate flavor and the right level of sweetness.

Tasters liked the creaminess of Hershey's Good Night Kisses Hot Cocoa, Swiss Miss Milk Chocolate, and Nestlé Rich Chocolate—again, a laundry list of stabilizers and emulsifiers provided adequate thickness. But Nestlé lost points for its "fake, sugary taste"—most tasters noticed the addition of sucralose, a modified sugar more often known by its brand name, Splenda.

Godiva Classic Milk Chocolate and Lindt Premium Hot Cocoa both scored near the bottom of the cocoas, turning off tasters with bitter flavors and chalky aftertastes. And too much sugar (a considerable 42 grams per serving) was Ghirardelli's undoing—tasters declared it "too sugary" and "undrinkable."

chocolate flavor, its ample sweetness, and its creaminess. Twenty-four grams of sugar per serving gave this cocoa just the right sweetness for most tasters. Since it also has a low fat content (just 3.5 grams per serving), cellulose gum and mono- and diglycerides were used to achieve the cocoa's "creamy" texture.

Second place went to Lake Champlain, a Vermont-based gourmet chocolate company. Tasters thought their All-Natural Traditional Hot Chocolate was rich and complex and tasted like homemade cocoa made the old-fashioned way. Containing only sugar, cocoa, and vanilla, it was the

TECHNIQUE:
Measuring Cocoa Neatly

To prevent dirtying a counter when measuring cocoa powder, run a double strip of masking tape across the opening of the container. Scoop up a heaping teaspoonful of the cocoa and level it off by scraping it against the tape. Try this method with baking powder, too.

Rating Hot Cocoa Mixes

TWELVE AMERICA'S TEST KITCHEN MEMBERS TASTED EIGHT COCOA MIXES PREPARED ACCORDING TO PACKAGE instructions. The hot cocoa mixes are listed in order of preference and are available in supermarkets.

RECOMMENDED

Land O' Lakes Supreme Chocolate Hot Cocoa

$5.95 for 18 ounces (12 servings)

Tasters liked this brand's buttery milk chocolate flavor, which reminded one taster "of the instant hot cocoas I grew up with." Others praised its creamy sweetness, and one taster thought this cocoa "was like eating a milk chocolate bar."

RECOMMENDED

Lake Champlain All-Natural Traditional Hot Chocolate

$6.99 for 16 ounces (21 servings)

Tasters found this brand rich and sweet, with "a nice flavor without being overly sugary." One taster likened it to homemade cocoa made with just cocoa powder, sugar, and milk. Although some complained of a chalky aftertaste, most liked this mix's dark chocolate flavor.

RECOMMENDED

Hershey's Good Night Kisses Hot Cocoa

$1.99 for 5 ounces (4 servings)

Tasters had mixed feelings about Hershey's: Some thought it had "the perfect sweetness," while others complained it was "a little sugary" and "a tad gritty." One taster compared it to white chocolate, another to "hazelnut or French almond." Almost all commented on the chocolate's milky creaminess.

RECOMMENDED

Swiss Miss Milk Chocolate Hot Cocoa

$2.09 for 10 ounces (10 servings)

One taster thought this cocoa was creamy and delicious, and that "kids would love this." Other comments ranged from "very chocolatey" and "very good" to "artificial tasting" and "bland."

RECOMMENDED WITH RESERVATIONS

Nestlé Rich Chocolate Hot Cocoa

$2.09 for 7.1 ounces (10 servings)

Most tasters thought the cocoa was too sweet. Some also thought the overwhelming sweetness masked its chocolate flavor. Some detected a fake, saccharine taste (the result of the addition of sucralose) and another picked up a "powdery" aftertaste. One taster thought the cocoa was a sugar-free product.

RECOMMENDED WITH RESERVATIONS

Godiva Classic Milk Chocolate Hot Cocoa

$10.00 for 15.4 ounces (14 servings)

Tasters thought Godiva's Milk Chocolate Cocoa lacked sufficient chocolate flavor, while one suggested that because it was "not too sweet" it would be "good for adults." Some tasters detected "odd" and "fruity" flavors, and others thought it tasted chalky, acidic, and slightly bitter.

RECOMMENDED WITH RESERVATIONS

Lindt Premium Hot Cocoa

$12.99 for 5.3 ounces (6 servings)

Tasters wished for more sweetness from this cocoa, which they also found chalky and somewhat bitter. One taster said, "Would get a higher mark if it was creamier." Another thought it had a nice chocolate flavor, while a third detected a "slightly fake aftertaste."

RECOMMENDED WITH RESERVATIONS

Ghirardelli Double Chocolate Premium Hot Cocoa

$4.49 for 16 ounces (12 servings)

Some tasters detected hints of hazelnut, while others picked up more cherry than chocolate flavor. Almost all tasters thought this cocoa was too sugary—one called it "candy-like," while another declared it "undrinkable."

A folding technique, similar to what's used in making puff pastry, helps make our fresh blueberry scones flaky and light.

COFFEEHOUSE
treats

CHAPTER 24

Scones seem to have a bit of an identity problem in the U.S. Hotel tea rooms typically offer diminutive English-style scones, which are delicate and biscuit-like—all the better to be enjoyed with spoonfuls of clotted cream and jam. Coffeehouses tend to go in the other direction, boasting supersized versions smothered under a thick blanket of icing. And then there's the health food scone, bulging with fruit, nuts, and grains—you just might need to don Birkenstocks to eat one. We set aside these myriad versions to create what we wanted in a scone; one that is moist, flaky, rich (but not overly so), and lightly sweetened. And we wanted our scone to be jam-packed with fresh blueberries—an embellishment rarely seen in scones on either side of the Atlantic.

A stalwart leftover from the '70s health food craze, bran muffins aren't exactly healthy (they contain a fair amount of butter and sugar), but their fiber content is impressive compared to most other breakfast offerings. Health issues aside, bran muffins taste good—we love their robust richness—and they make a satisfying breakfast, keeping our hunger in check for hours. Many recipes for good bran muffins contain unprocessed bran, which can easily be found at natural foods stores. But what if you don't want to make a special trip just for a batch of muffins? Could we make moist, hearty bran muffins from one of the many bran cereals our supermarket offers? We headed into the test kitchen to find out.

IN THIS CHAPTER

THE RECIPES
Blueberry Scones
Make-Ahead Blueberry Scones

Better Bran Muffins

EQUIPMENT CORNER
Commuter Coffee Mugs

TASTING LAB
Strawberry Preserves

BLUEBERRY SCONES

WHAT WE WANTED: A moist, tender scone, lightly sweetened and chock-full of fresh blueberries.

Real British scones are like British humor—steeped in tradition, dry as a bone, and often tasteless. A distant relative of the crumpet and the English muffin, the first scones were cooked without the aid of an oven; they were prepared on a cast-iron griddle, like thick pancakes. With the addition of baking soda in Victorian times, scones in England took on the role of customizable teatime accompaniments. The dry, bland biscuits were rendered palatable by the addition of plenty of butter, clotted cream, or jam.

Americans, however, are used to having breakfast quickly and on the move. We like our pastries ready to go in single servings with the sweetness, richness, and fruit built in. We've been gradually remodeling scones to fit this image. These days, coffee shop samplings run the gamut from misshapen muffin-like objects to big-as-your-head cakes. It seemed like it was time to redefine the American scone.

Rather than reworking just one style, we decided to try to bring together the best qualities from the sweetness of a coffeehouse confection; the moist freshness of a muffin; the richness and fruit of clotted cream and jam; and the super-flaky crumb of a good biscuit. We wanted scones light enough to be eaten on the go, with a healthy dose of fresh blueberries.

Traditional scone recipes call for a minimal amount of sugar and 2 to 3 tablespoons of butter per cup of flour. We found that a full 4 tablespoons of butter per cup of flour was ideal—any more and the dough became difficult to work with and baked up greasy. Adding ¼ cup sugar per cup of flour gave the scones subtle sweetness without being cloying, and a combination of sour cream and milk offered a contrasting tang.

Unfortunately, with all the added richness and sweetness, our scones were turning out heavy and under-risen. We were using the biscuit mixing method common to most scone recipes, cutting the cold butter into the dry ingredients with our fingertips and then quickly mixing in the wet ingredients. If we were going to capture the light flakiness we were after, our technique was going to need an overhaul.

We took a hint from puff pastry, where the power of steam is used to separate super-thin layers of dough into striated flakes. In a standard puff pastry recipe, a piece of dough will be turned, rolled, and folded about five times. With each fold, the number of layers of butter and dough increases exponentially. Upon baking, steam forces the layers apart and then escapes, causing the dough to puff up and crisp. We weren't after the 768 layers produced by the standard five-turn puff pastry recipe, but adding a few quick folds to our recipe allowed the scones to gently rise and puff. Tasters appreciated that the scones were now much lighter, but we wondered if we could lighten them even more.

A good light pastry depends on distinct pieces of butter distributed throughout the dough that melt during baking and leave behind pockets of air. For this to happen, the butter needs to be as cold and solid as possible until baking. The problem with trying to cut butter into the flour with your fingers or a food processor is that the butter gets too warm during the distribution process. We tried every alternative form of butter incorporation we could think of before discovering that freezing a stick of butter and grating it on the large holes of a box grater works best. The butter could then be quickly and evenly cut into the flour while remaining cold. This new method of distributing the butter kept the interior of the scones tender and moist without being dense.

Now that we'd made the ultimate plain scone, it was time to add the blueberries. Many recipes call for mixing blueberries in with the flour and butter and then adding the wet ingredients to form a dough. The result: scones that have been dyed blue by bludgeoned berries. What if we incorporated the berries into the already-mixed dough?

No dice. We had to knead the dough an extra 10 to 12 times, which introduced friction and heat. The butter we'd taken such care to add in small flakes was melting into a homogenous mass that wreaked havoc on the texture of the finished scones.

Low on ideas, we were running through a list of other foods that attempt a seamless marriage of distinct elements (sandwiches, napoleons, sushi) when inspiration finally struck—cinnamon rolls. What if we were to distribute the berries evenly over a large, thin square of dough, roll the whole thing up like a cinnamon roll (or jelly roll), and then flatten the log into a rectangle before cutting the scones out of it?

This worked even better than we had hoped. Rolling the blueberries and dough into a log not only distributed the berries much better but also created more flaky layers. Our technique had captured the best elements from several styles of scone—sweet, moist, rich, flaky, tender, crisp, and full of fruit. Now we really might have a reason to take a break for tea every afternoon.

WHAT WE LEARNED: Increasing the amount of butter adds richness and adding a moderate amount of sugar gives the scones a subtle sweetness without being cloying. Sour cream and milk add a contrasting tang. For light, tender scones, freeze the butter to keep it cold when it is being cut into the flour. Use a couple of quick folds (like puff pastry) to create layers of butter that help the dough rise. To evenly distribute the berries without mashing them, press the berries into the dough, and then roll the dough into a jellyroll-like log that can be flattened into a rectangle before cutting out the scones.

BLUEBERRY SCONES

makes 8

It is important to work the dough as little as possible—work quickly and knead and fold the dough only the number of times called for. The butter should be frozen solid before grating. In hot or humid environments, chill the flour mixture and work-bowls before use. While the recipe calls for two whole sticks of butter, only 10 tablespoons are actually used (see step 1). If fresh berries are unavailable, an equal amount of frozen berries, unthawed, can be substituted. An equal amount of raspberries, blackberries, or strawberries can be used in place of the blueberries. Cut larger berries into ¼- to ½-inch pieces before incorporating. Refrigerate or freeze leftover scones, wrapped in foil, in an airtight container. To serve, remove the foil and place the scones on a baking sheet in a 375-degree oven. Heat until warmed through and recrisped, 8 to 10 minutes if refrigerated, 16 to 20 minutes if frozen. See page 297 for information on making the scone dough in advance.

16   tablespoons (2 sticks) butter, frozen whole (see note)

1½   cups (about 7½ ounces) fresh blueberries, picked over (see note)

½   cup whole milk

½   cup sour cream

2   cups (10 ounces) unbleached all-purpose flour, plus extra for the work surface

½   cup (3½ ounces) sugar, plus 1 tablespoon for sprinkling

2   teaspoons baking powder

¼   teaspoon baking soda

½   teaspoon salt

1   teaspoon finely grated zest from 1 lemon

1. Adjust an oven rack to the middle position and heat the oven to 425 degrees. Score and remove half of the wrapper from each stick of frozen butter. Following the photo on page 297, grate the unwrapped ends on the large holes of a box grater (you should grate a total of 8 tablespoons). Place the grated butter in the freezer until needed. Melt 2 tablespoons of the remaining ungrated butter and set aside. Save the remaining 6 tablespoons butter for another use. Place the blueberries in the freezer until needed.

2. Whisk together the milk and sour cream in a medium bowl; refrigerate until needed. Whisk the flour, ½ cup of the sugar, baking powder, baking soda, salt, and lemon zest in a medium bowl. Add the frozen butter to the flour mixture and toss with your fingers until thoroughly coated.

3. Add the milk mixture to the flour mixture; fold with a spatula until just combined. With a rubber spatula, transfer the dough to a liberally floured work surface. Dust the surface of the dough with flour; with floured hands, knead the dough 6 to 8 times, until it just holds together in a ragged ball, adding flour as needed to prevent sticking.

4. Roll the dough into an approximate 12-inch square. Following the photos below, fold the dough into thirds like a business letter, using a bench scraper or metal spatula to release the dough if it sticks to the countertop. Lift the

---

TECHNIQUE: Folding and Shaping the Scones

1. Fold the dough into thirds (like a business letter).

2. Fold in the ends of the dough to form a 4-inch square. Chill the dough.

3. Reroll the dough into a 12-inch square. Press berries into the dough.

4. Roll the dough into a jellyroll-like log to incorporate the blueberries.

5. Lay the log seam-side down and press into an even 12 by 4-inch rectangle.

6. Cut the dough into 8 triangular pieces.

short ends of the dough and fold into thirds again to form an approximate 4-inch square. Transfer the dough to a plate lightly dusted with flour and chill in the freezer for 5 minutes.

5. Transfer the dough to a floured work surface and roll into an approximate 12-inch square again. Sprinkle the blueberries evenly over the surface of dough, then press down so they are slightly embedded in the dough. Using a bench scraper or a thin metal spatula, loosen the dough from the work surface. Roll the dough, pressing to form a tight log. Lay the log seam-side down and press it into a 12 by 4-inch rectangle. Using a sharp, floured knife, cut the rectangle crosswise into 4 equal rectangles. Cut each rectangle diagonally to form 2 triangles and transfer to a parchment-lined baking sheet.

6. Brush the tops with the melted butter and sprinkle with the remaining 1 tablespoon sugar. Bake until the tops and bottoms are golden brown, 18 to 25 minutes. Transfer to a wire rack and cool for 10 minutes before serving.

VARIATION
MAKE-AHEAD BLUEBERRY SCONES

1. Follow the recipe for Blueberry Scones through step 5, then wrap the unbaked scones (on the parchment-lined baking sheet) in plastic wrap and place in the refrigerator overnight. If freezing the unbaked scones, wrap the scones in plastic wrap and then foil and freeze for up to 3 months.

2. To bake refrigerated scones, heat the oven to 425 degrees and follow step 6.

3. To bake frozen scones, transfer the scones to a parchment-lined baking sheet, heat the oven to 375 degrees, and follow the directions from step 6, extending the cooking time to 30 minutes.

TECHNIQUE: Grating Butter
Use the wrapper to hold the frozen butter while grating it on the large holes of a box grater. Grate 4 tablespoons from each stick of butter.

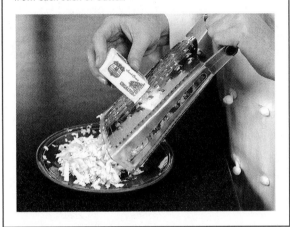

GETTING IT RIGHT: Scone Confusion
Americans have embraced scones, but something has been lost in translation.

Traditional
The British original is lean, dry, and barely sweetened. Spoonfuls of jam and clotted cream are a must.

Artificially Sweet
This scone is shellacked with icing and has tiny flecks of artificial blueberries that add color but not flavor.

Big Blob
This scone is too large and amorphous to cook through, leaving the center doughy and unbaked.

BRAN MUFFINS

WHAT WE WANTED: Really great-tasting bran muffins—tender and moist, not dense and dry—that can be made without a trip to the natural foods store.

The idea of using bran cereal to make muffins is nothing new. One of the first such recipes appeared on packages of Kellogg's Krumbled Bran in 1916, a time when mass-marketed bran cereals were a novel concept. Today, store shelves are chockablock with bran-based cereals that come in various shapes and sizes, fashioned as twigs, flakes, and granules. Many have other ingredients added, such as oats, corn, rice, barley, figs, raisins, and fruit juices. Most have accompanying bran muffin recipes.

In the past, we have made bran muffins with unprocessed wheat bran from the natural foods store. So we know what the real thing should be—a moist, hearty muffin redolent of bran's rich, earthy flavor. But these muffins require a special shopping trip. Could a commercial cereal sold at the supermarket deliver good results? If so, which one?

We wanted cereals in which wheat bran—the wheat kernel's papery, nutritious outer skin—was the major ingredient. That narrowed the field (goodbye to oat bran) and lightened our shopping cart, though not the "health nut" look from the checkout lady. After trying a number of back-of-the-box recipes, we'll admit we found a few muffins with decent bran flavor. But all of them came out squat and dry, desperate for moisture. Certainly none of them would inspire us to jump out of bed in the morning and get out the mixing bowl. We had our work cut out for us.

Our first goal was to clearly determine how each bran cereal functioned when baked into a muffin. We stitched together a recipe consisting of all-purpose flour, butter, sugar, molasses, milk, eggs, baking powder, and raisins and began testing cereals one at a time.

The recipes we tested with flakes came out flavorless and looked like springy cupcakes instead of the rustic muffins we had in mind. The muffins made with granules were also flavorless, and their texture was dense and pasty. The twigs provided a deep bran flavor, but getting them to bend to our will was another matter. They weren't fully dissolving into the batter and were even sticking out of the tops of the baked muffins.

Presoaking the twigs in the milk (as recommended in most recipes) didn't really work and made the muffins as dense as hockey pucks. The cereal was soaking up all the moisture, which dried out the batter. Heating the cereal in milk before adding it to the batter made it even worse, causing the muffins to bake up gummy. We decided to switch gears. Rather than soaking the cereal and then building the batter in the same bowl, we made the muffin batter first and tried adding the bran later. We hoped this would eliminate the guesswork regarding how much liquid the cereal was going to absorb.

Just adding the twigs to the batter didn't soften them enough. For our next test, we tried grinding the twigs to a powder in a food processor before adding them to the batter. Much better—the muffins had an even crumb, but they were a bit heavy. A compromise was in order. We pulverized half of the cereal and kept the other half whole. When we combined the pulverized and intact bran and added them to the batter, they softened perfectly in only five minutes. We finally had the chewy, rustic texture we wanted.

We had been using Kellogg's All-Bran Original for our testing, but we circled back to try other brands of twig-style bran cereal. General Mills Fiber One produced bland muffins—which made sense when we read the label more carefully and saw that wheat, not bran, was the primary ingredient. And tasters had a hard time getting past Post 100% Bran's malted, fruity flavor, which was explained by an ingredient list containing malted barley flour as well as fig and prune juice concentrates. In the end, tasters deemed Kellogg's All-Bran Original the winner for its deep, complex bran flavor.

With the cereal mystery finally solved, we could fine-tune our recipe. We discovered that one egg didn't add enough structure, and two eggs made the muffins too springy. A whole egg plus a yolk worked best, giving the muffins a fluffy, but not bouncy, texture. But our muffins still seemed too lean and dry. More than 6 tablespoons of butter made the muffins greasy, so we turned to the dairy element. Swapping the milk for sour cream was overkill. Buttermilk was an improvement over plain milk, but whole milk yogurt was the tasters' first choice. And replacing the baking powder with baking soda gave us a coarser crumb that tasters liked.

Mixing some whole-wheat flour with the all-purpose flour reinforced the flavor of the bran, as did replacing the granulated sugar with brown sugar and increasing the molasses. After complaints that the raisins didn't soften enough during baking, we plumped them in the microwave with a little water. We had finally found a way to use a supermarket cereal to create a moist, tender muffin with big bran flavor.

WHAT WE LEARNED: For muffins with an earthy bran flavor, bran cereal (specifically Kellogg's All-Bran Original, twig-style) is best. For a chewy, rustic texture pulverize half of the cereal and keep the other half whole—the twigs soften perfectly in only five minutes. Whole milk yogurt provides needed moisture. Swap baking soda for baking powder (the traditional choice) for muffins with a hearty crumb. For soft, moist raisins, plump them in the microwave with a little water before baking.

SHOPPING NOTES: Bran Cereal

Bran is the outer layer of the wheat grain that is removed during milling. Bran cereal comes in various forms. Here's how they stack up in muffins.

Twigs
We found that All-Bran Original gave our muffins the most robust bran flavor.

Flakes
Bran flakes use whole wheat and made muffins with very little bran flavor.

Granules
Small granules of bran buds made dense muffins with almost no bran flavor.

With Raisins
This cereal seemed like a good idea, but the raisins cooked up dry and tough.

BETTER BRAN MUFFINS

makes 12 muffins

The test kitchen prefers Kellogg's All-Bran Original cereal in this recipe. Dried cranberries or dried cherries may be substituted for the raisins. Low-fat or nonfat yogurt can be substituted for whole milk yogurt, though the muffins will be slightly less flavorful.

1	cup raisins
1	teaspoon water
2¼	cups (5 ounces) All-Bran Original cereal
1¼	cups (6¼ ounces) unbleached all-purpose flour
½	cup (2½ ounces) whole wheat flour
2	teaspoons baking soda
½	teaspoon salt
1	large egg plus 1 large egg yolk
⅔	cup (4⅔ ounces) packed light brown sugar
3	tablespoons mild or light molasses
1	teaspoon vanilla extract
6	tablespoons (¾ stick) unsalted butter, melted and cooled
1¾	cups plain whole milk yogurt

1. Adjust an oven rack to the middle position and heat the oven to 400 degrees. Spray a standard-sized muffin pan with nonstick cooking spray. Combine the raisins and water in a small microwave-safe bowl, cover with plastic wrap, cut several steam vents in the plastic with a paring knife, and microwave on high power for 30 seconds. Let stand, covered, until the raisins are softened and plump, about 5 minutes. Transfer the raisins to a paper towel–lined plate to cool.

2. Process half of the bran cereal in a food processor until finely ground, about 1 minute. Whisk the flours, baking soda, and salt in a large bowl to combine; set aside. Whisk the egg and egg yolk together in a medium bowl until well-combined and light-colored, about 20 seconds. Add the sugar, molasses, and vanilla; whisk until the mixture is thick, about 30 seconds. Add the melted butter and whisk to

TECHNIQUE: Softening the Bran

When we added the cereal directly to the batter, the muffins were marred by crunchy bits and twigs sticking out of the top. When we processed all of the cereal into a fine powder, the muffins were too dense. By processing just half of the cereal and leaving the other half in twig form, we created muffins with an even, but not heavy, texture.

Whole Bran Cereal Twigs   **Processed Bran Cereal Twigs**

combine; add the yogurt and whisk to combine. Stir in the processed cereal and unprocessed cereal; let the mixture sit until the cereal is evenly moistened (there will still be some small lumps), about 5 minutes.

3. Add the wet ingredients to the dry ingredients and gently mix with a rubber spatula until the batter is combined and evenly moistened. Do not overmix. Gently fold the raisins into the batter. Using a ⅓-cup measure or an ice cream scoop, divide the batter evenly among the muffin cups, dropping the batter to form mounds. Do not level or flatten the surfaces of the mounds.

4. Bake until the muffins are dark golden and a toothpick inserted into the center of a muffin comes out with a few crumbs attached, 16 to 20 minutes, rotating the pan halfway through baking. Cool the muffins in the pan for 5 minutes, then transfer to a wire rack and cool for 10 minutes before serving.

GETTING IT RIGHT:
Ensuring Big Muffins

For big, hearty muffins, fill the muffin cups to the rim. And for nicely domed muffins, mound the batter in the cups and don't level it off.

TASTING LAB: Strawberry Preserves

TRAILING ONLY GRAPE JELLY, STRAWBERRY PRESERVES are America's second-favorite spreadable fruit. We rounded up eight nationally available brands of strawberry preserves and headed into the tasting lab to see which one tastes best.

Two familiar names—Welch's and Smucker's—were our big winners. Our tasters preferred these brands because they didn't taste too sweet, and they packed big, distinct strawberry flavor. Interestingly, Welch's and Smucker's preserves contain more total sugar (from fruit as well as sugar and/or corn syrup) per serving than most other brands, and yet they weren't perceived as too sweet. Why?

First, not all sugars are equally sweet. Bonne Maman and Welch's both contain 13 grams of sugars per tablespoon, but Bonne Maman's primary sweetener is sugar, which tastes sweeter than the corn syrup listed first on the Welch's label. Second, the amount of acid (citric acid or lemon juice concentrate) added to balance the sugar had a big impact on overall flavor. We measured the pH (the acidity or alkalinity of a substance) of each sample and found that the brands tasters had called too sweet (like Bonne Maman and Cascadian Farm) had the highest pH readings, indicating that they were the least acidic. Lower pH readings—signifying more added acid—generally translated into better, more-rounded strawberry flavor.

Our lowest-scoring brands, Polaner and Cascadian Farm, were judged to have the weakest strawberry flavor—no surprise considering neither brand uses strawberries as its primary ingredient. Cascadian Farm lists sugar first (at least it's organic), while the Polaner product is made with more pear and grape juices than strawberries.

Testers weren't too concerned about texture. As long as there was a noticeable combination of "jellied" matter and fruit chunks, they were pretty happy. The preserves are listed below in order of preference.

Rating Strawberry Preserves

TWENTY-ONE AMERICA'S TEST KITCHEN STAFF MEMBERS TASTED EIGHT NATIONALLY AVAILABLE BRANDS OF STRAWBERRY jam. Each jam was tasted plain and spread on toast. The jams are listed in order of preference and are available at supermarkets.

RECOMMENDED

Welch's Strawberry Preserves

$3.49 for 16 ounces

Tasters praised this brand for its "great" and "natural-tasting" strawberry flavor, a result of being perceived as "not too sweet," with a "perfect sugar level." These preserves won top scores for their "thick" and "spreadable" texture.

RECOMMENDED WITH RESERVATIONS

Dickinson's Pure Pacific Mountain Strawberry Preserves

$4.79 for 10 ounces

Tasters liked the "appealing," "chunky" texture, but not the "Jolly Rancher–like flavor" that was deemed much too sweet.

RECOMMENDED

Smucker's Strawberry Preserves

$3.59 for 18 ounces

Tasters praised the "sweet with a slight tartness" of Smucker's, which scored very well for its "straightforward" strawberry flavor. Tasters also appreciated its "thick and chunky texture."

RECOMMENDED WITH RESERVATIONS

Bonne Maman Strawberry Preserves

$4.19 for 13 ounces

Tasters likened this sample to strawberry "lollipops" and "syrup" because of its "sickly sweetness." Many thought the texture was "too runny" and "not well-mixed."

RECOMMENDED

Smucker's Simply Fruit Strawberry Spreadable Fruit

$2.69 for 10 ounces

With about a third less sugar than the top two choices, Smucker's Simply Fruit was lauded for being "very fruity" and "very strawberry-y" but "without too much sweetness." A few tasters would have appreciated a chunkier texture.

RECOMMENDED WITH RESERVATIONS

Polaner All Fruit Strawberry Fruit Spread

$3.49 for 15.25 ounces

The "weird brown color" and "generic, nonstrawberry fruit flavor" (pear and grape juice concentrates are the first two ingredients) were big turnoffs.

RECOMMENDED WITH RESERVATIONS

Smucker's Strawberry Low Sugar Preserves

$3.69 for 15.5 ounces

With the least sugar of any brand, this sample was liked for its "mellow strawberry flavor." It was disliked for its "unnatural" color (it has red color added).

NOT RECOMMENDED

Cascadian Farm Organic Strawberry Fruit Spread

$3.19 for 10 ounces

"All sugar syrup and no strawberry flavor" and "so sweet it made my teeth hurt," said our tasters. Comments like "slimy" and "gloppy" are never good signs.

EQUIPMENT CORNER:
Commuter Coffee Mugs

WHEN WE POLLED OUR STAFF ABOUT THE BEST—AND worst—features of commuter coffee mugs, we were surprised at the passion and frustration in the responses. Our test kitchen director gave a typical response: "I have very strong feelings about them and can't recommend one to you because I haven't found the perfect one yet." It turns out there are a lot of mugs that fall over on a bumpy road, cool down too quickly to survive a traffic jam, or are just plain awkward to handle while turning a wheel or holding a subway strap. So we ordered 11 mugs of different materials, shapes, and sipping structures and organized a battery of tests designed to define the ideal mug, which left us feeling a little like test drivers as we careened around corners trying to spill the coffee or dislodge the mugs. What did we discover?

No one wants his or her coffee to cool off during a long commute, so we began by measuring heat and cold retention over two hours. Material proved to be the determining factor. Ceramic mugs failed miserably, not holding enough heat for even 30 minutes (in fact, the exteriors quickly became too hot to comfortably handle). Regular plastic performed a bit better, with the coffee cooling down after an hour. Both "thermoplastic" and plain stainless steel mugs were judged to be fair heat retainers. The best performers were the stainless steel mugs with vacuum layers, which kept coffee warm even after two hours. (To test your current mug, feel the outside five minutes after adding hot coffee—if it's warm, it's losing too much heat.)

The mug's material also affects taste. An optimal mug should not transmit flavor or odors from one beverage to the next. Plastic mugs proved inferior in this regard.

What about design? A good mug shouldn't spill coffee whether it's in the car or being jostled on the subway. The styles that worked well had both a tight connection of lid to body and an effective method of sealing off the sipping holes. Designs that worked well were those in which the lid was twisted entirely or an internal structure was pushed down to block the holes.

We also prefer mugs without handles. Unless the lid had 360-degree sipping (such as holes that rimmed the entire lid), handles often proved difficult to align with the sip hole. Drivers also found it easier to grab the mug around its body than to look down to locate the handle. And many of our commuters found that handles made it difficult to slip their cups in a coat pocket or backpack. Handles don't even provide the most secure grip—we found that nonhandled mugs with rubberized bands around the body gave the best grip.

Sipping from a commuter mug should not be hazardous. Liquid should flow from the cup easily but not too fast, and any excess liquid should drain quickly to prevent splashing at the next swallow. The best lids had either a slope leading down to a medium-sized sipping hole or numerous small holes rimming the cup and set in a deep enough trough to capture the liquid.

One feature we didn't consider off the bat, but is important, is visibility (especially if you're driving). When inverted for a last swallow, the mug shouldn't block visibility or hit the face. While none of the mugs bumped every tester, some testers were hit by protruding handles or especially high rims.

Another important feature to those who drive is fit. We tested the mugs in a variety of car cup holders, finding that most built-in cup holders did well. However, older, pull-out type cup holders (which suspend the cup from the dashboard) posed problems for a few candidates.

Once you arrive at your destination, you might still have some coffee left, so what about stability? We tested whether the mug could rest safely on a desk without tipping. Two of the mugs with top-heavy bodies had "docking stations" (rubber mats that the mugs screw into) to ensure stability, but we lost those pretty fast in a pile of papers. All the other mugs had rubber bases, which gave them sufficient stability.

Lastly, commuter cups should be easy to clean. We found that most higher-end commuter mugs cannot be machine washed; it's important to be able to thoroughly hand-clean all the crannies and crevices in the lid. This feature was especially important for those who add milk or cream to their coffee, as this makes it easy for a mug to become—as one tester put it—"gunked up."

Did we find the perfect cup? No, but we found two that we can recommend. The Thermos Stainless Steel Travel Mug with TherMax has a lid that was secure; it was even a little resistant to turning when wet. It has sip holes all around the rim, so users can drink from any location. The cup provided good insulation, and the rubberized band that covered almost the entire base earned a rating of "most comfortable to hold." We also liked the OXO Click LiquiSeal Travel Stainless Mug. This mug is comfortable to hold and has excellent insulation (we also tested the plastic version, which is not recommended; see the chart on page 305). A button in the middle of the lid lowers and locks an inner plastic lid, opening a space large enough to allow the liquid to flow through the sipping hole at a good speed. The hole itself is located in a little trench that provides excellent drainage. We also felt that one travel mug earned a special recommendation, Nissan Dual Purpose Can Insulator/ Travel Cup (by Thermos). Although an unsatisfactory beverage cup—the lid doesn't have any closure, and it leaked like a sieve—it's a good can insulator and holder. A soda can fit in snugly and stayed well chilled. The cup fit well in all of our car cup holders, and the grip band around the perimeter made the drink more comfortable and a lot less slippery to hold than a bare can.

Rating Commuter Coffee Mugs

WE TESTED 11 MUGS OF DIFFERENT MATERIALS, SHAPES, AND SIPPING STRUCTURES IN A VARIETY OF AREAS INCLUDING heat retention, clean taste, drainage, and visibility. The commuter mugs are listed in order of preference. See www.americastestkitchen.com for up-to-date prices and mail-order sources for top-rated products.

RECOMMENDED

Thermos Travel Mug with TherMax, #2610

$19.59; 14-ounce capacity

This mug has good heat retention, and the 360-degree sipping lid has holes completely around the rim for easy drinking, regardless of how the cup is held.

RECOMMENDED

OXO Click LiquiSeal Travel Mug, #1055291

$19.95; 14-ounce capacity

The mug is insulated superbly and, with two lids, was especially leakproof.

RECOMMENDED WITH RESERVATIONS

Trudeau Drive Time Double Wall Insulated Travel Mug, #B0006FYMP8

$22.95; 18-ounce capacity

For those who insist on a mug with a handle, this is our preferred model. But it does not have a vacuum structure, so heat retention was only fair.

NOT RECOMMENDED

Starbucks Thermoplastic Mug with Sealing Lid, #226185

$14.95; 14-ounce capacity

This thermoplastic mug retained odors, the snap-back lever on the lid was difficult to clean, and it also didn't fit in wire-rim cup holders.

NOT RECOMMENDED

Nissan Travel Tumbler (by Thermos), #JEN400

$19.95; 14-ounce capacity

This mug retained heat well but the seal was not sufficient; the cup leaked and coffee splattered even when the sipping hole latch was closed.

NOT RECOMMENDED

OXO LiquiSeal Travel Mug, #392580

$9.95; 14-ounce capacity

This is the plastic version of our recommended OXO model. Heat retention was poor, and the plastic gave an off-smell and off-taste.

NOT RECOMMENDED

Timolino Spill Proof Travel Mug with Red Lever, #PCA-46VDG1

$15.99; 14-ounce capacity

Testers found the shape (wide top and narrow bottom) to be awkward and bulky. And none of the testers liked the hard-to-use "Press 'N' Sip" lever for opening and closing the hole.

NOT RECOMMENDED

Avantro Cobalt Blue Leakproof Vacuum Travel/Desk Mug, #LTM40/COB

$29.95; 14-ounce capacity

Like the Timolino model (above), the misaligned lever is in an even more awkward position that made it almost impossible to use.

NOT RECOMMENDED

Highwave Autotray Stoneware Mug, #B000MS608Q

$15.99; 12-ounce capacity

This mug had a plethora of problems: poor heat retention, the mug body became too hot for comfort, and it leaked like a sieve.

NOT RECOMMENDED

Highwave Wide Base Ceramic Coffee Travel Mug, #B0009YIPSQ

$15.95; 14-ounce capacity

This model had poor heat retention, with the additional burden of an especially wide base that could not fit in any car cup holders, nor was it stable when placed on a dashboard (as advertised).

NOT RECOMMENDED

Nissan Dual Purpose Can Insulator/Travel Cup (by Thermos), #JCA350

$12.95; 10-ounce capacity

While this is advertised as both a can holder and a beverage holder, it failed as a hot beverage holder. But as a can insulator, it was successful. It kept the can cold, and the rubber grip made for a secure hold.

Some lemon layer cakes are too cloying and sweet—similar to the candies you find in an Easter basket. In developing Lemon Layer Cake, the test kitchen keeps the sweetness balanced and turns out a cake that shines with bright, citrusy flavor.

LEMON LAYER cake

We're not going to lie—a layer cake is not a dessert
you can whip together on a weeknight to serve after dinner. But then,
why should it be? Layer cakes are special occasion desserts to be savored
at birthday parties, holidays, and any other time that warrants celebra-
tion. One particularly impressive layer cake is the lemon layer cake.
Ideally, the cake's tender layers offset the bracing, citrusy lemon filling,
and the whole is swathed in a glossy pale frosting. This is a cake that
should taste as great as it looks. Unfortunately, past experiences have
proved the opposite. Most often, each component (the cake, the filling,
and the frosting) is simply too rich for them all to work together in
harmony. And the lemon flavor isn't always as prominent as we'd like.
We sought to restore balance to this cake and to bring the fresh, bright
flavor of lemon to the fore.

Layer cakes are also as much about construction as they are about
flavor. The layers should be level, so that the cake stacks evenly—
leaning cakes are charming only if they were baked by a 12-year-old.
The filling also needs to be thick enough to stay sandwiched between
the cake layers—not squirt out the sides once a knife cuts through a
slice. After all, we wanted this ultimate lemon layer cake to be a beauty,
inside and out.

LEMON LAYER CAKE

WHAT WE WANTED: Tiers of tender cake sandwiched with an intensely flavored lemon filling and swathed in billowy, sweet icing.

Special occasions deserve an exceptional dessert, and nothing fits the bill better than a sophisticated lemon layer cake. When made well, it is delicate and stylish, with an ideal contrast of sweet and tart. And yet this cake seems to have fallen out of favor, perhaps because most versions are poorly executed concoctions of heavy cake stacked with filling and frosting that taste more like butter than lemon. We wanted to produce a recipe for this old-fashioned cake in which tangy, creamy lemon filling divides layers of tender, delicate cake draped in sweet frosting.

Most layer cakes are made with substantial butter cakes, but we suspected that the light, fresh flavor of lemon would be better served by something more ethereal. We tried the test kitchen's recipes for all-purpose sponge cake, classic yellow cake, and white butter cake in a basic lemon layer cake recipe. The yellow cake was somewhat dense and rich—great for a birthday cake, but not what we had in mind for a lighter lemon layer cake. And while the sponge cake was indeed light and fluffy, its crumb was coarse and not refined enough. The white butter cake, however, was the perfect compromise: nicely flavored by butter yet lighter than the yellow cake due to the use of egg whites only (no yolks), with a fine crumb and tender texture.

Lemon layer cake is often filled with lemon-scented buttercream, but this monotonic arrangement mutes the lemon flavor and makes the cake far too rich. We prefer the brightness of lemon curd, a combination of sugar, lemon juice, butter, and eggs cooked together until it reaches the consistency of custard. The mixture is simmered gently so as to not overcook the eggs, and the acidic lemon juice denatures the egg proteins, allowing them to form a fluid gel. The result is a creamy, smooth custard with lively lemon flavor.

Starting with 1 cup of lemon juice and 1½ cups of sugar for the right level of lemony tang, we tinkered with different amounts of eggs and butter, ultimately settling on a middle-of-the-road recipe containing four whole eggs plus six yolks and 8 tablespoons of butter. This curd was silky smooth and tasted great, but when we attempted to spread it over the cake, we realized it was too runny. We needed to create something sturdier. Adding more eggs thickened the curd so much that it became gluey. More butter thickened the curd but muted the lemon flavor. Cornstarch made the curd too pasty.

We were racking our brains for more ideas when a colleague suggested fruit pectin or gelatin. These ingredients can be a baker's secret weapons in helping to set finicky fillings. After a few tests, we found that both did a beautiful job of firming up the curd without marring its lush texture or changing its intense flavor. In the end, gelatin was easier to add, as it just needed to be hydrated in a little lemon juice, whereas pectin needed to be boiled with the sugar and lemon juice.

Having successfully avoided rich buttercream for the filling, we were determined to find something lighter for the icing as well. We eventually landed on an old-fashioned classic: seven-minute icing. This pure white icing is exceptionally light and glossy, and tasters found it to be an ideal topping for our delicate cake. Prepared in the same manner as a Swiss meringue, it is made by whipping egg whites and sugar with a touch of water for precisely seven minutes over a pot of simmering water.

But this old model needed a new paint job. First, it was a little too sweet, almost candy-like. Second, it was slightly thick and chewy. Last, the cooking technique had us enduring the arm-numbing vibration of a handheld mixer for longer than was comfortable.

Cutting back on the sugar (by a quarter) and adding a squeeze of lemon juice easily solved the first two problems, but the cooking technique took some finagling. We knew we needed to expose the egg mixture to a certain amount of

heat (without it the mixture would not be stable; see "The Magic of Seven-Minute Frosting," page 312), but we wanted to rely on our standing mixer. After some trial and error, we learned that if we heated the mixture to at least 160 degrees and then transferred it to the standing mixer for whipping, the end result was just as billowy and shiny as the version whipped over constant heat.

With our adjustments to the recipe, it actually took 10 minutes, not seven, for the icing to form stiff peaks, but the mixer did the work—not us. (We also developed some flavor variations to use with other cakes.) Finally, we added a spoonful of corn syrup to the icing, which lent an impressive luster. With swirling peaks of white icing, this light, lemony cake is fashionable enough for any special occasion.

WHAT WE LEARNED: A white butter cake is preferred for its fine crumb and tender texture as well as its ability to show off (not overshadow) a bright lemon filling. Adding a little gelatin to the lemon curd helps it firm up enough to spread over the cake, without muting its flavors. Seven-minute icing, made with a little less sugar than usual and with a squeeze of lemon juice, makes a not-too-sweet, perfectly textured icing.

TECHNIQUE:
Assembling a Four-Layer Cake

To create an elegant, four-tiered cake, you must split two cake layers in half horizontally. If you cut the layers a bit unevenly (which is bound to happen), the cake can lean to one side. Here's how to compensate for less-than-perfect cutting.

1. Place the cooled cake layers on top of each other and make a ⅛-inch-deep cut into the side of each cake layer.

2. With a long, serrated knife, use a sawing motion to cut the cakes in half horizontally so that each cake forms 2 layers.

3. Assemble the cake, aligning the cuts in each layer. Stacking the layers in their original orientation conceals uneven cutting.

LEMON LAYER CAKE

serves 10 to 12

The filling can be made a day ahead and refrigerated, but it will become quite stiff; fold it with a rubber spatula to loosen it before spreading onto the cake. For neater slices, dip a knife into hot water before cutting the cake. Leftovers can be stored covered in the refrigerator, with the cut side of the cake covered tightly with plastic wrap, for up to three days.

lemon curd filling

1	cup juice from about 6 lemons
1	teaspoon powdered gelatin
1½	cups (10½ ounces) sugar
⅛	teaspoon salt
4	large eggs
6	large egg yolks (reserve egg whites for cake)
8	tablespoons (1 stick) unsalted butter, cut into ½-inch cubes and frozen

cake

2¼	cups (9 ounces) cake flour, plus extra for pans
1	cup whole milk, room temperature
6	large egg whites, room temperature
2	teaspoons vanilla extract
1¾	cups (12¼ ounces) sugar
4	teaspoons baking powder
1	teaspoon salt
12	tablespoons (1½ sticks) unsalted butter, cut into 12 pieces, softened but still cool

fluffy white icing

2	large egg whites
1	cup (7 ounces) sugar
¼	cup water
1	tablespoon juice from 1 lemon
1	tablespoon corn syrup

1. FOR THE FILLING: Measure 1 tablespoon of the lemon juice into a small bowl; sprinkle the gelatin over the top. Heat the remaining lemon juice, the sugar, and salt in a medium nonreactive saucepan over medium-high heat, stirring occasionally, until the sugar dissolves and the mixture is hot but not boiling. Whisk the eggs and yolks in a large nonreactive bowl. Whisking constantly, slowly pour the hot lemon-sugar mixture into the eggs, then return the mixture to the saucepan. Cook over medium-low heat, stirring constantly with a heatproof spatula, until the mixture registers 170 degrees on an instant-read thermometer and is thick enough to leave a trail when the spatula is scraped along the pan bottom, 4 to 6 minutes. Immediately remove the pan from the heat and stir in the gelatin mixture until dissolved. Stir in the frozen butter until incorporated. Pour the filling through a fine-mesh strainer into a nonreactive bowl (you should have 3 cups). Cover the surface directly with plastic wrap; refrigerate until firm enough to spread, at least 4 hours.

2. FOR THE CAKE: Adjust an oven rack to the middle position and heat the oven to 350 degrees. Grease and flour two 9-inch-wide by 2-inch-high round cake pans and line with parchment paper. In a 2-cup liquid measure or medium bowl, whisk together the milk, egg whites, and vanilla.

3. In the bowl of a standing mixer fitted with a paddle attachment, mix the flour, sugar, baking powder, and salt at low speed. With the mixer running at low speed, add the butter one piece at a time; continue beating until the mixture resembles moist crumbs with no visible butter chunks. Add all but ½ cup of the milk mixture to the crumbs and beat at medium speed until the mixture is pale and fluffy, about 1½ minutes. With the mixer running at low speed, add the remaining ½ cup milk mixture; increase the speed to medium and beat for 30 seconds more. Stop the mixer and scrape the sides of the bowl. Return the mixer to medium speed and beat for 20 seconds longer. Divide the batter evenly between the cake pans; using a rubber spatula, spread the batter to the pan walls and smooth the tops.

4. Bake until a toothpick inserted in the center of the cakes comes out clean, 23 to 25 minutes. Loosen the cakes from the sides of the pans with a small knife, cool in the pan for 10 minutes, then invert onto a greased wire rack; peel off the parchment. Invert the cakes again; cool completely on the rack, about 1½ hours.

5. TO ASSEMBLE: Following the illustrations on page 309, use a serrated knife to cut each cake into 2 even layers. Place the bottom layer of 1 cake on a cardboard round or cake plate. Using an icing spatula, spread 1 cup of the lemon filling evenly on the cake, leaving a ½-inch border around the edge; using a cardboard round, gently replace the top layer. Spread 1 cup of the filling on top. Using the cardboard round, gently slide the bottom half of the second cake into place. Spread the remaining cup filling on top. Using the cardboard round, replace the top layer of the second cake. Smooth out any filling that has leaked from the sides of the cake; cover with plastic wrap and refrigerate while making the icing.

6. FOR THE ICING: Combine all the ingredients in the bowl of a standing mixer or a large heatproof bowl and set over a medium saucepan filled with 1 inch of barely simmering water (do not let the bowl touch the water). Cook, stirring constantly, until the mixture registers 160 degrees on an instant-read thermometer, 5 to 10 minutes. Remove the bowl from the heat and transfer the mixture to a standing mixer fitted with the whisk attachment. Beat on medium speed until soft peaks form, about 5 minutes. Increase the speed to medium-high and continue to beat until the mixture has cooled to room temperature and stiff peaks form, 5 minutes longer. Using an icing spatula, spread the frosting on the cake. Serve. (The cake can be refrigerated for up to 1 day before serving.)

VARIATIONS
FLUFFY VANILLA ICING
makes 3 cups, enough to frost one 4-layer cake
Follow step 6 of Lemon Layer Cake, substituting 1 teaspoon vanilla extract for the lemon juice. Proceed as directed.

TOASTED ALMOND ICING
makes 3 cups, enough to frost one 4-layer cake
Follow step 6 of Lemon Layer Cake, increasing the water to ¼ cup plus 1 tablespoon and substituting ½ teaspoon almond extract for the lemon juice. Once the icing has been beaten, remove the bowl from the mixer and use a rubber spatula to gently fold in ¾ cup toasted and cooled chopped almonds.

TANGY ORANGE ICING
makes 3 cups, enough to frost one 4-layer cake
Follow step 6 of Lemon Layer Cake, substituting ¼ cup fresh orange juice for the water and 1 teaspoon grated orange zest for the lemon juice, and adding the orange zest to the icing during the last minute of beating the icing.

COCONUT ICING
makes 3 cups, enough to frost one 4-layer cake
Follow step 6 of Lemon Layer Cake, increasing the water to ¼ cup plus 1 tablespoon and substituting ½ teaspoon vanilla extract for the lemon juice. Once the icing has been beaten, remove the bowl from the mixer and use a rubber spatula to gently fold in ¾ cup toasted and cooled unsweetened coconut.

SCIENCE DESK:
The Magic of Seven-Minute Frosting

ALONG WITH ITS FLUFFY TEXTURE AND GLOSSY SHEEN, seven-minute icing offers the fringe benefit of retaining its volume for at least three days. What makes the egg whites in this old-fashioned recipe more stable than egg whites whipped for a mousse or a soufflé?

Beating raw egg whites and sugar temporarily relaxes the tightly wound egg proteins, allowing air to be trapped inside the resulting matrix. The foam this produces is impermanent, however, and will begin to deflate soon after being whipped.

Cooking the egg whites and sugar to 160 degrees causes the coiled egg proteins to permanently relax. When the warm mixture is then whipped, the egg proteins remain unraveled as they cool, forming a stable network that traps sugar and water. So the icing stays shiny, airy, and smooth long enough for you to enjoy the entire cake.

No Heat = Weak Foam
After just 30 minutes, the foam made by whipping raw egg whites with sugar and other ingredients has lost most of its volume.

Heat = Stable Foam
After 24 hours, the foam made by heating the egg whites with sugar and other ingredients and then whipping still holds its volume.

TASTING LAB: Boxed Cake Mixes

WHILE WE PREFER THE RICH FLAVOR OF A HOMEMADE cake, we know that many cooks invite Duncan Hines and Betty Crocker into their kitchens to help speed up the proceedings. But can any compete with homemade? We bought eight boxed yellow and gold cake mixes and headed into the test kitchen to find out. We served the plain, unfrosted cakes to 22 tasters, who rated each cake for flavor, texture, and overall appeal.

Our tasters weren't fooled by these mixes. All eight cakes had an unnaturally uniform crumb and extremely light, fluffy texture. Cake mixes are formulated to maximize the volume of air and moisture the batter can hold, which results in a very moist, tender, and delicate cake. Ingredients such as shortening, emulsifiers (mono- and diglycerides as well as lecithin), xanthan gum, and cellulose gum give cakes made from boxed mixes their distinctive texture.

Without these ingredients, a from-scratch cake doesn't rise as much and you end up with a tighter, more irregular crumb, which is able to withstand a heavy coating of frosting. Fluffy boxed cakes almost collapse under the weight of a rich frosting. Several of the cakes in our tasting were disliked for being particularly fluffy (more like cotton candy than cake).

The flavor of a boxed cake mix, even one that calls for the addition of butter, won't fool an observant taster, either—but some came surprisingly close. Tasters said that the cakes made from top-rated mixes tasted like butter and vanilla. Other mixes had an obvious artificial smell and flavor, which landed them at the bottom of our ratings.

The four top-rated cakes (three Betty Crocker mixes and one Pillsbury) all fall under the umbrella of General Mills; the two Duncan Hines mixes followed, with the two "independents," the Jiffy and King Arthur Flour mixes, bringing up the rear. Our conclusion: Betty Crocker knows how to make an appealing cake mix, Duncan Hines less so, and forget about the "alternative" brands you might find at the supermarket.

Rating Boxed Cake Mixes

TWENTY-TWO MEMBERS OF THE AMERICA'S TEST KITCHEN STAFF TASTED UNFROSTED CAKES MADE FROM EIGHT yellow and gold cake mixes, rating them on flavor, texture, and overall appeal. The cake mixes are listed in order of preference and are available in supermarkets.

RECOMMENDED

Betty Crocker Super Moist Butter Recipe Yellow Cake Mix

$2.49

This cake, which calls for a stick of butter, was praised for its "rich butter flavor" and "moist and tender" texture. Very "vanilla-y."

RECOMMENDED

Duncan Hines Moist Deluxe Butter Recipe Golden Cake Mix

$1.79

Some tasters detected hints of "coconut and lemon," while others complained about a "chemical" aftertaste. This cake was substantially darker than the others.

RECOMMENDED

Betty Crocker Super Moist Golden Vanilla Cake Mix

$1.69

Tasters appreciated the "very smooth," "nicely spongy" texture of this cake. Its flavor was deemed "mild but very good."

RECOMMENDED WITH RESERVATIONS

Duncan Hines Moist Deluxe Classic Yellow Cake Mix

$1.69

One taster likened this sample to a "spongy Twinkie," while other panelists were more generous and praised its "nice and light" crumb.

RECOMMENDED

Pillsbury Moist Supreme Classic Yellow Cake Mix

$1.39

This cake was "extremely tender and moist, with a very even crumb." So sweet "there's no need to add icing," quipped one taster.

NOT RECOMMENDED

Jiffy Golden Yellow Cake Mix

$.89

"Tastes like the box it came from," said one taster. Overall, this cake mix was panned for its insipid, stale flavor and "dry and terrible" texture. Note that this mix makes only one 9-inch cake while the other mixes make two cakes.

RECOMMENDED

Betty Crocker Super Moist Yellow Cake Mix

$1.69

With its "nice flavors of butter and vanilla," this cake was deemed the best-tasting. However, some tasters complained about the "chalky," "mushy" texture.

NOT RECOMMENDED

King Arthur Flour Vanilla-Butter Cake Mix

$4.95

This mix contains fewer additives than the rest, but tasters were not impressed by the cake's "grainy," "crumbly" texture and strong "almond extract" aftertaste.

Our Apple Galette's flaky layers rely on a fraisage technique, which involves smearing butter pieces into flour. After Julia has used the fraisage technique, she rolls the rested dough into a rectangle ready to be topped with sliced apples.

FRENCH APPLE *tart*

CHAPTER 26

There's no doubt about it—the French have flair.
Take their apple tart, called apple galette. A suave, open-faced tart, it contains thinly sliced shingles of caramelized apples set off by a thin, buttery crust so delicious you could eat it on its own. And although this tart appears delicate, it is actually sturdy enough to be eaten out of hand without falling apart—making it a wonderful menu choice whether you're packing for a picnic or wanting to end a cocktail party with something sweet, yet sophisticated.

Initial examination of this recipe indicates that the tart should be easier to prepare than the typical double-crust American pie. But developing a flaky crust that is sturdy enough to support the fruit—without being tough—is a bit tricky. And getting the apples to caramelize by the time the crust is baked is also a challenge. We were ready to tap into our American ingenuity to help uncover the secrets behind this Gallic treat.

FRENCH APPLE TART

WHAT WE WANTED: An apple tart with flair—with a thin and flaky crust sturdy enough to support tender slices of caramelized apple.

One bite of French apple tart, or apple galette, and we knew we had found a tart that we loved as much as apple pie. Apple galettes come in various shapes and sizes—from ones in which the dough is folded over a pile of apples to others that feature layers of sweet pie dough, almond filling, and meticulously layered apples. We wanted to re-create the one we first fell in love with. This galette features a thin, crispy, flaky, sugary crust topped with a generous layer of apples sliced a mere ⅛ inch thick. There's not much to this galette besides flour, sugar, butter, and fruit, and you don't even need a fork to eat it. When baked properly, the pieces are sturdy enough to eat out of hand, just like a slice of pizza.

What we thought would be a simple task proved—over the course of several dozen galettes—to be surprisingly tricky. Nearly all the recipes we tried were made from a simple dough (flour, sugar, salt, butter, and ice water) that claimed to produce the texture we were after. But in nearly every case the dough was tough, cracker-like, and bland. But we did learn a few things. Because of their size and thinness, round galettes were difficult to roll out and transfer to a baking sheet. We decided to stick with a rectangular galette. And from the way even our mediocre attempts were being devoured by tasters, we knew that this dessert had to feed a crowd.

For early tests, we used a food processor to cut the butter completely into the dry ingredients. Although this is the test kitchen's preferred technique for classic American pie dough, we thought that a French dough might require a French technique. A few years ago, one colleague experimented with fraisage in developing a free-form fruit tart.

This technique calls for partially cutting the butter into the dry ingredients, leaving large pea-sized pieces of fat unmixed. But what makes fraisage truly unique is how the dough is combined. Small bits of the barely mixed dough are pressed firmly against the counter with the heel of the hand to create a uniform dough. As a result, the chunks of butter are pressed into long, thin sheets that create lots of flaky layers when the dough is baked.

Fraisage did indeed produce a flakier crust than had our initial tests, but tasters said it was tougher than they would have thought. Something wasn't making sense. Upon closer examination of the free-form fruit tart recipe, it dawned on us. That recipe called for piling juicy summer fruit onto the dough and then folding the edges of the dough over the fruit. Our recipe called for shingling a single layer of fairly dry apples on top. Without a mound of fruit to keep the dough moist, our crust was drying out before the apples could brown and caramelize. Adding a bit more butter to the dough increased tenderness slightly, but not enough.

We wondered if using a different flour could be the answer. Until now, we had been using all-purpose flour, even though many recipes for French pastry call for pastry flour. It was time to give this flour a try. Basically, the difference between these two flours is protein content. When mixed with water, the proteins (gliadin and glutenin) in flour create a stronger, more elastic protein called gluten. The higher the gluten content, the tougher the dough. Pastry flour has a protein content of 9 percent, and the protein content of all-purpose flour ranges from 10 percent to 12 percent. This difference might not seem like much, but when we made galettes from each type of flour the results were dramatic. The galette made with all-purpose flour was tough, and the one with pastry flour was flaky, tender, and sturdy. The only problem is that pastry flour is not available in supermarkets, just through mail order.

Looking for a more practical alternative, we tried cake flour, which is sold in supermarkets and has a protein content of just 8 percent. But when we substituted 1 cup, ½ cup, and even ¼ cup of cake flour for the equivalent amount of all-purpose flour, the dough—though tender—crumbled. It turns out that cake flour goes through a bleaching process (with chlorine gas) that affects how its proteins combine with water. As a result, less gluten is formed—perfect for a delicate cake but not for a pastry that must be tender and sturdy.

Casting a wider net, we looked through numerous French cookbooks. Although most recipes were nearly identical in ingredients, there were two that stood out. Tart doughs in Julia Child's *From Julia's Kitchen* and André Soltner's *Lutèce Cookbook* both touted instant flour (also called quick-mixing flour) as the essential ingredient for flaky yet tender tart crusts. We keep instant flour in the back of the cabinet to make lump-free gravies, but we had never thought of it for pie-making. Instant flour is made by slightly moistening all-purpose flour with water. After being spray-dried, the tiny flour granules look like small clusters of grapes. Since these preclumped flour granules are larger than those of finer-ground all-purpose flour, they absorb less water, making it harder for the proteins to form gluten.

We replaced some of the all-purpose flour with various amounts of instant flour. We found that ½ cup of instant flour kept the dough tender yet sturdy enough to cut neat slices of galette that could be eaten out of hand. An unlikely supermarket ingredient, along with a classic French mixing technique, had helped us create a remarkable crust.

The ideal galette should have both a crust and apples that are a deep golden-brown color. After several tests, most tasters felt that 400 degrees struck the right balance between intense caramelization and simply burnt. Now the galette was almost perfect. Although not all galette recipes call for it, many brush the hot-out-of-the-oven tart with apricot preserves. This glaze provided an attractive sheen and fruity tartness that tasters praised as they picked up another slice.

WHAT WE LEARNED: To mix the dough, use the fraisage technique, where chunks of butter are pressed into long, thin sheets to create lots of flaky layers in the baked crust. Supplement some of the all-purpose flour with instant flour for a more tender pastry. Instant flour absorbs less water than regular flour, thus inhibiting the formation of gluten. And a moderately hot oven—400 degrees—caramelizes the apples without burning them.

APPLE GALETTE

serves 10 to 12

The two common brands of instant flour are Wondra and Shake & Blend. They are sold in canisters in the baking aisle, usually alongside the cornstarch. The galette can be made without instant flour, using 2 cups of all-purpose flour and 2 tablespoons of cornstarch. However, you might have to increase the amount of ice water. Although any apple will work in this recipe, we prefer a combination of Golden Delicious, Granny Smith, and Empire. Make sure to cut the apples as thin as possible. If they are cut thicker than 1/8 inch, they will be hard to shingle. If the dough has chilled longer than 1 hour, let it stand at room temperature for 15 to 20 minutes to soften. If the dough becomes soft and sticky while being rolled, transfer it to a baking sheet and refrigerate it for 10 to 15 minutes. Check the bottom of the galette halfway through baking—it should be a light golden brown. If it is darker, reduce the oven temperature to 375 degrees. Serve with ice cream, sweetened whipped cream, or crème fraîche.

dough

1½	cups (7½ ounces) unbleached all-purpose flour, plus extra for rolling out the dough
½	cup (2½ ounces) instant flour (see note)
½	teaspoon salt
½	teaspoon sugar
12	tablespoons (1½ sticks) cold unsalted butter, cut into ⅝-inch cubes
7–9	tablespoons ice water

apple filling and glaze

1½	pounds (3-4 medium or 4-5 small) apples (see note)
2	tablespoons unsalted butter, cut into ¼-inch pieces
¼	cup sugar
2	tablespoons apricot preserves
1	tablespoon water

1. FOR THE DOUGH: Combine the flours, salt, and sugar in a food processor with 3 pulses. Scatter the butter pieces over the flour, pulse to cut the butter into the flour until the butter pieces are the size of large pebbles, about ½ inch, about 6 pulses.

2. Sprinkle 1 tablespoon water over the mixture and pulse once quickly to combine; repeat, adding water 1 tablespoon at a time and pulsing, until the dough begins to form small curds that hold together when pinched with your fingers (the dough should look crumbly and should not form a cohesive ball).

3. Empty the dough onto a work surface and gather into a rough rectangle about 12 inches long and 5 inches wide.

4. Starting at the farthest end, use the heel of your hand to smear a small amount of dough against the counter, pushing firmly down and away from you, to create separate piles of dough (the flattened pieces of dough should look shaggy). Continue the process until all dough has been worked. Gather the dough into a rough 12 by 5-inch mound and repeat the smearing process. The dough will not have to be smeared as much as the first time and should form a cohesive ball once the entire portion is worked. Form the dough into a 4-inch square, wrap in plastic, and refrigerate until cold and firm but still malleable, 30 minutes to 1 hour.

5. FOR THE APPLES: About 15 minutes before baking, adjust an oven rack to the middle position and heat the oven to 400 degrees. Peel, halve, and core the apples. Cut the apples into ⅛-inch-thick slices.

6. TO ROLL AND ASSEMBLE THE GALETTE: Place the dough on a floured 16 by 12-inch piece of parchment paper and dust with more flour. Roll the dough until it just overhangs all four sides of the parchment and is about ⅛ inch thick, dusting the top and bottom of the dough and rolling pin with flour as needed to keep the dough from sticking. Trim the dough so the edges are even with the parchment paper.

7. Roll up 1 inch of each edge and pinch firmly to create a ½-inch-thick border. Transfer the dough and parchment to a rimmed baking sheet.

8. Starting in one corner, shingle the sliced apples to form an even row across the bottom of the dough, overlapping each slice by about one-half. Continue to layer the apples in rows, overlapping each row by half. Dot the apples with the butter and sprinkle evenly with the sugar. Bake until the bottom of the tart is deep golden brown and the apples have caramelized, 45 to 60 minutes.

9. TO GLAZE THE GALETTE: While the galette is baking, combine the apricot preserves and water in a medium microwave-safe bowl. Microwave on medium power until the mixture begins to bubble, about 1 minute. Pass through a fine-mesh strainer to remove any large apricot pieces. Brush the baked galette with the glaze and cool on a wire rack for 15 minutes. Transfer to a cutting board. Cut in half lengthwise and then crosswise into individual portions; serve.

TECHNIQUE: Preparing Apple Galette

1. Cut in the butter.

2. Add water to form a dough.

3. Form a mound.

4. Fraisage and chill.

5. Cut the apples.

6. Roll and trim the dough.

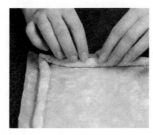
7. Form a border.

8. Layer the apples and bake.

Rating Essential Bakeware

DOES THE TYPE AND BRAND OF PAN MAKE A DIFFERENCE BETWEEN A GREAT BAKED GOOD AND A MEDIOCRE ONE? IN most cases, yes. After a dozen years of testing, we've compiled a list of what we believe to be the best of the best (so far) in the world of bakeware. See www.americastestkitchen.com for up-to-date prices and mail-order sources for top-rated products. And for more information on bakeware materials and finishes, see page 322.

BEST BAKING PAN
Pyrex Bakeware 13 by 9-Inch Baking Dish
$8.95

Sturdy Pyrex is our first choice here: dishwasher-safe, handy handles, and scratch-resistant. The 13 by 9-inch pan is the best all-around option, but the 17 by 11-inch model turns out super-sized casseroles, while the 8-inch- and 9-inch-square pans are good for smaller batches of cornbread or brownies. Be careful, however, with Pyrex and sudden temperature changes (see information on tempered ovenproof glass on page 322).

BEST ROUND CAKE PAN
Chicago Metallic Professional Nonstick
$14.95

We're still searching for the ultimate round cake pan: one with high, straight sides; a dark, nonstick finish; and handles, which most manufacturers consider unnecessary. Until then, Chicago Metallic Professional Nonstick scores two out of three. Nine-inch cake pans are the standard size, and you'll need two for most recipes.

BEST SQUARE CAKE PANS
Williams-Sonoma Goldtouch Nonstick
$21

The Williams-Sonoma Goldtouch Nonstick is deeper than the competition and yields nicely browned cakes with perfectly straight sides.

Calphalon Classic Nonstick
$16.95

Nearly identical to the Williams-Sonoma pan, but with a dark, charcoal gray surface. This pan yielded baked goods with deep, evenly golden sides and bottoms.

BEST BAKING SHEET
Vollrath Cookie Sheet
$24.95

When it comes to light-versus-dark-colored metal bakeware, the baking (or cookie) sheet is the exception. All of the dark-colored nonstick cookie sheets we tested consistently overbrowned the bottoms of cookies. Light-colored sheets, on the other hand, were prone to sticking (including the Vollrath), but because we always bake cookies on parchment paper, we chose the lesser of two evils.

BEST PIE PLATE
Pyrex (9-Inch) Pie Plate

$5.99

The Pyrex pie plate is scratch-resistant, its wide lip makes it easy to shape decorative fluted crusts, and its see-through glass is the best choice for monitoring a crust's browning progress.

BEST MUFFIN TIN
Wilton Ultra-Bake Muffin Tin

$9.99

Thanks to excellent heat absorption, dark-colored metal pans, like the Wilton Ultra-Bake, produce muffins and cupcakes that not only brown better but also rise higher and sport more nicely domed tops when compared with those baked in shiny, reflective tins.

BEST LOAF PAN
Williams-Sonoma Goldtouch Nonstick Loaf Pan

$19

The gold surface on the Williams-Sonoma Goldtouch Nonstick Loaf Pan yielded baked goods with a perfectly even, honey-coppered crust. Note that many recipes yield two loaves, so you might as well buy two pans.

BEST FLUTED TART PAN
Tinned Steel Fluted Tart Pan with Removable Bottom

About $8, depending on diameter

We love these clever pans—the fluted edges and false bottom allow even a novice baker to turn out elegant-looking desserts with not much effort. But we can't condone splurging on pricey nonstick models when the generic tinned steel pans, sold in most stores for around $8, work just as well.

BEST SPRINGFORM PAN
Frieling Handle-It (9-Inch) Glass Bottom Springform

$31.95

The disappointing truth: All springform pans leak. This means that using them in a water bath can be problematic (we recommend double-wrapping the pan with aluminum foil to make it leakproof). We picked out the least leaky contenders, then chose the only model, the Frieling Handle-It Glass Bottom Springform, with helpful handles and a clear glass bottom to boot.

GETTING IT RIGHT: The Low-down on Bakeware Materials and Finishes

All the usual jargon about clad aluminum cores and anodized coatings remains in full force, but after baking dozens of cookies and cakes over the years we are even more skeptical than usual about bells and whistles when it comes to shopping for bakeware. Here's what to look for—and what to avoid.

Tempered, Ovenproof Glass: Better known by the brand name Pyrex, thick tempered glass retains plenty of heat, so pans made from it ensure deep and even browning. They also make it easy to monitor the browning as it develops. Because Pyrex is scratch-resistant, you can cut and serve right from the pan with sharp knives and metal spatulas. What's not to like? Just the occasional explosion or shattering of the dish, a manageable risk as long as you take precautions. Do not add cold liquid to a hot Pyrex dish or place a hot Pyrex dish directly on a cold or wet surface. It is considered safe, however, to transfer a Pyrex dish directly from the refrigerator or freezer to a hot oven, provided the oven has been properly preheated—some ovens use the broiler element to heat up to the desired temperature, which could prove unsafe.

Dark-Colored Finishes: When it comes to metal pans, neither the type of metal nor its thickness matters much. What does matter is the color of the pan. Dark-colored nonstick pans allow metal to absorb more heat inside the oven than reflective, lighter-colored materials. The result: darker browning of baked goods, which is almost always a good thing. Combine that with the clean release and easy cleanup of nonstick, and pans in this category are often the ones to beat.

Light-Colored Finishes: A well-browned crust releases more easily from a pan than a pale crust. Because light-colored reflective pans brown more slowly than dark-colored pans, and because they also lack a nonstick coating, we're generally reluctant to recommend them. In a few situations, however, this controlled browning can be an advantage, such as when baking cookies. (Because it's only the bottom of a cookie that's in contact with the metal, it can easily burn before the rest of the cookie bakes through.)

Insulated: To protect against overbrowning (not usually a problem for us), insulated pans incorporate a layer of air sandwiched between two sheets of metal. Unfortunately, this "insulation" works all too well: The pans produce pale, underdeveloped crusts. The interior chamber also becomes waterlogged if submerged in water during cleanup.

Silicone: These flexible, rubbery pans are the most useless things to appear in the kitchen since salad shooters. These "pans" don't brown well, and getting them into the oven when loaded down with batter is awkward.

TASTING LAB: Supermarket Teas

IN OUR 2003 TASTING OF SUPERMARKET BLACK TEAS, the test kitchen preferred Lipton, but we really weren't that impressed with any of them. Recently, tea companies have created many more options, including what they present as higher-quality offerings in the form of loose leaves, special blends, or new pyramid-shaped tea bags. We decided it was time to find out if the supermarket has the makings of a great cup of tea.

While you can find black, green, and even white tea on the shelves these days, it's all from the same plant, an evergreen called Camellia sinensis. The color and flavor differences come from the way the tea leaves are processed. Because 87 percent of all tea drunk in America is black, we decided to focus our tasting on black teas. We bought the more "upscale" offerings distributed by national brands, all labeled simply black tea or English breakfast–type blends, a popular mix of black teas designed to stand up to the milk and sugar popular among the British. We chose loose tea when it was available and tea bags when it was not, including three teas that came in the new pyramid-shaped bags, which are touted as having more room for the tea to expand for better flavor. A panel of 20 tasters from our staff sampled 10 teas, both plain and with milk.

An ideal cup of black tea should taste fresh, with no stale overtones, and should not taste burnt, though a smoky or earthy flavor is acceptable. It should not be yeasty or sour. It should have a pleasing aroma, a bright color, and a crisp rather than heavy flavor, with some of the astringency tea professionals call "briskness." Black tea gets these characteristics from a number of factors, including where it is grown (cooler temperatures at higher elevations slow down the plant's growth and let it build more flavor), when it is picked (the often-prized "first flush" is the earliest), how it is picked (by hand is considered better; machines can be rough and tear up older, tougher leaves in addition to the desired top two leaves and bud), and how it is processed. When making black tea, processors let the harvested leaves wither for up to 24 hours, then roll or cut them. This breaks the cell walls and releases enzymes that oxidize to develop the tea's flavor and color—in the case of black tea, turning the leaves black. Then they heat (or "fire") the leaves to stop oxidation before drying them until they look like familiar dry tea. The leaves are then sold to tea companies, which generally blend tea from several sources, although really fine-quality leaves are often kept unblended as single-estate teas.

Our tasters began by assessing the tea samples' aroma, followed by complexity of flavor, astringency, and overall appeal. Tasters' scores for aroma most closely tracked with their overall ranking of the teas. Whenever the tea failed to deliver on that aromatic promise, however, our tasters downgraded it. Our tasters also preferred teas with smoother, less astringent profiles.

For our next test, we examined the leaves, opening up the tea bags as needed. The leaves varied in size and texture from half-inch twig-like pieces of tightly rolled leaves to tiny flakes no bigger than coarse coffee grounds. While tea aficionados will tell you that bigger is better when it comes to leaf size, we disagree. Our top two teas had the seventh- and sixth-smallest leaves, respectively, out of the 10 teas we tasted. "While a larger leaf may give you more complexity of flavor, you always have to judge by what you taste in the cup," said Donna Fellman of the Specialty Tea Institute in New York.

In the plain tasting, our two highest-ranked teas were from British companies: Twinings English Breakfast (a loose tea) and PG Tips (in pyramid bags). These teas offered strong, bright flavor with just a little astringency—the balance that our tasters liked best without milk.

TECHNIQUE: Brewing Tea

Tea experts recommend brewing black tea for three to five minutes, claiming that longer brewing brings out a harsh, bitter flavor. We put this to the test, tasting tea samples at three, four, and five minutes, and determined that four minutes was the best for full flavor without harshness. Clean-tasting water is the foundation of good tea, so we took fresh, cold spring water, brought it to a full boil, then immediately poured it over the tea bags in a prewarmed thermal carafe. (Boiling the water too long lets dissolved oxygen escape, leading to a flat-tasting cup of tea.) We used T-Sacs, fill-it-yourself paper tea bags sold in tea shops, to hold our loose tea and settled on $1/10$ ounce (about 2 teaspoons, not packed down) of loose tea per T-Sac as an equivalent to one tea bag. We also used the tea industry standard of 6 ounces of water per teacup. For our second tasting, with milk, we tested proportions and decided to add 1 cup of milk to each half-gallon of tea before serving.

We had one more experiment. All three teas in pyramid-shaped bags had shown well, and the teas in traditional bags performed poorly. We decided to see if it was the bag or the tea by taking tea out of two traditional bags and brewing it instead in T-Sacs, fill-it-yourself paper bags with gusseted bottoms that give them a shape similar to the pyramid bags. Regular Lipton tea still failed to impress tasters but, removed from its disk-shaped bag, Tetley performed much better. Evidently, the roomier pyramid bags (or T-Sacs) helped. Finally, better flavor didn't mean higher prices. While the teas in our lineup ranged from $.38 to $3.99 per ounce, our top two teas were $1.41 and $.47 per ounce.

Surprisingly, when we tried the teas again with milk, the results were nearly the opposite. Tea gets its astringency from tannic substances called catechins. Tasted plain, the teas that tasters rated lowest for astringency and highest for complexity of flavor rose in the rankings. When milk was added, teas formerly deemed too harsh became quite palatable, and those that were smoother but less robustly flavored sank in our tasters' estimation.

There's a chemical explanation for this: Proteins in the milk called caseins bind with the tea's catechins, taking the edge off the astringent effect on your palate. A little astringency is considered a good characteristic in a black tea. But too much turned off tasters, unless it was masked by milk. Tea drinkers among us were firm about our preference for always drinking tea with—or without—milk. So we decided to present the top-ranked teas in each tasting and let you focus on the section that applies to the way you drink your tea.

TASTING LAB: Gourmet Teas

PREMIUM TEAS ARE ALMOST ALWAYS PICKED BY HAND, sold loose, and mail-ordered. We chose English breakfast blends from five high-end tea companies—Harney & Sons, Upton Tea Imports, Mariage Frères, Mighty Leaf, and Adagio—and tasted them plain against our winning supermarket tea, Twinings English Breakfast, and again with milk against Tazo Awake, our favorite supermarket tea when milk is added. In the plain tasting, Mighty Leaf Organic English Breakfast Tea ($7.95 for 4 ounces, or $1.99 per ounce) won by a landslide. With milk, results changed dramatically. Harney & Sons English Breakfast Tea ($19 for 1 pound, or $1.19 per ounce) moved from fifth place in the plain tasting to the top. As for supermarket teas, Twinings and Tazo performed respectably in such rarified company, ranking in the middle of the pack in both the plain and with milk tastings.

Rating Supermarket Teas

TWENTY AMERICA'S TEST KITCHEN STAFF MEMBERS TASTED 10 TEAS, PLAIN AND WITH MILK ADDED. NOTE THAT BRANDS that showed well when tasted plain were generally quite dull when tasted with milk; likewise, brands that showed well when tasted with milk were generally too strong when tasted plain. The teas are listed in order of preference. See www.americastestkitchen.com for up-to-date prices and mail-order sources for top-rated products.

BEST TEAS PLAIN

RECOMMENDED
Twinings English Breakfast Tea

$9.95 for 7.05-ounce tin; loose tea

"Fruity and smooth," "floral, fragrant, nice and balanced," agreed tasters, who liked that this tea was "not too strong" but packed "a lot of flavor."

RECOMMENDED
PG Tips

$12.50 for 240 pyramid paper bags

"Not too astringent—clean-tasting and very nice," most tasters agreed, with a "lovely woodsy smell" and "a nice balance that matches the aroma."

RECOMMENDED
Bigelow Novus Kenilworth Ceylon

$6.30 for 15 pyramid nylon mesh bags

Tasters appreciated an "earthy" quality in this tea, which had a "lightly floral aroma and a super-smooth, almost honeyed flavor" and "moderate body."

RECOMMENDED
Lipton Black Pearl

$3.39 for 20 pyramid nylon mesh bags

This "good and smooth" tea was "fruity, pleasant, and mild," with a "clean taste" that "builds in the mouth." Some tasters noted a "surprisingly good aftertaste" and "slight astringency." Others, however, found it "nothing special."

RECOMMENDED
Stash English Breakfast Tea

$5.95 for 3.5 ounces; loose tea

"A strong smoky flavor and low astringency. I love it," said one taster, and others agreed, calling it "quite smooth," and "woodsy, floral, and sweet-smelling." However, a few found it "hoppy" and "musty like a barn."

BEST TEAS WITH MILK

RECOMMENDED
Tazo Awake

$21.58 for 17.6 ounces; loose tea

"Wow! Extremely smoky, with a strong, clean taste. Very good." "Fruity, delicious, and smooth, with a most pleasant aroma; perfumed but not overly precious." Tasters liked its spicy notes of clove, cinnamon, and vanilla. "Great balance of flavor and intensity."

RECOMMENDED
Tetley Specialty Tea English Breakfast

$3.19 for 20 disk-shaped paper bags

"Balanced; stands up to milk," said tasters, with a "big flavor" that is "full-bodied" and "good and complex." They praised its "rich, steeped aroma."

RECOMMENDED
Red Rose

$3 for 8 ounces; loose tea

"Tea flavor comes through the milk." Tasters liked this tea's "almost savory," "strong," "complex and assertive" taste that has notes of "pumpkin" and "clove."

RECOMMENDED
Lipton Tea

$4.99 for 100 folded dual paper bags

Smelling "sweet," like "honey," and "yeasty, like dough," this tea came across as "plain-tasting," "not jarring," "strong but flavorful—very drinkable."

NOT RECOMMENDED
Celestial Seasonings Devonshire English Breakfast

$2.99 for 20 square paper bags

"Light aroma, light flavor, light everything" was the consensus here, with a few tasters liking its "roundness," but others calling it "one-note" or "dull and boring."

A NOTE ON CONVERSIONS

SOME SAY COOKING IS BOTH A SCIENCE AND AN ART. We would say that geography has a hand in it, too. Flour milled in the United Kingdom and elsewhere will feel and taste different from flour milled in the United States. So we cannot promise that the loaf of bread you bake in Canada or England will taste the same as a loaf baked in the States, but we can offer guidelines for converting weights and measures. We also recommend that you rely on instincts when making our recipes. Refer to the visual cues provided. If the bread dough hasn't "come together in a ball," as described, you may need to add more flour—even if the recipe doesn't tell you so. You be the judge. For more information on conversions and ingredient equivalents, visit our Web site at www.cooksillustrated.com and type "conversion chart" in the search box.

The recipes in this book were developed using standard U.S. measures following U.S. government guidelines. The charts below offer equivalents for U.S., metric, and Imperial (U.K.) measures. All conversions are approximate and have been rounded up or down to the nearest whole number. For example:

1 teaspoon = 4.9292 milliliters, rounded up to 5 milliliters

1 ounce = 28.3495 grams, rounded down to 28 grams

Volume Conversions

U.S.	METRIC
1 teaspoon	5 milliliters
2 teaspoons	10 milliliters
1 tablespoon	15 milliliters
2 tablespoons	30 milliliters
¼ cup	59 milliliters
⅓ cup	79 milliliters
½ cup	118 milliliters
¾ cup	177 milliliters
1 cup	237 milliliters
1¼ cups	296 milliliters
1½ cups	355 milliliters
2 cups	473 milliliters
2½ cups	592 milliliters
3 cups	710 milliliters
4 cups (1 quart)	0.946 liter
1.06 quarts	1 liter
4 quarts (1 gallon)	3.8 liters

Weight Conversions

OUNCES	GRAMS
½	14
¾	21
1	28
1½	43
2	57
2½	71
3	85
3½	99
4	113
4½	128
5	142
6	170
7	198
8	227
9	255
10	283
12	340
16 (1 pound)	454

Conversions for Ingredients Commonly Used in Baking

Baking is an exacting science. Because measuring by weight is far more accurate than measuring by volume, and thus more likely to achieve reliable results, in our recipes we provide ounce measures in addition to cup measures for many ingredients. Refer to the chart below to convert these measures into grams.

INGREDIENT	OUNCES	GRAMS
I cup all-purpose flour*	5	142
I cup whole wheat flour	5½	156
I cup granulated (white) sugar	7	198
I cup packed brown sugar (light or dark)	7	198
I cup confectioners' sugar	4	113
I cup cocoa powder	3	85
Butter†		
4 tablespoons (½ stick, or ¼ cup)	2	57
8 tablespoons (1 stick, or ½ cup)	4	113
16 tablespoons (2 sticks, or 1 cup)	8	227

* U.S. all-purpose flour, the most frequently used flour in this book, does not contain leaveners, as some European flours do. These leavened flours are called self-rising or self-raising. If you are using self-rising flour, take this into consideration before adding leavening to a recipe.

† In the United States, butter is sold both salted and unsalted. We generally recommend unsalted butter. If you are using salted butter, take this into consideration before adding salt to a recipe.

Oven Temperatures

FAHRENHEIT	CELSIUS	GAS MARK (IMPERIAL)
225	105	¼
250	120	½
275	130	1
300	150	2
325	165	3
350	180	4
375	190	5
400	200	6
425	220	7
450	230	8
475	245	9

Converting Temperatures from an Instant-Read Thermometer

We include doneness temperatures in many of our recipes, such as those for poultry, meat, and bread. We recommend an instant-read thermometer for the job. Refer to the above table to convert Fahrenheit degrees to Celsius. Or, for temperatures not represented in the chart, use this simple formula:

Subtract 32 degrees from the Fahrenheit reading, then divide the result by 1.8 to find the Celsius reading.

EXAMPLE:

"Roast until the juices run clear when the chicken is cut with a paring knife or the thickest part of the breast registers 160 degrees on an instant-read thermometer." To convert:

$160°F - 32 = 128°$
$128° \div 1.8 = 71°C$ (rounded down from 71.11)

INDEX

P

Pancetta, Penne alla Vodka with, 47

Pan-Roasted Chicken Breasts
with Artichokes and Cherry Tomatoes, 21
with Baby Carrots, 20–21
with Potatoes, 19–20, *261*

Pans
baking, ratings of, 320
cake, round, ratings of, 320
cake, square, ratings of, 286–87
loaf, ratings of, 321
materials and finishes for, 322
roasting, ratings of, 126–28
springform, ratings of, 321
tart, ratings of, 321

Pan-Seared Thick-Cut Steaks, 212–14, *262*

Parmesan cheese
Baked Manicotti, *82,* 84–87
Baked Manicotti with Prosciutto, 87
Baked Manicotti Puttanesca, 87
Baked Manicotti with Sausage, 87
Cherry Tomatoes, Peas, and Ham, Rice Salad with, 176
-Crusted Chicken Cutlets, 14–17, *70*
Four-Cheese Lasagna, 56–59, *67*
Four-Cheese Lasagna with Artichokes and Prosciutto, 59
mail-order, taste tests on, 93
Skillet Baked Ziti, 4–5, *68*
Skillet Baked Ziti with Puttanesca Sauce, 5
Skillet Baked Ziti with Vodka-Cream Sauce, 5
supermarket, taste tests on, 89–92

Pasta
Baked Manicotti, *82,* 84–87
Baked Manicotti with Prosciutto, 87
Baked Manicotti Puttanesca, 87
Baked Manicotti with Sausage, 87
Caprese, 48–50, *263*
Cool and Creamy Macaroni Salad, 42–43
Four-Cheese Lasagna, 56–59, *67*
Four-Cheese Lasagna with Artichokes and Prosciutto, 59
penne, taste tests on, 50–51
Penne alla Vodka, 46–47
Penne alla Vodka with Pancetta, 47
Salad, Antipasto, 191–92, *267*
Skillet Baked Ziti, 4–5, *68*
Skillet Baked Ziti with Puttanesca Sauce, 5
Skillet Baked Ziti with Vodka-Cream Sauce, 5
Skillet Beef Stroganoff, 8–9, *77*

Peas
Ham, Cherry Tomatoes, and Parmesan, Rice Salad with, 176
Potatoes, Cauliflower, and Chickpeas, Indian-Style Curry with, 222–24, *268*
snow, preparing, for stir-fries, 241

Penne
alla Vodka, 46–47
alla Vodka with Pancetta, 47
taste tests on, 50–51

Pepperoni
Antipasto Pasta Salad, 191–92, *267*
Pan Pizza, 188–89, *266*

Pepper(s)
Antipasto Pasta Salad, 191–92, *267*
preparing, for stir-fries, 241
Roasted Red, and Basil, Shrimp Salad with, 27
see also Chiles

Pickles, bread-and-butter, taste tests on, 154

Pie plates, ratings of, 321

Pineapple
and Cucumber Salsa with Mint, 162
preparing, 162

Pizza
frozen, taste tests on, 193–94
Pepperoni Pan, 188–89, *266*
Sauce, Basic, 190

Pork
chops
buying, 38
searing, 37
Skillet-Barbecued, 34–37, *264*
ribs
St. Louis, about, 150
Sticky, Kansas City, *80,* 148–50
Sticky, Kansas City, Easiest, 150
Sticky, Kansas City, on a Gas Grill, 150
see also Bacon; Ham; Sausage(s)

Potatoes
Cauliflower, Peas, and Chickpeas, Indian-Style Curry with, 222–24, *268*
Mashed, Creamy, *75,* 144–45
Mashed, Garlic and Olive Oil, 217–18
Pan-Roasted Chicken Breasts with, 19–20, *261*
Sweet, Eggplant, Green Beans, and Chickpeas, Indian-Style Curry with, 225

Pots de Crème
Chocolate, 203–5
Milk Chocolate, 205

Poultry
game hens, butterflying and skewering, 172